Schiller's Early Dramas

The interpretation of the works of Friedrich Schiller, with Goethe one of the co-founders of German classicism, has long been a central concern of German critics. In a country known as "the land of poets and thinkers," the achievements of great writers have been a matter of national pride and identity. But special problems are raised by Schiller, whose dramas address political questions more directly than those of his fellow-classicist Goethe, yet tend to end in a manner that shifts the focus to a general moral or metaphysical level, leaving politically engaged readers dissatisfied. The reception of Schiller's works is thus not only a topic in the history of criticism, but forms a chapter in the history of German political and national consciousness. Given this situation, Professor Pugh's study of the plays' fortunes at the hands of the various schools of German literary scholarship from Schiller's day down to the present is useful both to literary scholars seeking orientation in the field and also to readers with a wider interest in German intellectual traditions.

David V. Pugh is associate professor of German at Queen's University, Kingston, Ontario, Canada, and is the author of *The Dialectic of Love: Platonism in Schiller's Aesthetics*.

Studies in German Literature, Linguistics, and Culture:
Literary Criticism in Perspective

Editorial Board

Literary Criticism in Perspective

About *Literary Criticism in Perspective*

Books in the series *Literary Criticism in Perspective* trace literary scholarship and criticism on major and neglected writers alike, or on a single major work, a group of writers, a literary school or movement. In so doing the authors — authorities on the topic in question who are also well-versed in the principles and history of literary criticism — address a readership consisting of scholars, students of literature at the graduate and undergraduate level, and the general reader. One of the primary purposes of the series is to illuminate the nature of literary criticism itself, to gauge the influence of social and historic currents on aesthetic judgments once thought objective and normative.

David Pugh

Schiller's Early Dramas

A Critical History

CAMDEN HOUSE

First published 2000
by Camden House

Camden House is an imprint of Boydell & Brewer Inc.
PO Box 41026, Rochester, NY 14604–4126 USA
and of Boydell & Brewer Limited
PO Box 9, Woodbridge, Suffolk IP12 3DF, UK

ISBN: 1–57113–153–1

Library of Congress Cataloging-in-Publication Data

Pugh, David, 1952–
    Schiller's early dramas : a critical history / David Pugh.
        p. cm. — (Studies in German literature, linguistics, and culture. Literary
    criticism in perspective)
    Includes bibliographical references and index.
    ISBN 1–57113–153–1 (alk. paper)
        1. Schiller, Friedrich, 1759–1805—Criticism and interpretation. I. Title.
    II. Studies in German literature, linguistics, and culture (Unnumbered).
    Literary criticism in perspective.

    PT2492 P83 2000
    832'.6—dc21
                                                    00–036097

A catalogue record for this title is available from the British Library.

This publication is printed on acid-free paper.
Printed in the United States of America.

Contents

Acknowledgments   vii

Abbreviations   ix

Introduction   xi

1. The Neoclassical Establishment:
   The Contemporary Reception   1

2. Romantics, Liberals, Hegelians, Positivists:
   The Nineteenth Century   12

3. The Age of *Geistesgeschichte:* 1905–45   57

4. Schiller Scholarship since 1945   91

5. *Die Räuber:* A Political Play?   144

6. *Fiesco:* The "Republican Tragedy"   159

7. *Kabale und Liebe:* The Domestic Tragedy   166

8. *Don Carlos:* The Drama of Freedom   182

9. Conclusion   199

Works Cited   201

Index   223

Acknowledgments

I am grateful to the series editors for entrusting me with the task of writing this book, and for their patience in awaiting its completion. I should like to thank the Advisory Research Committee of Queen's University for making it possible for me to collect materials at the Deutsches Literaturarchiv in Marbach in summer 1995. My thanks are due finally to Dennis Mahoney of the University of Vermont for his careful reading of the manuscript and for his thoughtful suggestions, many of which I have adopted.

D. P.
November 1999

Abbreviations

CG	*Colloquia Germanica*
DU	*Der Deutschunterricht*
DVjs	*Deutsche Vierteljahrsschrift für Literaturwissenschaft und Geistesgeschichte*
EG	*Études germaniques*
GLL	*German Life and Letters*
GR	*Germanic Review*
GRM	*Germanisch-Romanische Monatsschrift*
JDSG	*Jahrbuch der Deutschen Schillergesellschaft*
JEGP	*Journal of English and Germanic Philology*
JFDH	*Jahrbuch des Freien Deutschen Hochstifts*
PEGS	*Publications of the English Goethe Society*
PMLA	*Proceedings of the Modern Language Association of America*
ZfdPh	*Zeitschrift für deutsche Philologie*

Introduction

THE STATUS OF FRIEDRICH SCHILLER (1759–1805) in German letters is epitomized by Ernst Rietschl's monument of 1857, in which Schiller's statue stands alongside Goethe's before the National Theater in Weimar. Schiller appears here as a noble and resolute visionary, looking boldly into the future while the older Goethe restrains him by laying an arm gently on his shoulder. Schiller's reputation, which earned him the right to stand here in Weimar, the central shrine of German literature, is based on the nine completed dramas (counting the *Wallenstein* trilogy as a single work) that together earn him the title of Germany's greatest dramatist. In addition to his dramas, Schiller wrote a body of philosophical and didactic poetry that includes the ode "An die Freude" [To Joy, 1785] (which was famously set to music by Beethoven in his Ninth Symphony), and a series of essays of the mid-1790s in which, on the foundation of Kant's philosophical system, he designed an anthropology and an aesthetics that he hoped would assist in the peaceful progress of human civilization. He also left a large number of letters, including a correspondence with Goethe that extended over the last ten years of his life. The publication of this correspondence in two volumes in 1828–29, as well as of his correspondence with Wilhelm von Humboldt (1830), did much to cement his reputation and to keep him before the eyes of the public, not merely as a proponent of liberal ideals, but also as an attractive individual and as a participant in the lively culture of Weimar, which continues today to fascinate a wide public, both in Germany and around the world.

Schiller's first four works for the theater — the prose plays *Die Räuber* [The Robbers, 1781], *Die Verschwörung des Fiesco zu Genua* [The Conspiracy of Fiesco in Genoa, 1783], and *Kabale und Liebe* [Intrigue and Love, 1784], followed by the verse play *Don Carlos* (1787) — are the products of the author's first creative period and were written before the encounters with Kant and Goethe that provided the impulse for his final, classical, decade. The three prose plays, of which two deal with contemporary and one with historical subject matter, are easily recognizable as a triptych. At a superficial level, they resemble each other in their melodramatic plots, their violent emotions, and their exclamatory language, while at a deeper level they are linked by substantive themes such as generational conflict, the quest for individual greatness, and the challenging of divine providence. *Don Carlos* is rather different. Here a calmer spirit prevails, and although the cast contains two young rebels, the work displays many new features, notably the involvement of controversial political ideas in the plot and a new ability to create complex and rounded individuals. King Philip II of Spain, whom Schiller initially conceived as an uncomplicated tyrant, is portrayed in the completed work with a remarkable degree of sympathy. Despite this apparent gulf between the prose plays and *Don Carlos*, however, it still makes sense to discuss them together. After *Don Carlos*, Schiller gave up writing drama for seven years, and the *Wallenstein* trilogy was published only in 1800. The dramas of his so-called classical period, which encompasses the years of his partnership with Goethe up to his death in 1805, are thus chronologically distinct from the early works.

All four early plays were recognized at once by the German public as the products of a powerful new talent. Yet the initial response was divided, with some critics acclaiming the young author as a new Shakespeare, others ridiculing him for the unnatural bombast of his language and the implausibility of his plots. Even now, when the works have become canonical, they tend to provoke mixed responses. With their emotional excesses and their manipulated plots, all are clearly the works of a young man inexperienced in theatrical writing, and they all, in their different ways, pose deep questions of interpretation. Of the first one, *Die Räuber*, Schiller wrote in his preface that it deserved "einen Platz unter den moralischen Büchern" [a place among the moral books].[1] And yet, while working on the same play, he is alleged by a credible witness to have said that he was aiming to write a book "das aber durch den Schinder absolut verbrannt werden muß" (cited Hecker, ed. 1904, 162) [that must be absolutely burnt by the horse slaughterer]. The two remarks hint at an uncertainty as to whether the completed work was written with revolutionary or conservative intentions. This uncertainty, which can still be felt in the scholarly literature, applies in different ways to each of the four plays. The abortive coup d'état in *Fiesco* ends with Verrina, a staunch republican, returning to the duke whom he had aimed to depose. Is this a mature recognition of the futility of revolution, does it signify resignation to absurdity, as in the conclusion of Georg Büchner's later masterpiece *Dantons Tod* [The Death of Danton, 1835], or is it something quite different? In *Kabale und Liebe*, it is unclear whether the young protagonist, Ferdinand von Walter, should be seen as hero or villain. As for *Don Carlos*, Schiller published a series of letters (the *Briefe über Don Carlos*) the year after the completion of the work in which he directed criticism at the Marquis Posa, a figure whom the play itself appears to idealize as a champion of freedom. To this day the debate rages among critics as to whether Schiller wrote these letters for tactical reasons or whether they reflect his own opinion. Such uncertainty has had its effect on the critical reception of all these works.

But Schiller is a controversial author in a way that goes beyond such interpretative questions arising from individual works. It may be helpful, especially for readers who are unfamiliar with the outlines of German literary history, if I place the story to be traced here in a somewhat wider context. Although Schiller represents half of the great duumvirate of Weimar Classicism as the poetic collaborator of Goethe, there has never been a consensus as to his literary stature. In the years since his death he has received extremes of praise and censure, ranging from the triumphant heights of the centenary celebrations in 1859 to the depths of rejection and even ridicule with which prominent authors including Georg Büchner (1813–37) and Bertolt Brecht have responded to his work (although, as Hans Mayer argued in 1955, *Die Räuber* exemplifies a realism that is akin to Büchner's own dramatic approach [153]). Although Schiller was acclaimed by a mass readership in the nineteenth century, literary sophisticates, starting with the Jena Romantic circle of the 1790s, have tended to look down their noses at him. The bon mot by Friedrich Nietzsche (1844–1900) in his book *Götzendämmerung* [Twilight of the Idols, 1889], characterizing Schiller as "der Moraltrompeter von Säckingen" [the moral trumpeter of Säckingen, 991] had a particularly deadly effect.[2] Thomas Mann (1875–1955), to be sure, portrays the young Tonio Kröger in the story of that name (1903) as being profoundly moved by *Don Carlos*. For the centenary of Schiller's death in 1905 he wrote a fine story called "Schwere Stunde" [Difficult Hour] depicting the author's agonies over *Wallenstein*, and for the anniversary fifty years later he paid a masterly tribute in his *Versuch über Schiller* [Essay on Schiller, 1955], the last completed work of his career. But Thomas Mann was a self-consciously conservative writer, and his son Klaus (1906–49) is more typical of writers of this time when, in his posthumously published autobiography *Der Wendepunkt* [The Turning Point, 1952], he provides a list of the authors who inspired him most in his early years. It includes Heinrich von Kleist, Georg Büchner and Heinrich Heine, but Schiller is notably absent. More recently, we see the contemporary writer Hans Christoph Buch quoted as saying of Schiller: "I do not love him, I do not even like him" (Ugrinsky 1988, vii). Even among academics, it is not uncommon to come across statements impugning Schiller's poetic credentials in a surprisingly harsh way. This occurs particularly often with scholars for whom Goethe represents the acme of poetic achievement. An influential example is Friedrich Gundolf, a disciple of the poet Stefan George and the author of a famous book on Goethe (1916), in which Schiller's (allegedly only) rhetorical and philosophical talents are systematically contrasted with Goethe's more spontaneous and organic genius.

This sort of disdain has given rise to a characteristic defensiveness among Schiller scholars, who have often found it easier to respond to the detractors by accusing them of snobbery than by answering their objections fairly. Such divergences of opinion can be described up to a point as a matter of literary taste; a reader might thus legitimately claim, on purely aesthetic grounds, to find Goethe more skilful than Schiller in the use of poetic rhythm or imagery. But the objection also goes beyond taste, and sometimes hints at an underlying conviction that Schiller possessed some fundamental flaw of temperament, some combination of naiveté, pharisaism and lack of empathy, that caused his works always to fall short of the highest standards.

Such disparagement, however, goes back to Schiller himself, who throughout his life was uncertain and defensive about his talents. This is especially true during his partnership with Goethe, and the essay *Über naive und sentimentalische Dichtung* [On Naive and Sentimental Poetry, 1795] is usually seen as Schiller's act of resistance to the threat posed to his self-confidence by the older poet. As early as 1784, however, Schiller described *Die Räuber* as "ein Ungeheuer" [a monster], although when he continued that the play was the product of "der naturwidrige Beischlaf der *Subordination* und des *Genius*" [the unnatural copulation of *subordination* and *genius*], he showed that he did not regard it as devoid of all merit.[3] The passage of time was to make him less charitable toward his early work. On 4 September 1794, as he struggled with his *Wallenstein*, the massive first drama of his classical period, he wrote to his friend Christian Gottfried Körner that none of his previous dramatic work was calculated to give him confidence, and "ein Machwerk wie der Carlos ekelte mich nunmehr an" [a hotchpotch like *Carlos* would disgust me now]. Twenty years after Schiller's death, Goethe recalled that in the years of their partnership Schiller "could not stand" his early plays and refused to let them be produced in Weimar (Eckermann, 1836–48, 180), and there can be little doubt that the experience of working with Goethe hardened Schiller's attitude toward them.[4] Besides Goethe, a fateful role has also been played by Shakespeare, to whom the young Schiller was at once compared by contemporaries, and from whom he also tried to distinguish himself in *Über naive und sentimentalische Dichtung*. It has always been easy to belittle

Schiller by placing him beside the great English dramatist, not least (in view of the Shakespearian echoes in *Die Räuber* and *Don Carlos*) since Schiller appeared to court that comparison himself. Once more, Gundolf is a notable example of a critic who took this path.

But again, more is at stake than aesthetic taste and more even than the assessment of his personality in the question of Schiller's reputation, and here we must return to the political uncertainty to which I have already referred. Schiller was adopted posthumously as literary champion by the German liberals of the nineteenth century who, largely on the strength of *Don Carlos*, saw in him the poet of freedom. The political events of the second half of the century — the defeat (partly self-inflicted) of the liberals in 1848–49, the mass emigrations that followed it, the unification of Germany by the Prussian monarchy and the imposition of a veiled authoritarianism in the constitution of the new Reich — led, as historians have argued, to the ruin and demoralization of the German liberal movement. In a remarkable and unflinching study of Schiller's reputation during this period, Christian Grawe (1994) argues that the 1859 celebrations to mark Schiller's centenary — probably, as Grawe writes (643), the greatest festival to a poet in human history — marked a fateful watershed between the dynamic and the decadent phases of German liberalism; the subsequent veneration of Schiller, which soon took on pseudoreligious traits, turned into a delusionary compensation for the bourgeoisie's abandonment of the humane and cosmopolitan values with which Schiller had earlier been associated.

Bismarck and his successors denied political power to the middle classes and fobbed them off with a campaign against German Catholics, with the profits of a protected economy, and with the ersatz satisfactions of military and colonial adventures. Of this period A. J. P. Taylor wrote in 1945: "The majority of liberals washed their hands of public affairs and withdrew into a liberalism of the spirit, as Luther had done three hundred years before" (142). Throughout the Second Reich Schiller was the favorite poet of this middle class with its "liberalism of the spirit," and his works were drummed into middle-class children by German teachers at the Gymnasium. (Heinrich Mann gives us a particularly damning picture of such instruction in his 1905 novel *Professor Unrat.*) Sometimes, however, and again following the Zeitgeist, the official picture of Schiller could change from that of an earnest moralist to that of an aggressive nationalist or even anti-Semite, a version of course lacking all foundation in fact. This image of Schiller, which returns with greater force during the Third Reich, is propagated as early as 1901 in a deplorable speech by Carl Weitbrecht. (For further examples, see Grawe 1994, 661–66.) It is not an exaggeration to say that Schiller's reputation has still not completely recovered from the treatment he received during the demoralized Wilhelminian years. As we shall see, it was this age above all that glorified Schiller as an idealist, paying him a tribute of adulation that nowadays rings so hollow that it still prevents many readers from taking him seriously. The degeneration of the moral and political commitment of 1848 to the vapid and hypocritical idealism of 1905 (the centenary of Schiller's death) still represents a crushing burden on his reputation. Moreover, as we shall see in chapter 3, the abstract, rhetorical and oracular criticism produced by the *Geistesgeschichte* movement [literally: history of mind or spirit] in the first half of this century was barely an improvement.

The failures of the German middle class in the early part of this century — the ultimate consequences of Bismarck's work — are too familiar a subject to be dwelt on here, and I do not intend to deny that part of the blame for the catastrophic story rightly belongs with other nations. It might seem out of place to raise such subjects at all in a book on literary criticism, and I should make it clear that there are some admirable trends in the scholarship on Schiller, living up to Germany's finest traditions of academic research. Such trends range from the positivism of the nineteenth century, through the *Werkimmanenz* of the 1950s and 60s (a movement focusing on precise textual analysis and related to the American New Criticism), to the painstaking historical work that present-day scholars engage in. I will not overlook these trends in the following chapters. But the political issues have to be raised if the reader, especially the nonspecialist, is to understand the discomfort with which many readers and scholars still approach this apparently so progressive author. Wolfgang Paulsen, for example, detected an underlying note of "Hilflosigkeit" [bewilderment] in the celebratory speeches given by Western scholars and writers during the anniversary years of 1955 and 1959 (1962, 401). (I shall discuss the East German picture, which was very different, in chapter 4 below.) It is not too much to claim that such "bewilderment" is linked to the discomfort that many Germans feel about their country's political traditions and even about their nationality in the widest sense. If the German liberals failed so disastrously to prevent their country's descent into barbarism, and if Schiller was their favorite poet, must not — so goes the unspoken question — some of the blame be attached to Schiller himself, to limitations, compromises or evasions in his personality and in his work? It will be a central theme in my discussion of criticism since 1945 that, while Schiller's detractors are seeking a historical culprit for modern disasters, his defenders are in search of an al-

ternative to the old idealistic image of him, for this is the only way to
rescue Schiller from his Wilhelminian admirers. One can compare these
newer defenders to art restorers clearing away the Victorian additions
to a rococo building; their efforts to chip away the accretions of Bismarck's Empire allow the modern reader to see Schiller in his proper
historical surroundings. But only time will tell whether this restoration
work will turn out to have an effect on Schiller's image with the wider
German public.

The reader of a study such as this has a right to know the author's
views on the interpretative questions whose history he is trying to tell.
To state my position briefly: I regard the works as deeply problematic
and the debate about them as incapable of final resolution. All four
works are flawed masterpieces. Their aesthetic stature is undeniable if
one compares them with the works of the Storm and Stress movement
of the previous decade, over which (with the exception of Goethe's
early dramas) they tower by virtue of both their intellectual substance
and their extraordinary emotional tension. On the other hand, it is impossible to deny that they contain numerous misjudgments as to language, characterization, motivation, and general plausibility, as well as
(in the case of the Queen's handwriting in *Don Carlos*) one plain error
of consistency. It is hard to imagine a modern production, especially of
the first three plays, that without careful editing would not raise a good
deal of inappropriate laughter in a theater today.

Regarding their interpretation, I believe that it is a mistake to overrate the plays' political import (in a "progressive" sense) and to neglect
their religious element, an error that often arises when a scholar holds
too secular a concept of the German Enlightenment. Despite his allusions to the revolutionary ideas circulating in his time, the young
Schiller guides his plays towards conclusions that seem to me to reaf-
firm the existing social order, even when its temporary rulers stand
convicted of wrongdoing. I do not believe that he did this for tactical
reasons. At the same time, I feel that it is wrong to assume, as some
scholars do, that an interpretation must unequivocally designate the
work as a particular type of play to the exclusion of other kinds, for instance as a character tragedy and not a political tragedy or tragedy of
providence (or "theodicy"). Such categories are merely aids to interpretation. It makes no sense to portray them as absolutes and to claim
that if a play is one thing, it cannot be another as well. Where, as we
should expect of rich texts such as these, the events depicted have
ramifications of different kinds and on different levels, the interpreter
should attempt to do justice to all of these levels rather than to dwell
on one at the expense of the others. In particular, it seems undeniable

that in these plays Schiller displays a deep preoccupation, first, with the materialist theory of psychological motivation, second, with the workings of divine providence in human history, and third, with the mutual rights and obligations of rulers and subjects. The combination, especially of the first two, is perhaps paradoxical, but we would do better to accept it as such than to give an unequivocal picture by suppressing awkward facets of the truth.

No previous work has attempted to describe the reception of the four plays under discussion here, and so in a sense I am breaking new ground. But the subject runs parallel to, and sometimes merges with, two other narratives, of which we shall remain aware throughout the following pages and that will have to be mentioned from time to time. These are the history of Schiller's reputation in general, on which much has been written, and the history of the academic study of German literature, which has itself recently become a subject of academic study. Schiller has attracted the attention of many of the most eminent scholars since the birth of the discipline, and so the history of his reception bears an inevitable resemblance to the history of German literary scholarship itself. I should stress here that, as with the other volumes in the series *Literary Criticism in Perspective*, the subject of this book is the efforts of academic critics to reach a satisfactory interpretation of specific texts. For the story of Schiller's image and reputation with the wider public and of the role played by that image and reputation in the political history of Germany, the reader must go elsewhere.

This investigation would have been much more difficult if I had not been able to draw on several surveys of the scholarship on Schiller (although not all periods are equally well covered) as well as on some less systematic discussions of Schiller's reputation and standing in Germany. Among the discussions of the latter type, Reinhard Buchwald's book of 1938 and Hans Mayer's article of 1959 stand out for their acuity. Of the attempts at a more comprehensive treatment, I must first note those by Norbert Oellers; in addition to a detailed monograph (1967) on Schiller's reputation up to 1832, he has also edited two collections of documents covering the periods 1782–1859 (1970) and 1860–1966 (1976), in the introductions to which he has sketched the broad lines of Schiller's changing reputation. For the nineteenth century Albert Ludwig's monograph of 1909 still provides a helpful vade mecum. For the pre-Second World War period, there are overlapping reports on research by Herbert Smith, Rudolf Unger, and Georg Keferstein; although the last two authors were writing in Hitler's Germany, they nonetheless provide useful orientation. The story of Schiller's treatment during the Third Reich is well told by Georg Ruppelt (1979). Claudia

Albert has edited a thought-provoking volume on the same period (1994) that contains useful references to other contributions on the history of the discipline. For the immediate postwar period we have overlapping reports by Walter Müller-Seidel (1952) and Benno von Wiese (1953), and for the periods 1955–59 and 1962–65 we have splendidly comprehensive and intelligent surveys by Wolfgang Paulsen (1962) (Kurt Vansca's report of 1961 is less comprehensive) and by Wolfgang Wittkowski (1966). Writing in 1961, William Witte summarizes the attempts of British scholars to overcome the negative image of Schiller prevalent in their country. Helmut Koopmann, finally, in addition to outlining the key contributions on each play in his indispensable book in the Sammlung Metzler series (1977), has also written a thorough, if somewhat pessimistic, report on the work of the 1970s (1982), in which he offers thoughtful comments on a wide range of contributions. While for a long time a new edition of the Metzler book seemed overdue, its place has now been taken by a *Schiller-Handbuch*, also edited by Koopmann (1998), in the series published by Kröner. The last section of this volume is devoted to the story of Schiller's reception, with excellent essays by Ute Gerhard and Claudia Albert on the nineteenth and twentieth centuries respectively, and by Peter Boerner on the record in non-German countries. Koopmann himself contributes a lengthy history of scholarly research on Schiller, in which the emphasis falls on recent developments, and in which his own expertise is well in evidence. The Schiller scholar is also well served by bibliographies from both parts of Germany. In the East, Wolfgang Vulpius edited two volumes (1959, 1967), and the series continued with two more edited by Peter Wersig (1977) and Roland Bärwinkel and collaborators (1989), so that the whole period from 1893 to 1985 is covered. In the West, there have been bibliographies every four or five years in the *Schiller-Jahrbuch* following from Vulpius's first volume and now covering the years from 1959 to 1994; they were started by Paul Raabe and Ingrid Bode (1962) and continued by Bode alone.[5] The British and the American literature are covered respectively by R. Pick (1961) and John R. Frey (1959).

In the greater part of this book (chapters 2–4), I proceed chronologically. The fact that I am dealing with four plays and not one has necessitated a certain selectiveness in my discussions. Thus I do not include each critic's views of each work, but have instead tried to say enough to indicate the general nature of his/her contribution to the subject. The recent scholarship on each of the individual plays is dealt with in chapters 5–8, where it is possible to be more specific about the problems posed by each one, although in view of the quantity of material now available it has proved necessary to be selective. Quotations from Schiller's works come from the five-volume Hanser edition, still the most convenient for everyday use while being perfectly reliable. (The two other standard editions are the *Nationalausgabe*, which commenced publication in 1943, and the new *Frankfurter Ausgabe*.) The three prose plays are contained in volume 1, *Don Carlos* in volume 2 (in the edition of 1801 but incorporating amendments in Schiller's own hand; the *Thalia* fragment appears in the Appendix). Quotations are identified in the text, in the case of the prose plays, by references to act and scene number, and, in the case of *Don Carlos*, by line references. These will be followed by page references to the appropriate volume of the Hanser edition. Hence a quotation from *Fiesco* might be referenced as follows: (III/4; 702), and a quotation from *Don Carlos* as follows: (4010; 160). Unless otherwise stated, the texts of primary reference will be the book editions of the three prose plays and the late version of *Don Carlos* (that is, not any of the stage versions). Although the use of the late version of *Don Carlos* (and not the original one of 1787) is highly questionable, this has until recently been the practice among scholars, and so there is no alternative to adopting it here also. Regarding quotations from the secondary sources, I provide translations for readers without German, but I have also included the original German where I have found the formulation to be distinctive or difficult to convey in English. As Eberhart Lämmert has written (1967), *Germanistik* is a *German* discipline, and the story of Schiller's reception is a German story. Something of the spirit of this story is lost if it is told only by summary and translation.

Some readers may need to refresh their memories as to the plots of the four plays, and for their benefit I shall end this chapter with summaries. *Die Räuber* deals with the fate of the noble Moor family. Franz, the younger son, conspires against Karl, the elder son, who is away at university, and with the aid of forged reports persuades their father to disinherit him. Karl, who is guilty only of the usual misdeeds of young noblemen, has counted on his father's forgiveness so that he can return home, marry his sweetheart Amalia, and resume his aristocratic life. He is cast into despair by the receipt of his father's letter, which has in fact been forged by Franz. His earlier tirades against conventional society suddenly take on substance in his new situation, for Spiegelberg, one of his cronies, has urged the other members of their circle to take to the Bohemian forest as robbers, to which they agree on condition that Karl become their leader. Karl agrees in a spirit of despair and hatred, but when we see him as a robber in act II he has become a Robin Hood-like figure, punishing the mighty and distributing their goods to the

poor. Plenty of members of the band, however, follow the evil Spiegelberg and lack any such higher aspirations. Karl falls once more into despair when he discovers that the rescue of one of his men from hanging
has caused the deaths of innocent people, but he is prevented from
fleeing the band by the arrival of an army in pursuit of them. Karl repeats his earlier oath never to leave his comrades and then leads them
to victory. In act III, the arrival of Kosinsky, a new recruit with a life
story resembling Karl's own, impels Karl to return home in disguise.
Here he is told that his father is dead but also that his banishment was
the result of his brother's plots. Karl's despair is therewith redoubled;
whereas before he was in revolt against a universe that denied him the
paternal love to which he was entitled, he now sees that he has thrown
away his life and salvation for nothing. In a nocturnal scene, he spurns
the temptation to commit suicide, but on hearing voices discovers his
father, imprisoned in a ruin and starving. Reversing his plans to leave
Franz in possession of lands, title, and sweetheart, Karl now sends a
group of robbers to seize and deliver Franz. Although his father is still
alive, Karl's intention seems to be to a sacrificial punishment of the parricide. But Franz (whose progress as a tyrant has counterpointed Karl's
story) is in torment over an apocalyptic nightmare induced by his guilt.
Mistaking the robbers for devils coming to fetch him, he kills himself
before they reach him. The play's climax comes as the robbers bring
Amalia before Karl, and she declares that she still loves him. Karl's father, who had vainly urged the unknown robber chief to be merciful to
Franz, expires suddenly on being told that this chief is really his beloved son. For a moment Karl believes that he can still leave the robbers and marry Amalia, but the robbers remind him of the oath that
binds him to them. Acknowledging that he is trapped, Karl frees himself from the oath by killing Amalia and then leaves the stage declaring
his intention to restore the moral order of the universe by accepting the
due punishment for his crimes. The *Trauerspiel* version (1782) reflects
the changes to the published *Schauspiel* version that Dalberg, the intendant of the Mannheim theater, demanded before the work could
have its first performance on 13 January 1782. The most important
changes are that the action is transferred from the present back to the
sixteenth century, and that, instead of committing suicide, Franz is actually brought before Karl, who casts him into the dungeon from
which the father has been freed. There is also a conciliatory gesture as
Karl tells his men to find a king to serve who will fight for the rights of
man.

The plot of *Fiesco*, which is loosely based on historical events, deals
with an attempted coup d'état against the rule of the Doria family in

sixteenth-century Genoa. Fiesco, a young nobleman of exceptional gifts, appears in the opening ball scene to be devoting himself to a life of hedonism. His wife, Leonore, is distraught over his flirtation with Julia, the niece of the ruling Doge Andreas Doria, and an approach by the conspiratorial republican faction led by Verrina fails to break through his cynicism. Fiesco is dissembling, however. The roguish Moor Hassan is sent by Gianettino Doria, the Doge's brutal nephew and heir, to assassinate Fiesco at the ball; he fails, whereupon Fiesco recruits him as a messenger and helper in his own budding plans for revolution. Summoning the republicans to his home, Fiesco reveals that he will join them, but only on the condition that they accept his leadership, to which they agree. In two monologues, Fiesco debates his intentions, and decides that, instead of restoring freedom, he will seize the dukedom for himself. Meanwhile Verrina warns Bourgognino, his daughter's fiancé, that Fiesco will prove to be the worst enemy of the republic and will have to be murdered. The coup then takes its course, although Fiesco comes close to calling it off when he learns that the Doge, despite warnings of treachery, has dismissed his guards before retiring to sleep. Fiesco is tempted by this sign of trust to enter into a contest with Andreas over which of them can show more greatness. Next morning, Gianettino, the real target of the conspiracy, is quickly killed by Bourgognino, but disaster strikes as Fiesco kills his wife Leonore, who as a passionate republican has ventured on to the streets and has put on the dead tyrant's cloak and hat. On discovering what he has done, Fiesco claims that this deed was a test set him by the gods to prove his worthiness to rule. In the final scene he appears in ducal regalia. Verrina challenges him to give it up, and, when Fiesco refuses, Verrina pushes him into the harbor where he drowns. Voices announce that Andreas is returning to the city, and the play ends with Verrina declaring that he is going to join him. The Mannheim stage version of 1784 has a radically different conclusion from the published version of 1783, with Fiesco demonstrating his greatness by an act of renunciation. Breaking the scepter, he gives the Genoese the freedom for which they have fought. A further stage version, prepared for performances in Leipzig and Dresden in 1785, returns to the tragic conclusion, with Verrina stabbing Fiesco instead of drowning him. The authenticity of this version, however, is doubtful.

The events of *Kabale und Liebe* occur in a small German principality in Schiller's own time. The Duke's leading official, President von Walter, is an unprincipled man, interested only in maintaining his power. His son Ferdinand, recently returned from university, has fallen in love with Luise, the daughter of the musician Miller, and has promised to marry her. Miller is displeased at this course of events, believing that Luise will inevitably be seduced and abandoned. The President is also displeased when he hears the news from his scheming secretary Wurm, since the former is planning to secure his own influence at court by marrying his son to Lady Milford, the Duke's English mistress. Sent by his father to visit Lady Milford, Ferdinand is surprised to find, not the vicious figure he expects, but a woman of noble character who has used her relationship with the Duke to alleviate some of the harshness of his rule (although this benign influence is unknown to the servant who graphically describes to her the forced departure of local troops to fight as mercenaries in America). But Lady Milford loves Ferdinand, and, on being told of his plan to marry Luise, vows to thwart him. The President's next step is to invade the home of the Miller family and publicly to insult Luise, but this provokes Ferdinand into open defiance. The debacle ends with the President's withdrawal after Ferdinand threatens to reveal the criminal means by which he has obtained his office. On Wurm's advice, the President resolves on a more devious strategy, the "cabal" of the title. Luise's parents are to be arrested, and she is to be told that, in order to free them, she must write a letter to Hofmarschall von Kalb, a foolish courtier who is in fact unknown to her, but implying that the two of them are engaged in a liaison. She is then to be forced to swear on the sacrament never to admit that the letter was written against her will, while the letter is to be passed to Ferdinand. The point of Wurm's strategy is that the lovers' own qualities, that is, Luise's piety and Ferdinand's jealousy, will destroy the relationship more effectively than force. His calculation proves to be justified, for even before Luise has written the letter, she tells Ferdinand of her wish to end the relationship, which appears sacrilegious to her, and Ferdinand responds by accusing her of having another lover. The cabal works according to plan, with Ferdinand believing in Luise's deceit even when the terrified Kalb tries to tell him the truth. But the plan to marry him to Lady Milford miscarries when the latter, after a confrontation with Luise, decides impulsively to leave the principality. Although no outer obstacles now remain to their marriage, Luise and Ferdinand are both no longer capable of it. As Wurm calculated, Luise feels bound by her oath, but she plans to commit suicide and has to be dissuaded by her father's Christian arguments. But then, to Luise's horror, Ferdinand enters and gets rid of Miller by asking him to deliver a letter in return for a bag of gold. Alone with Luise, he reproaches her for her faithlessness, and, together with her, he drinks the lemonade that he has poisoned while her back was turned. When she realizes that she is dying, she at last feels released from her oath and tells Ferdinand that he has been deceived. The play ends with the President, shaken at his son's death, submitting to arrest for his crimes. In the published version the dying Ferdinand gives his father his hand in a token of forgiveness, but the Mannheim stage version, the so-called Mannheimer Soufflierbuch (published in 1963), ends without this conciliatory gesture.

Don Carlos, finally, tells the story of the death of the son of King Philip II of Spain. Though there was a historical Don Carlos, who died in obscure circumstances, Schiller's is a fictional version based on a *nouvelle historique* of 1672 by the Abbé de Saint-Réal. It is full of intrigues and counter-intrigues, which it is necessary to simplify somewhat. The play opens in the royal gardens of Aranjuez. Carlos is suffering from a secret love for his young stepmother Elisabeth, to whom he had been betrothed until Philip decided to marry her himself. Carlos is cheered by the arrival of his friend Marquis Posa, whom he had known at university, but the latter is perplexed by Carlos's low spirits. Posa holds progressive political ideas, to which he has earlier converted Carlos, and he is now counting on his friend's help in advancing the cause of Dutch independence. On learning that Carlos loves his "mother" (his real mother died in childbirth), Posa arranges for Carlos to meet the Queen in confidence and to receive the dispatches from the Netherlands from her hands, for she also sympathizes with the Dutch cause. At their meeting, the Queen persuades Carlos to give up all hopes of ever marrying her and rekindles his zeal for political freedom. The meeting has to end abruptly at the approach of the King, who harshly rebukes the Queen for being without attendants. In act II, Carlos obtains an audience with his father, and, after pleading for a closer relationship with him, asks to be given charge of the Netherlands instead of the Duke of Alba. Although flatly refusing this request, Philip is touched by Carlos's personal pleas. Carlos is next approached by a page with a letter from a lady asking for an assignation. Carlos agrees in the belief that it is from the Queen, but when he arrives he discovers not her but Princess Eboli, a lady-in-waiting who loves him. The outcome of their long conversation is that each learns a secret, Carlos that his father has amorous designs on Eboli and Eboli that Carlos loves the Queen. Eboli, angered by Carlos's rejection of her, hatches a plot with Alba and Domingo, the King's confessor, to undermine the Queen's position. Carlos tells Posa that he can influence the Queen by showing her the King's letter to Eboli, but Posa tells him that the plan is unworthy of him and tears the letter up. As act III opens, the King has received evidence from Alba and Domingo pointing toward an illicit liaison between Carlos and the Queen, but instead of reacting as the two had hoped, he accuses them of scheming and dismisses them in a rage. At this point chance intervenes. Hoping to find a new and uncontaminated adviser, Philip leafs through an index and pulls out at random the name of Marquis Posa. On discovering that Posa is a hero of the Turkish war, Philip summons him, and this leads to the great audience scene, the most famous of the play and possibly in Schiller's whole oeuvre. Posa refuses to enter into the King's service, and, on being pressed for his reasons, he gives a long and passionate statement of his liberal political beliefs, culminating in the line "Geben Sie Gedankenfreiheit" [Grant freedom of thought]. As at his meeting with Carlos in act II, Philip responds with sympathy at the personal level though without taking Posa's ideas seriously. He insists that Posa enter his service and orders him to find out what is going on between Carlos and the Queen. Act IV is filled with particularly dense intrigues and contains several obscurities as to the characters' motives. Briefly, Posa fails to inform Carlos of his new status, and Carlos, when informed that Posa has been seen showing some of his letters to the King, wrongly assumes that Posa has decided to betray his (Carlos's) secret to the King in order to strengthen his own influence. When Carlos rushes to Eboli to beg for access to the Queen, Posa abruptly has him arrested and comes close to killing Eboli. Next, believing that this is his only remaining means of aiding the Dutch, Posa writes an incriminating letter and allows it to fall into the hands of Philip's spies. The letter is brought to Philip, who astonishes his court by weeping over his betrayal by the one man he thought he could trust. In act V Posa is duly arrested and murdered, but not before a long and emotional farewell from Carlos, who happens to be in the same cell. The King now arrives to release Carlos, who ridicules his father for believing that a man like Posa could ever have been his friend. The King responds by vowing to redouble his efforts to suppress the cause of freedom. In a chilling scene with the ancient Grand Inquisitor, the King learns that the Inquisition has long known of Posa's conspiracies and he is rebuked for having tried to govern without the tutelage of the Church. The Inquisitor insists that Philip now hand over Carlos for execution, comparing this to God's sacrifice of His son for man. In the last scene Carlos meets the Queen to bid her farewell before leaving for the Netherlands, where he intends to declare openly against his father, but he is forestalled by the entry of the King and his retinue, who overhear the last part of their conversation. The play thus ends with the arrest of Carlos but also of the Queen. Besides the first complete published version of 1787 and several shortened published versions which appeared before Schiller's death, there are stage versions prepared for performances in Hamburg and Riga in 1787. The latter is in prose and ends with Carlos's suicide instead of his arrest.

Notes

[1] Quoted from Schiller, *Sämtliche Werke*, ed. Gerhard Fricke and Herbert G. Göpfert, 1: 488. This and all further unattributed translations are my own.

[2] The reference is to *Der Trompeter von Säkkingen* [The Trumpeter of Säkkingen, 1853], a once popular, now largely forgotten work by Johann Viktor Scheffel (1826–86), and so Nietzsche is combining the accusation that Schiller is a moralist and a rhetorician (hence the trumpet) and not a poet, with the smear that he appeals to the same parochial and middlebrow readership as the later author.

[3] The passage is from Schiller's announcement of his journal the *Rheinische Thalia*. By the term "subordination" he means his oppressive education at the Karlsschule, the ducal academy in Stuttgart at which he was educated against his will.

[4] Schiller's preference for his classical works over the less polished and more naturalistic prose works has been followed in some periods and by some critical schools but rejected by others. From a present-day perspective, the undeniable flaws in the classical works, particularly in *Die Jungfrau von Orleans* and *Die Braut von Messina,* disprove the notion that his early works are mere juvenilia in comparison with the mastery of his later years. His flight from the contemporary world into history and legend in search of subject matter for the classical dramas is for most critics today rather a cause for regret than for celebration. Without entering into a debate setting the early Schiller against the late, we should note first that the tendency for scholars to prefer one group of works at the expense of the other is probably unavoidable, and second that the early works can be preferred to the later on various grounds, aesthetic, moral, or political.

[5] These bibliographies appeared in the years 1966, 1970, 1974, 1979, 1983, 1987, 1991, and 1995, from 1974 under the name Hannich-Bode.

Works Cited

Albert, Claudia, ed. 1994. *Deutsche Klassiker im Nationalsozialismus: Schiller — Kleist — Hölderlin.* Stuttgart: Metzler.

———. 1998. "Schiller im 20. Jahrhundert." In *Schiller-Handbuch*, ed. H. Koopmann, 773–94.

Bärwinkel, Roland, Natalija I. Lopatina, and Günther Mühlpfordt. 1989. *Schiller-Bibliographie 1975–1985.* Berlin: Aufbau.

Bode, Ingrid. 1966. "Schiller-Bibliographie 1962–65." *JDSG* 10: 465–505.

———. 1970. "Schiller-Bibliographie 1966–69." *JDSG* 14: 584–636.

Boerner, Peter. 1998. "Schiller im Ausland: Dichter-Denker und Herold der nationalen Befreiung." In *Schiller-Handbuch*, ed. H. Koopmann, 795–808.

Buchwald, Reinhard. 1938. *Wandlungen unseres Schillerbildes.* Leipzig: Liebisch.

Eckermann, Johann Peter. 1836–48. *Gespräche mit Goethe in den letzten Jahren seines Lebens.* Munich: Beck, 1982.

Frey, John R. 1959. "American Schiller Literature: A Bibliography." In *Schiller 1759/1959. Commemorative American Studies*, ed. J. R. Frey. Urbana: U of Illinois P, 203–13.

Gerhard, Ute. 1998. "Schiller im 19. Jahrhundert." In *Schiller-Handbuch*, ed. H. Koopmann, 758–72.

Grawe, Christian. 1994. "Das Beispiel Schiller: Zur Konstituierung eines Klassikers in der Öffentlichkeit des 19. Jahrhunderts." In *Wissenschaftsgeschichte der Germanistik im 19. Jahrhundert*, ed. Jürgen Fohrmann and Wilhelm Vosskamp. Stuttgart: Metzler, 638–68.

Gundolf, Friedrich. 1916. *Goethe.* Berlin: Bondi.

Hannich-Bode, Ingrid. 1974. "Schiller-Bibliographie 1970–73." *JDSG* 18: 642–701.

———. 1979. "Schiller-Bibliographie 1974–78 und Nachträge." *JDSG* 23: 549–612.

———. 1983. "Schiller-Bibliographie 1979–82 und Nachträge." *JDSG* 27: 493–551.

———. 1987. "Schiller-Bibliographie 1983–86 und Nachträge." *JDSG* 31: 432–512.

———. 1991. "Schiller-Bibliographie 1987–90 und Nachträge." *JDSG* 35: 387–459.

———. 1995. "Schiller-Bibliographie 1991–94 und Nachträge." *JDSG* 39: 463–531.

Hecker, Max, ed. 1904. *Schillers Persönlichkeit. Urtheile der Zeitgenossen und Dokumente.* Vol. 1. Weimar: Gesellschaft der Bibliophilen.

Keferstein, Georg. 1939. "Zur Wiedergeburt Schillers in unserer Zeit." *GRM* 27, 165–91.

Koopmann, Helmut. 1977. *Friedrich Schiller I: 1759–1794.* Sammlung Metzler. 2nd revised ed. Stuttgart: Metzler.

———. 1982. *Schiller-Forschung 1970–1980: Ein Bericht.* Marbach am Neckar: Deutsche Schillergesellschaft.

———. 1998. "Forschungsgeschichte." In *Schiller-Handbuch*, ed. H. Koopmann, 809–932.

———, ed. 1998. *Schiller-Handbuch.* Stuttgart: Kröner.

Lämmert, Eberhard, ed. 1967. *Germanistik — eine deutsche Wissenschaft.* Frankfurt a. M.: Suhrkamp.

Ludwig, Albert. 1909. *Schiller und die deutsche Nachwelt.* Berlin: Weidmannsche Buchhandlung.

Mann, Heinrich. 1905. *Professor Unrat.* Hamburg: Rowohlt, 1951.

Mann, Klaus. 1952. *Der Wendepunkt: Ein Lebensbericht.* Munich: Nymphenburger Verlagshandlung, 1969.

Mann, Thomas. 1903. *Tonio Kröger.* In his *Sämtliche Erzählungen*, Frankfurt a. M.: Fischer, 1963, 213–66.

———. 1905. "Schwere Stunde." In his *Sämtliche Erzählungen*, Frankfurt a. M.: Fischer, 1963, 294–300.

———. 1955. *Versuch über Schiller.* Berlin: Fischer.

Mayer, Hans. 1955. "Schillers Vorreden zu den *Räubern*." In his *Von Lessing bis Thomas Mann: Wandlungen der bürgerlichen Literatur in Deutschland.* Pfüllingen: Neske, 1959, 134–53.

———. 1959. "Schillers Nachruhm." *EG* 14: 374–85.

Müller-Seidel, Walter. 1952. "Zum gegenwärtigen Stand der Schiller-Forschung." *DU* 4, H.5, 97–115.

Nietzsche, Friedrich. 1889. *Götzendämmerung.* In vol. 2 of *Werke*, ed. Karl Schlechta. 6th ed. 3 vols. Munich: Hanser, 1969, 941–1033.

Oellers, Norbert. 1967. *Schiller: Geschichte seiner Wirkung bis zu Goethes Tod.* Bonn: Bouvier, 1967.

———, ed. 1970. *Schiller — Zeitgenosse aller Epochen: Dokumente zur Wirkungsgeschichte in Deutschland. Teil I: 1782–1859.* Frankfurt a. M.: Athenäum.

——, ed. 1976. *Schiller — Zeitgenosse aller Epochen: Dokumente zur Wirkungsgeschichte in Deutschland. Teil II: 1860–1966.* Munich: Beck.

Paulsen, Wolfgang. 1962. "Friedrich Schiller 1955–1959: Ein Literaturbericht." *JDSG* 6: 369–464.

Pick, R. 1961. "Schiller in England 1787–1960: A Bibliography." *PEGS*, N.S. 30.

Raabe, Paul and Ingrid Bode. 1962. "Schiller-Bibliographie 1959–1961." *JDSG* 9: 465–53.

Ruppelt, Georg. 1979. *Schiller im nationalsozialistischen Deutschland: Der Versuch einer Gleichschaltung.* Stuttgart: Metzler.

Saint-Réal, César Vichard, Abbé de. 1672. *Dom Carlos: Nouvelle Historique.* Repr.: Geneva: Slatkine Reprints, 1979.

Schiller, Friedrich. 1943– . *Werke.* (Nationalausgabe), founded by Julius Petersen. Weimar: Böhlau. Vol. 3, *Die Räuber*, 1953. Vol. 4, *Fiesco*, 1983. Vol. 5, *Kabale und Liebe*, 1957. Vols. 6, 7/1, 7/2, *Don Carlos*, 1973, 1974, 1986.

——. 1963. *Kabale und Liebe: Das Mannheimer Soufflierbuch*, ed. Herbert Kraft. Mannheim: Bibliographisches Institut.

——. 1980–84. *Sämtliche Werke*, ed. Gerhard Fricke and Herbert G. Göpfert. 5 vols. Munich: Hanser; licensed edition, Darmstadt: Wissenschaftliche Buchgesellschaft. Vol. 1, including *Die Räuber, Die Verschwörung des Fiesco zu Genua, Kabale und Liebe*, 7th ed., 1984. Vol. 2, including *Don Carlos, Briefe über Don Carlos*, etc., 6th ed., 1981.

——. 1988– . *Werke und Briefe* (Frankfurter Ausgabe), ed. Klaus Harro Hilzinger et al. Frankfurt a. M.: Deutscher Klassiker Verlag. Vol. 2 (*Dramen I*), *Die Räuber, Fiesco, Kabale und Liebe.* Vol. 3 (*Dramen II*), *Don Carlos.*

Smith, Herbert. 1935. "Present-Day Tendencies in the German Interpretation of Schiller." *PEGS*: 20–36.

Taylor, A. J. P. 1945. *The Course of German History.* 2nd ed. London: Methuen, 1961.

Ugrinsky, Alexej. 1988. Preface to *Friedrich von Schiller and the Drama of Human Existence*, ed. A. Ugrinsky. New York: Greenwood Press, vii-viii.

Unger, Rudolf. 1937. "Richtungen und Probleme neuerer Schiller-Deutung." *Nachrichten von der Gesellschaft der Wissenschaften zu Göttingen: Philologisch-historisch Klasse: Neue Folge: Fachgruppe IV: Neuere Philologie und Literaturwissenschaft*, I, 9: 203–42.

Vansca, Kurt. 1961. "Das Ernte der Schiller-Jahre 1955–59." *ZfdPh* 79: 422–41.

Vulpius, Wolfgang. 1959. *Schiller-Bibliographie 1893–1958.* Weimar: Arion.

———. 1967. *Schiller-Bibliographie 1959–1963*. Berlin (East): Aufbau.

Weitbrecht, Carl. 1901. "Schiller in der Gegenwart." In his *Schiller und die deutsche Gegenwart*. Stuttgart: Bonz, 51–92.

Wersig, Peter. 1977. *Schiller-Bibliographie 1964–1974*. Berlin (East): Aufbau.

Wiese, Benno von. 1953. "Schiller-Forschung und Schiller-Deutung von 1937 bis 1953." *DVjs* 27: 452–83.

Witte, William. 1961. "Das neue Schillerbild der britischen Germanistik." *JDSG* 5: 402–13.

Wittkowski, Wolfgang. 1966. "Friedrich Schiller 1962–65: Ein Literaturbericht." *JDSG* 10: 414–64.

1: The Neoclassical Establishment: The Contemporary Reception

WHILE CONTEMPORARY REVIEWS MIGHT not belong to every definition of the critical history of a literary work, it is worth beginning with them in the present instance. From our twentieth-century perspective, it is all too easy to take for granted Schiller's status as classical author and from there to assume the canonical character of all his works. That classical status was not won overnight. Schiller's first reviewers knew nothing of it, and hence were able to evaluate his early works, if not with an unprejudiced eye, then at least with one unclouded by the personal prestige in which the author would later be held. In the nineteenth century, furthermore, Schiller's reputation rested largely on his verse dramas; to the extent that the early prose dramas found favor, it was mainly because they were allowed to share in the reflected glory of the later achievements. Full recognition of the prose dramas has only come about in the present century. It is thus of interest to observe the first reaction aroused by those early works before the later and more palatable dramas came along to sweeten the public's appetite. This reaction, ranging from qualified approval to vehement rejection, brings home to us the intractable, almost rebarbative character of the works under discussion and consequently leads us to appreciate the obstacles that prevented them from gaining unqualified recognition.

Most dramatic criticism in the 1780s was still guided by the spirit of Gotthold Ephraim Lessing (1729–81) and the Aristotelian values of the mid century. At least one writer found that Schiller's challenge to these standards undermined not only public taste but also morality. We come across adjectives like "ekelhaft" [disgusting] and "zurückstoßend" [repulsive] for the situations in *Die Räuber*, and the spirit of the first three plays is described as monstrous and even cannibalistic. The most frequently heard complaint among more sober critics, despite Schiller's aspiration to a radical psychological realism — "die Seele gleichsam bei ihren geheimsten Operationen zu ertappen" [to catch the soul so to speak in its most secret operations; preface to *Die Räuber*, 484] — is that his prose plays are unnatural in characterization, situation, and language. An instructive example is the review of the first edition of *Die Räuber* in the *Erfurtische Gelehrte Zeitung* in 1781, where the author,

Hermann Timme, is plainly divided between his recognition of young Schiller's extraordinary achievement and his inability to account for his own positive response within the canons of critical orthodoxy. Quibbling with Schiller's declared aim of writing a dramatized novel, Timme writes that this might be suitable for a talent of the second rank, but an author of Schiller's evident genius should aim at nothing but the best. Interpreting Schiller's style as a Shakespeare-inspired naturalism, he compares it to the painting style of Rembrandt or Teniers (another seventeenth-century Dutch painter). Against this, he asserts the superiority of the classicism of Raphael and Adolf Mengs, and the literary equivalent of this classicism, as Timme makes clear, is Aristotle as interpreted and put into practice by Lessing. What Timme seems not to consider is whether Schiller could have followed this advice without sacrificing those very qualities of fiery energy and imagination that have marked him as such a phenomenon. Like many readers, Timme is impressed by the characterization of Karl Moor, but also by the strict causality that governs his fate; in this latter point especially we can observe the influence of Lessing's dramatic criticism. Timme is less impressed by Franz, who is, despite Schiller's professed commitment to psychological realism, "ein . . . vollkommenes Ideal eines menschlichen Ungeheuers" (953) [a perfect ideal of a human monster]. Nonetheless, Timme displays a certain critical acumen by pointing out the consistency of Franz's miserable behaviour in the last act with his character as presented in the previous acts. In his appreciation of Amalia, he shows the sentimental taste to which Schiller was of course catering in his creation of this character. From here on, his review degenerates into a succession of points, praising the beauties and blaming the faults after the fashion of the times, and we should note his criticism of Schiller's language, on the grounds, first, of indecency, second, of the use of obscure dialect expressions, and third, of Schiller's penchant for, he says, exaggerated and artificial similes and metaphors.

Many of the same points can be heard in a longer review by a Jesuit author, P. Klein, in the *Pfälzisches Museum* two years later (1783–84). Klein shares Timme's neoclassical tenets, and he too objects to Schiller's language — "künstlich, gezwungen und undeutlich" (48) [artificial, forced and unclear] — although, interestingly, he also employs the term "Schwulst" [bombast] that had been directed by both Lessing and Gottsched against the hated Baroque style. This may seem a minor point, but it suggests that Schiller's first plays did not annoy merely through reviving the Storm and Stress fashion of the previous decade; they also appeared to older readers to threaten the humanizing and civilizing accomplishments of the previous generations, a factor that accounts, more satisfactorily than instinctive distaste, for the deep hostility aroused by the works in some quarters. We may note also that, behind the frequent allusions to Schiller's alleged imitation of Shakespeare, there lurks a Voltairean hostility to the English playwright as often as a Lessing-inspired admiration.

Klein is more specific than Timme in his criticisms of Schiller. The plot of *Die Räuber*, he finds, lacks the clarity and simplicity of the ancients; it is overloaded and confused, strains for significance by means of philosophical digressions, and seeks to attract attention to itself by drawing on the lowest strata of society for material. Not content to condemn the characterization of Franz, Klein offers a lengthy literary comparison to prove that his objections do not rest on simple moralism; despite her equally great crimes, he writes, Medea was turned by both Euripides and Seneca into a more truly theatrical character than is Franz by Schiller. And Klein is also less than impressed by Karl, whose words and deeds he finds simply too erratic, too reminiscent of the "Genieritter" [cavaliers of genius] to exert the fascination of a great dramatic figure (the reference is to the ranting heroes made fashionable by the Storm and Stress in the previous decade). Despite these various criticisms, Klein too concedes that Schiller has extraordinary talent, although, like Timme, he has been largely unable to explain why he thinks so.

We should mention finally an anonymous review of 1783 that W. Kurrelmeyer has plausibly attributed to Johann Joachim Eschenburg, the friend of Lessing and Nicolai and an early translator of Shakespeare. If the attribution is correct, it shows how even one of the leaders of the Shakespearian revival failed to appreciate the wave of imitations by young writers inspired by Goethe's *Götz von Berlichingen* (1773). More in sorrow than in anger, this critic laments the way in which even the brighter members of the young generation have seen fit to copy those aspects of Shakespeare's work that no rational person can admire; for this he blames "ein mißverstandener Begriff von Natur und Kraft" (74) [a misunderstood concept of nature and force]. Thus even what is promising in Schiller's play is spoiled by "Uebertreibung und Unnatürlichkeit" (75) [exaggeration and unnaturalness]. Beyond this, the author has little to say about the work beyond some tut-tutting about its possible harmful influence and some suggestions as to how the plot might have been made less implausible.

On *Fiesco*, we must attend first to a notice in the *Allgemeine deutsche Bibliothek* in 1783 by Adolf Freiherr von Knigge (1751–96), a leading member of the Illuminati (a secret society devoted to Enlightened ideals) and soon to be famous as the author of the best-selling

Über den Umgang mit Menschen [On Human Society, 1788]. Knigge had contributed a short review of the book version of *Die Räuber* in the previous year, praising the work's extraordinary power, but with *Fiesco* he deplores the fact that the author has not learnt to use his talents properly. Knigge lists a number of implausibilities and inconsistencies, no less evident today than two hundred years ago, and, like others, he finds Schiller's language "zu bilderreich, zu voll von Wortspielen und Gleichnissen" [too rich in images, too full of wordplays and similes], a feature he attributes to Shakespeare worship. He recommends that, instead of pandering to the fashionable belief that "was plump ist, wäre stark" [clumsiness is the same as strength], Schiller should devote himself to mastering the technical aspects of his art. A similar note of disappointment is sounded by the anonymous reviewer of the *Nürnbergische gelehrte Zeitung*, who advises Schiller to study "true nature" and the classics if he wishes to remedy his shortcomings.

A more substantial review of a later production of the play has been discovered and published by Christian Grawe. Writing in his short-lived *Dramaturgisches Wochenblatt für Berlin und Deutschland* in 1792, Gottfried Lucas Hagemeister gives a general (and, considering the year, courageous) justification of political drama as promoting an enlightened public opinion, and then considers the merits of the nontragic conclusion to the play that was evidently used in the version staged in Berlin. Although there is no real connection between Hagemeister's general and specific arguments, the review is notable for initiating the critical debate about the variant conclusions of *Fiesco*; Hagemeister argues on the grounds of psychological consistency that the protagonist's dominant motivation throughout is ambition, and that if at the end he renounces the ducal purple, it can only be through fear of a violent revenge. But Hagemeister clearly finds the conclusion to the first edition, in which the Republican Verrina drowns Fiesco, to be the most satisfying. Otherwise, he is unusual for his time for recognizing and appreciating Schiller's extravagant dramatic language.

Walter Pape (1988) has summed up the consensus on *Kabale und Liebe* that emerges from the contemporary reviews: it is a drama "mit übertriebenen und psychisch unwahren Charakteren, mit einer allzu groben Intrige und einer unnötigen Katastrophe" (199) [with exaggerated or psychologically untrue characters, with an all too clumsy intrigue and with an unnecessary *dénouement*].[1] As drastic as it sounds, Pape's summary is in fact perfectly accurate. One of the most famous early responses to the play, and to Schiller's prose dramas in general, came from Karl Philipp Moritz (1757–93), by then a leading voice of the Berlin Enlightenment, in a pair of reviews in the Berlin *Staats- und gelehrte Zeitung* in 1784. Moritz had noted the appearance of the book version of *Kabale und Liebe* with a brief and hostile paragraph in July, calling Ferdinand "ein Geck" [a conceited ass] and Luise "ein dummes affektirtes Mädchen" [a stupid and affected girl]. Called upon to substantiate his charges, he then wrote a longer review the following September repeating and detailing them. What emerges from the longer piece is chiefly Moritz's distaste for the apocalyptic religious imagery in which Schiller's protagonists express their love, an aspect of the play that still causes many readers to balk. The language, he says, is distasteful, extravagant and implausible, and he quotes numerous passages that he finds unacceptable. The term "Galimathias" [farrago] occurs, and, after a quotation, the rhetorical question "Ist das Sprache des Herzens und der Natur?" (1375) [Is that the language of the heart and of nature?]. In addition, Moritz finds the language of the President, Ferdinand's father, undignified, that of Lady Milford precious, while the language of Miller to his wife is so vulgar as to be entirely beyond the pale. Regarding the plot, he argues that a good drama might have been written around Lady Milford, but that Schiller has overloaded the play with events at the expense of clarity and plausibility. Like other critics, Moritz concludes by holding up Lessing as a paragon of good dramatic practice, and in so doing shows that he speaks for a fairly broad section of the literary public.

These plays had their admirers, of course. An anonymous reviewer in the *Gothaische gelehrte Zeitungen* (1784) defends the use of exaggerated characters and even ventures to cite Lessing in support of Schiller's creation, in the Hofmarschall, of a character too comic to suit normal conceptions of tragedy. This reviewer also associates Schiller with Lessing's campaign against Baroque tragedy. Lessing was by now safely dead and could not protest at this misuse of his name. Another favorable review appeared in the *Allgemeine deutsche Bibliothek* (1784). The author was once more Eschenburg, the translator of Shakespeare, who however can only say that *Kabale und Liebe* is better than he had expected, in that its plot structure is superior to those of its two predecessors. Eschenburg then considerately lists for the author's benefit a number of instances where his plot developments are insufficiently motivated; like other critics, he seems unwilling or unable to explain what it is about the play that he admires.

Finally, it is worth noting an article of 1788 in the *Tagebuch der Mainzer Schaubühne*, in which Aloys Wilhelm Schreiber claims, with reference to *Kabale und Liebe*, to be seeking the middle ground between those who praise Schiller uncritically and those who condemn him outright. Although flawed as works of art, his plays contain signs of fiery imagination and true "Menschenkenntnis" [psychological insight]; the latter compliment must have pleased Schiller, who had underlined psychological accuracy as one of his aims in the preface to *Die Räuber*. Even the faults in these plays, Schreiber writes, are aberrations of genius. Unfortunately, his article does not deliver the kind of balanced analysis that these remarks lead us to hope for. Despite two promising insights, first, that Schiller aims not to move but to shatter, and second, that the implausible accumulation of incident can be understood from this perspective, Schreiber proves unable to transcend the dominant critical principles of his time, cataloguing like so many others Schiller's inconsistencies of plot and characterization and allowing the "beauties" to speak for themselves. In fact, the insight that Schiller's goals in these plays differed from the conventional ones might have alerted this critic to the inappropriateness of the usual evaluative criteria.

In view of its milder spirit, one might think that *Don Carlos* would have had a less controversial reception, and to some extent this is true. For example, an anonymous reviewer of the 1787 book version in the Berlin *Ephemeriden* noted that, together with Lessing's *Nathan der Weise* [Nathan the Wise, 1779] and Goethe's *Iphigenie auf Tauris* (1787), the play formed "ein vortreffliches Kleeblatt" (186) [a glorious trio]. A Jena reviewer employed the same metaphor, although he tempered his praise by pointing out Schiller's inconsistency regarding Carlos's recognition of the Queen's handwriting, as well as his departure from historical accuracy (Koch 1962). By 1803, the critic Johann Friedrich Schink, a leading spokesman of the Enlightenment, was writing of *Don Carlos* as an established masterpiece, although, to be sure, the contrast with Schiller's earlier "false Shakespearianism" causes the new play's qualities of maturity and restraint to stand out so strongly. Clearly, this was a play that fitted more easily into the contemporary landscape. However, even this work provoked some comment from critics whose resistance to Schiller's talents had been, if not confirmed by the new work, then at least not disarmed.

Schiller had published parts of the first three acts in the *Rheinische Thalia* and had called for suggestions from his public as to how the work should be concluded and its existing parts improved. An unnamed reviewer took up this invitation in the *Neue Bibliothek der schönen Wissenschaften und der freyen Künste* in 1786, launching the kind of attack on Schiller's imagery that we have seen already:

> Die sämtlichen Personen des Stückes sprechen, als wenn sie eben erst von dem Land der Metaphern zurückgekommen wären; sie schwimmen (wie Haller sich über Lohenstein ausdrückt) auf Metaphern wie

auf leichten Blasen; sie häufen Figur auf Figur, Bild auf Bild. . . . Das Bild schmiegt sich nie nach dem Gedanken; der Gedanke muß sich immer nach dem Bilde bequemen. (155)

[All the characters speak as if they had just returned from the land of metaphors; they float (as Haller expresses himself about Lohenstein) on metaphors as on light bubbles; they pile figure upon figure, image upon image. . . . The image never fits the thought; the thought has to accommodate itself to the image.]

What is expressed here is the hostility of the middle-aged to the allegedly self-indulgent and superficial art of the younger generation, and the reference to Lohenstein once more conveys the apprehension that this new art signals a return to the presumed horrors of the previous century. This reviewer casts doubt on Schiller's claim (in the *Räuber* preface) to illuminate the human heart. Instead, we hear an anticipation of the later criticism that, as a poet, Schiller could invent new images and fit them to abstract ideas but had no talent for anything of a more personal nature. Here we can see, beside the fear of a Lohenstein *redivivus*, the emergence of the fatal stereotype of Schiller the philosophical poet.

Two lengthy reviews of the book version of 1787 are of special interest, since they elicited a response from Schiller in the *Briefe über Don Carlos*, which were published the following year in Wieland's *Teutscher Merkur*. The two reviews are remarkable in that they level the charges against the work's coherence that have never been entirely dispelled. The reviewer of the Jena *Allgemeine Literatur-Zeitung* (Johann Friedrich Jünger, according to Kluge's conjecture) gave the work an on the whole polite reception, attributing to it poetic excellence, the fulfillment of its moral purpose, and a greater mastery of versification than had been achieved by Lessing in *Nathan der Weise*. Although generally admiring the first three acts, the reviewer wonders whether too much space has been devoted to the mechanics of the plot and to bringing the protagonists together; he is thinking of the intrigue of Princess Eboli with Domingo and Alba, and of the scene between Carlos and the Page. We notice the predilections of the neoclassical critic when this writer asserts: "Das Intrigen und Plane machen ist überhaupt nicht fürs Trauerspiel, in welchem die Leidenschaften der Menschen handelnd vorgeführt werden sollen" (1118). [Intriguing and scheming are definitely not for tragedy, in which human passions are supposed to be presented by means of action.] It is from this standpoint that he goes on to criticize the plot from act IV onward, calling it "unerträglich verwickelt" [intolerably complicated]. In view of the difficulties that this matter continues to cause to modern readers, we should perhaps note that the neoclassical requirement of unity of plot was not always the pedantic excrescence for which it is usually taken nowadays but could be used as a way of making valid observations. The criticism of psychological inconsistency in Posa — "Posa verleugnet die einfache Größe seines Charakters, um ein abentheuerlicher Intrigant zu werden" (1118) [Posa belies the simple greatness of his character in order to become a bizarre intriguer] — is another application of the insistence on unity, as is the demand that a figure's actions should harmonize with his character. The reviewer's moral outrage over Posa's conduct is thus not the decisive element of his criticism.

A part of this early review that is less well known (presumably since Schiller did not deign to respond to it) is directed against act V, scene 10 between the King and the Grand Inquisitor, and once again unity of plot is the touchstone. The reviewer is indignant over the late introduction of a plot element which causes all the foregoing events to appear in a new light. This manipulation annoys us, the reviewer writes, and again his *a priori* method is on display:

> Eine solche Idee, an welche der ganze Faden der Geschichte sich knüpfen soll, muß gleich vom Anfange in die Handlung so verwebt werden, daß man sie nie ganz aus dem Gesichte verliert, damit das Interesse ja nicht auf einen falschen Weg gerathe, von dem der Zuschauer oder Leser nicht ohne Unmuth wieder abgebracht wird. (1119)

> [This kind of idea, to which the whole thread of the story ought to be attached, must be woven into the plot right from the outset in such a way that one never loses sight of it, so that one's interest never gets onto a false trail, from which the spectator or reader will not be diverted again without annoyance.]

Although he does not mention this, the reviewer might well have had in mind Lessing's use of Orsina's letter in *Emilia Galotti* as a piece of deft plot management that would show up Schiller's shortcomings.

The other review, written by Christian Viktor Kindervater, appeared in the *Kritische Uebersicht der neusten schönen Litteratur der Deutschen*. While covering some of the same ground as the article just outlined, it also expresses distaste for Schiller's theological imagery (for example the overuse of the terms "Unendlichkeit" [eternity] and "Weltgericht" [day of judgment]), and adds some points of criticism of the plot that are worth recording. In the early acts, which had found the approval of the reviewer in the *Allgemeine Literatur-Zeitung*, Kindervater finds a general lack of focus and forward movement, and the entire Eboli in-

trigue he finds implausible. The chief problem, in his view, is the un-
suitability of Carlos himself as tragic protagonist. In both the important
scenes with the Queen and with the Princess, Carlos behaves and
speaks in a way that the reviewer finds ridiculous, leaving a vacuum
where the tragic hero is supposed to be. Posa's whole intrigue is thus
vitiated, not only because of his lack of openness in conducting it, but
also because of a fundamental lack of judgment on his part: how could
so rash and unstable a youth as Carlos fulfill the hopes that Posa has
placed in him? The intrigue itself is not only overcomplicated, the disproportion between Posa's preparations and the outcome infringes a
basic rule of dramatic economy:

> In der wirklichen Welt geschieht das freylich oft genug, aber im Dra-
> ma, und zumal im Trauerspiel, darf eine solche Person nichts thun, als
> was der ihr gegebene, deutlich bezeichnete Charakter und die Um-
> stände nicht anders als nothwendig machen. (1126)

> [In the real world of course this happens often enough, but in drama,
> especially in tragedy, such a person is permitted to do nothing but
> what his . . . clearly defined character and the circumstances make ab-
> solutely necessary.]

Here we again see that a recourse to *a priori* neoclassical principle can
reveal real weaknesses in the structure of the play. The consequence of
all these miscalculations in the character and actions of Carlos and Posa,
the reviewer believes, is the emergence of King Philip as the figure
arousing the highest degree of sympathy, and, while this might seem to
be in some degree inadvertent on Schiller's part, Kindervater allows
Schiller much credit for the creation of this fine tragic figure.

Albert Ludwig, the historian of Schiller's reputation to the end of
the nineteenth century, wrote (1909, 10) that the rationalistic critics
treated Schiller as a teacher treats a promising student who still has to
be cured of some bad habits before he can receive unqualified praise.
While the ironic tone of his remark is perhaps not wholly unfair, it is
also worth considering whether Ludwig's view of the matter is not
distorted to some extent by his own assumption of Schiller's monumental stature. Far from schoolmasterly pedantry, the criticisms of the
structure of *Don Carlos* expressed in the two reviews just outlined go to
the heart of this work, raising objections that are still at the centre of
the critical debate today. While much of the response to the three prose
plays simply reflected the reviewers' shock at works that confounded all
their expectations, the reviewers of *Don Carlos* show that neoclassical
critical principles were also capable of yielding analyses whose validity is
not confined to a particular time and place.

Notes

[1] There is a useful collection of early reviews in *Schillers Kabale und Liebe in der zeitgenössischen Rezeption*, edited by Hans Henning (Leipzig: Zentralantiquariat der Deutschen Demokratischen Republik, 1976).

Works Cited

Anon. 1783. [Review of *Fiesco*.] *Nürnbergische gelehrte Zeitung* 47: 377–79. Cited in Schiller 1988, *Dramen I*: 1196–98.

Anon. 1784. [Review of *Kabale und Liebe*.] *Gothaische gelehrte Zeitungen*, 29.5.1784. Cited in Schiller 1988, *Dramen I*: 1371–72.

Anon. 1786. [Review of excerpts of *Don Carlos* in *Rheinische Thalia*.] *Neue Bibliothek der schönen Wissenschaften und der freyen Künste* 32, 1: 289–323. Cited in Braun 1882, 1: 147–69.

Anon. 1787. [Review of *Don Carlos*.] *Ephemeriden*, 10 and 17.11.1787. Cited in Braun 1882, 1: 185–88.

Anon. 1787. [Review of *Don Carlos*.] *Jenaische Zeitungen von gelehrten Sachen*, 1787, 708. Cited in Koch 1962, 179–80.

Braun, Julius W. 1882. *Schiller und Goethe im Urtheile ihrer Zeitgenossen. Abteilung 1: Schiller*. 3 vols. Leipzig: Schicke.

Eschenburg, J. J. (?). 1783. [Review of *Die Räuber*.] *Jahrbücher des Geschmacks und der Aufklärung*. Cited in Kurrelmeyer 1919.

———. 1784. [Review of *Kabale und Liebe*.] *Allgemeine deutsche Bibliothek* 58, 2: 477–80. Cited in Schiller 1988, *Dramen I*: 1381–85.

Grawe, Christian. 1982. "Zu Schillers *Fiesko*: Eine übersehene frühe Rezension." *JDSG* 26:9–30.

Hagemeister, Gottfried Lucas. 1792. [Review of *Fiesco*.] *Dramaturgisches Wochenblatt für Berlin und Deutschland*. Cited in Grawe 1982, 13–30.

Henning, Hans, ed. 1976. *Schillers Kabale und Liebe in der zeitgenössischen Rezeption*. Leipzig: Zentralantiquariat der Deutschen Demokratischen Republik.

Jünger, Johann Friedrich (?). 1788. [Review of *Don Carlos*.] *Allgemeine Literatur-Zeitung* 139–140a: 529–42. Cited in Schiller 1989, *Dramen II*: 1116–21.

Kindervater, Christian Viktor. 1788. [Review of *Don Carlos*.] *Kritische Uebersicht der neusten schönen Litteratur der Deutschen* 1, 2: 9–62. Cited in Schiller 1989, *Dramen II*: 1122–31.

Klein, P. 1783–84. [Review of *Die Räuber*.] *Pfälzisches Museum* 1: 225–90. Cited in Braun 1882, 1: 32–64.

Knigge, Adolf, Freiherr von. 1782. [Review of *Die Räuber.*] *Allgemeine deutsche Bibliothek* 49, 1: 127. Cited in Schiller 1988, *Dramen I*: 958–59.

——. 1783. [Review of *Fiesco.*] *Allgemeine Deutsche Bibliothek* 56, 1: 959. Cited in Schiller 1988, *Dramen I*: 1198–99.

Koch, Herbert. 1962. "Zwei unbekannte Schiller-Rezensionen." *JDSG* 6: 178–83.

Kurrelmeyer, W. 1919. "A Contemporary Critique of Schiller's *Räuber.*" *JEGP* 18: 72–79.

Ludwig, Albert. 1909. *Schiller und die deutsche Nachwelt.* Berlin: Weidmann.

Moritz, Karl Philipp. 1784. [Review of *Kabale und Liebe.*] *Königlich privilegierte Berlinische Staats- und gelehrte Zeitung*, 4.9.1794. Cited in Schiller 1988, *Dramen I*: 1373–79.

Oellers, Norbert, ed. 1970. *Schiller — Zeitgenosse aller Epochen.* Vol. 1. Frankfurt a. M.: Athenäum.

Pape, Walter. 1988. "'Ein merkwürdiges Beispiel produktiver Kritik': Schillers *Kabale und Liebe* und das zeitgenössische Publikum." *ZfdPh* 197: 190–211.

Schiller, Friedrich. 1988. *Dramen I*, ed. Gerhard Kluge. Vol. 2 of *Werke und Briefe*. Frankfurt a. M.: Deutscher Klassiker Verlag.

——. 1989. *Dramen II*, ed. Gerhard Kluge. Vol. 3 of *Werke und Briefe*. Frankfurt a. M.: Deutscher Klassiker Verlag.

Schink, Johann Friedrich. 1803. [Review of *Don Carlos.*] *Neue allgemeine deutsche Bibliothek* 83, 1: 86–102. Cited in Oellers, ed. 1970, 98–109.

Schreiber, Aloys Wilhelm. 1788. "Ueber *Kabale und Liebe.*" *Tagebuch der Mainzer Schaubühne* 3: 44f., 5: 68–74. Cited in Schiller 1988, *Dramen I*: 1395–1400.

Timme, Hermann. 1781. [Review of *Die Räuber.*] *Erfurtische Gelehrte Zeitung*, 24.7.1781. Cited in Schiller 1988, *Dramen I*: 950–57.

2: Romantics, Liberals, Hegelians, Positivists: The Nineteenth Century

Scholarly examination of Schiller's life and works begins with the publication of Karl Hoffmeister's five-volume work *Schiller's Leben, Geisteshaltung und Werke im Zusammenhang* in the years 1838–42. This is not to say that Schiller did not receive the attention of the literary public in the years following his death, rather that that attention (in many cases veneration would be a more accurate term) expressed itself mainly through popular interest in the story of his life. Indeed, as Oellers has commented (Oellers 1970, 32, 36), the veneration of Schiller in these early years contributed remarkably little in the way of literary understanding. Works such as the biographies by Caroline von Wolzogen (1830) and Andreas Streicher (1836), which catered to that public interest, convey valuable information as to the circumstances in which Schiller wrote his first four plays, but contain little that could properly belong in the present study. The autobiography of Schiller's friend Friedrich Wilhelm von Hoven (1840) should also be mentioned here, for this is the source of our knowledge that *Die Räuber* was inspired by Christian Friedrich Daniel Schubart's story "Zur Geschichte des menschlichen Herzens" [On the History of the Human Heart, 1775]. Wilhelm von Humboldt's expansive preface to his correspondence with Schiller (1830) deals entirely with the latter's intellectual development, mentioning *Don Carlos* only as an example of its author's passion for abstract ideas. His distaste for the prose plays is barely concealed: "Ungeachtet aller Mängel der Form, ungeachtet vieler Dinge, die dem gereiften Künstler sogar roh erscheinen mußten, zeugten die *Räuber* und *Fiesko* von einer entschiednen großen Naturkraft" (288). [Regardless of all formal defects, regardless of many things that must even have seemed crude to the mature artist, *The Robbers* and *Fiesco* testified to a decided great natural power.]

A similar judgment was passed on the prose plays by Goethe, who, in an essay of 1815 *Über das deutsche Theater*, referred to the trio as "Produktionen genialer, jugendlicher Ungeduld und Unwillens über einen schweren Erziehungsdruck" (322) [products of the impatience of youthful genius and of resentment about a heavily oppressive education]. Three further comments by Goethe noted by Eckermann (1836–48) have, thanks to Goethe's unique authority, influenced much subsequent scholarship. The first, recorded by Eckermann for 17 January 1827, is the most trivial, but it illustrates how shocking *Die Räuber* was felt to be in its time. Goethe recalls getting into a profound conversation with an unnamed nobleman one summer at a spa (we are not told in which year):

> Wir kamen auch auf Schillers "Räuber," und der Fürst äußerte sich folgendermaßen: "Wäre ich Gott gewesen," sagte er, "im Begriff, die Welt zu erschaffen, und ich hätte in dem Augenblick vorausgesehen, daß Schillers 'Räuber' darin würden geschrieben werden, ich hätte die Welt nicht erschaffen." (181)

> [We got onto the subject of Schiller's *Robbers*, and the Prince expressed himself thus: "If I had been God," he said "on the point of creating the world, and if I had in that moment foreseen that Schiller's *Robbers* would be written in it, I would not have created it."]

This prince would no doubt have been surprised to learn that most scholars now regard the play as essentially antirevolutionary. The amusing anecdote, besides revealing much about Schiller's reputation, also points to a serious issue, which is the discrepancy between the play's surface gestures, which are shocking and even offensive, and its core, which offers little in the way of a substantive challenge to the status quo.

In the next statement (18 January 1827), Goethe coins a distinction between the spirit of Schiller's pre- and post-Kantian dramas while uniting both periods under a single idea:

> Durch Schillers alle Werke . . . geht die Idee von Freiheit, und diese Idee nahm eine andere Gestalt an, sowie Schiller in seiner Kultur weiterging und selbst ein anderer wurde. In seiner Jugend war es die physische Freiheit, die ihm zu schaffen machte und die in seine Dichtungen überging, in seinem spätern Leben die ideelle. (187)

> [The idea of freedom runs through all of Schiller's works, and this idea took on a different form as Schiller progressed in his cultivation and became a different person. In his youth it was physical freedom that was of concern to him and that overflowed into his poetic works; in his later ones it was ideal freedom.]

Like all brilliant aphorisms, the remark obscures as much as it illuminates, and it has perhaps led some critics to overstress the concept of freedom and to overlook the religious dimension in the plays.

Goethe's last comment to Eckermann (3 May 1827), published in the later third part of the *Gespräche* [Conversations], will also have reached a wide readership:

> Es ist wahr, Schiller war recht jung, als er seine "Räuber," seine "Kabale und Liebe" und seinen "Fiesko" schrieb. Allein wenn wir aufrichtig sein wollen, so sind doch alle diese Stücke mehr Äußerungen eines außergewöhnlichen Talents, als daß sie von großer Bildungsreife des Autors zeugten. Daran ist aber nicht Schiller schuld, sondern der Kulturzustand seiner Nation und die große Schwierigkeit, die wir alle erfahren, uns auf einsamem Wege durchzuhelfen. (541)

> [True, Schiller was very young when he wrote his *Robbers*, his *Intrigue and Love*, and his *Fiesco*. However, if we are to be honest, all these plays are more expressions of an extraordinary talent than that they testify to any great cultural maturity on the part of the author. But that is not Schiller's fault, but rather the fault of his nation's cultural state, and the great difficulty that we all experience in making our way along our solitary path.]

Goethe's comments fit in with his abiding preoccupation with the growth of German culture in his time, and aim to place Schiller's supposed juvenilia in their historical context. Nonetheless, his words will have had the effect of causing readers to expect little more from these plays than an outburst of unbridled youthful energy.

Implicit in Goethe's last comments is an apparent shift of paradigm; where the neoclassical critics had reproached Schiller for a deficiency of nature and an excess of art, the charge now seems to be the opposite. It might be argued that there is less to this than meets the eye; after all, the ideal for both the neoclassical reviewers and for Goethe is a "true nature," that is, a nature tamed and disciplined by art, such as was later advocated by Schiller himself in *Über naive und sentimentalische Dichtung*. Nonetheless, we can still note a shift of focus here, away from the old preoccupation with the propriety of Schiller's language and dramatic situations (in accordance with the neoclassical principle of decorum) and toward the hermeneutical and biographical method favored in the nineteenth century. Where the former method notices the "unnaturalness" of the text as imitation of reality, the latter absorbs the text into a master-narrative of Schiller's personal development, conceived as a tale of nature restrained by discipline and reflection and purified in the direction of ideality. This narrative is particularly evident in the influential anonymous obituary that appeared in the *Allgemeine Literatur-Zeitung* in June 1805, where we read of *Don Carlos*: "Des Mannes gereifte Weltansicht vereinigte sich in diesem Stück mit der Wärme des Jünglings, ein milderes Kolorit ist über das Ganze verbreitet, und nur der furchtbare Schluß erinnert an den *einstigen* Schiller" (186, emphasis original). [The man's mature view of the world was united in this work with the warmth of youth, a more gentle color is spread over the whole, and only the dreadful conclusion is reminiscent of Schiller *as he had been.*]

Two celebrated works that were written during these early years contributed greatly to Schiller's fame outside Germany but do not fit easily into any categories. The first is Madame de Staël's *De l'Allemagne* (1813), the book that, more than any other, drew the attention of Europe to the literary life of contemporary Germany. Madame de Staël (1766–1817) had visited Weimar in the winter of 1803–04, and she leaves her reader in no doubt of her close acquaintance with Schiller. In the second part of the book, she paints a glowing picture of "le meilleur ami, le meilleur père, le meilleur époux" [the best friend, the best father, the best husband], and the only shadow that she admits falls on his early life: "Schiller s'était fait tort, à son entrée dans le monde, par des égarements d'imagination; mais avec la force de l'âge il reprit cette pureté sublime qui naît des hautes pensées" (1: 140). [Upon his entry into the world, Schiller had wronged himself by his aberrations of the imagination; but with the strength of age he regained that sublime purity which is born of lofty thoughts.] The term "égarement" here is an accurate translation of "Verirrung," a central concept for the early Schiller and one that he applied to Karl Moor in his preface (486). We wonder if de Staël hit upon the term fortuitously, or if she applied Schiller's judgment on Karl to Schiller himself.

A later chapter is devoted to *Die Räuber* and *Don Carlos*, the others being passed over in silence. Her comments on these two works are capricious, and she regards them as of less significance than *Wallenstein* and its successors. But two common themes can be discerned in her discussion. One is an interest in the historical accuracy of the dramas. She wrongly believes that Schiller intended the action of *Die Räuber* to take place in the sixteenth century, whereas this was in fact a concession he made under pressure and applies only to the *Trauerspiel* version. De Staël's criticism of a French translation that places the action in the present is thus misplaced. However, she believes that the action would be better motivated if situated in that earlier period. She similarly faults *Don Carlos*, despite her praise for several scenes, for being a hybrid work, part history and part imagination, and this is a shortcoming that in her view Schiller avoids in his later plays.

Her other concern, both here and in *De l'Allemagne* as a whole, is with the German national character. Comparing French and German drama, she had written that, where the French excelled in the depiction of action, "tout ce qui tient au developpement des impressions du coeur, aux orages secrets des passions fortes, est beaucoup plus approfondi chez les Allemands" (1: 113). [Everything that pertains to the development of the heart's impressions, to the secret storms of strong passions, is much more profound with the Germans.] The rampant subjectivity of the Germans, for de Staël their dominant characteristic, is particularly susceptible to the influence of the theater, and de Staël deplores the bad effect that *Die Räuber* has had on youth. As for *Don Carlos*, she rejects the widespread criticism that Schiller had anachronistically placed eighteenth-century sentiments in Posa's mouth. Instead, she argues that, while Schiller may indeed be faulted for attributing his personal views to Posa, Posa does not display the modern philosophical spirit familiar to herself and her readers: "Le marquis de Posa, tel que l'a peint Schiller, est un enthousiaste allemand; et ce caractère est si étranger a notre temps, qu'on peut aussi bien le croire du seizième siècle que du nôtre" (212). [Marquis Posa, as Schiller has painted him, is a German enthusiast, and this character is so foreign to our age that one could just as well believe him to be of the sixteenth century as of ours.] Her remark is of interest in that it illustrates differences between countries that shared what was in some respects a common Enlightenment culture.

The other work we should mention here is the *Life of Friedrich Schiller* (1825) by Thomas Carlyle (1796–1881), an impassioned book that formed part of its author's lifelong mission to bring German literature before the English public.[1] Like de Staël, therefore, Carlyle has an interest in presenting Schiller's works from their most favorable aspect, so that, while he gives a hearing to the objections that others have made, he ends by downplaying them and praising the excellence of the works. He is unimpressed by the allegation of structural disunity in *Don Carlos*: "Intent not upon applying the dramatic gauge, but on being moved and exalted, we may peruse the tragedy without noticing that any such defect exists in it" (77). Carlyle's critical method consists mainly of an empathetic identification with the characters and situations; he will have nothing to do with the "dramatic gauge" applied by critics of the older generation.

As biographer as well as critic, Carlyle has learned the story of Schiller's youth, education at the Karlsschule, and escape from Württemberg. He is by no means the only writer to allow his excitement at this story to affect his response to *Die Räuber*, the play which, of the four under consideration, inspired the most enthusiasm in him. Carlyle had been forestalled by Schiller himself in this biographical approach to the work, and he quotes at length from the "Ankündigung der *Rheini-*

schen Thalia" in which Schiller cites the circumstances of his early life in his defense against the critics of *Die Räuber*. But Carlyle clearly relishes this personal approach to the work and he portrays the young Schiller as an unchained Titan: "he stood forth as a Man, and wrenched asunder his fetters with a force that was felt at the extremities of Europe" (15). The passage leads effortlessly into some rhapsodic pages on Karl Moor, who is conceived to be the poet's alter ego: "Moor is animated into action by feelings similar to those under which his author was then suffering and longing to act" (16).

But it would be wrong to reduce Carlyle's discussion to a naive confusion of author and character. In fact, he raises the discussion to a universal level, portraying Karl's situation as epitomizing the perennial confrontation between idealistic youth and mediocre reality, and he does so with an eloquence and insight surpassing anything to be found among German critics to that date (with the possible exception of Hegel). To convey the flavor of Carlyle's prose, it is necessary to cite a longer passage:

> Since the world is not the abode of unmixed integrity, he [Karl Moor] looks upon it as a den of thieves; since its institutions may obstruct the advancement of worth, and screen delinquency from punishment, he regards the social union as a pestilent nuisance, the mischiefs of which it is fitting that he in his degree should do his best to repair, by means however violent. Revenge is the mainspring of his conduct; but he ennobles it in his own eyes, by giving it the colour of a disinterested concern for the maintenance of justice, — the abasement of vice from its high places, and the exaltation of suffering virtues. (16–17)

We can hardly miss the echoes of Hamlet's great soliloquy here: "The insolence of office, and the spurns / That patient merit of th'unworthy take" (III/1). Schiller had been castigated by many German critics for an exaggerated imitation of Shakespeare. In Carlyle, however, it is plain that a critic immersed in Shakespeare from an early age and understanding how to express his appreciation in critical prose also proves capable, despite his awareness of the work's technical weaknesses, of putting into words the emotional message to which in large measure *Die Räuber* owed its effect.

Before leaving Carlyle, we should note also that, in his review of the Goethe-Schiller correspondence in 1831, he alludes once more to *Die Räuber*, contrasting the scene by the Danube and Karl's monologue in act IV/5 with a scene from *Die Jungfrau von Orleans* in order to point up the author's zeal for self-cultivation. As so often, this type of context highlights the wildness of the earlier text. In *Die Jungfrau*, Carlyle writes, "that volcanic fury has assuaged itself; instead of smoke and red lava, we have sunshine and a verdant world" ("Schiller" 215). What is overlooked, both here and in the earlier passage, is that Schiller put as much of himself into Franz Moor as he did into Karl.

Romanticism

The relationship between Schiller and the Jena circle, with its heady mixture of philosophical disagreement and personal antipathy, is one of the most entertaining stories to be found in German literary history. The episode yields remarkably little, however, that is of relevance to our study. Apart from Friedrich Schlegel's study "Über Goethes Meister," the Romantics produced little by way of analyses of specific works, preferring to pursue criticism at a more exalted theoretical level. The Schiller who fell foul of the Romantics, moreover, was the editor of the *Horen* and the *Musenalmanache*, not to mention the poet of the notorious "Würde der Frauen" [Women's Dignity, 1796]. The works that concern us here lay a decade in the past at the time of the confrontation; not only were they not at the focus of interest for the Romantic circle, Schiller had even repudiated them himself.

The canonical document of the Romantics' reception of Schiller is the icy treatment accorded him by August Wilhelm Schlegel (1767–1834) in the fifteenth of his Vienna lecture series *Über dramatische Kunst und Literatur* (delivered 1808, published 1811). Schlegel passes over the early plays in an offhand fashion, referring collectively to the three prose plays as "Ausschweifungen" [extravagances]. *Die Räuber* exerted its powerful and harmful influence, we read, by virtue of being "wild und gräßlich" [wild and horrible]. *Kabale und Liebe*, Schlegel writes, "kann schwerlich durch den überspannten Ton der Empfindsamkeit rühren, wohl aber durch peinliche Eindrücke foltern" [can hardly move us with its exaggerated tone of sentimentality, but can certainly torture us with embarrassing impressions]. Of *Fiesco* he can only write that it is the worst of the trio. Schlegel's praise, finally, for *Don Carlos* is so faint as to be inaudible. While some situations have "viel pathetische Kraft" [much pathetic power], the play as a whole manifests, besides the old unnaturalness, Schiller's unfortunate reflective nature that prevents him from treating his themes in a truly dramatic fashion:

> Seine [Schillers] teuer errungnen Gedanken über die menschliche Natur und die gesellschaftliche Verfassung waren dem Dichter so wert, daß er sie ausführlich darlegte, statt sie durch den Gang der Handlung auszudrücken. (129–30)

[His dearly won thoughts about human nature and the constitution of society were of such value to the poet that he set them out in detail instead of expressing them through the course of the plot.]

Compared to his treatment of *Wallenstein* and the later dramas, Schlegel's comments on the early plays are perfunctory, corresponding to his sense of their relative unimportance. We can surmise that, in the stereotypical condemnation of the reflective style of *Don Carlos*, Schlegel is to some extent relying on his and his younger brother's critique of Schiller in the 1790s rather than on an unbiased reading of the play. Even so, there is little in the substance or manner of Schlegel's comments to justify the pretensions of his circle to have brought literary criticism to a higher level than earlier generations. In his lengthy review of these lectures (1819), Karl Wilhelm Ferdinand Solger (1780–1819) concurs with Schlegel in attaching little aesthetic significance to the four plays. What unites them, he claims, despite the distinctness of *Don Carlos*, is a bitterness of tone that is attributable to social conditions, for Schiller had not yet managed to transcend his resentment of these. Despite the brevity of his remarks, Solger's discovery of an almost masochistic undertone in the four plays is nonetheless of interest.

As Oellers observes (1970, 29), it is inaccurate to portray Friedrich Schlegel (1772–1829) as an unrelenting opponent of Schiller, for in his lecture series *Geschichte der alten und neuen Literatur* (delivered in Vienna in 1812, published 1815) he manages to recognize Schiller's importance as a writer in a way that had eluded his older brother. In a wide-ranging survey of the growth of German literature, the value of which is by no means undermined by its (one can only say) fanatically Catholic presuppositions, the younger Schlegel allocates Schiller to the third generation. Where the founders (led by Klopstock, Wieland and Lessing) had had to struggle to establish a German literature in unpropitious circumstances, the second generation (Goethe and his contemporaries) had been able to rest on their laurels. Schlegel accuses this second generation of lotus-eating:

Sie . . . waren unbekümmert um alle politischen Verhältnisse und Begebenheiten nicht nur, sondern sogar um die ganze übrige und äußere Welt, nur sich und ihrer Kunst lebend, und sich ihrer genialischen Kraft erfreuend. (394)

[They . . . were unconcerned, not only with all political conditions and occurrences, but even with the whole of the rest of the external world, living merely for themselves and their art and delighting in the force of their genius.]

Schiller's generation, the third, was much more deeply engaged in the events of the time. Schlegel has the French Revolution in mind here, and he names this epoch the revolutionary one, implying not that all the writers supported the Revolution, but rather that their lives were marked by an inner struggle alien to the writers of Goethe's generation.

In Schiller's case, this means that the critic's focus shifts to the manner in which the work mirrors the spirit of the age. Schlegel comments first on the gulf in style and content separating *Don Carlos* from its three predecessors (and also *Wallenstein* from *Don Carlos*) as a consequence of Schiller's inner struggle. Here we see an attempt to draw a connection between Schiller's cultural environment and his unusual development as a writer. Second, Schlegel seems to deduce a general law that, while works of harmonious beauty cannot be produced in a strife-torn age, such an age will give rise to a literature of ideas, and this is of course an attempt to place the notorious philosophical quality of Schiller's work in a wider context. Finally, Schlegel adduces the general phenomenon of "das Mißverhältnis zwischen der Poesie und der Bühne in Deutschland" (403) [the disproportion between poetry and the stage in Germany] to explain how Schiller was forced to choose between poetic quality and popular success. After his first three plays, Schiller chose to strive for a higher poetic niveau and forfeited popularity as a result. Nonetheless, Schlegel writes, Schiller deserves to be called

> der wahre Begründer unsrer Bühne . . . , der die eigentliche Sphäre derselben, und die ihr angemessene Form und Weise bis jetzt noch am glücklichsten getroffen, sich ihr wenigstens am meisten genähert hat. (404)

> [the true founder of our stage . . . who has found the form and manner appropriate to it in the happiest fashion to date, or has at least approached it the most closely.]

Despite (or perhaps because of) the qualifications, this must count as a serious attempt to give Schiller his due, and Schlegel deserves credit for overcoming his earlier hostility to him. As examples of criticism in the hermeneutical mode, the three insights of Friedrich Schlegel, as perfunctory as they are, compare favorably with his brother's sarcastic and mean-spirited performance and lend substance to Oellers's claim that, despite their sometimes hostile attitude, the Romantic critics contributed more to an understanding of Schiller than all the legions of worshippers.

Regarding popular reviewing in this period, Oellers divides writers into two categories, those still holding the attitudes of the Enlightenment, which underlay the liberalism of the new century, and those influenced by the views of the Jena Romantic circle. The former tended strongly to favor *Don Carlos* and had difficulty in accounting for their conviction that Schiller was a great writer. The Göttingen critic Ernst Brandes (1758–1810), a foremost member of this camp, regarded *Don Carlos* as "die Krone Schiller's und wenigstens aller Deutschen dramatischen Dichtungen" (1806, 143) [the crown of Schiller's and, at the least, of all German dramatic writings], but he devotes more space to a point-by-point denunciation of *Die Räuber*. As Oellers sardonically observes, the implied view of Brandes and those who agreed with him is that, although a great poet, Schiller only managed to write mediocre works (Oellers 1967, 203).

Among critics inspired by the Romantics, Franz Horn (1781–1837) denies Schiller the noble title of "Dichter" [poet, as opposed to a writer] which is reserved for Shakespeare and Goethe, but he still shows more willingness to enter into the spirit of the prose works, particularly *Die Räuber*, than Brandes managed. One can detect, he writes in 1804, in the work's wholehearted rejection of art an art of a different kind: "Himmel, Erde und Hölle sind hier in kolossalen Formen, durch schroffe Kluften auseinandergerissen, hingestellt mit einer Kraft und Fülle, die vielleicht noch niemals ganz und gar gewürdigt ist" (110). [Heaven, earth and hell are here, separated by deep gulfs and represented with a power and fullness that has perhaps never been fully appreciated.] Here at last is a willingness to consider that the neoclassical rules might not be universally valid. Horn also has reservations toward *Don Carlos*, in which he finds Schiller writing as prophet rather than as poet, with the result that the play is flawed; he states that it is dominated by two incompatible spirits, the spirit of music and the spirit of the picturesque (111). If he had taken the time to explain this Delphic remark, he might have been able to say something of interest.

In an interesting review of an 1814 performance of *Kabale und Liebe* in Vienna, Clemens Brentano (1778–1842) shows himself to be surprisingly close to the Enlightenment tradition. He was so disgusted by the play's language — "unnatürlich, geschwollen, bombastisch, manchmal beinahe lächerlich" [unnatural, swollen, bombastic, sometimes almost ridiculous] — and by the figures of Wurm and the President, who lack all tragic dignity, that he left the theater during the third act. However, Brentano's overall theme is Schiller's superiority to the popular playwrights Kotzebue and Iffland, and, although he views *Die Braut von Messina* as the summit of Schiller's achievement, he is prepared to concede some signs of genius to the younger Schiller as well. The following passage is worth quoting for a truly extraordinary simile:

> Dieses Trauerspiel [*Kabale und Liebe*] gehört in die Periode Schillers, in welcher er noch mit sich selbst kämpfte; es ist die Arbeit eines jungen Gefühlshelden; der Pegasus, statt mit goldenem Hufe den kastalischen Quell aus grüner Erde hervorzuschlagen, beträgt sich wie ein arabisches Roß, das, sich die strotzenden Adern zu erleichtern, sie aufbeißt, und wir erhalten daher oft etwas Pferdeblut, zwar von edelster Abkunft, aber es ist doch nur Pferdeblut. (153)

> [This tragedy [*Kabale und Liebe*] belongs in the period when Schiller was still struggling with himself; it is the work of a young hero of emotion; Pegasus, instead of striking forth the Castalian spring from the earth with his hoof, behaves like an Arabian horse which, in order to relieve its bursting veins, bites them open, and we thus often get some horse blood, of the noblest pedigree of course, but still only horse blood.]

The review also contains an interesting sketch of Schiller's career: in his early plays the plots are more beautiful than the language and in the later ones the language more beautiful than the plots, but in *Don Carlos* the two are in equilibrium.

Ludwig Tieck (1773–1853), known as a Schiller critic primarily for his fine discussion of *Wallenstein*, shows surprising sympathy for the early Schiller as well. In the tenth of his *Dramaturgische Blätter* [Dramaturgical Pages], first published in a Dresden newspaper in 1827, Tieck praised the prose plays not as reflections of their time, but for their apparently effortless command of stage effect. He thus adopts not so much the hermeneutic approach of Friedrich Schlegel as the neoclassical focus on the play as artifact. Instead of applying a ready-made set of rules, however, Tieck, the translator of Shakespeare, speaks from a deep practical understanding of the theater. He thus does not pass over those aspects of Schiller's prose plays that had aroused distaste ever since their appearance, and he alludes to exaggerations, false *Pathos* (in the sense of the rhetorical expression of strong emotion) and manipulation of the plot for effect. But behind all this, he is able to recognize Schiller's instinctive mastery of the techniques that cause a play to seize the attention of an audience:

> In jeder Rede schreitet die Handlung vor, jede Frage und Antwort gibt Theaterspiel, die Spannung steigt, alles was hinter dem Theater und in den Zwischenakten geschieht, belebt die sichtbar gemachte Gegenwart. (173)

[In every speech the action advances, every question and answer gives rise to drama, the suspense rises, everything that happens offstage or between the acts enlivens what is visibly present.]

Tieck also points out that Goethe, though a greater writer than Schiller, lacked this theatrical mastery and was never able to acquire it. Here at last we can see an incipient recognition of why these plays had provoked such an overwhelming response on their first appearance. In view of Schiller's study of Shakespeare during his school years, it can hardly be coincidental that it was Tieck, one of the early translators of Shakespeare, who was able to recognize and analyze Schiller's theatrical genius for the first time.

To Tieck's eye, *Don Carlos* represents a retrograde step. Although he acknowledges that the climate of the age demanded the treatment of political themes in the theater, he still wishes that this could have happened in a manner more consistent with the requirements of the stage. But the figure of Posa, who is the ideological focus of the play, brings the whole play to a standstill, and his great audience scene with the King in act III has no plausibility or truth. In general, Tieck finds, the play has little in the way of plot, substituting untragic intrigue and a great deal of static material: "Gesinnungen, in welchen die Szenen stillstehen, Meinungen, Reflexionen, Untersuchungen und Seelenzustände ersetzen die eigentliche Handlung" (174). [Opinions, during which the scenes stop dead, reflections, investigations and states of mind replace the real plot.]

Liberalism

In a helpful article on the reception of Schiller in these years, Siegbert Prawer (1950) cites a remark from the *Ästhetische Feldzüge* (1834) by the Young German author Ludolf Wienbarg (1802–72) distinguishing two meanings of the word "liberal." These correspond roughly to two generations. On the one hand, there is the older and unpolitical conception, by which the word means little more than "right-thinking." On the other, there is the younger generation's commitment to specific political change. Prawer identifies liberals in the first sense with the term *Biedermeier*, in the second with the term *Vormärz*. The Biedermeier attitude to Schiller is the veneration to which I have referred above. Prawer distinguishes three main grounds for such veneration: Schiller's establishment of "a native tradition of drama strong enough to keep at bay undesirable foreign influences"; his inspiration of the young patriots of the anti-Napoleonic campaign of 1813; and his exertion through his works of "a spiritually uniting force" for the politically divided German nation (190). Such veneration was directed as much toward the man as to the work, tended to stress personal integrity at the expense of political commitment, and had a nationalistic undertone that would be heard more strongly later in the century. Although it is not always easy to draw a firm line between the two attitudes, the authors we shall examine next belong to the younger of the generations as defined by Wienbarg.

In his *Die Romantische Schule* (1833), which forms part of his reply to Mme. de Staël's *De l'Allemagne*, Heinrich Heine (1797–1856) gives a critical but telling outline of the aesthetic views of Goethe and his circle:

> [Sie] betrachten . . . die Kunst als eine unabhängige zweite Welt, die sie so hoch stellen, daß alles Treiben der Menschen . . . unter ihr hin sich bewegt. . . . Ich kann aber dieser Ansicht nicht unbedingt huldigen; die Goetheaner ließen sich dadurch verleiten die Kunst selbst als das Höchste zu proklamieren, und von den Ansprüchen jener ersten wirklichen Welt, welcher doch der Vorrang gebührt, sich abzuwenden. (393)

> [They consider . . . art as an independent second world that they exalt so far that all human doings . . . are beneath it. . . . But I cannot give my unconditional assent to this view; the Goetheans let themselves be misled by it into proclaiming art itself as the highest value, and to turn away from the first, the real world, to which precedence is due.]

For Heine, attentive as he is to the political import of literature, Schiller contrasts positively with this circle, for he addressed the needs of his time in his work: "Schiller schrieb für die großen Ideen der Revolution, er zerstörte die geistigen Bastillen, er baute an der Tempel der Freiheit." [Schiller wrote for the great ideas of the Revolution, he destroyed the intellectual Bastilles, he helped to build the temple of freedom.] Heine next unleashes his incomparable wit:

> Er begann mit jenem Haß gegen die Vergangenheit, welchen wir in den *Räubern* sehen, wo er einem kleinen Titan gleicht, der aus der Schule gelaufen ist und Schnaps getrunken hat und dem Jupiter die Fenster einwirft.

> [He began with that hatred of the past that we see in *Die Räuber*, in which he resembles a young Titan who has run away from school, drunk some liquor, and thrown stones through Jupiter's windows.]

But if that is how Schiller starts, he finishes according to Heine with the cosmopolitan humanitarianism of *Don Carlos*, which is of course the work that supports the Bastille-storming view of Schiller most strongly. In line with his usual method of placing the author before the work, Heine identifies Posa as his author's alter ego. In his brief discussion, there is no room for any of the later works that would cast doubt on his view of Schiller as an author who used the theater to comment on the vital issues of his age.[2] But the essay as a whole leaves us in no doubt that Heine regarded Goethe as a greater artist than Schiller, and that the latter's great protagonists like Posa are ultimately only "Theaterhelden" [stage heroes].

With his contrast between a politically indifferent Goethe and a committed Schiller, Heine is reflecting a widespread politicization during this period. As Wellek writes (1965a, 182): "German criticism became more and more subservient to the national, political, and social aims of the time." The most famous and most extreme opponent of Goethe's aestheticism was actually Wolfgang Menzel (1798–1873), Heine's nemesis, although, where Heine sees Schiller as a cosmopolitan adherent of revolutionary ideas, Menzel offers more a nationalistic picture of Schiller as moral paragon for German youth. Menzel is loud in his praise for the ideals of the later Schiller, and in his *Die Deutsche Literatur* of 1828 he praises the early dramas only in so far as they adumbrate the later ones:

> Welche Torheiten man in Karl Moor, auch in *Kabale und Liebe* und im Fiesko finden mag, ich kann sie nicht anders betrachten, als die Torheiten jenes altdeutschen Parzifals, der als roher Knabe noch im kindlichen Kleide zur Beschämung aller Spötter sein adeliges Heldenherz erprobte. (243)

> [Whatever follies one may find in Karl Moor, and also in *Kabale und Liebe* and *Fiesko*, I cannot think of them other than as the follies of that old Germanic Parzifal, who, even as a raw youth in childish raiment, put his heroic heart to the test and shamed all the scoffers.]

Despite these reservations, Menzel sees Karl Moor, Ferdinand von Walter and Posa as embodiments of Schiller's warlike angel that will lead Germany toward a better future.

Despite his greater stature as a scholar, Georg Gottfried Gervinus should be dealt with in this section, for, in the five volumes of his *Geschichte der poetischen Nationalliteratur der Deutschen* (1835–42), he too accords systematic primacy to the political sphere, and his literary judgments bear the imprint of that decision. From this somewhat skewed perspective, *Fiesco* is the most significant of Schiller's prose plays, since it marks most clearly the turn toward history and politics that Gervinus sees as Schiller's decisive contribution. *Kabale und Liebe*, by contrast, is dismissed with contempt. Seeing Schiller as essentially a man of deeds not words, Gervinus argues that, paradoxically, the pursuit of an artistic vocation was his natural outlet in an environment that otherwise thwarted his desire for action, and, by no means implausibly, he attributes the exaggerated and garish (grell) spirit of *Die Räuber* to these personal circumstances. Less promisingly, Gervinus takes the famous motto "*in tyrannos*" as a truthful reflection of the play's spirit. (The motto, which only appears in the Löffler edition of 1782, was in fact added without Schiller's knowledge.) No less imprecise are his portrayal of *Fiesco* as an anticipation of the French Revolution and his claim that Posa's ideals, which elicit his enthusiastic praise, helped to bring about the German resistance to Napoleon in 1813. Clearly, a critic carrying such heavy political baggage as Gervinus is badly placed to carry out the careful assessment required by texts as complex as these. We can also agree with a wry comment by Albert Ludwig (1909, 300): Gervinus's conviction that his countrymen should turn their attention from literature to politics makes him quicker to see the flaws than the merits in the literature of the past.

Another prominent author of this period is August Friedrich Christian Vilmar, whose popular *Geschichte der deutschen National-Literatur* began to appear in 1844. Although he is now known chiefly as the austere Protestant churchman who dared to castigate Goethe and Schiller for their deficient zeal for Christianity, Vilmar's judgments on individual works, as Albert Ludwig points out (1909, 305), often follow those of Gervinus. This is true here, in that Vilmar prefers *Fiesco* to *Kabale und Liebe* on account of its political subject matter, while the latter is denounced as a caricature that is both morally and aesthetically repellent. He expands on Gervinus's account by suggesting that Schiller's artistic progress from *Die Räuber* to *Don Carlos* resembles the progress of the French Revolution in reverse order, starting with the criminality of the Convention and working backwards toward the idealism of the National Assembly. More promising than this piece of dilettantism, however, is Vilmar's claim that Schiller retained some features of his Storm and Stress into his classical period, for example,

> Die Neigung, . . . nicht so sehr die Wirklichkeit poetisch zu erfassen und poetisch zu gestalten, als Ideen in die Wirklichkeit hinein zu werfen, die Neigung zu lebhafter Darstellung und starker oratorischer Färbung. (490)

> [the tendency, . . . not so much to grasp reality poetically and to portray it poetically, as to throw ideas into reality, the tendency toward vivid representation and strong rhetorical coloring].

Hence there is a line connecting what Vilmar sees as Schiller's "Haschen nach Effect" [straining for effect] in *Die Räuber* and the later achievement of a classical style. This insight goes beyond the usual clichés about Schiller's progress from unnaturalness to ideality and pre-figures, if only embryonically, the view of Schiller taken in our century by Emil Staiger.

The anniversary of Schiller's birth in 1859 was celebrated through-out Germany with such fervor that we cannot help seeing in it an emo-tional compensation for the defeat of the revolution in 1848–49. The year thus forms an important chapter in the story of Schiller's poetic afterlife, although the recorded speeches contain virtually nothing that is specific enough to belong in the present volume. It is nonetheless true that the attitude to Schiller's works among readers and critics re-mains colored by the political history of Germany in the mid-nineteenth century. Schiller came to be adopted as spokesman and prophet by the liberal bourgeoisie, and the failures of that class were thus deemed to be his failures also. The importance of such considera-tions, which are even today often implicit in discussions of Karl Moor and Posa, emerges most clearly if we look briefly at Marx and Engels. Although they were neither liberals nor literary scholars, they belong in this story owing to the inordinate influence that their views on Schiller have exerted in the twentieth century, and not only on socialist scholars.[3]

Three comments need to be cited, of which the first is also the best known. In an essay of 1847 on a book about Goethe by Karl Grün, Engels writes that Goethe was conquered by the German "Misere," an imprecise but highly suggestive term that refers to the internal and ex-ternal obstacles, preeminently parochialism and submissiveness to authority, that stand in the way of a revolutionary politics in Germany. Engels continues:

> Goethe war zu universell, zu aktiver Natur, zu fleischlich, um in einer Schillerschen Flucht ins Kantische Ideal Rettung vor der Misere zu su-chen; er war zu scharfblickend, um nicht zu sehen, wie diese Flucht sich schließlich auf die Vertauschung der platten mit der über-schwenglichen Misere reduzierte. (468)

> [Goethe was too universal, of too active a nature, too carnal, to seek refuge from wretchedness in a Schillerian flight into the Kantian ideal; he was too sharp-sighted not to see that this flight after all meant nothing more than exchanging a banal wretchedness with a high-flown one.]

As the reference to Kant shows, this is of course an attack on the later Schiller. However, since there are few comments that have had such a subversive effect on the way in which readers have viewed Schiller and his relation to German political traditions (it can only be compared to Nietzsche's "moral trumpeter"), it deserves to be cited here. The term "überschwenglich" [high-flown] could moreover be easily construed to include some of the speeches of Karl Moor, Ferdinand von Walter and the Marquis Posa. What Engels's brilliant and cruel remark suggests is that the exaltedness of Schiller's rhetoric is in inverse proportion to its political effectiveness, that the emotion occasioned by hearing or reading it in effect forms a substitute to any real political response on the part of the recipient. In an argument that one can see as descended from Rousseau's criticism of the theater in his famous *Letter to D'Alembert* (1758), Engels insinuates that Schiller's treatment of political themes paradoxically provides the German bourgeois audience with a psychological excuse for its political passivity.

The other references can be passed over briefly. In a letter of 19 April 1859 to the Socialist leader Ferdinand Lassalle about the latter's play *Franz von Sickingen* (in which Lassalle had used events from the time of the Reformation to deal with the failure of the revolution of 1848), Marx criticizes him for writing in too Schillerian a manner, by which he means "das Verwandeln von Individuen in bloße Sprachröhren des Zeitgeistes" (181) [transforming people into mere mouthpieces for the spirit of the age], and wishes he had shown more of the Shakespearian style of characterization. This judgment, anticipated of course by Schiller himself in *Über naive und sentimentalische Dichtung*, is followed by remarks about the excessive abstractness and reflectiveness of Lassalle's characters, criticisms that in the context are implicitly directed at Schiller also. The last comment, this time a favorable one, is taken from a letter of 26 November 1885 from Engels to Minna Kautsky, in which he praises *Kabale und Liebe* as "das erste deutsche politische Tendenzdrama" (484) [the first politically committed German drama]. The authority of this statement can still be felt in Alexander Abusch's book on Schiller of 1955.

Positivism and its Critics

The biographies began to appear soon after Schiller's death. Given the low standard of most of these, an early book by the Viennese author Johann Schwaldopler (1806) surprises us with its quality. Confining the biographical material to an introductory sketch, he devotes more space to a consideration of the works. Although he has little rapport with the prose plays, he reveals his enlightened convictions by his vehement praise of *Don Carlos*. But Schwaldopler does not merely vent his emotions, he attempts also to answer the widespread criticisms of the play's structure, arguing that its unity becomes evident if one takes the relationship of Posa and King Philip as the axis around which the whole revolves. His remarks on Philip, in which he recognizes this character's dramatic weight in the overall structure, are perceptive and go well beyond the customary endorsement of Posa's political ideas.

As said above, there is no question that Karl Hoffmeister's massive critical biography (1838–42) is a landmark in the application of scholarly standards to the study of Schiller. His achievement in bringing to light new facts about the poet's life has been recognized ever since the appearance of his book. As to his treatment of the works, an example of his scrupulousness is that, in contrast to all his predecessors, he compared the final version of *Don Carlos* with the "*Thalia*-Fragment," although he had to obtain the original publications in order to do so. In his foreword, Hoffmeister pays homage to the progress achieved by the natural sciences in his time, expressing the bold hope that his work, conceived as a "wissenschaftliche Naturgeschichte des Schiller'schen Geistes" [scientific natural history of the Schillerian mind/spirit], may pioneer a new biographical method. Although aware that a poet's fame rests on his works, Hoffmeister still believes that a work such as his must focus first and foremost on the development of the subject's personality, leading to what Hoffmeister calls "die innere Auslegungskunst" [the art of inner interpretation]. He is thus impatient of any mere textual approach, arguing instead that the proper method must pursue "alle zu erklärende [*sic*] Werke bis in die Denkweise und Persönlichkeit ihres Verfassers hinein" (1838, vii) [all the works to be explained (sic) right into the mentality and personality of their author]. True, Hoffmeister is also committed to elucidating the material circumstances of the composition of the works, a procedure we can more readily see as scientific. But his impatience with parallels and precedents in other literary texts and his eagerness to plumb the depths of Schiller's psyche open the way to much speculation of an unverifiable kind. His view of what is to be admitted as scientific evidence is perilously arbitrary. Hoffmeister is thus no exception to the tendency, which was to predominate until the middle of the twentieth century, of glorifying the author and setting him above the work.

Given these fundamentals, it is not surprising that Hoffmeister's discussions of the early plays in his first volume, although always thorough and thoughtful, have obvious shortcomings. First, with reference to *Die Räuber*, we hear the familiar topos of immaturity and inadequate education: "Da er diese Natur damals in sich noch nicht zum Idealen ausgebildet und geläutert hatte, so mußten die Menschen und die Welt, die er uns darstellt, ungeschlacht und formlos ausfallen" (73). [Since he . . . had at that time not yet educated and purified his nature to the ideal, the people and the world that he depicts for us had to turn out as uncouth and formless.] It is not surprising that a critic who brings these expectations to the text overlooks the great care Schiller devoted to the motivation of the two brothers. But besides Hoffmeister's professed "inner interpretation," of which this was an example, we also find a propensity to assume that the *external* circumstances of composition have fed directly into the content of the work. After describing how the conditions at the Karlsschule forced Schiller to write *Die Räuber* in secret, for example, Hoffmeister infers that the work is "der Angstruf eines Gefangenen nach Freiheit" (69) [a prisoner's fearful cry for freedom]. We read further that Schiller's "Privaterbitterung wuchs . . . zu einer allgemeinen Unzufriedenheit mit der Welt, zu einem Universalhaß gegen das ganze Menschengeschlecht an" (68) [private annoyance grew . . . to a general discontentedness with the world, to a universal hatred against the whole human race]. But this is simply to identify Karl Moor's misanthropic outburst of act I/2 as a direct expression of Schiller's own mood. Finally, we are told that Karl's speech in act IV/5 starting with "Ich bin mein Himmel und meine Hölle" [I am my heaven and my hell] represents "der ethische Gipfel des Schauspiels" (77) [the ethical peak of the play]. Such overhasty and disconnected inferences from the life to the work and back again, although purportedly scientific, in fact help us understand neither the one nor the other.

The hunt for biographical clues continues in the discussion of *Kabale und Liebe*. Once again ignoring the literary context, Hoffmeister takes it for granted that Ferdinand is a self-portrait of his author, and he is thus forced to assume a fracture in the conception of the character when the latter starts to run amok. Hoffmeister's method merges here with neoclassicism, in that Schiller is said to depart simultaneously from truthful self-expression and from the eighteenth-century tenets of truth and nature, but the erroneous premise prevents Hoffmeister from seeing the underlying consistency in Ferdinand's character, in both of the latter's manifestations as ardent lover and as murderer from deluded jealousy. The methodological error of placing integrity of self-expression before the coherence of the work, a mistake that — we can safely say — no scholar would commit today, illuminates the different priorities guiding the scholarship of Hoffmeister's age. It is Schiller himself, or rather the classical Schiller, who is to stand as a beacon to the bourgeois public, inspiring it to emulate his self-education and offering this as the path to a better collective future. Even with good scholars like Hoffmeister, the study of Schiller's works was made to serve this ulterior purpose.

Summarizing his discussion of the three prose plays, Hoffmeister faults them all for their lack of formal harmony and for the disharmonious state in which they leave the reader: "Der Dichter macht uns zu Theilnehmern seiner innern Leiden, seines Haders mit der ganzen Welt: versöhnt, besänftigt, erhoben können wir nicht werden" (196). [The poet makes us participants in his inner suffering, in his feud with the whole world; we cannot be reconciled, assuaged, elevated.] Earlier (85) he has deplored the preponderance of crudity ("das Rohe"), both aesthetic and moral, in *Die Räuber*, and has insisted on form as a prerequisite of beauty. In such passages, the aesthetic norms are drawn from Schiller's own writings of the 1790s, exemplifying the way in which the later Schiller can be used as a stick to beat the earlier. In such an ideologically motivated account, it is clear that the early dramas are fated to play an inglorious role.

In Hoffmeister's biographical narrative, *Don Carlos* fulfills two functions. First, it is said to represent the arrival of an emotionally milder phase in Schiller's life, such that the depressing emotions of the prose plays are succeeded by more affirmative ones. The change is expressed in his adoption of verse composition, hence

Die Iamben wurden alsbald der sprachliche Ausdruck seiner Gemüthlichkeit. . . . [D]er ungestüme Heroismus seiner Seele wurde durch diese rhythmische Form gemäßigt, welche alles Rohe und Widerliche abwies. (289)

[The iambuses forthwith became the linguistic expression of his geniality. . . . (H)is soul's uncouth heroism was moderated by this rhythmic form, which banished all that was crude or repulsive.]

Second, the play marks the growing ascendancy of philosophical reflection in Schiller's intellectual development; the "Naturpoesie" [natural poetry] of the early years is to be followed by a "Periode der wissenschaftlichen Selbstverständigung" [period of scholarly reflection] which is the title of Hoffmeister's second volume. *Don Carlos* was thus composed primarily as "eine begeisterte Enthüllung der Idee" (294) [an enthusiastic revelation of the idea], and its aesthetic form is said to be accordingly flawed. Despite his approval of these ideas, therefore, Hoffmeister has some severe words for the obscurities of plot and motivation in the second half of the play, and he finds a striking metaphor to express the resulting ramshackled structure:

Die herrlichen affektvollen Scenen liegen, wie einzelne leuchtende
Gruppen, durch dunkle Zwischenräume geschieden, auseinander, und
man kann den Weg nicht immer angeben, auf dem man von einer dieser Oasen zur andern gelangt. (311)

[The splendid emotional scenes lie apart from each other like distinct
glowing groups separated by dark spaces, and one cannot always explain the path by which one gets from one of these oases to the next.]

At the same time, Hoffmeister sees the dramatic characters less as human than as symbolic figures for the ideas they espouse, whether positive or negative. This leads him to elide the mutual differences of
character among the positive figures, and indeed to overlook the human complexities in all the relationships in the play, requiring him, for
example, to think up a rather weak argument (301) as to why, contrary
to his theory, King Philip emerges as such a powerfully human figure in
the drama. Such, we may reflect, are the consequences of circular argumentation.

In spite of the contrasts with the prose plays implicit in his dual clas-
sification of *Don Carlos* — gentler emotions, more philosophical content — Hoffmeister still insists that all four plays belong together as
products of the period in Schiller's life in which the moral-political
concern is paramount. This concern, according to Hoffmeister, is
manifested in *Die Räuber* primarily in negative and polemical form, but
finds positive and exegetic expression in *Don Carlos* owing to the poet's
greater maturity. In this respect, Hoffmeister can write that the later
play represents the harmonious sequel that, as he had earlier argued
(72), *Die Räuber* required and presupposed: "Denn die Welt, welche in
den Räubern zerschlagen worden ist, wird in Don Karlos auf idealem
Fundament wieder aufgebaut" (294). [For the world that has been
smashed to ruins in *Die Räuber* is rebuilt in *Don Carlos* on an ideal
foundation.] One cannot deny the elegance of this argument, for it allows for a high degree of contrast between the two plays while also
making them complement each other as the opening and closing phases
of a discrete period in their author's creative life. At the same time,
however, one wonders whether, for all his devotion to science, Hoffmeister is not making these plays tell a story of sacral import and dimensions. Besides, his attempt to treat all four plays under the rubric of
a youthful poetry of nature (in contrast to the mature art of the final
years) but also as ethically motivated (in contrast to the later preponderance of fate) sometimes makes his overall argument not so much
many-textured as muddled.

It was desirable to treat Hoffmeister's work at such length (and we shall be returning to him) because of its exemplary stature in the Schiller scholarship of the nineteenth century. Its combination of science and ideology, of scrupulousness and prejudice, of skepticism and naiveté, of clarity and confusion were worth dwelling on for what they tell us about the age in which it was written and about the reasons why Schiller had come to loom so large in the mind of the educated public. The main alternative to Hoffmeister's approach to Schiller was represented by the Hegelianism of H. F. W. Hinrichs, whose three-volume *Schillers Dichtungen nach ihren historischen Beziehungen und nach ihrem inneren Zusammenhange* appeared in the years 1837 to 1839. (The plays that concern us are discussed in the second volume, which appeared in 1838.) But before we review his opinions, we should take a look at what Hegel (1770–1831) himself had said about our subject.

Hegel's Olympian discussion of tragedy in the third volume of his *Ästhetik* (published posthumously in 1835) is structured as a contrast between the ancient and modern types; the chief differentia are the greater degree of subjectivity and particularity in the modern period, with a resulting multiplicity of possible plots, characters, themes and motivations — here he mainly has love and honor in mind — as well as the greater distance separating the characters from the moral institutions of God, country, and family that had effectively determined human life in antiquity. This situation creates both advantages and disadvantages for the modern tragedian, although Wellek is probably right to say that Hegel tends to accentuate the disadvantages: "But Hegel, in general, criticizes modern tragedy . . . for not posing [the tragic] conflict clearly, indeed for obscuring it by the contingencies of individual character" (1955, 331).

Hegel's direct comments on Schiller, although not many, are sufficiently frequent to show that he regards him as a paradigmatic modern tragedian, and that his general analysis pertains as much to Schiller as to anyone else. Hegel's observations on modern tragedy fall into three parts, dealing successively with the tragic ends ("Zwecke"), the characters, and the conclusion (or reconciliation). With reference to ends, he contrasts Schiller's early plays to his later ones in that the former better exemplify his theory. For where the later Schiller came to approach the objectivity of ancient tragedy, in the early plays "das Pochen auf Natur, Menschenrechte und Weltverbesserung [erscheint] mehr nur als Schwärmerei eines subjektiven Enthusiasmus" (14: 566). [The continual harping upon nature, the rights of man, and the improvement of the world appears more as the excess of a subjective enthusiasm.] A consequence of Hegel's theory thus seems to be that the occurrence of good tragedy in the modern period is a problem requiring explanation.

This charge of excessive subjectivity is at the heart of Hegel's most memorable comment on Schiller, which we should quote in full:

> Karl Moor, verletzt von der bestehenden Ordnung, und von den Menschen, welche deren Macht mißbrauchen, tritt aus dem Kreise der Gesetzlichkeit heraus, und macht sich, indem er die Schranken, welche ihn einzwängen, zu durchbrechen die Kühnheit hat, und sich so selbst einen neuen heroischen Zustand kreirt, zum Wiederhersteller des Rechts und selbstständigen Rächer des Unrechts, der Unbilde und Bedrückung. Doch wie klein und vereinzelt einer Seits muß diese Privatrache bei der Unzulänglichkeit der nötigen Mittel ausfallen, und auf der anderen Seite kann sie nur zu Verbrechen führen, da sie das Unrecht in sich schließt, das sie zerstören will. Von Seiten Karl Moors ist dies ein Unglück, ein Mißgriff, und wenn es auch tragisch ist, können doch nur Knaben von diesem Räuberideal bestochen werden. Ebenso quälen sich die Individuen in *Kabale und Liebe*, unter drückenden gegenwärtigen Verhältnissen, mit ihren kleineren Partikularitäten und Leidenschaften herum, und erst in *Fiesko* und *Don Karlos* erscheinen die Hauptgestalten erhobener, indem sie sich einen substantielleren Gehalt, die Befreiung ihres Vaterlandes, oder die Freiheit der religiösen Ueberzeugung zu eigen machen, und Helden aus Zwecken werden. (12: 266–67)

> [Karl Moor, injured by the existing order and by the men who misuse its power, steps outside the circle of legality; by being bold enough to burst through the bounds that hem him in and thus to create a new heroic condition, he makes himself into the upholder of law and the autonomous avenger of injustice, corruption and oppression. But how small and isolated must this private revenge turn out, in view of the inadequacy of the necessary means; and, on the other hand, it can only lead to crimes, since it includes in itself the injustice that it wishes to eradicate. From Karl Moor's point of view this is a misfortune, a blunder, and, even if it is tragic, only boys could be corrupted by this robber-ideal. In the same way the individuals in *Kabale und Liebe* wrestle with their smaller particularities and passions, and only in *Fiesco* and *Don Carlos* do the main figures appear more exalted, in that they lay claim to a more substantial content, that is, the liberation of their fatherland, and thus become heroes out of a real purpose.][4]

According to this magisterial argument, Schiller's path to maturity is simultaneously one from arbitrary subjectivity toward historical substance.

However, Hegel's view on this matter is not entirely clear. For one thing, he writes in his introduction to the *Ästhetik* (12: 54) that the

youthful flaw in Schiller's early works (and in Goethe's too), besides a
general "Roheit und Barbarei" [crudity and barbarism], is an excess not
so much of enthusiasm as of undigested prosaic elements, a deficiency,
we would think, rather than a surfeit of subjectivity. Further, he has
also conceded that even the earliest play tends to transcend the subjective by conferring general validity on a localized individual conflict. In
this context *Die Räuber* is set alongside Goethe's *Faust*, which is the
absolute philosophical tragedy; where the latter depicts "die tragisch
versuchte Vermittlung des subjektiven Wissens und Strebens mit dem
Absoluten" [the tragic attempt to mediate subjective knowledge and
striving with the absolute], the rebellion of Karl Moor is similarly expanded from a personal enterprise to one directed against the entire society of his age, and in this sense is said to incorporate an "allgemeiner
Weltzweck" [a general world-end]. (Here we sense that Hegel, admiring *Die Räuber* despite his awareness of its faults, is attempting to defend it against his own earlier strictures.) Ferdinand and Posa are cited,
in contrast, as cases in which individual ends are neither expanded nor
left as mere psychological contingencies, but rather are conceived as
being in themselves universally binding:

> So meint z.B. schon der Major Ferdinand in *Kabale und Liebe* die
> Rechte der Natur gegen die Konvenienzen der Mode zu vertheidigen,
> und vor allem fordert Marquis Posa Gedankenfreiheit als ein unveräu-
> ßerliches Gut der Menschheit. (14: 565)

> [Thus, for example, Major Ferdinand in *Kabale und Liebe* believes he
> is defending the rights of nature against the conventions of fashion,
> and most of all Marquis Posa demands freedom of thought as the in-
> alienable birthright of humanity.]

Hegel's contrast between Karl Moor on the one side, Ferdinand and
Posa on the other, is not entirely clear. Does he really mean, as he suggests, that, where Karl's misanthropic rebellion has transcendent validity, Posa's espousal of liberal principles is frivolous? Unfortunately, the
compactness of his discussion forces us to speculate in vain as to his real
meaning and as to how he would have reconciled the apparent contradictions.

We can pass rapidly over Hegel's treatment of character, noting
only that his remarks on figures who personify specific passions, love or
ambition for example, as well as those on internally divided characters,
could easily apply to at least some of Schiller's early heroes. Similarly, in
the final part we note merely that, in his remarks as to the danger of
randomness in the modern tragic plot, Hegel might well have been

thinking of the *dénouement* of *Fiesco*. Of most significance in this part
are two observations, with which I shall conclude my look at Hegel.

First, as we have seen, Hegel has noted a tendency for the modern
tragic hero, who lacks the ancient transcendental and collective contexts for his action, to appear as a mere criminal (14: 543). He now
mentions the arrest of President von Walter as an example of a dramatic
conclusion that lacks tragic dimensions, for all that happens is that a
scoundrel's deeds catch up with him (14: 572). Hegel, we may note,
has also said that it is possible to counteract this deficiency:

> Hier vor allem muß . . . die formelle Größe des Charakters und Macht
> der Subjektivität gefordert werden, alles Negative aushalten, und ohne
> Verleugnung ihrer Thaten und ohne in sich zertrümmert zu seyn, ihr
> Loos dahinnehmen zu können. (14: 543)

> [Here above all one must . . . demand formal greatness of character
> and power of subjectivity, in order that the character be able to with-
> stand all negativity and to bear its fate without denying its deeds or
> being shattered in itself.]

We can hardly help noticing how well these words apply to the Moor
brothers. But this criminal tendency in modern tragedy, although in
one sense a flaw, has in Hegel's view a higher philosophical necessity.
As he has stated, such tragedy, behind all its new multiplicity, deals
with the emergence of the modern subjectivity in its rebellion against
the old collective structures of meaning:

> Vertiefter noch ist es das Unrecht und Verbrechen, das der subjektive
> Charakter, wenn er es sich auch nicht als Unrecht und Verbrechen
> zum Zweck macht, dennoch, um sein vorgesetztes Ziel zu erreichen,
> nicht scheut. (14: 564)

> [More profound yet is the criminal wrongdoing that the subjective
> character, in order to reach the goal he has set himself, does not shirk,
> even though he has not made criminal wrongdoing his purpose.]

As a comment, however oblique, on the historical meaning of Schiller's
"erhabene Verbrecher" [sublime criminals], this is an analysis that still
deserves close attention.[5]

The second point is that, given the greater role of subjectivity, the
modern tragic hero must be personally reconciled to his fate as he dies.
Hegel offers three ways in which this can occur, the first religious, with
the hero anticipating bliss in the afterlife, and the second worldly,

> insofern die Stärke und Gleichheit des Charakters, ohne zu brechen,
> bis zum Untergange aushält, und so seine subjektive Freiheit, allen

Verhältnissen und Unglücksfällen gegenüber, in ungefährdeter Energie bewahrt. (14: 573)

[insofar as the character's strength and consistency of character holds out to the bitter end without breaking, thus preserving his subjective freedom in undiminished energy in the face of all situations and misfortunes.]

(This is presumably the same means that permits the dramatist to elevate his play above a criminal story.) The third category notes the possibility of the hero acknowledging that he has brought about his end by his own actions. Although Schiller is not mentioned in this passage, the last two categories seem to throw light on the closing scenes of the plays under discussion (with the possible exception of *Fiesco*); the last quotation, again, might well be a commentary on the death of Franz Moor.

Hegel's discussion therefore engages Schiller's early tragedy on a different level from Hoffmeister's, eschewing biography and textual exegesis but instead offering searching reflections on such issues as the role of subjectivity and its relation to the transcendental orders of religion and morality. A reader comparing, say, *Don Carlos* with Shakespeare's histories is bound to be struck by the greater degree of attention paid by Schiller to the delineation of individual characters; Hegel's thoughts on the subject, for all their philosophical terminology, thus address a feature of Schiller's drama that is by no means abstruse and is certainly a legitimate topic for literary criticism.

So great was the influence of Hegel that even Hoffmeister, despite his hostility to the Hegelians (which prompts some polemic against "an obsession with system" and "scholasticism" ["Systemsucht und Scholastik"] in his Foreword), is not immune to their influence. The final pages of his first volume (312–20) are thus devoted to a discussion of the difference between ancient and modern tragedy that clearly echoes Hegel. The concept of fate, says Hoffmeister, has been replaced in our times by divine providence, against which struggle is unthinkable. Fate has thus been dislodged as the opposition to the tragic hero by the forces of history, such that, in the tragic conflict, we always see the clash of the hero, as representative of the new, with the figures representing the established order. Unmistakably Hegelian is the dictum: "Der große neue Tragiker muß . . . ein kulturhistorisches, weltgeschichtliches Bewußtsein, der alte mußte einen religiösen Sinn haben" (315). [The great new tragedian must . . . have a cultural, world-historical awareness, the ancient one had to have a religious sense.] The results are an immanent and naturalistic drama in contrast to the transcendentalism of the Greeks, and a modern drama of action verging on the epic where the Greek, focusing on heroic endurance, tended toward the lyric mode.

Schiller, for Hoffmeister, is the modern tragedian *par excellence*, and for the purposes of this argument the early Schiller is preferred to the author of *Wallenstein*: "Er hatte den tiefen, immer auf das Allgemeine, auf das Ganze der Menschheit gerichteten universalhistorischen Blick" (316). [He had the deep, universal-historical gaze, always directed at the general, at the whole of humanity.] But, as becomes clear at this point, there are limits to Schiller's naturalism. Because, Hoffmeister writes, he experienced with exemplary intensity the universal conflict between freedom and determinism, he was able to express this in his works based on his own experience. History, we see, does not move blindly from one epoch to the next, but rather incorporates (again we can hear Hegel speaking) the progress of human freedom. Schiller was a witness to this heroic process, and this is reflected, not only in his avoidance of the fate motif, but in his affirmation of freedom in *Don Carlos*. Hoffmeister thus concludes by positing, as a new genre for his age, the historical tragedy of progress, a genre for which *Don Carlos* is to be the prototype. The hero's death is not to be required here, and where (as in *Carlos*) it does occur, this is not to throw the final victory of the cause in doubt. Hoffmeister concludes his discussion, and his first volume, with an open plea for more political and religious freedom and for the activist and committed literature that will help to bring them about.

Hoffmeister, we can say, is thus quite successful in absorbing the Hegelian influence without allowing "Systemsucht und Scholastik" to detract from the wider appeal of his book. We cannot say the same for Hinrichs. Where his master saw human history as the progressive self-realization of freedom, Hinrichs sees a similar process at work in Schiller's dramatic oeuvre, advancing dialectically from play to play and reaching its *dénouement* in *Wilhelm Tell*, where the concrete ideal is presented in definitive form, leaving Schiller nothing to do but die, exhausted but triumphant.

Hinrichs states his program as follows:

> Das Ideal ist bei Schiller die innere, reale Möglichkeit des Geistes selbst. Der Gegensatz von Ideal und Wirklichkeit ist, wenn gleich noch vorhanden, doch blos Voraussetzung der Einheit, zu dieser sich erhebend und deshalb zur Schönheit sich gestaltend. Er ist nur noch da, um sich aufzuheben. Der ganze Verlauf der Schillerschen Stücke ist kein anderer, als diese Vermittlung des Gegensatzes von Ideal und Wirklichkeit zur Einheit und Durchdringung. (2: lvi)

[With Schiller, the ideal is the inner, real possibility of the spirit itself. The contrast of ideal and reality, although it is still present, is merely the precondition of unity, to which it raises itself and thus shapes itself as beauty. The contrast is only there in order to eliminate itself. The whole course of Schiller's plays is no other than this mediation of the contrast of ideal and reality to the end of unity and interpenetration.]

Each play has thus to be portrayed as embodying a higher degree of fusion between ideal and reality than the previous one, but at the same time leaving unreconciled loose ends for the next work to tie up. Further, this progress is said to represent stages in the historical growth of the modern rational state, a type of allegorical application of his philosophy that Hegel himself had been too sensible to suggest. Despite the ingenuity that it unquestionably requires to pursue such a program through three thick volumes, Hinrich's book reads nowadays as the product of an obsession. While he rails untiringly against Hoffmeister on the grounds of subjectivity, dilettantism, and a host of other failings, Hoffmeister will no doubt have seen Hinrichs as a victim of the Hegelian "Systemsucht," and he will have been right to do so. We have to remind ourselves that this was no private obsession but rather a symptom of the Hegelian ascendancy in German universities during this decade. As Albert Ludwig tells us (1909, 273), it was Hinrichs's work that met with instant critical acclaim, while it took many years before Hoffmeister's work received proper recognition.

We can agree with Hinrichs when he describes Hoffmeister's position as more Kantian than his own. Where Hoffmeister takes the more conventional stance that moral reason is an instance that transcends the physical world, Hinrichs regards such a sundering as the problem that Schiller's oeuvre sets out to solve. A consequence is that he takes Schiller's theory of beauty and the play impulse ("Spieltrieb") as paradigmatic for his development, while regarding Schiller's theory of tragedy, based on the sublime, as falling short of the actual accomplishment of the dramas. Here again, Hinrichs rightly says that Hoffmeister accords more validity to the theory of tragedy.

However, a glance at Hinrichs's interpretation of *Die Räuber* shows that his Hegelian standpoint has led him badly astray. Starting from Hegel's remarks about Karl's "private vengeance," Hinrichs portrays the play as the starting-point of Schiller's dialectical odyssey, and hence as representing the maximum distance between ideal and reality:

> Die Räuber enthalten die entsetzliche, aber große Wahrheit, daß der Mensch, welcher in seiner selbstbewußten Vernunft so verblendet ist, die wirkliche Vernunft in der Welt nicht zu sehen, sich selbst zu Grunde richtet.

[*Die Räuber* contains the terrible but great truth that the man who is
so blinded in his self-conscious reason as not to see the reality of reason in the world destroys himself.]

Reason that is not embedded in actual history is designated by Hinrichs
as abstract, and he regards any action undertaken to realize such an entity in the world as inevitably destructive. Before he dies, Karl is thus
vouchsafed a glimpse of this great truth, "daß er, mit seinem vermein-
ten Rechte gegen das wirkliche Recht und Gesetz im Unrecht ist" (2:
74) [that he, with his supposed right, is in the wrong in relation to the
reality of right and law]. Rather than show in detail that this view mis-
represents the text, we should be clear that Hinrichs's characterization
of Schiller's position as Hegelian rather than Kantian is wholly unten-
·able, for Schiller warns constantly against the attempt to base moral
standards on any existing material reality. More generally, Hinrichs's
work stands as a warning of the consequences of treating literary works
as materials of philosophical argument with no regard for their aesthetic
character (and where Hinrichs descends to the literary level, his argumentation can be remarkably naive). How, we are entitled to ask, could
Schiller, writing his plays in the various circumstances and stages of his
life, have unwittingly prefigured Hegel's theory of the historical dialectic, presented by the latter two years after Schiller's death in the *Phä-
nomenologie des Geistes*? Running counter to all Hinrichs's claims of
intellectual sophistication is an assumption that can only be called su-
perstitious, viz., that Schiller acted as a Swabian John the Baptist making straight the way of the coming "Weltgeist."

Not much need be said about Gustav Schwab's popular biography
of 1840, for this draws mainly on Hoffmeister, partly on Gervinus and
Vilmar, for its evaluations. The book is evidence of a resistance among
common readers to the Hegelian fashion, for its author indulges in
some polemics against Hinrichs. At the same time, one can see Schwab
struggling honestly with the question how works containing such obvious flaws of construction and characterization can still exercise such a
powerful effect. His answer seems to be, first, that the prose plays also
contain strong elements of social realism, generally concentrated in individual characters, and second, that *Don Carlos* (and here we see the
patriotic spirit of the age at work) is redeemed by the typically German
character of its two young heroes. The latter point is of some interest
since Hoffmeister (319–20) had been embarrassed by the unfashionable cosmopolitanism of the ideas informing the play. We should perhaps give Schwab some credit for the boldness of his solution to this
tricky problem.

With Karl Grün's book of 1844 we see the Hegelian establishment striking back. And yet, in his defense of Hinrichs's readings, Grün generally manages to make the search for an inherent dialectic behind Schiller's development (636) appear more reasonable than his predecessor had done. His intimation, for example, of a sense in Schiller's repeated move from freely invented to historical material — *Die Räuber* and *Kabale und Liebe* followed by *Fiesco* and *Don Carlos* — should not be lightly dismissed. With reference to *Die Räuber*, while Grün abuses Hoffmeister with no less arrogance than Hinrichs, he also makes the important and valid point that Karl Moor is not a self-portrait of Schiller, but rather that Schiller, by creating Karl, has achieved a reflective mastery over what Karl represents. The play must be seen as a whole, he implies, not plundered piecemeal for biographical correspondences. Occasionally, Grün even ventures to criticize Hinrichs for his one-sided approach to the works, arguing that some awareness of aesthetic aspects is needed also, and suggesting at one point (651) that the methods of Hinrichs and Hoffmeister complement each other.

Grün accordingly distinguishes between the idea of a play and its execution, allocating the various flaws and implausibilities (and Karl Moor's "blunder" ["Mißgriff"] in Hegel's interpretation of *Die Räuber*) to the latter level while praising the former. Modern readers, who often feel torn between their sense of the prose plays' absurdities and of their underlying greatness, may well find this distinction helpful. Grün also makes the vital distinction between Schiller as empirical person and as author of a particular text, a step that allows him to set textual evidence above extraneous or anecdotal information as to what the text was supposed to mean. To be sure, Grün does this in order to legitimate what is still a fundamentally dogmatic approach to the works, but he nonetheless strikes a telling blow against Hoffmeister's principle of "inner interpretation." With his suspicion of biography, Grün points the way toward a modern style of close critical reading, while, with his exploration of parallels between the work and contemporary events (in which he is less reductive than his predecessors), he anticipates the positivistic method that emerged later in the century.

In a newspaper review of 1853, Theodor Fontane (1819–98) portrays Goethe and Schiller as precursors of the emergent literary realism "solange sie, 'unangekränkelt von der Blässe des Gedankens,' lediglich aus einem vollen Dichterherzen heraus ihre Werke schufen" (10). [So long as they, "unsicklied o'er with the pale cast of thought," composed their works out of nothing but a poetic fullness of heart.] The consequence of the Shakespearian qualification is that Schiller's prose plays are singled out for praise, although *Die Räuber* is found, because of its

"Phrase und Überschwenglichkeit" (11) [high-flown phrases] to be incompatible with the formal excellence required by true realism. The relationship with Goethe and Schiller remained a problem for realist writers and critics, for whom Schiller's early plays pose an ongoing dilemma. On the one hand, the early Schiller deserved to be upheld in contrast to what the realists saw as the lifeless classicism of the later works; on the other, his turbulent prose plays were a world away from the calmer and more contemplative style that they, as *poetic* realists, cultivated.

Although known chiefly for his opposition to Schiller (Wellek 1965b, 308), Otto Ludwig (1813–65), in his sketchy notes posthumously published as *Shakespearestudien* (1874), praises *Die Räuber* as coming closer to the ideal of tragedy than the author's later plays; he regards *Kabale und Liebe* as Schiller's best composed tragic plot; and he prefers *Don Carlos* to *Wallenstein*. Ludwig is free with his criticism, however, especially with regard to characterization. In *Kabale und Liebe* he is particularly vexed by the implausibility of Ferdinand's knowing how his father had obtained his high office. Would such a villainous man have entrusted this secret to his son? More damagingly, Ludwig contends that for Schiller the emotional effect of the individual scene is decisive, and that the characters are made to act in a way that maximizes this local effect even at the expense of overall psychological consistency; in Ludwig's words, "Schillers Figuren sind Schauspieler, die immer die Rolle spielen, die eben im Augenblicke die glänzendste scheint" (294) [Schiller's characters are actors who always play the role that in that moment seems the most dazzling].

Die Technik des Dramas (1863) by Gustav Freytag (1816–95) was an influential work of this period, in which Schiller's plays, along with those of Shakespeare and the Greek dramatists, are cited in order to exemplify general dramatic principles. The intrigue of *Kabale und Liebe*, for example, is analyzed into four phases in order to illustrate the process of intensification ("Steigerung," 112), one of five plot elements arranged by Freytag into a triangular diagram (102; Albert Ludwig could still refer to this in 1909 as "the famous triangle" and designate it as a "cabbalistic drawing," 436–37.) We can pass over Freytag, however, whose scattered remarks hardly amount to an interpretation of Schiller's works, and pass on to Julian Schmidt (1818–86), the chief theorist of poetic realism and a prolific literary historian. Schmidt, who discusses the early plays in *Schiller und seine Zeitgenossen* (1863), approves of their realism as against the idealism that set in after the Bürger review (1791). Where realist tragedy aims at shaking the spectator ("Erschütterung"), he tells us, idealist tragedy aims at catharsis ("Läuterung").

But Schmidt can recognize the young Schiller only as a partial precursor of the kind of realism that he is calling for, and he is therefore free with his faultfinding. Schiller's chief shortcoming at this time, he writes, is a lack of cultivation and taste that predisposes him to the crude and monstrous. His shift to idealism results from self-criticism with respect to these excesses, but in making the shift Schiller throws out the baby with the bathwater, abandoning his commendable attentiveness to motivation.

With regard to the individual plays, Schmidt displays little sensitivity. He regards *Die Räuber* as a mosaic of impressive scenes that only approaches the coherence proper to drama in the last act. *Fiesco* he views as marred by disunity of character and incoherence of motivation; the protagonist, for example, is a hybrid of libertine and republican hero. The material, in fact, is more suitable to comic than tragic treatment. With *Kabale und Liebe*, Schmidt praises the portrayal of milieu, especially the figure of Luise's father, but the representation lacks the poetic element that he is looking for. Schmidt's argument forces him to see the play as the high-water mark of Schiller's realism, after which the author had no alternative but to turn toward idealism. His comments are thus slightly mystifying; without explanation, he calls the dramatic technique superb ("vortrefflich"), but makes serious criticisms of the characterization. As for *Don Carlos*, Schmidt's aversion to Posa's idealism outweighs his sympathy for his liberalism. His discussion is remarkable for dwelling mainly on Schiller's self-interpretation in the *Briefe über Don Carlos*. Schmidt is the first in a line of critics who have followed the *Briefe* and have taken over Schiller's hostile analysis of the character, viz., that Posa's laudable ideals lead him to act in a culpable way toward Carlos and the King. The implication is that Schiller is concerned less with the moral and political ideal per se than with the psychological make-up of the idealist.

Schmidt returns to this material much later in the third volume of his *Geschichte der deutschen Literatur*, which appeared in 1886, the last year of his life. Two departures are worth mentioning here, first, a general comment, reminiscent of Otto Ludwig's view, that Schiller has difficulty in reconciling individual scenes of high emotion with the requirements of overall plot consistency. An example is Carlos's apparently sincere attempt at reconciliation with his father in act II, which sits uneasily with the hatred he has expressed in act I. Are we to assume he is a hypocrite? Second, Schmidt comments that, in *Don Carlos*, King Philip becomes the chief tragic figure, although this might not have been the author's conscious intention.

Hermann Hettner was a more distinguished literary historian than Schmidt, but his roots, like Schmidt's, lie in the realist movement of the mid-century. In *Die romantische Schule* (1850), a polemical early work, Hettner played off the realism of the early Schiller against the remote and escapist classicism of the later. By the time he wrote his great six-volume *Literaturgeschichte des achtzehnten Jahrhunderts* (1856–70), he had moderated his views somewhat, although even here he expresses regret that Schiller strayed from his beginnings. If he had remained true to these, Hettner writes in his third volume, Schiller could have become a German Shakespeare. Hettner is justly famous for having tried to rehabilitate the European, and especially the French, Enlightenment, an era that did not stand in high esteem in the Germany of his time. The influence of Rousseau thus stands at the center of his interpretation, and Rousseau's contrast between culture and nature is stated to give rise to the *Tragik* of Schiller's early dramas. (Wolfgang Liepe put an end to this overestimation of Rousseau's influence in an article of 1926.) Franz and Karl Moor are even stated to be the respective embodiments of the two principles.

The political meaning receives most attention in Hettner's discussions of *Fiesco* and *Kabale und Liebe*, and this gives rise to a rather one-sided view. Despite his generous estimation of the plays' ethical and social importance, however, negative tones prevail in Hettner's discussion of their aesthetic merits, the plots being criticized for implausibility and the character portrayal for exaggeration. Despite their merits as political plays, *Fiesco* and *Kabale und Liebe* are disparaged as plays of intrigue rather than tragedies proper, while, on the positive side, Hettner praises the sheer vividness of expression in some scenes as well as the swift movement of the plots. On *Don Carlos* as well we find the same mixture of praise as to generalities and condemnation in detail that is the hallmark of so much that was written about these works at this time.

Wilhelm Scherer, the next prominent literary historian and the doyen of literary positivism, may have been a harsh critic of Hettner (A. Ludwig 1909, 438–39), but his treatment of Schiller's first four plays in his *Geschichte der deutschen Literatur* (1883) falls well short of the level Hettner had attained. Description of the social environment and comparison to other works of the period prevail over attention to the texts, and the discussions get lost in generalities; this confirms Norbert Oellers's view (1976, xxv) that the literary historians of this school had particular trouble with Schiller. To discover the contribution of positivistic scholarship to our knowledge of Schiller, we must note Karl Goedeke's monumental achievement in publishing the first critical edition of Schiller's works (1867–76), and then turn to the great unfinished biographical projects of this era. (I shall pass over the popular bi-ographies by Emil Palleske [1858], Jakob Wychgram [1895] and Otto Harnack [1898].)

The greatest of the unfinished works is that of Jakob Minor, whose two volumes (1890) cover Schiller's life up to 1787 and hence include all the four plays under discussion here. Minor devotes most space to various extrinsic aspects of the texts. We learn much from him about the process of composition, about literary sources (with special atten-tion to Shakespeare and Rousseau), about parallels and precedents for each work in German letters, and about the relation of the plays to the author's character and experience. Minor is concerned above all to an-chor each play in its age and to provide orientations to known historical landmarks, and in this he does an admirable job. He also makes some perceptive judgments on the inner structure of the dramas. He argues, for example, that Fiesco is a divided character, with each side of him re-ceiving a different but appropriate "other," Gianettino for the patriot, Verrina for the usurper. Further, he notes a mutual affinity between the young despots Fiesco and Gianettino and the old patriots Verrina and Andreas; this cuts across the overt battle-lines and helps make sense of the conclusion. On the other hand, Minor's approach can lead to mis-judgments, as when he rushes to identify a character with the author. This leads to embarrassment in his interpretation of Ferdinand, where he finds a complete discontinuity between the noble idealist of the opening acts and the jealous lover of the last ones; a reader less preoc-cupied with authorial self-expression will spot the underlying consis-tency more easily. It also does not help us much to be told that, taken together, Posa and Carlos amount to a complete portrait of their author.

Otto Brahm's biography (1888–92) is another fine work that re-sembles Minor's in method. As Wellek tells us (1965b, 316–17), Brahm was a proponent of naturalism in the theater and thus had more sympathy with Schiller's early plays than with the later ones. (Carl Weitbrecht [1901] is another author to note this affinity of the early plays to the naturalistic trend of the 1890s.) This interest in the early plays may indeed have been the reason for Brahm's failure to complete the work, for his narrative stops in 1794. What is most distinctive in Brahm's treatment of the plays is the theatrical sense that alerts him to strengths and weaknesses that can elude the philologist. In *Die Räuber*, for example, he argues that Karl's repentance in act II/3 comes too early, with the result that act III lacks dynamism; it takes the arbitrary arrival of Kosinsky to get the plot moving again. (He sees a resem-blance between this scene and the moment when King Philip pulls

Posa's card from his index, since each of them represents the intrusion of chance to overcome a dramatic aporia.) In *Fiesco* Brahm points out Schiller's mastery in the control and pacing of an elaborate plot with a large cast; he praises the "affect-laden naturalism" of *Kabale und Liebe*, which is his favorite among the four plays; and in *Don Carlos* he observes most acutely that the love intrigue with Eboli is so inconsistent with Philip's character that it would have been impossible for Schiller to bring the two characters together on the stage.

But Brahm proves his acumen by making points of a more general nature too. He notes the connection between Schiller's method in *Die Räuber* and in his third medical dissertation, the *Versuch über den Zusammenhang der tierischen Natur des Menschen mit seiner geistigen* [Essay on the Connection of Man's Animal and Intellectual Nature, 1780] and suggests a connection to the thesis, which Schiller planned but never wrote, "Über die Freiheit und Moralität des Menschen" [On Man's Freedom and Morality]. Like Minor he is fascinated by the changes of conception during the composition of *Don Carlos*, and he exhaustively analyzes the difficulties in the plot. He proposes that the conception of Posa should be seen in the context of the secret societies in the 1780s, an idea that has recently been explored by Hans-Jürgen Schings (1996). And he has some perceptive comments about the conflict between rhetorical *Pathos* and psychological calculation in these plays. In general, Brahm's biography of Schiller stands up well to comparison with the more famous work by Minor.

Of our four plays, Richard Weltrich's unfinished biography (1899) discusses only *Die Räuber*. Weltrich repeats the Rousseauian interpretation of the play with great force and in rhapsodic style, and concludes with some hyperbolic statements as to the political impact of Schiller's work up to and including *Don Carlos*. Of more interest is the one-volume "life and works" by the American scholar Calvin Thomas (1901). Although well read in German scholarship, Thomas writes with all the elegance of Anglo-Saxon scholarship at this time and he brings a fresh common-sense perspective to Schiller's characters and situations. He succinctly states the central paradox of *Die Räuber*: on the one hand, it is full of palpable absurdities, on the other, it started a new era in German drama and is undeniably a great work. Thomas explains this greatness, first, by Schiller's ability to tap into the social tensions of the age ("He converted the dynastic tragedy of his predecessors into a tragedy of the social revolution"), and secondly, by his achievement of a universal sense of tragedy at the conclusion; citing the Greek concept of hubris, Thomas writes that we see in Karl's downfall "the verdict of the gods upon human presumption" (38–39). Although he regards *Kabale und Liebe* as the finest example of the domestic tragedy,[6] Thomas is still frustrated at the unnaturalness of Luise's words and deeds; he evidently feels that, in order to justify the play, it is necessary to dwell on its portrayal of conditions in Württemberg rather than of the characters. He is severe on the confusions and shifts of focus in *Don Carlos*, and he judges (in my view rightly) that the revelation of Posa's plotting in act IV is a late addition that, in a way that Schiller failed to grasp, has damaging implications for Posa's character as it has been portrayed up to that point. While not claiming to break new ground, Thomas offers a thoughtful and lively discussion of the plays for the English-speaking student, one that can still be read with profit.

No less valuable are Ludwig Bellermann's studies of the plays, which appeared first in 1888. Bellermann's analyses grow out of the kind of detailed textual examination practiced by Heinrich Düntzer in his series of commentaries on classic literary works. With his indifference to the author's biography and his surprising attention to the old doctrine of the unities, Bellermann even seems a throwback to neoclassicism; where other critics cultivate the description of Schiller's characters, Bellermann invokes Aristotle and emphasizes the primacy of plot. Although somewhat austere, his studies are in fact highly intelligent examinations of the structure of each play, and they make many of Bellermann's contemporaries seem impressionistic in comparison. They are still frequently consulted by scholars today.

Bellermann's procedure is to search for the sources of unity in each play and then scrupulously to weigh the features that have been portrayed by critics as incoherent or insufficiently motivated; his usual conclusion is that the flaws, where they are present, pertain to surface matters of language or characterization whereas the deeper structure is sound. Bellermann is thus a champion of Schiller, not on the basis of a rhapsodic celebration of his genius or his moral character, but rather of his measurable achievement. He is particularly vehement in his rejection of Julian Schmidt's view that, composing by inspiration, Schiller could only achieve a disjointed mosaic of scenes. Bellermann defends the coherence of *Fiesco* against the charges of Hettner and Minor, arguing that one must see the unity of the play as revolving around the actions and fate of the hero and not around the idea of republicanism. In *Kabale und Liebe* he defends the much criticized confrontation of Luise and Lady Milford in act IV; one cannot introduce a major figure for just one scene! Finally, he stands up for the unity of *Don Carlos*, basing himself upon Schiller's account in the *Briefe* and rejecting Hoffmeister's analogy of the finer passages to "oases" between long stretches of desert. In general, Bellermann reinforces Schiller's own request to his readers in the *Briefe über Don Carlos* that, before assuming an author to be incompetent, they should make a serious attempt to understand his intentions, a piece of advice that is unlikely ever to become obsolete.

Carl Weitbrecht's 1897 study of Schiller's dramas deserves mention on a number of grounds. First, Weitbrecht is not a scholar, and his opinions seem based less on time spent in libraries, more on extensive experience of seeing Schiller performed on the stage. Second, he writes with an engaging and forceful style and in an open spirit of advocacy, pleading Schiller's case both against the literati, with their preference for Goethe, and against the self-conscious moderns with their "nervöse Feminismus und die primanerhafte Früh- und Überreife" (10) [nervous feminism and schoolboyish precocity]. Weitbrecht's Schiller is a tragedian of world rank, but also a virile and down-to-earth writer, a good antidote to all effeteness and hypochondria. Third, Weitbrecht's interest is in the works, not the author's life, and he is thus free of the pious sentimentality of much of the popular literature. In my Introduction, I criticized a later essay by Weitbrecht for its nationalistic viewpoint, and it may be that his intention in this book is the same. He stresses, for example, Schiller's masterful character and the centrality of the struggle for mastery and freedom in his dramas ("Herrschaft und Freiheit," a pair of terms figuring prominently in the Prologue to *Wallenstein*), and he possibly hopes to inspire his young male readers to emulate these qualities in their lives, to the benefit of the Fatherland. It only remains a possibility, however, and the book can be read without this thought pressing itself on the reader's awareness.

The common thread running through Weitbrecht's analyses is the concept of the tragic, which he sees as applying to characters rather than to events and situations. He has several criteria for the tragic: first, the character must suffer; second, he or she must be of superior strength or vitality; third the drama must convey a sense of necessity in the course of the hero's life, a necessity generated in uncertain proportions by his/her character and surroundings. Last, the hero's physical end must be preceded by an inner destruction, and it must signal the intervention of a higher order of some metaphysical kind. Hence, the hero's guilt is not of a criminal variety, a point that Weitbrecht perhaps overdoes. Weitbrecht applies his model with admirable consistency; it leads him to argue, for example, that Carlos lacks tragic stature because of his passivity, while Posa's fate is determined by events that lack all necessity. Weitbrecht's judgment of Luise in *Kabale und Liebe* is distinct from his concept of the tragic, but is nonetheless of interest as a sign of the numerous ways in which this play can legitimately be

viewed. Many critics have found fault with Luise's readiness to renounce Ferdinand, and have blamed this on her overconventional
mentality; Weitbrecht is alone in attributing her choice to the literary
material with which, as the play tells us, Ferdinand himself has supplied
her. Luise emerges here as a prefiguration of Flaubert's Emma Bovary,
with the difference that, where Emma's reading leads her into sexual
adventures, Luise's reading undermines her natural determination to
fight for her rights, so that, in a flight of sentimental religiosity, she insists on renouncing erotic fulfillment and playing the martyr instead.

Another important book, which with its social perspective looks
forward to much modern scholarship, is Arthur Eloesser's history of
domestic (or bourgeois) drama (1898). In a few elegant pages (146–
55), the author ingeniously presents Schiller's three prose plays as a reca-
pitulation of the phases of German domestic drama up to that point,
and *Don Carlos* as a sign foretelling the Kantian and classical spirit to
come. He argues that, in the abstractness of its moral conflict, *Die
Räuber* harks back to the earliest domestic dramas (the brothers as embodiments of virtue and vice); *Fiesco* reflects the greater political concreteness of Lessing's work; and *Kabale und Liebe* repeats the social
criticism of the 1770s. *Don Carlos* is a companion-piece to Lessing's
Nathan, and Eloesser insists on its bourgeois character despite its
courtly setting. As a contextualization of Schiller's early dramas,
Eloesser's treatment is still valuable.

We must pass over Heinrich Bulthaupt's interesting discussions of
the plays in the first volume of his *Dramaturgie des Schauspiels* (1880),
and also Julius Petersen's exhaustive *Schiller und die Bühne* (1904),
works that approach the plays from the angle of performance without
offering an overall interpretation, and close this chapter by looking
briefly at two books that, while falling well below the highest standards
of the period, nonetheless represent different facets of the positivist
movement and thus deserve a place in our story. Julius Burggraf, a
Protestant pastor who in 1905 preached twenty sermons on Schiller's
Christianity (Oellers 1976, xxxix), gives a conscientious and reverential
account of Schiller's relations with the female sex throughout his life,
and works to dispel the prejudice that Schiller was better at portraying
men than women (1897). Predictably, Burggraf interprets Elisabeth
and Eboli as the two faces of Charlotte von Kalb. And Arthur Böhtlingk, on the lookout for literary rather than biographical influences,
seeks to show both that Schiller's career was motivated by a desire to
equal Shakespeare, and that his dramas draw on Shakespeare's to a degree hitherto undreamt of (1910). Against the background of such naive and pettifogging works as these, we can more readily understand

the rise of *Geistesgeschichte* in the new century, a school of criticism that seemed to offer better prospects of gaining worthwhile insights into the great literary works of the past.

Notes

[1] The book had appeared in installments in *The London Magazine* in 1823–24. For a full account of the reception of Schiller's works in Great Britain, see Ewen, whose well-documented study *The Prestige of Schiller in England* (1932) supersedes the older one by Rea (1906) and is still invaluable. William Taylor, who published an appreciation of Schiller in *The Monthly Magazine* (1821–22) deserves to be mentioned as Carlyle's most important predecessor. For a modern discussion of Carlyle's role as interpreter of Germany to England, see Ashton (1980, 67–104). As Ewen tells us, Schiller had been known in England almost exclusively for *Die Räuber* until the appearance of *De l'Allemagne* in 1813. Opinions were violently divided on the play, with enthusiasts, led by Coleridge (who read it in 1794 and was inspired to write a sonnet), being opposed by conservatives writing in the *Anti-Jacobin* (founded 1797). In the preface to a parodistic drama called *The Rovers* (1798) by George Canning and two associates, *Die Räuber* is said to be "a tragedy in which robbery is put in so fascinating a light that the whole of a German university went upon the highway in consequence of it" (cited in Ewen, 17). The reputation of German literature at this time as subversive is confirmed by the description of *The Rovers* in the same preface as "a play, which, if it has a proper run, will . . . do much to unhinge the present notions of men with regard to the obligations of Civil Society and to substitute in lieu of a sober sentiment, and regular discharge of duties incident to each man's particular situation, a wild desire of undefinable latitude and extravagance."

[2] See also Heine's poems "Georg Herwegh" (1843; *Sämtliche Schriften* 7: 421–22) and "Die Audienz" (1853; ibid., 11: 231–33) on the meeting of Herwegh, a prominent writer of the Young Germany movement, with King Friedrich Wilhelm IV of Prussia in 1842. The audience, which Heine compares with Marquis Posa's audience with King Philip, was a disaster and was followed by Herwegh's immediate banishment.

[3] See the article by S. S. Prawer (1975/76), who argues against Demetz (1959) that Marx's attitude to Schiller was not wholly negative. As a young man, Marx had written poems in a Schillerian style, and later on his scorn was directed more against Schiller's admirers among bourgeois politicians than it was against Schiller himself.

[4] Another famous comment of Hegel's would therefore appear to refer to *Die Räuber* and *Kabale und Liebe*: "Schiller . . . ist in eine Gewaltsamkeit verfallen, für deren hinausstürmende Expansion es an dem eigentlichen Kern fehlt" (14: 569). [Schiller . . . succumbed to a violence whose heaven-storming expansion lacks a real kernel.] Demetz (1959, 148) observes that Marx and Engels took over Hegel's fundamentally negative attitude to Schiller.

5 The authority for the term "erhabener Verbrecher" [sublime criminal], which will occur frequently in this discussion, comes from Schiller's anonymous "Selbstbesprechung" [self-discussion] of *Die Räuber* (1782), where he writes: "Rousseau rühmte es an dem Plutarch, daß er erhabene Verbrecher zum Vorwurf seiner Schilderungen wählte" (622). [Rousseau praised the fact that Plutarch chose sublime criminals as the objects of his description.]

6 "Domestic tragedy" is used here and throughout as the equivalent of the German "bürgerliches Trauerspiel." In view of the frequent appearance of noble characters in these plays, the term is more suitable than "middle-class" or "bourgeois tragedy."

Works Cited

Abusch, Alexander. 1955. *Schiller: Größe und Tragik eines deutschen Genius.* 4th ed. Berlin: Aufbau, 1965.

Anon. "Über Friedrich von Schiller." 1805. *Allgemeine Literatur-Zeitung, Intelligenzblatt* 98 (19 June), 785-806. Cited in Oellers, ed. 1970, 181–99.

Ashton, Rosemary. 1980. *The German Idea: Four English Writers and the Reception of German Thought, 1800–1860.* Cambridge: Cambridge UP.

Bellermann, Ludwig. 1888–91. *Schillers Dramen: Beiträge zu ihrem Verständnis.* 3rd ed. 3 vols. Berlin: Weidmann, 1905.

Böhtlingk, Arthur. 1910. *Schiller und Shakespeare.* Vol. 3 of his *Shakespeare und unsere Klassiker.* Leipzig: Eckardt.

Brahm, Otto. 1888–92. *Schiller.* 2 vols. Berlin: Hertz.

Brandes, Ernst. 1806. [Review of *Theater von Schiller*, 2 vols., 1805.] Cited in Karl Guthke, "Lessing-, Goethe- und Schiller-Rezensionen in den *Göttingischen Gelehrten Anzeigen* 1769–1836." *JFDH* 1965: 139–47.

Brentano, Clemens. 1814. [Review of *Kabale und Liebe.*] Cited in Oellers, ed. 1970, 153–56.

Bulthaupt, Heinrich. 1880. *Lessing, Goethe, Schiller, Kleist.* Vol. 1 of his *Dramaturgie des Schauspiels.* 11th ed. Oldenburg: Schulzesche Hofbuchhandlung, 1906.

Burggraf, Julius. 1897. *Schillers Frauengestalten.* 2nd ed. Stuttgart: Krabbe, 1900.

Canning, George, et al. 1798. Preface to *The Rovers.* Cited in Ewen 1932, 17.

Carlyle, Thomas. 1825. *The Life of Friedrich Schiller Comprehending an Examination of his Works.* 2nd ed. Philadelphia: Hazard, 1859.

——. 1831. "Schiller." In *Critical and Miscellaneous Essays*. 4 vols. in 2. London: Chapman, n.d., 2: 182–219.

Demetz, Peter. 1959. *Marx, Engels und die Dichter*. Stuttgart: Deutsche Verlags-Anstalt.

Eckermann, Johann Peter. 1836–48. *Gespräche mit Goethe in den letzten Jahren seines Lebens*. Munich: Beck, 1982.

Eloesser, Arthur. 1898. *Das bürgerliche Drama. Seine Geschichte im 18. und 19. Jahrhundert*. Berlin: Hertz.

Engels, Friedrich. 1847. [Review of Karl Grün, *Über Goethe vom menschlichen Standpunkte*, 1846.] Cited in Marx/Engels 1968, 1: 457–83.

——. 1885. Letter to Minna Kautsky. Cited in Marx/Engels 1968, 1: 484.

Ewen, Frederic. 1932. *The Prestige of Schiller in England: 1788–1859*. New York: Columbia UP.

Fontane, Theodor. 1853. "Unsere lyrische und epische Poesie seit 1848." In vol. 21/1 of *Sämtliche Werke*. Munich: Nymphenburger Verlagshandlung, 1963, 7–33.

Freytag, Gustav. 1863. *Die Technik des Dramas*. In vol. 14 of *Gesammelte Werke*. 22 vols. Leipzig: Hirzel, 1887.

Gervinus, Georg Gottfried. 1835–40. *Geschichte der deutschen Dichtung*. 5th ed. revised by K. Bartsch. 5 vols. Leipzig: Engelmann, 1874.

Goethe, Johann Wolfgang von. 1815. "Über das deutsche Theater." Cited in Oellers, ed. 1970, 321–23.

Grün, Karl. 1844. *Friedrich Schiller als Mensch, Geschichtsschreiber, Denker und Dichter*. Leipzig: Brockhaus.

Harnack, Otto. 1898. *Schiller*. Berlin: Hofmann.

Hegel, Georg Wilhelm Friedrich. 1835. *Vorlesungen über die Ästhetik*. Vols. 12–14 of *Sämtliche Werke*, ed. Hermann Glockner. 20 vols. Stuttgart: Fromann, 1928.

Heine, Heinrich. 1833. *Die Romantische Schule*. In vol. 5 of *Sämtliche Schriften*, ed. Klaus Briegleb. 12 vols. Frankfurt a. M.: Ullstein, 1981, 357–504.

Hettner, Hermann. 1850. *Die romantische Schule in ihrem inneren Zusammenhange mit Goethe und Schiller*. Reprinted in *Schriften zur Literatur*, ed. Jürgen Jahn. Berlin (East): Aufbau, 1959, 51–165.

——. 1856–70. *Geschichte der deutschen Literatur im achtzehnten Jahrhundert*. 3rd revised ed. Vol. 3/1. Braunschweig: Vieweg, 1879.

Hinrichs, H. F. W. 1837–39. *Schillers Dichtungen nach ihren historischen Beziehungen und nach ihrem inneren Zusammenhang*. 3 vols. Leipzig: Verlag der Hinrichsschen Buchhandlung.

Hoffmeister, Karl. 1838. *Schillers Jugendgeschichte und Periode der jugendlichen Naturpoesie bis zum Don Karlos 1786.* Vol. 1 of *Schiller's Leben, Geistesentwickelung und Werke im Zusammenhang.* 5 vols. Leipzig: P. Balz'sche Buchhandlung, 1838–42.

Horn, Franz. 1804. "Andeutungen für Freunde der Poesie." Cited in Oellers, ed. 1970, 109–13.

Hoven, Friedrich Wilhelm von. 1840. *Autobiographie.* Cited in Max Hecker, ed., *Schillers Persönlichkeit. Urteile der Zeitgenossen und Documente.* Vol. 1. Weimar: Gesellschaft der Bibliophilen, 1904, 140–46.

Humboldt, Wilhelm von. 1830. "Über Schiller und den Gang seiner Geistesentwicklung." In Oellers, ed. 1970, 287–309.

Liepe, Wolfgang. 1926. "Der junge Schiller und Rousseau. Eine Nachprüfung der Rousseaulegende um den *Räuber*-Dichter." *ZfdPh* 51, 299–328. Repr. in Liepe, *Beiträge zur Literatur- und Geistesgeschichte.* Neumünster: Wachholtz, 1963, 29–64.

Ludwig, Albert. 1909. *Schiller und die deutsche Nachwelt.* Berlin: Weidmann.

Ludwig, Otto. 1874. "Schiller." In vol. 5 of *Gesammelte Schriften.* 6 vols. Leipzig: Grunow, 1891, 285–323.

Marx, Karl. 1859. Letter to Ferdinand Lassalle. Cited in Marx/Engels 1968, 1: 179–82.

—— and Friedrich Engels. 1968. *Über Kunst und Literatur,* ed. Manfred Kliem. 2 vols. Berlin (East): Dietz. (Lizenzausgabe Frankfurt a. M.: Europa Verlag.)

Menzel, Wolfgang. 1828. *Die deutsche Literatur.* Cited in Oellers, ed. 1970, 240–45.

Minor, Jakob. 1890. *Schiller: Sein Leben und seine Werke.* 2 vols. Berlin: Weidmannsche Buchhandlung.

Oellers, Norbert. 1967. *Schiller: Geschichte seiner Wirkung bis zu Goethes Tod.* Bonn: Bouvier, 1967.

——, ed. 1970. *Schiller — Zeitgenosse aller Epochen. Teil 1: 1782–1859.* Frankfurt a. M.: Athenäum.

——, ed. 1976. *Schiller — Zeitgenosse aller Epochen. Teil II: 1860–1966.* Munich: Beck.

Palleske, Emil. 1858. *Schillers Leben und Werke.* Revised ed. Berlin: Weichert, 1912.

Petersen, Julius. 1904. *Schiller und die Bühne.* Berlin: Mayer und Müller. Repr. 1967.

Prawer, S. S. 1950. "The Schiller-Cult in 'Biedermeier' Times." *Modern Language Review* 45, 189–94.

———. 1975/76. "What *Did* Marx think of Schiller?" *GLL*, N.S. 29: 122–37.

Rea, Thomas. 1906. *Schiller's Dramas and Poems in England*. London: Fisher.

Scherer, Wilhelm. 1883. *Geschichte der deutschen Literatur*. 8th ed. Berlin: Weidmann, 1899.

Schiller, Friedrich. 1988. *Dramen I*, ed. Gerhard Kluge. Vol. 2 of *Werke und Briefe*. Frankfurt a. M.: Deutscher Klassiker Verlag.

———. 1989. *Dramen II*, ed. Gerhard Kluge. Vol. 3 of *Werke und Briefe*. Frankfurt a. M.: Deutscher Klassiker Verlag.

Schings, Hans-Jürgen. 1996. *Die Brüder des Marquis Posa: Schiller und der Geheimbund der Illuminaten*. Tübingen: Niemeyer.

Schlegel, August Wilhelm. 1811. *Über dramatische Kunst und Literatur*. Cited in Oellers, ed. 1970, 129–32.

Schlegel, Friedrich. 1815. *Geschichte der alten und neuen Literatur*. Vol. 6 of *Kritische Friedrich-Schlegel-Ausgabe*, ed. Hans Eichner. Paderborn: Schöningh, 1961.

Schmidt, Julian. 1863. *Schiller und seine Zeitgenossen*. Leipzig: Grunow.

———. 1886. *Geschichte der deutschen Literatur von Leibniz bis auf unsere Zeit*. Vol. 3: 1781–1797. Berlin: Hertz.

Schubart, Christian Friedrich Daniel. 1775. "Zur Geschichte des menschlichen Herzens." In *Werke in einem Band*, ed. Ursula Wertheim and Hans Böhm. Weimar: Volksverlag, 1967, 241–46.

Schwab, Gustav. 1840. *Schiller's Leben*. Stuttgart: Lieschung.

Schwaldopler, Johann. 1806. *Uiber Friedrich von Schiller und seine poetischen Werke*. Leipzig: Liebeskind.

Solger, Karl Wilhelm Ferdinand. 1819. "Ueber dramatische Kunst und Literatur: Vorlesungen von August Wilhelm Schlegel." In *Erwin: Vier Gespräche über das Schöne und die Kunst*, ed. W. Henckmann. Munich: Fink, 1970, 396–471. Cited in Oellers, ed. 1970, 156–58.

de Staël, Germaine. 1813. *De l'Allemagne*. 2 vols. Paris: Garnier, 1932.

Streicher, Andreas. 1836. *Schiller-Biographie*, ed. Herbert Kraft. Mannheim: Bibliographisches Institut, 1974. (First published as *Schiller's Flucht von Stuttgart und Aufenthalt in Mannheim von 1782 bis 1785*.)

Taylor, William. 1821–22. "Schiller." *Monthly Magazine* 52: 223–26, 393–96; 53: 402–3, 300–3.

Thomas, Calvin. 1901. *The Life and Works of Friedrich Schiller*. 2nd ed. New York: Holt, 1906.

Tieck, Ludwig. 1827. *Dramaturgische Blätter*. Cited in Oellers, ed. 1970, 172–77.

Vilmar, August Friedrich Christian. 1871. *Geschichte der deutschen National-Literatur*. 14th ed. Marburg: Elwert.

Weitbrecht, Carl. 1897. *Schiller in seinen Dramen*. Stuttgart: Fromann.

——. 1901. "Der junge Schiller und das moderne Drama." In *Schiller und die deutsche Gegenwart*. Stuttgart: Bonz, 147–75.

Wellek, Rene. 1955. *The Romantic Age*. Vol. 2 of *A History of Modern Criticism, 1750–1950*. 2nd ed. Cambridge: Cambridge UP, 1981.

——. 1965a. *The Age of Transition*. Vol. 3 of *A History of Modern Criticism, 1750–1950*. 2nd ed. Cambridge: Cambridge UP, 1983.

——. 1965b. *The Later Nineteenth Century*. Vol. 4 of *A History of Modern Criticism, 1750–1950*. 2nd ed. Cambridge: Cambridge UP, 1983.

Weltrich, Richard. 1899. *Friedrich Schiller: Geschichte seines Lebens und Charakteristik seiner Werke*. Vol. 1. Stuttgart: Cotta.

Wolzogen, Caroline von. 1830. *Schillers Leben verfaßt aus Erinnerungen der Familie, seinen eignen Briefen und den Nachrichten seines Freundes Körner*. 2 vols. Stuttgart: Cotta.

Wychgram, Jakob. 1895. *Schiller: Dem deutschen Volke dargestellt*. Bielefeld: Velhagen.

3: The Age of *Geistesgeschichte*: 1905–45

NORBERT OELLERS has identified Fritz Strich's monograph of 1912 as the arrival of the new methodology known as *Geistesgeschichte* in Schiller scholarship (1976, xlii). The term, which literally means the history of mind or spirit, is not usually applied in any very precise sense, however, and it seems to me reasonable to posit a continuity between the "idealistic" tones of the 1905 centenary and the methodological extravagances that one associates more with the 1920s, the movement's core decade. (The first of the five volumes of Hermann August Korff's monumental *Geist der Goethezeit*, the canonical work of the movement, appeared in 1923.) Even the nationalism that was to become so much more acute after the Treaty of Versailles can already be heard in the work of 1905, and this dragon was of course not slain until 1945. In his appraisal of the *Geistesgeschichte* movement, Eberhart Lämmert has drawn attention to the plurality of methods and insights that can be found even in the 1920s, and so it is legitimate to use the term loosely to characterize the whole period from the centenary to the end of the Second World War (1967, 15).[1] In my discussion of the scholarship of these years, I shall first discuss some of the publications of 1905. I turn next to some of the standard works of *Geistesgeschichte* (Gundolf, Strich, Korff, Fricke 1927), and then to a group of authors (Kommerell, Cysarz, Deubler, Pongs, Fabricius, Nadler) whose work, albeit in different degrees, illustrates the continuity between this intellectual school and the ideological aims of the Nazi regime. The chapter concludes with a discussion of those authors (Liepe, Borcherdt, Brüggemann, Fricke 1930, Böckmann, Schmid, Storz, von Wiese, Rehm) who seem to me to succeed in preserving their intellectual independence and whose work can still provide impulses today.

The year 1905, the centenary of Schiller's death, was marked by celebrations and public speeches throughout Germany, the aim of which was to express the awakening nation's veneration for its noble poet and to exhort the young to take him as their example in the conduct of their lives. This was also a busy year for German publishers, and four of the books that appeared in 1905 need to be considered here. First of all, however, we should mention the edition of Schiller's works, the Säkular-Ausgabe, published to mark the centenary and edited by prominent scholars. Erich Schmidt, a doyen of German positivism, was responsible for the volume containing the prose plays, and he contributed a magisterial and sardonic introduction underlining their theatrical qualities — he prefers *Die Räuber* to *Götz von Berlichingen* — while unflinchingly criticizing their weaknesses. In *Kabale und Liebe,* as he rightly points out, the President's statement (I/5; 769) that his position is based on Lady Milford's influence is supported nowhere else in the play, and the same is true of Lady Milford's claim (II/3; 787) to have alleviated the ruler's oppression of his people; her good works have certainly been kept a secret from the servant whose accusations make the scene II/2 so famous. Richard Weissenfels, the editor of the volume containing *Don Carlos*, is less positivistic than Schmidt, and his commentary dwells more on the play's status as a document of Schiller's personal growth and "purification" than as an autonomous work of literature. He accentuates the historical importance of Posa as harbinger of liberal ideas in the real world, but he finds him and Carlos to be poorly executed as dramatic figures. This disharmony between work and idea will remain at the forefront of scholarship throughout the century.

Unlike the works of his predecessors in the 1890s, Karl Berger's two-volume biography (1905/09) was completed and became the standard work until the appearance of the first version of Reinhard Buchwald's biography in the 1930s. Berger aimed for a fairly popular level of exposition; in this respect he is as much the successor of Wychgram and Harnack as of Minor, Brahm and Weltrich. His focus is more on the glorification of his subject than on precision, and his style is rich in rhetorical *Pathos.* Like his predecessors, Berger is deeply concerned with reflections of Schiller's "Erleben" [experience], but he has his distinctive techniques too. The hallmark of his treatment of the plays is a highly literary form of character description; the underlying assumption seems to be that the contemporary reader of Schiller's plays, accustomed to the breadth of nineteenth-century narrative writing, requires this kind of epic commentary to help him (or her) appreciate the full grandeur of the dramatist's achievement.

Another departure is the edifying and hortatory tone adopted by Berger. After making the most of the revolutionary content of the early acts of *Die Räuber*, for example, he assures his respectable readers that, in the light of act V, things are not so critical, for

> In der Beherrschung der Leidenschaften, nicht in ihrer wilden Entfesselung liegt die wahre sittliche Freiheit. . . . Und weil Schiller zu dieser höheren Freiheitsidee durchdrang, darum blieb er ästhetisch nicht stecken in revolutionärer Anklage und Auflehnung, sondern konn-

te . . . sein Drama zu einem ästhetisch, künstlerisch und sittlich befrie-
digenden Schluß führen. (1: 168)

[True moral freedom lies in mastering the passions, not in unleashing
them wildly. . . . And since Schiller progressed to this higher idea of
freedom, he did not remain stuck aesthetically in revolutionary accusation and recalcitrance, but was able to . . . lead his drama to a conclusion that was aesthetically, artistically and morally [*sic*] satisfying.]

This kind of rhetoric is also evident in Berger's definition of tragedy,
which calls for the sacrifice of something great in order to gain something yet greater (1: 167). This works well enough for *Die Räuber* but
causes problems with *Fiesco* and is quietly forgotten with *Kabale und
Liebe*. Here we can see the new spirit of idealism, commented on by
Oellers (1976, xxxviii), that asserted itself throughout this anniversary
year. The side-effect of this kind of writing is a diminished interest in
the text per se; Berger does not try very hard to make sense of *Don
Carlos*, preferring to dwell on its transitional status between Storm and
Stress and *Humanitätsepoche* [the era of humanity] and, in the biographical context, as "Denkmal der Entwicklung seines Schöpfers von
stürmischem Titanismus zu maßvoller Kraft" (1: 528) [a memorial to
its creator's development from tempestuous titanism to restrained
power].

Eugen Kühnemann's book aims at a more intellectual readership
and expresses the idealistic spirit of the age more strongly than
Berger's. (One of his students credited him with bringing about a
Schiller renaissance. See Unger 1937, 207.) In its more rhapsodic and
exclamatory passages, it anticipates one aspect of the *Geistesgeschichte*
movement. However, it shares Berger's hortatory and pedagogical intent. In comparison to the works of the previous decade, Kühnemann's
exposition makes a disorganized impression, which is not necessarily a
shortcoming. Minor and his colleagues had done their work so thoroughly that it was necessary to pose new questions; what, in particular,
was the *point* of the mass of information that had been accumulated
with such devotion? The question spoke to the needs of the new generation in an age of intellectual ferment. The homogeneous methodology of the positivists had served its purpose. Now, Kühnemann clearly
felt, a more exploratory approach was needed, with each play requiring
a distinct treatment. With its haphazard combination of positivistic and
more hermeneutical lines of inquiry, we can see his rather inchoate
book as a sign of scholarship in a time of transition.

Kühnemann writes forcefully on the religious meaning of the works.
Of *Die Räuber*, which receives the longest treatment, he writes (31)

that it is "ein Weltaufruhr und ein Weltgericht ohnegleichen" [an un-paralleled world-uproar and world-tribunal] in which the deity is the real protagonist. But Kühnemann is more concerned with morality than with theology per se, and his real theme is "die sittliche Weltordnung" [the moral world order], evidently a favorite text among German peda-gogues at this time (see Wedekind's *Frühlings Erwachen* [Spring Awak-ening, 1891]!). He regards *Fiesco* with some distaste, apparently because it does not come to grips with this moral theme. After seeming to disparage *Kabale und Liebe* as a work of mere "Tendenz" [political engagement], he rehabilitates it on the grounds that it elevates the tragedy of the bourgeoisie to a "sittliche Weltfrage" [moral world-question, 234].

Kühnemann is most at ease dealing with *Don Carlos*, which he por-trays as essentially optimistic and affirmative of the values that he wishes to commend to his readers: "Es ist sein [i.e., Schillers] an positiven Kräften so reicher Geist, der uns erhebt, auch wo die Tragik seiner Dichtung uns zermalmt" (277). [It is (Schiller's) mind, so rich in posi-tive powers, that elevates us, even where the tragic quality of his poetry crushes us.][2] This leads to a rather nontragic view of the conclusion, for Carlos is said to be defeated by sheer force, not by any inner flaws. In addition, Kühnemann draws our attention to an expansive lyricism in the work as a whole (rather a helpful insight), and, in general, he en-gages more deeply with the text of this play than with the others. Plac-ing the relationship of Carlos and Philip at the heart of the play, which he sees as a human and not a political tragedy, Kühnemann takes a drastic approach to the question of Posa's role, portraying this as a function of the father-son relationship rather than as an element of in-herent importance. The problem of act IV is thus no problem at all; all that matters is that, by dying at the right time, Posa should bring about a crisis between father and son. Kühnemann even suggests that, as a failed intriguer, Posa is really a comic figure out of place in a tragedy. This is surely to go too far to vindicate the coherence of a work. In the age of Kaiser Wilhelm II, caution was perhaps advisable for scholars when discussing the political content of this play.[3]

With Robert Petsch's *Freiheit und Notwendigkeit in Schillers Dra-men* we enter a scholarly world much closer to our own. Petsch's analy-sis places the issue in context by exploring the treatment of freedom in the philosophy of the German Enlightenment, and then considers Schiller's exposure to this debate at the ducal academy. He continues with a close reading of *Die Räuber*. Focusing on the inner dimension of the tragedy, Petsch identifies a striving for happiness as Karl's domi-nant motivation in the early acts, surely a more accurate diagnosis than the frequent assumption that he is an idealist. Petsch then turns his attention to the speech in act IV/5, during which Karl contemplates suicide and momentarily denies his freedom. Rather than pose the old-fashioned questions about unity or plausibility, Petsch attempts to define Karl's states of mind as influenced by the unfolding events until, at the end of the play, he comes to an understanding of what moral freedom requires of him. Petsch concludes with a deeply felt summary of Schiller's tragic philosophy, as realized both here and in later plays, that makes Kühnemann's statements about the "sittliche Weltordnung" sound glib. Petsch thus succeeds in going beyond the methods of positivism without falling into the trap of rhetorical froth, to which *Geistesgeschichte* was all too prone. His interpretations of the other three plays at issue are marked by an unsparing insight into the characters, but are unfortunately not set out as fully as that of *Die Räuber*.

The last German work of this anniversary year that I shall mention is very different. In his *Schiller: Ein Lebensbild für deutsche Arbeiter*, Franz Mehring aimed to present the apostle of freedom to German socialists in a way that was unclouded by a bourgeois academic tradition, showing them what Schiller offered that was of lasting political value. In so doing, he set the direction for future Marxist commentaries on Schiller (Oellers 1976, xxxvii).[4] It is not always clear, however, whether Mehring is quarrelling with the bourgeois reception or with Schiller himself. In his conclusion to the book, for example, Mehring castigates Gervinus and Vilmar for their failure to recognize the merits of *Kabale und Liebe*. On the other hand, he also aligns himself quite strongly with Friedrich Engels and his dictum about the German "Misere," and links Schiller's idealism itself (that is, not a bourgeois misapprehension of it) to the weakness of the German liberals in 1848.

Regarding the individual works, Mehring praises Schiller's decision to locate *Die Räuber* in the present. Interestingly, he sees the portrayal of Franz as revealing his author's doubts regarding revolutionary materialism, to which he is nonetheless attracted, whereas Karl represents revolutionary enthusiasm afflicted by sentimentality. Mehring is predictably sarcastic about the victory of the "Bau der sittlichen Welt" [the structure of the moral world] "zu deren Pfeilern ein Herzog Karl Eugen . . . gehörte" (20) [one of the pillars of which was Duke Karl Eugen]. In *Kabale und Liebe*, Luise's readiness to renounce her love is said to mirror the weakness of the German bourgeoisie. On the one hand, Mehring intends this as a reproach to Schiller, and it is one that will be repeated often in this century; but on the other, Mehring sees the close relation of the dramatic action to the actual social circumstances as a merit that is diminished but not invalidated by the drama's conclusion, with its unrealistic hope of earthly justice. *Don Carlos* causes Mehring extreme exasperation over a missed opportunity; Posa clearly reflects the political turbulence of the 1780s (Mehring's reference to the Illuminati is vindicated by recent research), and yet his tactics are confused and directed toward manipulating the monarchy rather than founding a republic. The reason for Mehring's irritation here becomes clearer at the end of the book, where he attacks the bourgeoisie for selecting Posa — "jenen flachen Phrasenhelden" [that shallow hero of clap-trap] — as its political hero, a choice that he implies is linked to the bourgeoisie's own disastrous illusions. All in all, Mehring's discussion is refreshing in its iconoclasm and its distance from the academic mainstream, but it of course aims at political utility rather than critical understanding, and is thus chiefly of historical interest.

Mehring's book provoked considerable discussion among German Social Democrats, and this has been documented in a volume edited by Gisela Jonas (1988) that contains, among other essays, one by Karl Kautsky on the rebellions in Schiller's dramas. Kautsky's verdict on the four early plays is that Schiller expresses the limitations of his age when he only envisages a personal, anarchistic ideal of freedom rather than a political one, and that even Posa's utopia cannot do without a king.

We should not overlook an outspoken contribution of English scholarship to the centenary year. John Robertson prefaces his *Schiller after a Century* with some harsh criticism of the celebrations, inveighing especially against "the German schoolmaster" for adopting Schiller "as a means of instilling moral principles, self-denial, and patriotism into the minds of his pupils" (9). Arguing that Schiller must be understood historically, not as a timeless moral paragon, Robertson gives an appreciative account of *Die Räuber* ("one of the phenomenal works of the eighteenth century," 25) arguing that, in the Moor brothers, Schiller succeeded in encapsulating the dominant conflict in the Europe of his time. With *Fiesco* and *Kabale und Liebe*, Schiller makes advances in technique and in portrayal of milieu, so that, if only he had stayed on this naturalistic path, he would have created an authentically national drama. With *Don Carlos*, however, Robertson portrays Schiller as falling back into the trap of the French courtly style from which German drama had only just escaped. In an astoundingly damning judgment, he claims that Schiller "betrayed the Germanic drama to Voltaire" (68), even "led German tragedy back to the Canossa of French classicism" (125), and his discussions of the remaining dramas are accordingly negative. While Robertson is evidently influenced by nineteenth-century nationalism — there is much talk of national character — his attack on Schiller's change of direction has considerable force. In particular, his view that in Don Carlos Schiller learned from Voltaire how to modernize the seventeenth-century tragic style by an admixture of French sentimentality deserves to be taken more seriously.

Wilhelm Dilthey, the originator of *Geistesgeschichte*, did not leave us a satisfactory treatment of Schiller's early dramas. However, in an unfinished essay on Schiller, written in 1895 and published in 1933, he offers some rudiments of a new approach. While the longest section is devoted to *Wallenstein*, the essay contains some remarks about the early plays, which he views as preparatory steps to the fully realized historical trilogy. As a historian of ideas, Dilthey ruminates suggestively about the tradition of German idealism and its interaction with "the natural system" of the early modern period. (The term refers to the emerging naturalism of Western thought in reaction to the transcendentalism of the Middle Ages; it is one of Dilthey's great themes.) But the application of these ideas to the dramas is only fragmentary. Dilthey jumps to the usual conclusion that *Die Räuber* is inspired by the revolutionary spirit of Rousseau, and portrays the robbers' life in the woods as a proverbial return to nature. His passage on the structure of the prose plays, which he sees as a clash of idealism and worldly intrigue, is suggestive but imprecise. What is perhaps of most value in his essay is his attention to the theme of greatness, both as a personal aspiration on Schiller's part and as a theme in his works, and to the relation of this concern with greatness to themes such as idealism and history. Here Dilthey's essay anticipates the work of post-Second World War critics such as Staiger and Kayser for whom the theme of greatness becomes a means of escaping from the image of Schiller the idealist.

Friedrich Gundolf and Max Kommerell are two of the prominent figures of this time. They have their intellectual roots in the circle of the poet Stefan George, and as such they represent a widespread spirit among younger literary intellectuals in the interwar period. Instead of empirical biography or the analysis of texts, both critics also give precedence to the *Erlebnis* [experience] of the poet. This concept, a hallmark of *Geistesgeschichte*, is a hybrid combination of psychological and metaphysical impulses that we can see as mediating between the biographical and philosophical criticism of the previous century (that is, between Hoffmeister and Hinrichs).[5] As this was also the period that saw the high tide of Nietzsche's influence, it is not surprising that Schiller receives rather uncharitable treatment at Gundolf and Kommerell's hands.

Gundolf, whose glorification of Goethe in his monograph of 1916 will no doubt have influenced Korff's view of the *Goethezeit*, presents a fundamentally hostile view of Schiller in his earlier study *Shakespeare und der deutsche Geist* (1911). In accordance with George's view, Schiller emerges here as an active rather than a productive spirit, a rhetorician and pedagogue rather than a poet, a theatrical rather than a dramatic writer. Like Kühnemann, Gundolf stresses Schiller's allegiance to the "sittliche Weltordnung," but unlike Kühnemann he sees this as a sign of Schiller's inferiority. Where for Shakespeare things have their meanings in themselves, for Schiller they point beyond themselves to the transcendent moral order; Gundolf illustrates this quite persuasively with reference to Schiller's version of *Macbeth*. But he goes some way to mitigate the harshness of the criticism when he distinguishes between the content of Schiller's moral view, which he identifies as superficial rationalism, and the surprising new *Pathos* with which Schiller expresses a basically conventional outlook.

In his broad outlines, Gundolf follows Goethe's view that Schiller's early plays communicate a struggle for freedom against external obstacles. The common denominator of the prose plays is that they depict "der Titanismus verirrter Freiheitshelden, die sich durch Verletzung des Sittengesetzes ins Unrecht bringen gegen eine Welt welche schlechter ist als sie selbst" (295) [the titanism of aberrant heroes of freedom, who put themselves in the wrong against a world that is worse than themselves]. He continues with an insight that typifies the strength and limits of *Geistesgeschichte*. The enormous gulf separating social reality from the moral order, he writes, leads to a "Pathos der Distanz" (a Nietzschean phrase). This explains the "kolossalische Verstiegenheit" [colossal exaggeratedness] of the plays, as well as the "moralische Wucht, die eben auf der Überfliegung dieser Distanz ... beruhte" (195) [the moral impetus that ... rested precisely on the overflying of that distance]. On the one hand, this is a notable attempt to account for a stylistic feature by reference to a spiritual situation. On the other, the insight is couched in such metaphorical terms (including mixed metaphors) that it has to succeed or fail as a momentary *aperçu*. Gundolf offers no answer to the interesting question *why* Schiller should have expended so much *Pathos* in defense of an outworn morality. And one might object that since the action and language of *Die Räuber* have an "exaggerated" quality to them even before Karl starts explaining his revolt in moral terms, the moral explanation can hardly be sufficient.

Gundolf's most interesting comments address Schiller's absorption of the Shakespearian influence, which he claims is confined to externalities. Franz Moor, Gundolf writes, performs similar actions to Edmund in *King Lear*, but he has nothing of his essence. The same is true of the relation of Wurm to Iago. Schiller is interested in the deed and not the doer, and the deed not in itself but as it is related to an unequivocal and undisputed moral law. This gives a "fratzenhaft" [distorted] quality to Schiller's villains. Shakespeare's Richard III has the power to grip and disturb the most ethically unassailable spectator, "während Franz Moor eben jenes moralische Hochgefühl des Besserseins ungetrübt mitteilt" (297) [while Franz Moor communicates just that euphoric feeling of undiluted moral superiority]. This deadly comment goes to the heart of the Nietzschean generation's objections to Schiller: they see him as the moral trumpeter, a Pharisee who reinforces the moral prejudices of the self-satisfied "Bildungsphilister" [educated philistine]. While the charge may not be groundless with reference to Schiller's villains, what this one-sided account suppresses is that, in his portrayal of the "sublime criminal," Schiller was every bit as disdainful of middle-class morality as were the Nietzschean *jeunesse dorée*. Certainly, his statement in the Preface to *Die Räuber*, "vielleicht hat der große Böse-wicht keinen so weiten Weg zum großen Rechtschaffenen, als der klei-ne" (I: 487) [perhaps the great miscreant is not separated from the man of great integrity by as far a distance as is the small] seems to ex-press a sentiment that Nietzscheans ought to endorse.

Nonetheless, despite his rather bullying approach to Schiller, Gun-dolf is a fine critic who attempts to go beyond dogmatic assertion, vali-dating his judgment by reference to specific features of the plays. Schiller's verse, his *sententiae* and his stage directions are thus distin-guished from Shakespeare's on the grounds that, where Shakespeare's are organically connected to the situation depicted, Schiller's are extra-neous and superimposed. Perhaps Gundolf's most interesting contri-bution is his comparison of Karl's monologue from *Die Räuber* (IV/5) to Hamlet's "To be or not to be," which it echoes. After a fairly close reading, he comes to the conclusion once again that, whereas the Shakespearian speech arises naturally from the dramatic context, "das Abstrakte ist bei Schiller immer zuerst da" (301) [in Schiller's case the abstraction is always there first].

Fritz Strich's account, referred to above as the breakthrough of *Geistesgeschichte*, is informed by Dilthey's concept of *Erlebnis*. Schiller seems an eminently suitable case for this treatment for, as Strich argues, what distinguished him from the Storm and Stress writers was precisely that he elevated his personal experiences to philosophical ones. Hence Schiller's conflict with the restrictions of the Karlsschule becomes a universal conflict between reality and ideal. He surpasses the Storm and Stress in his use of the theme of fraternal strife, for he universalizes it to a "Symbol für die unbrüderliche Menschheit, in der doch die Liebe

herrschen soll" (1912, 70) [symbol of unfraternal humanity, in which
after all love ought to prevail].

At times, this new hermeneutic is capable of posing questions that
go beyond the ken of the positivists, and of offering bold speculative
answers that can convince us intuitively even where they cannot be
proven. The method is perhaps most impressive when the critic draws
connections between the wider intellectual argument and specific formal or stylistic features of the work, as when Strich notes the juxtaposition of metaphysical abstraction and obscenity in the language of *Die
Räuber*. But the danger of *Geistesgeschichte* is that, with its pontifical
and dogmatic style of writing, this method lures the interpreter into
making impressive-sounding assertions that cannot be verified or vali-
dated with reference to the text. Is there anything more than rhetorical
validity to Strich's assertion of *Die Räuber* that "die Idee der Nemesis . . . war für Schiller . . . die Versöhnung zwischen den allzu schrof-
fen Gegensätzen des Idealismus und des Materialismus" (70) [the idea
of nemesis . . . was for Schiller . . . the reconciliation between the all
too harsh contrasts of idealism and materialism]? And does he go beyond banality when, of *Kabale und Liebe*, he writes: "Es ist ein Drama
der Kultur überhaupt: denn es zeigt, daß in der Kluft, welche die Menschen zwischen sich geschaffen haben, die Liebe versinken muß" (102)
[It is a drama of culture in general, for it shows that, in the gulf that
human beings have created between themselves, love must sink].
Friedrich Engels would surely have castigated this kind of writing as
"überschwengliche Misere" [extravagant wretchedness]. Would he
have been wrong to do so?

Strich's interpretation of *Kabale und Liebe* begs the important
questions. Since he assumes that, for Schiller, the lovers' ideals have absolute validity, he refuses to admit the grotesqueness of their language,
which was recognized by all the contemporary reviewers. The hybrid
concept of *Erlebnis* might, we feel, have enabled Strich to see that
Schiller is a psychologist as well as an idealist in these plays, and that the
lovers' ideals might equally well be delusions that Schiller intended us
to see as dubious. And in *Don Carlos*, Strich allows both the biographical and the philosophical arguments to lead him away from the text.
On the one hand, the switch to iambics is attributed to the emotion
caused by Schiller's friendship with Körner. On the other, the underlying idea of "Steigerung," that is, the intensification of individual love
and friendship to universal emotions, is said to unify the play despite all
surface complexity and confusion.

Hermann August Korff's version of *Geistesgeschichte* is less biographical than Strich's. Indeed, it would be possible to describe his

Geist der Goethezeit (vol. 1 1923, vol. 2 1930) as an absorption of literary history into the history of ideas, and his work has both the merits
and the shortcomings that such a program leads us to expect. While the
argument struggles for a more lofty perspective than the concern with
personalia and with philological detail in the previous century, there is a
tendency for the individual text, even the individual author, to get lost
from view and for particular intractabilities to be elided in the dialectical sweep of abstractions.

The watchword in Korff's treatment of the Storm and Stress movement is irrationalism (the dialectical antithesis to the rationalism of the
Enlightenment), and, before he turns his attention to particular literary
works in his fifth chapter, this concept is expounded at four different
levels: as irrational "Kulturphilosophie" [philosophy of culture], as
"Weltanschauung" [world-view], as "Kunstauffassung" [conception of
art], and finally in a general treatment of irrationalistic poetry. What is
striking about these preparatory chapters is how little room they have
for Schiller, even in the treatment of "irrationalistic drama" in the
fourth chapter. The reason for this is that Korff is chiefly interested in
the work of the young Goethe as influenced by the ideas of Herder and
Hamann; but, instead of treating these writers as individuals, Korff
tends to inflate them (and also to conflate them) into universal cultural
forces. His method (a particularly inappropriate one given the cultural
diversity of pre-Bismarckian Germany) thus makes it difficult for him to
account for a writer like Schiller who came from a different milieu and
who had quite different concerns.

Korff resorts to something of a subterfuge to fit Schiller into his exposition: whereas the introductory chapter on the irrationalistic Weltanschauung dwells on the idea of nature, Korff gives his fifth chapter (in
which Schiller's early dramas are discussed) an introduction of its own
in which the concept of freedom comes to the fore. In this way the
distance separating Schiller from the line of succession Hamann-
Herder-Goethe is camouflaged rather than acknowledged. On the
other hand, the focus on freedom allows Korff now to give a more differentiated description of the relation between Enlightenment and
Storm and Stress than he had done previously, which in turn enables
him to avoid the error of presenting Schiller as a simple opponent of
the Enlightenment. He concedes the proximity of Karl Moor's "sittliche Weltordnung" to the standard Enlightenment view, specifically to
the "Confessions of a Savoyard Vicar" from Rousseau's *Emile* (1: 278).
(By contrast, his exposition of Karl's "Ich bin mein Himmel und meine
Hölle" [I am my heaven and my hell] in act IV/5 in terms of Deism
misses the echo of Milton's Satan.) While such differentiation is helpful,

it remains true that different parts of Korff's overextended exposition tend to lead us in different directions.

Korff's attention to the switch from an Enlightened to a Storm and Stress concept of freedom gives him a useful perspective on the plays, and he writes suggestively on what we might call the moral-immoral dilemma. Do the heroes aspire to greatness on the basis of strength alone, or because they turn their strength to good ends? In act II, Karl Moor is shown fighting against oppression and injustice, but the original motivation for his revolt was a desire for leadership and glory (combined of course with the "Menschenhaß" [misanthropy] provoked by Franz's letter). Fiesco is even more obviously torn between the desire to do good and the desire to rule; but is his desire to restore the republic, for as long as it lasts, itself merely a desire to reap personal glory? Korff returns to this theme in his second volume, in which he describes the heroes of the three plays as "verirrte Idealisten" [idealists gone astray] (2: 221) and notes the ambiguous motif of the moral "Kraftprobe" [trial of strength]. Here, taking his cue from Goethe's statement to Eckermann of 18 January 1827 (see chapter 2 above), Korff argues that, even before reading Kant, Schiller was developing away from a merely natural ideal of freedom toward the Kantian freedom realized in submission to the moral law. While this seems to capture rather well an ambivalence in the prose plays, it remains a moot point whether the later ones are well served by portraying them as dramas of the categorical imperative.

The body of Korff's chapter is divided into categories of freedom (political, social, love, metaphysical), a frustrating method for a reader interested primarily in specific works. Korff seems to say different things about *Fiesco* in sections 2 and 3, for example, arguing first for the play's revolutionary quality and then that the hero's republicanism is only a mask for his will to power. In section 2, in a much-quoted phrase, Korff calls *Kabale und Liebe* "ein Dolchstoß in das Herz des Absolutismus" (1: 209) [a dagger-thrust into the heart of absolutism], but he barely returns to the play later on to explore the problems inherent in Luise and Ferdinand's understanding of their love. Again, the conclusion Korff draws from the audience scene in *Don Carlos*, "die Freiheit ist die Voraussetzung der wahren Humanität" (1: 217) [freedom is the precondition of true humanity], looks like abstract sloganeering. In general, Korff's focus on ideas and (to a lesser degree) on *Erlebnis* leads to a technique of detaching aspects of the play from their context in order to make points that the text as a whole may not support.

Gerhard Fricke's book *Der religiöse Sinn der Klassik Schillers* (1927) was one of the two most ambitious monographs to be written on

Schiller during the interwar years. (The other was by Herbert Cysarz, 1934.) Fricke castigates Dilthey and his followers for having too secular an attitude to the literature of classicism and idealism, and indeed his own emphasis is on transcendental absolutes rather than on anything as subjective as *Erlebnis*. We can nonetheless think of Fricke as a practitioner of *Geistesgeschichte* in the sense that he treats literary texts as evidence of great spiritual movements, while the aesthetic or poetic aspects of the texts tend to get short shrift. (For the unfortunate story of Fricke's career after 1933, see the essay by Gabriele Stilla 1994.) Fricke turns to Schiller in search of guidance amidst the religious disorientation of his own day, and his book has been linked by Buchwald (1938, 11–12) to the discovery of Kierkegaard by innovating Protestant theologians in the 1920s. Schiller emerges from Fricke's book as a spiritual genius with the power to overcome the moralistic rationalism of the Enlightenment and to communicate a religious experience of an authentically Lutheran kind to his contemporaries. Schiller, we are to understand, can provide the same to Fricke's contemporaries, who are struggling to extricate themselves from the materialism and historicism of the nineteenth century. Although Fricke's emphasis naturally falls on the later Schiller, there is a serious discussion of *Die Räuber* that traces Karl Moor's relation to God and states the text's special significance to be its rediscovery of the conscience as an unconditional religious experience. Fricke is bold enough to argue that, in the play's conclusion, Schiller allowed his religious concern to override what was aesthetically or tragically appropriate. There is no heroism in Karl's surrender, therefore, and no submission to fate, but instead an act that satisfies our moral judgment even as it perplexes our aesthetic judgment. Although argued with great passion, Fricke's view in my view encounters an insuperable obstacle in the fact that, before leaving the stage, Karl invokes the "Bau der sittlichen Welt" (V/2; 617) [structure of the moral world]. This is a construct of rationalist metaphysics and not the kind of "unconditional" instance that would support Fricke's existentialist reading. To be the kind of religious thinker that Fricke and others want him to be, Schiller would have had to be a disciple of J. G. Hamann and not the student of Adam Ferguson that we know him to have been.

I shall now deal with a handful of works that, from the perspective of the present, seem to represent the excesses of the scholarship of this period. I shall pass over those contributions that serve a primarily propagandistic purpose, making an exception only of Hans Fabricius's notorious *Schiller als Kampfgenosse Hitlers*. (For a general survey of Schiller's fate during the Third Reich, the 1979 study by Ruppelt can be highly recommended, but see also the response by Lesley Sharpe, 1982/83.) After that we shall move on to a further group of critics who, while participating to a greater or lesser degree in the *Geistesgeschichte* movement, seem to me to have nonetheless aided the development of the more fruitful trends of research since 1945. The distinction is admittedly a rather arbitrary one, and it is based as much on how these groups of critics have been regarded in the postwar period as on the inherent merit of their arguments. As we shall see, valuable insights can be found even in books that are in other respects contaminated by the nationalistic spirit of these years.

Max Kommerell published his unfortunately titled *Der Dichter als Führer in der deutschen Klassik* (1928) seventeen years after Gundolf's book on Shakespeare, and, while he has much the same attitude to Schiller, his book carries far more clearly the baleful stamp of German authoritarianism.[6] Kommerell rhapsodizes about Schiller's early plan for a drama about the Hohenstaufen prince Konradin and about the unfinished drama *Die Malteser* [The Knights of Malta]. Each work would have employed the motif of the ardent male friendship inspired by devotion to a cause, but the cause in each case would have been free of what Kommerell sees as the rationalistic cant espoused by Posa. Posa and his creator were ignorant of the components which, so Kommerell informs us, are essential to the foundation of a state: "Stufung Zucht Gesetzlichkeit des körperlichen und unbedingt geltende Maße des geistigen Lebens" (217) [Hierarchy, discipline, obedience to law in bodily life and unconditionally valid norms in spiritual life].

As appalling as such statements are, it would be unfair to reduce Kommerell's treatment to them. Although he starts by echoing Gundolf as to the rhetorical nature of Schiller's talents, he in fact goes on to develop a new and original perspective, at least with regard to Schiller's first two plays. (*Kabale und Liebe* is passed over in silence, and the discussion of *Don Carlos* focuses, embarrassingly enough, on the heroic "Männerbund" [male bond] of Carlos and Posa.) Kommerell claims first that Schiller's ruling passion in these works is fundamentally that of a conspirator, that his works are a response to external oppression and a diversion of energies that would have found natural expression in desperate deeds. Schiller's character, Kommerell claims, is better expressed in the song of the robbers (IV/5) than in all his philosophical poetry.

Up to this point, such views merely elaborate Goethe's statement about Schiller's quest for physical freedom, but now Kommerell adds that Schiller's peculiarity is that he is "eine Täternatur von allerdings leidenschaftlicher Vergeistigung" (185) [the nature of a doer, but one of passionate intellectuality], and thus a conspirator who needs a bind-

ing idea: "So eng wohnte das Sprengende und das Verpflichtende bei-
einander in einer Brust" (181) [the explosive and the morally binding
dwelt so close together in one breast]. The discovery of this paradox
enables Kommerell to make some suggestive remarks about Schiller's
self-identification with Satan and Catiline (as suggested in the "Suppressed Sheet B" to *Die Räuber*), and with the further paradox of a religious urge that expresses itself through blasphemy and destruction. In
Fiesco Kommerell sees Schiller's moral-immoral *Erlebnis* as divided
neatly between the protagonist and Verrina. He draws the following
balance: "In den *Räubern* und im *Fiesko* birst eine Gemeinschaft, die
rohe Sinnenkräfte unvermittelt an den höchsten Gedanken bindet,
auseinander" (193) [In *Die Räuber* and *Fiesco*, a community that binds
crude physical forces directly to the highest idea bursts asunder]. Like
Gundolf's remark quoted above, Kommerell's statement, with its
speculative boldness and metaphorical expression, illustrates the merits
and limits of *Geistesgeschichte*. But the insight that Schiller's supposed
moralism, which still arouses the ire of some readers, has a dark and destructive side to it, is an important one that makes him (to some, at
least) aesthetically more appealing. Despite the two critics' different
idioms and methodologies, we can perhaps see here a continuity of
conviction between Kommerell and Emil Staiger's notable monograph
of 1967.

We can pass over the speech of 1934 by Ernst Bertram, another
prominent George disciple, who besides touting a "Doric" Schiller
(whatever that is supposed to mean) sticks close to Kommerell's views,
and turn to the substantial volume of 1934 by Herbert Cysarz. Modern
readers are likely to blanch and lay aside Cysarz's monograph when, in
the introductory chapter, they come upon the view that Schiller's messianic "Sendung" [vocation] was to prepare the German people to enter on to the stage of world history. But the book is better than the
preface suggests. Despite his showy and exclamatory style, which was
extreme even for his time, Cysarz still has much to offer. While not
going so far as Fricke in *Der religiöse Sinn der Klassik Schillers*, Cysarz's
interest in Schiller's relation to the spirit of Protestantism addresses a
matter of genuine interest. But Cysarz combines this theological
awareness with a broad cultural perspective which, while sometimes
wrongheaded, nonetheless contrasts with the tendency of most modern
writers to look no further than the Enlightenment when establishing
the relevant context for Schiller's works.

Building upon Kommerell's reading of *Die Räuber*, Cysarz is preoc-
cupied by the notion of religious rebellion. He attaches great importance to Schiller's early poem "Der Eroberer" [The Conqueror, 1777],

in which he finds the same idea expressed. The title figure is the prototype for Schiller's sublime criminals, and he is treated by Schiller with a paradoxical combination of pagan glorification and Christian abhorrence. Cysarz finds this mixture of pagan and Christian to be characteristic of Schiller in general. (It returns later with his evocation of the ascension of Hercules to Olympus in "Das Ideal und das Leben" [The Ideal and Life, 1795].) Although we may doubt whether this two-sided "Verlangen, den Menschen mit dem Weltgrund zu verknüpfen" [longing to join man to the foundation of the world] is "urdeutsch" [primally German], as Cysarz claims (49), we can agree that he is saying something true and important about Schiller here.

Cysarz seeks also to rebut Gundolf's charge as to Schiller's moralism. Based on his analysis of Karl Moor as religious rebel, he states that the work is neither libertine nor moralistic in spirit but is rather "eine tragische Kommunion zwischen Einzelseele und Weltall" (65) [a tragic communion between the individual soul and the universe]. But Cysarz then makes room for Franz within this religious argument. This figure is not just a collection of Shakespearian grimaces, but rather "der Apostat des nämlichen Glaubens, dessen Karl der Apostel, der Saulus und Paulus wird" (64) [the apostate of the same creed of which Karl becomes the apostle, both the Saul and the Paul]. This is not special pleading, I think. Despite the stylistic fireworks (and the brilliance of the comparison of Karl to St. Paul cannot be denied), Cysarz is arguing in a spirit that would later be called New Criticism, seeking to prove the organic unity of the text by relating its various parts to one central theme.

Cysarz makes a fresh start in dealing with *Fiesco* and *Kabale und Liebe*, placing these dramas in the context of the bourgeois theater with its anticourtly ethos. His argument (rather an original one) is that Schiller saw that a bourgeois and Puritan theater was a *non sequitur*, for the theater cannot do without the element of pomp and splendor ("Gepräng"). In both plays, therefore, Schiller re-establishes contact with the immoral court that it had been customary to excoriate, producing a new hybrid: "Hie . . . bürgerliche Schaubühne als moralische Anstalt; hie Fest und Glanz und Spiel einer unbürgerlichen Arena" (93) [On the one hand, . . . bourgeois stage as moral institution; on the other, festival, splendor and play of an unbourgeois arena]. (This insight perhaps explains an aspect of *Kabale und Liebe* that had vexed numerous critics, that is, why Schiller had brought Luise and Lady Milford together in act IV. The solution is that the confrontation of the courtly and the noncourtly is at the core of Schiller's dramatic program and so must be contrived even where, as here, the plot does not require it.) And while Schiller had himself advertised the generic character of *Kabale und Liebe* as a domestic tragedy, Cysarz's discovery of the same spirit in *Fiesco*, which he describes as "eine Haupt- und Staatsaktion, der ein Rührstück eingesetzt ist" (98) [a political play into which a tearjerker has been inserted], is once again original and illuminating, for it places the conflict in the protagonist's mind (and in the author's mind too) in the context of theatrical as well as of political history.

The title of Cysarz's next chapter, "Das Reich des *Don Carlos*," is unpromising. Despite some alarming rhetoric about dying for a cause, however, Cysarz has interesting things to say about this play also, in particular its religious dimension. He concedes that the play is more "this-worldly" than the others, but argues nonetheless that, in absorbing the religious telos into human history, Schiller has turned historical development into a religious process. Schiller's vision of a happy and perfected human community, which appears here for the first time, is an essentially religious one and is the result of the redemption of humanity, not by a divine redeemer, but by itself. Once again, therefore, the play is a hybrid of Baroque drama and bourgeois "Rührstück," the whole being placed between cosmic horizons.

Cysarz is a brilliant and learned guide on matters of this kind. Despite its unfashionable style and despite some political excesses, his book still deserves to be read more widely than it is. It would be quite wrong to equate it with such repellent contributions as Werner Deubler's article of the same year, which is contaminated by the nationalist spirit to an incomparably greater degree. Deubler, an enthusiast for Ludwig Klages, proceeds from the latter's antithesis of (good) biocentrism and (bad) logocentrism. His defense of Schiller against Gundolf's charge of shallow rationalism thus entails forcing him into a mythical framework of Germanic heroism and sacrifice. Hermann Pongs also adopts a Klagesian paradigm in his essay *Schillers Urbilder*. In practise, the term "Urbild" [archetype] seems to be not very different from *Erlebnis*. But Schiller's "Urbild" is stated to be "der Mensch der Gruppe, gebunden an Gott und Mitwelt" (11) [the man of the group, bound to God and to the surrounding world], and the source of his *Tragik* is said to lie in the conflict between these two bonds. Cysarz seems closer to the mark here when he writes about Schiller's Lutheran attention to the individual conscience. While starting out in more judicious tones than Deubler, Pongs still ends up ranting about "Volk" and "Führer." It would really be better to leave Schiller with the stigma of rationalism than to hand him over to defenders such as these.

As his notorious title *Schiller als Kampfgenosse Hitlers* [Schiller as Hitler's Comrade-in-Arms] tells us, Hans Fabricius (1932) goes even further than Deubler and Pongs in mobilizing Schiller, as "feurig[er] Künder deutschen Wollens" (5) [fiery herald of the German will], for the coming struggle, and in denouncing as "Volksverderber" [corrupters of the people] those critics who had portrayed him as an ally of liberalism. Fabricius's book is remembered now mainly for its account of Spiegelberg as "Ein Jude wie er im Buche steht" (13) [a textbook Jew]. As loathsome as it is, one cannot deny that there is a certain opportunistic flair in the way Fabricius pounces on quotations that will support a nationalistic view of his subject. Hence Karl Moor's early lines about the spirit of Hermann and a German republic are made into a prophecy of Hitler's expansionist foreign policy: "Karl Moor, eines deutschen Kleinfürsten Sohn, träumt von einem großen deutschen Volksstaat der Zukunft." [Karl Moor, son of a German princeling, dreams of a great German nation-state [Volksstaat] of the future.] Karl's admiration of Rome and Sparta is glossed with no less ingenuity, for these are "Republiken, in denen Adel nicht Mehrheit entschied; in denen wehrhaftes Volkstum, nicht friedensseliges Weltbürgertum sich eine Form schuf" (8) [republics in which nobility and not the majority decided, in which robust nationhood, not pacifistic cosmopolitanism created a form for itself]. And so it goes on. We may be surprised to find Karl Moor praised here as an exemplar of socialistic "Führertum," but Fabricius's perspective seems to be that of the Strasser wing of the Nazi party, which had not yet been purged. Instead of any liberal message, Fabricius praises in *Kabale und Liebe* the determination of Ferdinand, the "deutscher Jüngling," to spurn the foreign courtesan and to seek love, and national regeneration too, among the lower classes, for "[d]as einfache Volk ist der Jungbrunnen der Nation" (32) [the simple people are the nation's fountain of youth]. Of the four plays, Fabricius understandably has the most trouble with *Don Carlos*, although he struggles bravely to dress Posa in nationalist garb. This is perhaps the only discussion of the play that actually *praises* Posa for his manipulation of Carlos in act IV: "So bestätigt er durch die Tat die Wahrheit, daß jede menschliche Freiheit ihre Grenze findet, wo sie Notwendigkeiten entgegensteht, die die Gesamtheit betreffen" (35). [So, by the deed, he confirms the truth that every human freedom finds its limit where it runs into necessities that concern the collectivity.]

We should conclude this list of scholars of the Nazi period with the Austrian scholar Josef Nadler's famous attempt to place literary history on a "tribal" basis (he employs the term "Stämme" in his title). In the revised fourth edition of his work (1938), he presents Schiller as a typical representative of the Swabians of the time, but he does so only by making the Swabians sound rather like characters from an early Schiller play: "Zorn, Ingrimm, aufbrausendes Rechtsgefühl, immer auf Wirkung bedacht" (231) [anger, rage, a flaring-up sense of justice, always intent on effect]. *Die Räuber* is implausibly stated to be the artistic culmination of the constitutional strife in the state of Württemberg, while *Fiesco* and *Kabale und Liebe* are said to epitomize "die staatenbildende Anlage der Alamannen" (242) [the state-creating disposition of the Alamannen].

Turning now to the studies that seem less bound to the time in which they were written, we must first mention Wolfgang Liepe's article of 1926, alluded to in chapter 2 above, in which he attacks the prevalent consensus that these plays, particularly *Die Räuber*, contain a strong element of Rousseauian "Kulturpessimismus." In the process, he discredits the belief that Rousseau preached that people should return to living in the woods. In a careful analysis of the evidence, and eschewing the rhetoric and dogmatism of *Geistesgeschichte*, Liepe shows that Schiller only had the vaguest knowledge of Rousseau at this time, and that his social and moral views at this time were decisively influenced by Adam Ferguson, a thinker more representative of the Enlightenment's favorable assessment of civilization, who had drawn for his political views on the ideas of Montesquieu, not on Rousseau's. Liepe's findings remain as valid today as when he wrote them.

With respect to *Die Räuber*, Liepe argues against finding any revolutionary message in the play; Karl's aspirations in this direction begin and end in act II/3. Liepe makes two pertinent observations in this regard. First, we are told by Razmann in the same scene that Karl gives his share of the booty "damit arme Jungen von Hoffnung studieren" [so that poor boys of promise may study], hardly the action of "Kulturpessimist." And secondly, Karl, on hearing Kosinsky's tale of oppression (III/2) is not impelled to political action, but rather merely to return home to see Amalia again. Liepe concludes that the psychological interest in the play is stronger than the political, with the dominant influence coming from Abel's theory of "Seelenstärke" [strength of soul]. He concedes finally that the play's climax is hard to reconcile with an orthodox harmonious view of society, and suggests that the tragedy of the ending points forward to Schiller's later dualism. All of these views, based as they are on a scrupulously historical method, have been fruitful in modern discussions.

The first scholar to put Liepe's findings to use was Hans Heinrich Borcherdt, whose short study of Schiller's development (1929) still reads surprisingly well today (despite a recurrent use of the term

"Urerlebnis" [primal experience]). The thread running through Borcherdt's discussions is the insistence that in these works Schiller is not a
cultural pessimist and should not be grouped with the Storm and Stress
movement. The Storm and Stress authors were led by their belief in the
self-sufficient man of genius to produce dramas of character, whereas
the young Schiller, primarily concerned with moral and religious ideas,
wrote "Handlungsdramen" [dramas of plot]. The latter, which Borcherdt implies to be aesthetically superior, show the conflict of the individual with the great supra-individual forces of the universe.

Where Herder's pantheism was the dominant literary credo of the
1770s, Borcherdt sees Schiller's beliefs as more conventionally dualistic,
and moreover as more firmly grounded in the beliefs of the Enlightenment. Schiller's early philosophy of love receives its due attention here.
Borcherdt presents Karl and Franz Moor as critical embodiments of
two recent cultural types, the "genius" of the 1770s and the disciple of
French materialism, and he (in my view rightly) argues that, for Schiller, Karl's titanism is already historical (51). Finally, Borcherdt downplays the political theme in the plays; where this is present, he argues, it
is either derived from the wider religious concern (as in *Die Räuber*,
Kabale und Liebe and *Don Carlos*), or, where it is independent of that
wider concern (as in *Fiesco*), it leads to shallow and unconvincing work.
The message left by Borcherdt's treatment is the strongly religious tone
of the plays, an emphasis that was to be pursued soon after by Gerhard
Storz and Benno von Wiese. Of *Die Räuber*, to which he devotes the
most space, Borcherdt writes: "Es ist ein Kampf der Menschen gegen
Gott, und der Sieger ist die göttliche Weltordnung" (45). [It is a
struggle of men against God, and the victor is the divine order of the
world.] But he disparages *Don Carlos*, the favorite of the political critics, for its lack of unity, both intellectual and artistic.

The question whether to classify Schiller's first three plays as works
of the Storm and Stress has been a contentious one throughout the
twentieth century. Fritz Brüggemann (1925) offers an alternative perspective to Borcherdt's and places Schiller firmly in this movement.
From a present-day perspective, of course, it is unclear why this question requires a unequivocal answer. Why can we not say that in some
respects he is a member, in other respects not? Our terms for literary
periods and movements are no more than heuristic conventions. But
nominalism of that kind was unknown to the *Geistesgeschichte* movement. Although Brüggemann attempts a sociological approach, his argument is still strongly colored by the abstractions of *Geistesgeschichte*;
he distinguishes between three succeeding human types who appear in
prominent literary texts and who allegedly represent the actual progres-

sion of "Weltanschauungen" in the eighteenth century. These are: the prebourgeois man, an intellectualist and intriguer like Franz Moor; the bourgeois man, a resigned and passive believer in providence like Luise Miller and her father; and the "postbourgeois" man ("überbürgerlicher Mensch"), an active and emotional being like Werther, Karl Moor and Ferdinand. As a piece of sociology the analysis must be rejected as being based entirely on intuition. Moreover, its teleological character leads Brüggemann to assume with Korff that, as the more "advanced" type, Ferdinand must have Schiller's sympathy and Luise cannot, which of course is to prejudge the central issue of the play. However, Brüggemann's discussion of the eighteenth century's belief in divine providence and the changing attitudes to this doctrine is of lasting interest.

Gerhard Fricke's long article "Die Problematik des Tragischen im Drama Schillers" (1930), has proved to have a more lasting influence than his 1927 book. Fricke here takes issue with Fritz Strich's categorization in *Deutsche Klassik und Romantik* (1922), one of the most famous works of *Geistesgeschichte*, which placed Schiller under the heading of classical "Vollendung" [perfection] in antithesis to Romantic "Unendlichkeit" [infinity]. Fricke's primary focus is therewith on the classical Schiller, but his thorough article deals with each drama in turn, including the four at issue here. Despite the reference to Strich, Fricke is no less concerned with Gundolf's charge that Schiller is too much of a moral dogmatist to be a good dramatist. The thread running through his article is the admission that the charge is justified up to a point, but that beyond that point, and in varying degrees, Schiller's dramas escape moralism and enter into a world with a tragic "Tiefendimension" [dimension of depth]. Fricke proposes a general definition of *Tragik* as the experience of "das Verfallensein des Menschen an ein Übermächtiges, Unentrinnbares, Zerstörendes" (3) [man's subjection to an almighty, inescapable, destructive force]. Depressingly, he concludes that only in the unfinished *Demetrius* did Schiller realize a vision comparable to the achievements of the great tragedians of earlier times.

Fricke is certainly doing Schiller a favor in detaching him from the criterion of "Vollendung," which condemns him to be compared perpetually, and unfavorably, to Goethe. On the other hand, the article is peppered with references to Kleist, and so we wonder whether Fricke is still judging Schiller by an alien standard, merely switching the author from whom that standard is abstracted. But Schiller's moralism is indeed a problem that cannot be wished out of existence, for, unquestionably, his plays often leave this impression, and we are justified in thinking that moral dogmatism is inconsistent with good tragedy. (A spectator who saw in *Macbeth* nothing but a tale of a criminal getting his just deserts would, we feel, be missing the point.) Karl Moor's line (V/2) about destroying "den ganzen Bau der sittlichen Welt" is as much of an irritant in this regard as the lemonade in *Kabale und Liebe.* And so it would seem to be a helpful step to determine to what extent the charge of moralism is true and to what extent it is not.

Fricke deserves credit for contradicting Goethe's statement about the struggle for physical freedom, which, in his view, applies to Klinger, Lenz and Heinse but not to Schiller. The "inner form" of these dramas, he argues, is constituted by Schiller's sense that the individual is under the sway of a higher power and that his freedom consists in a recognition of this. The objections to Fricke's article are, first, that he tends to prejudge certain scenes so as to overstate the degree of moralism that they contain or imply, and second, to overlook the complexity of the characters in order to sustain his charge that Schiller had no interest in individual psychology. Thus Karl Moor is wrongly said to be motivated by a moral impulsion right from the outset, and the conclusion of the play is said (as in Fricke's 1927 monograph) to trivialize the aesthetic effect for the sake of morality, a rather extreme way of seeing the matter. In *Kabale und Liebe* the situation depicted is said to be so morally outrageous as to leave no room for any response of a nonmoral kind. Fricke regards this as the weakest of the early plays from the tragic point of view, arguing that the lovers remain abstract "Menschen" rather than concrete individuals, and that the potential for tragedy subsisting in their incompatibility never gets beyond being a quiet "Begleitmusik" [background music] for the ethical main theme. Again, most readers would surely regard this as one-sided.

On the other hand, Fricke's discussion of *Don Carlos* is rather illuminating. Fricke posits here a contrast between an idealistic and a tragic impulse in the author. The former sees the characters simply as vehicles for the idea, which is the true hero of the drama, and tests them against their readiness to die for the idea. This idealistic type of drama Fricke sees as derived from the Baroque age, in which the transcendental framework is so prominent as to forestall the contingent particularity of character and plot indispensable in tragedy proper. Neither Posa nor Carlos, Fricke writes, suffers a death that has any individual necessity to it, as should occur in tragedy. But despite this, the play embodies a tragic impulse that is focused on the figure of Philip (who would, if the idealistic conception had been the only one, have been portrayed as a monster). From Philip's perspective, the death of Carlos (and, we might add, of Posa also) does seem to have tragic meaning. However, in the finished play the idealistic conception prevails, so that the tragic impulse asserts itself only intermittently.

A final shortcoming in Fricke's study is perhaps the mirage-like quality of the concept of *Tragik* itself, such that it tends to vanish, or worse, to turn into banality, if one tries to come too close to it, as Fricke does with his definitions. *Tragik* is realized differently in different works, we might object, and part of its power resides in its ineffability. Besides, it is surely just as mistaken to deny that morality is involved in the tragic as it is to identify the two. A nonmoral view of tragedy is in danger of turning into a kind of masochistic power-worship. (Macbeth is an outstanding individual, but he is destroyed not by a malignant fate but by the consequences of his own evil deeds.) The antithesis of the moral and the aesthetic, from which Fricke's argument proceeds, is therefore vulnerable. But the question of the extent of Schiller's moralism and its effect on his dramas remains inescapable.

In his study "Die innere Form in Schillers Jugenddramen" (1934), which deals solely with the three prose plays, Paul Böckmann seeks answers to similar questions to those that concerned Fricke, although, oddly, he does not refer to him directly. As we saw, Fricke was also inquiring into the "inner form" of the plays, and he too was concerned with the relationship of morality and tragedy. Böckmann differs, however, in insisting on a historical mode of inquiry (as opposed, presumably, to an atemporal paradigm of *Tragik*), and, in general, he succeeds in producing a more differentiated and searching analysis than Fricke's.[7]

Böckmann's starting-point is Schiller's attentiveness to psychological motivation, which he rightly connects to his third medical dissertation. Although it is only the villains Franz Moor and Wurm who directly affirm the belief in the absolute calculability of human actions, this problem in fact concerns Schiller throughout these works, being reflected in his portrayal of all the characters, and it stands in a sharp contrast to the high emotionality of most of the scenes. The importance of such a "Seelenmechanik" [mechanistic psychology] is brought out especially well in Böckmann's discussion of *Kabale und Liebe*, where it is shown to be the premise for the existence of the courtly milieu. But the determinism that is implied by this psychology has a limit, and this is constituted by the conscience or (to cite the Kierkegaardian term that Böckmann takes over from Fricke) the experience of "Unbedingtheit" [unconditionality]. For Schiller, this represents a heterogeneous and incalculable force, the moment where human beings escape a purely mechanical existence.

Böckmann is thus providing his own solution to what I have called the moral-immoral dilemma: he admits that morality has a central role in the plays, but, by insisting on the irrational quality of Schiller's view of moral experience, he is able to dispute the view that there is something fundamentally untragic about it. As the sole incalculable factor in the operations of the psyche, the Schillerian conscience does not give rise to a cozily didactic drama in the manner of Gottsched's prescriptions. On the contrary, Schiller reveals the tragic potential of morality itself. Despite his strong moral concerns, therefore, Böckmann (and here he contradicts Borcherdt) allocates Schiller more firmly to Storm and Stress than Korff had done, although, like Korff, he views this movement as essentially irrationalistic, a view that is now discredited.

Further, the Schillerian conscience makes claims of frightening totality that the physical world cannot satisfy, hence giving rise in act I of *Die Räuber* to the sin of despair. Later Karl Moor finds himself caught between nemesis, which is the province of God, and human justice with its inevitable imperfections. Neither of these will directly satisfy the demands of conscience, and Böckmann sees this fact as a matter for tragedy. He thus asserts that a dialectical "Dreigliedrigkeit" [triadic structure] underlies the tragic mood in these dramas, and goes on to argue that, just as Karl Moor's inner conflict is more important than his conflict with Franz, so also the political themes in *Fiesco* and *Kabale und Liebe*, with their proximity to didactic "Schwarzweißmalerei" [black-and-white portrayal], are only secondary. Precedence goes to the inner dialectic of politics and love, an inherently tragic process arising from the incommensurability of the conscience with experience: "Stets trifft die Unbedingtheit des Geistes nicht nur auf eine wertlose Gegenwelt, sondern immer zugleich auf die Bedingungen seiner eigenen Verwirklichung" (41). [The unconditionality of spirit continually encounters not only a external world that is devoid of value but also the conditions of its own realization.] This is and remains an impressive solution to the problem of Schiller's moralism, with the qualification that (as is not uncommon with dialectical arguments) it inclines toward ex cathedra dogmatism and tends to override the concrete dynamics of the drama in its search for a dynamic of a more abstract kind.

A final and slightly mysterious strand in Böckmann's argument is his stress on the concept of *Pathos*, which he removes from its rhetorical roots and transforms into a formal category that can be applied to character portrayal, dramatic situation and plot structure also. He is persuasive when he affirms Schiller's great achievement to be the conquest of the pathetic style for the German stage. However, without quite explaining why, Böckmann seems to view this *Pathos* as the expressive form commensurate to the tragic dialectic that he has identified as the inner form of the dramas. When he writes that the characters and situations of *Fiesco* are "pathoserfüllt, weil durch sie das Reich der Idee zugleich verwirklicht und in Frage gestellt wird" (36) [filled with *Pathos*, because the realm of the idea is simultaneously realized and put into question by them], the nature of the causal connection asserted through the word "because" is by no means obvious.

Karl Schmid's monograph of 1935 addresses similar problems to the articles by Fricke and Böckmann, but does not offer such interesting answers. Schmid is guided in part by Wilhelm von Humboldt's statement that thought was Schiller's "life-element," in part by Schiller's analysis of the sentimental poet from the essay *Über naive und sentimentalische Dichtung*; Schmid's constant theme is that, where Goethe is "naive," that is, a poet of experience with an empathetic ability to create rounded characters, Schiller is a poet of the idea and the will, whose dramatic psychology is derived from his reading of theoretical and literary texts. In accordance with the program of *Geistesgeschichte*, the scholar's task is taken to consist in the attempt to divine Schiller's artistic and intellectual "Eigenart" [particular nature]. The fact that this occurs here largely in terms of Schiller's own conceptual vocabulary leads to a critical method in which a juggling with concepts replaces a close reading of the texts. The presence of the "idea" in each text is assumed rather than proved. We are thus told that Karl Moor and Ferdinand are spokesmen of enlightened reason, a dubious proposition at best, and that there is nothing left of Posa if one removes the speeches in which he serves as Schiller's mouthpiece. There are unresolved problems here, in the tension, for example, between the claims that Schiller lacks empathy and that his central characters are self-portraits, and in the contradiction between the critic's stress on thoughts and ideas and the wild emotionality of the texts themselves.

The appearance of Reinhard Buchwald's two-volume biography in 1937 marked a major step forward in Schiller studies. I shall pass over this work for the moment, discussing the second edition (1953/54), which is still the standard biography, in the next chapter. However, the two scholars who were to dominate the field in the immediate postwar decades each published a monograph on Schiller's dramas in the year 1938. Although these works, by Gerhard Storz and Benno von Wiese, are normally skipped nowadays in favor of their longer works of the year 1959, they are still worth reading both for their own sake and as proof that honest scholarship was not impossible during the Nazi dictatorship. (Storz deserves credit for his suggestion, after some general words in praise of obedience, that obedience *properly understood* excludes both the "Erstarrung des Fanatikers" [the fanatic's rigidity] and "dumpf[es] Massenbewußtsein" [dull mass consciousness, 17].)

As in his later book, Storz in 1938 presents himself as an analyst of the formal features of the plays. If this is supposed to mean that the interpretations will be more technical in nature and will abstain from the *weltanschaulich* issues investigated by mainstream critics, the claim is misleading, for Storz's interpretation of *Die Räuber* deserves to be remembered as the most strongly religious and antipolitical of all that we have met so far. While there is indeed a good case for seeing the play as conservative rather than revolutionary, there seems to be little point in camouflaging this view as somehow more "formal" than the rival one.

The form of *Die Räuber*, Storz tells us, is determined by the two brothers' struggle against God, in which Karl and Franz represent respectively a dissociated heart and mind ("Verstand"). He is thus opposed to Wilhelm Spengler's view of the early plays as dramas of character (see note 6 to this chapter), and he has no interest in Böckmann's psychological subtleties. For Storz, character is wholly subordinate to the plot, which in turn can only be grasped in theological terms. Although he makes a forceful case, Storz is clearly one-sided here, passing over Schiller's detailed attention to motivation with barely a word, and portraying the characters as little more than marionettes. He also makes the surprising statement that God is a more central figure in the dramatic structure than Spiegelberg, who he says is merely there for decorative purposes.

As a professed formalist, Storz decries the biographical approach that deduces a revolutionary message to the play from the allegedly oppressive environment of the Karlsschule. But Storz is inconsistent in this regard, for he is happy enough to employ a biographical argument when it suits him, that is, when he relates his theological view of the play to Schiller's childhood ambitions to enter the priesthood. As to insights of a genuinely formal character, these are rather sparse and impressionistic, although he has some good things to say about the verbal rhythms and about Schiller's lack of interest in creating mood ("Stimmung"). But Storz concludes his argument by returning to his theological theme, arguing that the play has more affinity with Greek tragedy, which served a ritual function, than with the allegedly more psychological drama of Shakespeare.

Storz's discussion of *Kabale und Liebe* is in the same vein, and leads to even more extreme results. On the one hand he reduces the central figures to embodiments ("Figuranten") of a theological message and denies their autonomy as individuals. On the other, he dismisses all aspects of the play that are derived from the tradition of the domestic tragedy (including even so important a figure as Miller) as mere decoration, inserted merely for reasons of superficial audience appeal. Storz goes badly astray here, and not merely in his high-handed treatment of the bourgeois drama, which would be unthinkable in post-1945 schol-

arship. He also leaps from the lovers' use of religious language to the
highly dubious conclusion that their love has divine sanction; Luise's
early statement that her love is "Kirchenraub" [stealing from a church]
is a warning ignored by Storz, although it seems to be borne out by the
subsequent course of the plot. A more psychologically attentive reading
would also be less inclined to take Ferdinand's theological claims at face
value.

Storz's rather odd dislike of the world of theatrical spectacle comes
to the fore in his discussion of *Fiesco*, which is presented merely as a vehicle for empty "Selbstdarstellung" [self-presentation]. The discussion
of *Don Carlos* is more weighty, although even here Storz sees the play's
untheatrical character as a point in its favor. We also sense Storz's aversion to politics and history as dramatic subjects and his determination
to maximize the religious content. His most interesting insight is into a
certain heterogeneity between the characters like Posa and Alba, whom
he sees as mere bearers of ideas, and Philip, who is conceived in Shakespearian fashion as a fully rounded figure. The play thus embodies a
clash between different types of drama, and the reason why Posa and
Philip talk past each other in the audience scene is that they each belong in different types of play. Here at last is an argument that lives up
to Storz's claim to offer criticism of a formal kind, and it is significant
that he ignores the usual genetic approach to the difficulties of this
text.

Von Wiese's 1938 book, in some respects a polemical response to
Storz, is deeply impressive but not easy to summarize briefly. Where
Storz rejects political interpretation in favor of the religious, von Wiese
attempts a dialectical resolution of the two, and where Fricke devalues
Schiller by reference to an alien norm, von Wiese seeks to prove that
Schillerian tragedy has its own distinctive character. Böckmann is his
most important precursor here, although von Wiese manages to make
the argument as to the "irrationality" of Schiller's vision more convincing than Böckmann had himself. Von Wiese's central argument is
that in these plays Schiller orchestrates a confrontation between private
values, whether of a religious or a sentimental kind, and the great forces
of the historical world. Schiller's vision of the latter is not determined
by the Enlightenment's concept of progress but rather by the concept
of nemesis, a mechanism by which human deeds lead to unforeseen
guilt and punishment but also, in a dark modulation of the doctrine of
theodicy, to an unexpected fulfillment of the divine will. (The word
"Politik" in the book's title alludes to this vision of history rather than
to any commitment to political ideals.) In a helpful passage (referring
to *Fiesco* but applicable to all the works), von Wiese portrays Schiller's

tragedy as the attempt, "die moralischen, privaten und innerlichen Kräfte des deutschen Bürgertums, denen die kalte Staatsautorität und die unpersönliche Staatsvernunft fremd gegenüberstand, auch noch im Bereich der Haupt- und Staatsaktionen wirksam zu machen und den individuellen Anspruch des Gewissens mit weltgeschichtlichen Notwendigkeiten zu verschmelzen" (36) [to make effective, even in the realm of political drama, the moral, private and inward powers of the German bourgeoisie (which were at odds with the cold authority of the state and with the impersonal *raison d'état*); and to fuse the individual claim of conscience with world-historical necessities]. This remark, which anticipates Koselleck's influential analysis of the mentality of the German bourgeoisie in his *Kritik und Krise* (1959), strives at once to elucidate the "inner form" of the dramas and also to define their socio-historical position as a synthesis of Baroque and bourgeois domestic drama.

In *Die Räuber*, the transcendental framework is for von Wiese only one pole of the dialectic, that is, the private one that he terms "worldless" ("weltlos"); the other is the actual course of events, the fateful "Weltlauf," at the end of which the divine purpose emerges as an immanent force at once moral and destructive. The dialectical structure is clear when von Wiese interprets the conclusion of the play as "der tragische Ausgleich zwischen dem individuellen Anspruch auf Gewissensentscheidung, dem unentrinnbar waltenden Schicksal und der göttlichen Nemesis" (25) [the tragic settlement between the individual claim to decide by conscience, inescapably powerful fate, and divine nemesis]. Two points bearing on the play's conclusion should be stressed: first, contrary to political critics such as Mehring, von Wiese sees Karl Moor not as surrendering meekly to earthly authorities but rather as deciding freely to view those authorities as representative of the divine order. Secondly, although Karl's decision turns him from a "complainant" to a "witness" for the deity (from "Kläger wider die Gottheit" to "Kronzeuge der Gottheit") in the moment where he accepts his own death, von Wiese insists on the immanent ("innerweltlich") character of the play.

In *Fiesco*, which von Wiese sees as a precursor of *Wallenstein*, the prevailing dilemma is between the private values of greatness and heroism that *Fiesco* entertains and the constraints imposed on him by the external world. The demands of the two spheres are irreconcilable, and lead to a series of events, the "Weltlauf" again, that lead by unpredictable steps to disaster. In *Kabale und Liebe*, the clash of courtly intrigue and pure human values is only the starting point, giving rise here to a tragic series of deeds and consequences that reveals the inner fragility of the private values themselves, but at the same time (by von Wiese's dialectic) justifies them: "Die tragische Vernichtung der Liebe bringt erst das ewige Recht der Liebe an den Tag" (44). [The tragic destruction of love paradoxically highlights love's eternal right.] Although he regards the social element of the play as superficial, von Wiese is also at pains once again to refute the transcendental interpretation, defining the Schillerian nemesis (in terms echoing a famous passage of *Wallenstein*) as "die späte Frucht, die die Saat der menschlichen Taten verborgen in sich trägt und die den freien Willen des Menschen zum Träger des göttlichen Willens werden läßt" (45) [the late fruit which the seed of human deeds carries hidden within itself and which causes man's free will to become the bearer of the divine will].

Von Wiese's interpretation of *Don Carlos*, finally, reads like a direct response to Storz. The audience scene, far from being a symptom of the play's hybridity, in fact embodies the central dialectic in that it confronts the "weltlos" idealist with the realist who embodies the "Weltlauf," drawing both into the fateful sequence of events. Posa is thus seen, in line with Schiller's assessment in the *Briefe*, as a tragic not an exemplary figure, in that his blindness to reality makes him guilty in fact of the crimes that in theory he deplores. All in all, von Wiese's rigorous and lucid study, despite some occasional comments that reflect the time in which it was written, deserves to be rescued from the neglect to which it has been condemned not least by the author's own postwar treatments of the same material.

We should mention in conclusion Rehm's 1941 article on the Baroque echoes in Schiller's dramas. While Rehm has little explicit here to say about the early dramas, he makes some suggestive remarks about the cultural atmosphere of Schiller's youth, and gives weighty expression to the view, heard intermittently in the scholarship, that Schiller's work is in some respects a throwback to the seventeenth century. The article can be seen as a precursor of Michelsen's postwar study of *Die Räuber* (1964) in relation to the Baroque tradition, which we shall consider at the proper place.

Notes

[1] Two points of interest arising from Lämmert's study should be mentioned: first, Julius Petersen, the founder of the Schiller Nationalausgabe, was an advocate of *Germanistik* as a source of political recovery. As early as 1924 (and thus with no excuse of duress) he wrote: "Wo können führerlos wir besser leitende Kräfte hernehmen als aus der vaterländischen Geschichte und aus dem Nacherleben großer Persönlichkeiten unserer Vergangenheit?" (qtd. Lämmert, 15). [Whence can we, leaderless as we are, derive powers of guidance better than from the history of our fatherland and from re-experiencing the great personalities of our past?] Second, and more general, *Geistesgeschichte*, despite its intention of identifying the suprapersonal determinants of great literary texts, continually fell back into celebrating the greatness of individual authors as incarnations of the national spirit or the spirit of the age. Claudia Albert is thus justified in writing of "Unterwerfung als Haltung des Interpreten" [submission as the posture of the interpreter] (1998, 788) even before 1933.

[2] Kühnemann is here echoing Schiller's description of tragic fate in his later poem "Shakespeares Schatten" (1: 302): "das große gigantische Schicksal, / Welches den Menschen erhebt, wenn es den Menschen zermalmt." [Fate, great and gigantic, that elevates man even as it crushes him.]

[3] In order to convey Kühnemann's tone at its most hortatory (and also in order to explain, at least in part, Schiller's unpopularity in this century), it is worth quoting the conclusion of his chapter on *Don Carlos*: "Sollte doch jeder deutsche Jüngling in die Welt treten mit dem Mut des Eroberers, sollte tief durchdrungen sein von der Gewißheit: ein Kron der Wahrheit bin auch ich, und auch in mir wächst die große kommende Sache der Menschheit heran. Sie braucht mich, und ihr allein will ich leben. Die Tragödie dieser echten deutschen Jünglingsgesinnung ist der *Carlos*. Solang es deutsche Jünglinge gibt, mögen sie sich in diesem ihrem Gedicht erkennen." [Every German youth ought to step into the world with a conqueror's courage, ought to be permeated with the certainty: "I too am a crown of truth, and in me too the great future cause of humanity is ripening. It needs me, and for it alone I desire to live." *Don Carlos* is the tragedy of this mentality of pure young German manhood. So long as there are young German men, may they recognize themselves in this their poem.] Berger and Kühnemann's books support Hans Mayer's devastating judgment (1959, 383) on Schiller's reception in the Wilhelmine age: "Eine Idealität der Zitate, des Festrednerschmucks, eine Umdeutung des Nationalen ins Nationalistische wurde angestrebt." [One aspired to an ideality of quotations, of decorative speeches for festive occasions, a reinterpretation of the national into the nationalistic.]

[4] Demetz (247–48) underlines the contrast between Mehring's attitude and the more negative one of Marx and Engels, and observes that Mehring's re-

appraisal of Schiller led to the efforts of scholars in East Germany to appropriate him as a precursor of socialism.

[5] *Erlebnis* was introduced as a concept of criticism by Wilhelm Dilthey (1833–1911), the intellectual progenitor of *Geistesgeschichte*. For an analysis and critique of the concept, see Wellek's discussion in his treatment of Dilthey (1965b, 322–23).

[6] To be fair to Kommerell, it should be recalled that *Der Dichter als Führer* was an early work, and that the author's later studies, "Schiller als Gestalter des handelnden Menschen" (1934) and "Schiller als Psychologe" (1934) escape this charge. Since they deal mainly with Schiller's later dramas, these studies will not be discussed here, although the former one contains some sensitive remarks on *Don Carlos* as well as the aphorism that the prose plays are "die Rache des Jünglings dafür, daß die Welt nicht sein Bild ist" (142) [the young man's revenge for the fact that the world is not his image of it].

[7] We should give passing mention here to Wilhelm Spengler's 1932 study, which also addresses the issue of inner form, but from a perspective that is disadvantageous to the works under discussion. Spengler sees the prose plays as essentially formless works of genius, that are dominated by character rather than plot. As his strategy is to play them off against the "objective" formal mastery of the later works, his readings have little to offer.

Works Cited

Albert, Claudia. 1998. "Schiller im 20. Jahrhundert." In *Schiller-Handbuch*, ed. Helmut Koopmann. Stuttgart: Kröner, 773–94.

Berger, Karl. 1905/1909. *Schiller. Sein Leben und seine Werke.* 2 vols. Munich: Beck.

Bertram, Ernst. 1934. "Schiller." *Jahrbuch der Goethe-Gesellschaft* 20: 213–49.

Böckmann, Paul. 1934. "Die innere Form in Schillers Jugenddramen." *Euphorion* [*Dichtung und Volkstum*] 35: 439–80. Repr. in Klaus Berghahn and Reinhold Grimm, ed., *Schiller: Zur Theorie und Praxis seiner Dramen.* Wege der Forschung, 323. Darmstadt: Wissenschaftliche Buchgesellschaft, 1972, 1–54.

Borcherdt, Hans Heinrich. 1929. *Schiller: Seine geistige und künstlerische Entwicklung.* Leipzig: Quelle und Meyer.

Brüggemann, Fritz. 1925. "Der Kampf um die bürgerliche Welt- und Lebensanschauung in der deutschen Literatur des 18. Jahrhunderts." *DVjs* 3: 94–127.

Buchwald, Reinhard. 1938. *Wandlungen unseres Schillerbildes.* Leipzig: Liebisch.

Cysarz, Herbert. 1934. *Schiller.* Tübingen: Niemeyer.

Demetz, Peter. 1959. *Marx, Engels und die Dichter.* Stuttgart: Deutsche Verlags-Anstalt.

Deubler, Werner. 1934. "Umrisse eines neuen Schillerbildes." *Jahrbuch der Goethe-Gesellschaft* 20: 1–64.

Dilthey, Wilhelm. 1933. *Schiller.* Ed. Hermann Nohl. Göttingen: Vandenhoeck & Ruprecht, n.d.

Fabricius, Hans. 1932. *Schiller als Kampfgenosse Hitlers: Nationalsozialismus in Schillers Dramen.* Bayreuth: N. S. Kulturverlag.

Fricke, Gerhard. 1927. *Der religiöse Sinn der Klassik Schillers: Zum Verhältnis von Idealismus und Christentum.* Munich: Kaiser.

——. 1930. "Die Problematik des Tragischen im Drama Schillers." *JFDH*: 3–69.

Gundolf, Friedrich. 1911. *Shakespeare und der deutsche Geist.* 8th ed. Berlin:: Bondi, 1927.

Jonas, Gisela, ed. 1988. *Schiller-Debatte 1905.* Berlin (East): Akademie.

Kautsky, Karl. 1905. "Die Rebellionen in Schillers Dramen." Repr. in Jonas, ed. 1988, 149–78.

Kommerell, Max. 1928. *Der Dichter als Führer in der deutschen Klassik.* 2nd ed. Frankfurt a. M.: Klostermann, n.d.

———. 1934. "Schiller als Gestalter des handelnden Menschen." In his *Geist und Buchstabe der Dichtung.* 5th ed. Frankfurt a. M.: Klostermann, 1962, 132–74.

———. 1934. "Schiller als Psychologe." In his *Geist und Buchstabe der Dichtung.* 5th ed. Frankfurt a. M.: Klostermann, 1962, 175–242.

Korff, Hermann August. 1923. *Geist der Goethezeit, I. Teil. Sturm und Drang.* Leipzig: Weber.

———. 1930. *Geist der Goethezeit. II. Teil. Klassik.* Leipzig: Weber.

Koselleck, Reinhard. 1959. *Kritik und Krise: Eine Studie zur Pathogenese der bürgerlichen Welt.* Frankfurt a. M.: Suhrkamp, 1973.

Kühnemann, Eugen. 1905. *Schiller.* 5th ed. Munich: Beck, 1914.

Lämmert, Eberhard. 1967. "Germanistik — ein deutsche Wissenschaft." In *Germanistik — eine deutsche Wissenschaft,* ed. E. Lämmert. Frankfurt a. M.: Suhrkamp, 7–41.

Liepe, Wolfgang. 1926. "Der junge Schiller und Rousseau. Eine Nachprüfung der Rousseaulegende um den Räuber-Dichter." *ZfdPh* 51: 299–328. Repr. in Liepe, *Beiträge zur Literatur- und Geistesgeschichte.* Neumünster: Wachholtz, 1963, 29–64.

Mayer, Hans. 1959. "Schillers Nachruhm." *EG* 14: 374–85.

Mehring, Franz. 1905. *Schiller: Ein Lebensbild für deutsche Arbeiter.* Leipzig: Leipziger Buchdrückerei.

Nadler, Josef. 1938. *Literaturgeschichte des deutschen Volkes: Dichtung und Schrifttum der deutschen Stämme und Landschaften.* 4th ed. Vol. II: Geist. Berlin: Propyläen. (First ed. 1912–28.)

Oellers, Norbert, ed. 1976. *Schiller — Zeitgenosse aller Epochen. Teil II: 1860-1966.* Munich: Beck.

Petsch, Robert. 1905. *Freiheit und Notwendigkeit in Schillers Dramen.* Munich: Beck.

Pongs, Hermann. 1935. *Schillers Urbilder.* Stuttgart: Metzler.

Rehm, Walther. 1941. "Schiller und das Barockdrama." *DVjs* 19: 55–107. Repr. in Berghahn/Grimm, ed. 1972, 55–107.

Robertson, John G. 1905. *Schiller after a Century.* Edinburgh: Blackwood.

Ruppelt, Georg. 1979. *Schiller im nationalsozialistischen Deutschland: Der Versuch einer Gleichschaltung.* Stuttgart: Metzler.

Schmid, Karl G. 1935. *Schillers Gestaltungsweise: Eigenart und Klassik.* Frauenfeld: Huber.

Schmidt, Erich. 1905. "Einleitung." Vol. 3 of Schiller, *Sämtliche Werke*. Säkular-Ausgabe. Stuttgart: Cotta, v–xlviii.

Sharpe, Lesley. 1982–83. "National Socialism and Schiller." *GLL*, N.S. 36: 156–65.

Spengler, Wilhelm. 1932. *Das Drama Schillers: Seine Genesis*. Leipzig: Weber.

Stilla, Gabriele. 1994. "Gerhard Fricke: Literaturwissenschaft als Anweisung zur Unterordnung." In *Deutsche Klassiker im Nationalsozialismus: Schiller — Kleist — Hölderlin*, ed. Claudia Albert. Stuttgart: Metzler, 18–47.

Storz, Gerhard. 1938. *Das Drama Friedrich Schillers*. Frankfurt a. M.: Societäts-Verlag.

Strich, Fritz. 1912. *Schiller: Sein Leben und sein Werk*. Vol. 13 of *Sämtliche Werke*. Tempel-Klassiker. Leipzig: Tempel, n.d.

———. 1922. *Deutsche Klassik und Romantik: oder Vollendung und Unendlichkeit, ein Vergleich*. Munich: Meyer & Jessen.

Unger, Rudolf. 1937. "Richtungen und Probleme neuerer Schiller-Deutung." *Nachrichten von der Gesellschaft der Wissenschaften zu Göttingen: Philologisch-historische Klasse: Neue Folge: Fachgruppe IV: Neuere Philologie und Literaturwissenschaft*, I, 9: 203–42.

Weissenfels, Richard. 1905. "Einleitung." Vol. 4 of Schiller, *Sämtliche Werke*. Säkular-Ausgabe. Stuttgart: Cotta, v–xliv.

Wellek, René. 1965b. *The Later Nineteenth Century*. Vol. 4 of *A History of Modern Criticism. 1750–1950*. 2nd ed. Cambridge: Cambridge UP, 1983.

Wiese, Benno von. 1938. *Die Dramen Schillers: Politik und Tragödie*. Leipzig: Bibliographisches Institut.

4: Schiller Scholarship
   since 1945

IT WOULD BE PARTLY BUT NOT ENTIRELY TRUE to say that the end of the Second World War marked a caesura in Schiller studies. While of course the more rabid nationalistic and irrationalistic treatments ceased abruptly, some contributions continued lines of inquiry that had been started during or before the Third Reich. This is hardly surprising, in that the dominant figures in Schiller scholarship in the new Federal Republic, Benno von Wiese, Gerhard Storz, and Reinhard Buchwald, had all entered the scene in the 1930s, while Paul Böckmann's first book had appeared as early as 1925. Besides the burden of the past, the ideological conflict between East and West was of course another inescapable feature of intellectual life during this period, and it inevitably impinged on Schiller scholarship. One must be grateful, however, that, thanks to the determination and discretion of its editors, the Nationalausgabe, which had been started during the war years, continued despite delays and obstacles to be published as a venture sponsored by both German states. The volumes containing the texts that occupy us here have all appeared, starting with *Die Räuber* in 1953 and finishing with the commentary to *Don Carlos* in 1986. In a lecture of 1991, Norbert Oellers, currently the general editor, gives us a revealing survey of the edition's troubled history.

The Schiller centenaries of 1955 and 1959 provided occasions for a good deal of tension and polemic between the two German states, and the story is well told by Maximilian Nutz in an essay of 1990. If there was little foundation to the charges from the German Democratic Republic that western scholars were lending themselves to a defense of capitalism and American imperialism, there is more truth to the criticism that they overcompensated for the abuse of scholarship in the Nazi years by eschewing all sociopolitical commentary on Schiller's works. We thus see a continuation of the existentialist trend of the interwar years, with its attention to religious themes and to intense inner states, but also the appearance of the formalistic approach known as *Werkimmanenz* referred to in the introductory chapter. The deficient awareness of social context became the chief criticism directed at the older western scholars when a new generation began to assert itself in the late 1960s. The opening sections of this chapter discuss first the contributions of West German scholarship in the years up to 1959 and secondly the views on Schiller emerging from East Germany up to its demise in the late 1980s, returning thirdly to the late 1960s to examine the work of the rebellious younger generation in the West.

Political Quietism?

Two works that can be passed over briefly are late echoes of the George-Gundolf school. The title of Friedrich-Wilhelm Wentzlaff-Eggebert's book *Schillers Weg zu Goethe* [Schiller's Path to Goethe, 1949] indicates the underlying conviction that only after the transforming touch of his senior Weimar partner did Schiller become a poet at all. Hence the only early drama mentioned is *Die Räuber*, which is stated merely to be inferior to *Götz von Berlichingen*. The same view is stated at greater length by Melitta Gerhard (1950), although she is also concerned to find anticipations in these plays of Schiller's later classical attainments. This method leads to an oddly vehement denial that the plays have any genuine sociopolitical component and an insistence that their experiential core is a self-alienation for which the aesthetic education of the 1790s will of course turn out to be the remedy. The result is an astonishingly teleological argument, in which any component of the plays that the author can relate to the classical Schiller is said to be based on experience and thus (in accordance with the privileged status that *Geistesgeschichte* accorded to *Erlebnis*) timeless, while whatever she cannot is dismissed as merely observed and a reflection of passing circumstances. The method reaches its peak with the assertions that Carlos's friendship with Posa is an anticipation of his creator's friendship with Goethe, and that their dream of a new state is a hazy vision of the aesthetic state of Schiller's later essay *Über die ästhetische Erziehung des Menschen* [On the Aesthetic Education of Man, 1795]. With its resolutely antihistorical method and its open hostility to the Enlightenment, Gerhard's book now has only curiosity value.

Kurt May's 1948 monograph remains within the camp of *Geistesgeschichte*, and is largely an attempt to answer Fricke's 1930 study. Schiller is portrayed here as oscillating between realistic and idealistic poles — May alludes to the Goethean paradigm of "Verselbstung" und "Entselbstigung" [selfing and de-selfing] from book 8 of *Dichtung und Wahrheit* — so that, in addition to the idealistic element (Fricke's untragic "Ethik"), the plays are said to contain, albeit in varying degrees, a realistic counter-plot. For the works under consideration May sketches a dialectical movement. The Karl- and Franz-plots of *Die Räuber* he sees as embodying idealism and realism respectively. This synthesis is followed by shifts to the realistic pole in *Fiesco* (described as "sehr stark eingeweltlichte [!] tragische Dramatik," 41 [very strongly worldly tragic drama]) and back to the idealistic pole in *Kabale und Liebe*. In a comment that neatly epitomizes the method of *Geistesgeschichte*, May writes that, when taken together, these two plays represent "eine höhere Einheit und Ganzheit . . . , die als solche im Schillerschen Geist angelegt gewesen sein muß" (43) [a higher unity and totality . . . that must have been latent as such in the Schillerian mind/spirit]. The texts are thus taken as significant not in themselves but as signs to the ineffable *Geist* that produced them. This goes along with an overhasty reduction of characters to terms in a philosophical argument and (one might argue) of the specifically Christian content to an abstract "idealism." May's treatment of *Don Carlos* seems the most satisfactory of the four. Here he again finds, as in *Die Räuber*, the juxtaposition of ideal and reality, but what takes this play further is in his view the working of the dialectic *within* the character Posa, that is, not merely in the confrontation between Posa and the "realistic" King. But May's attempt at a dialectical unravelling of the arguments of these plays falls well short of von Wiese's of 1938.

Von Wiese himself restated his views on Schiller in his lengthy study of German tragedy (1948). The chief concern in the book, which is more difficult than the 1938 monograph, is the concept of *Tragik*, and hence the discussions proceed at some distance from the text. Von Wiese aims to integrate a broader variety of perspectives than before, and the cost of this is a certain loss of critical focus. Three general points can be made, however. First, von Wiese resists the idolization of Goethe by saying that, where Goethe's drama is a vehicle for authorial self-exploration, Schiller's proceeds from the intellectual, religious and political *Ordnungen* [orders] of the world he lives in (170). Second, von Wiese again aims to refute Fricke by means of a dialectical view of *Tragik* into which morality and "idealism" are absorbed; to quote an example of the multiple paradoxical formulations to which this gives rise, von Wiese writes that Schillerian drama "stellt . . . jeden reinen Gedanken, jedes 'unbedingte' Gefühl in Gefahr und Verschuldung hinein und läßt auch umgekehrt den scheiternden, zugrunde gerichteten Menschen zum Arm 'höherer Majestäten' werde," (207–8) [places . . . every pure thought, every 'unconditional' feeling into danger and guilt, and conversely causes the defeated and shipwrecked individual to become the arm of 'higher majesties']. Von Wiese finally aims to defend a religious view of tragedy in which the concepts of theodicy and nemesis play a prominent role, while also rejecting Rehm's association of Schiller with the Baroque tradition as too other-worldly; this attempted integration of immanent and transcendental perspectives only accentuates von Wiese's proneness to complicated chains of abstract paradoxes in his attempts to circumscribe Schillerian *Tragik*.

The individual interpretations are as wide-ranging as this framework suggests, and are full of impressive formulations (often italicized in case the reader misses them) of the tragic contradiction at various critical moments of the plays. Overall, the desire to find a middle course between religious and secular interpretations seems to be the thread running through these discussions, as it was through his 1938 study. Karl Moor, for example, is said to be the first of a series of martyr figures, not Christian, that is, but *tragic* martyrs, "die im Abgrund des Bösen und in der Verzweiflung am Schicksal noch den Weg finden, für den Willen Gottes im Irdischen Zeugnis abzulegen" (180) [who, even in the abyss of evil and in despair over fate, still find the way to testify to God's will on earth]. Von Wiese, it is fair to say, sees the plays as allegories of cosmic moral forces. Although he does not ignore the political dimension, therefore, he treats it as he did in his 1938 book, as a fateful realm of actions and consequences in which the individual clashes with the universal. *Fiesco* thus (to give a final sample) illustrates the tragic "Widerspruch von Heldentum und Staatsidee, von Machttrieb und Gewissensanspruch, von Größe und Berechnung, von Politik und Menschlichkeit als Antinomien des geschichtlichen Lebens" (184) [contradiction of heroism and the idea of the state, of power-drive and claim of conscience, of greatness and calculation, of politics and humanity as antinomies of historical life]. One may find this style excessively grandiloquent for a modern work, but it is hard to deny that the interpretation of *Don Carlos* in terms of a clash of the idea and the individual is a highly impressive attempt to deal with the difficulties of this work.

We can pass rapidly over Heinz Kindermann's *Theatergeschichte der Goethezeit* (1948), which contains some interesting pages on the clash between the dramatic styles of Iffland (bourgeois and complacent) and Schiller (cosmic and extreme) at the Mannheim *Nationaltheater* (243–60), and turn to Paul Böckmann, who also published on the early Schiller in these years. In a chapter of his *Formgeschichte der deutschen Dichtung* (1949), he returned to the concerns of his 1934 article, attempting once again to circumscribe the "inner form" in these works by means of the concepts of *Pathos* and conscience. This discussion seems to be more successful than the earlier one, and indeed to be one of the most insightful that we have. Böckmann again abstains from a detailed consideration of plot and character, and tries to discern the underlying forces that give rise to a drama of precisely this form. More explicit now as to the nature of his concern with *Pathos*, he asserts that for the young Schiller this is not merely a rhetorical manner, but arises from an existential anxiety as to the individual's ability to resist what the world foists upon him. *Pathos*, as Schiller made clear in his later essay *Über das Pathetische*, is not merely suffering but also resistance to suffering, and what enables man to resist is his awareness of an inner power that is independent of material circumstances. Although Schiller later drew on Kantian moral theory to define this inner power, Böckmann finds the outline of the theory applicable also to these pre-Kantian works, in which the inner space is occupied variously by love, conscience or enthusiasm.

So far the analysis is perhaps not strikingly original. But Böckmann goes further and explores the presence of a psychological naturalism in the works. This strand, which manifests itself not only in the machinations of Franz Moor and Wurm but also in Schiller's prefaces to *Die Räuber*, sits uneasily beside the pathetic manner that determines not merely the dramatic language but also the characters and situations. Böckmann attributes this naturalism to Schiller's medical researches at the Karlsschule, and argues that his underlying concern here is to identify the source of human freedom in an organism that is subject to physical laws. Hence the expertly contrived intrigues of the plays represent the knowable and calculable element of human existence, which functions as a kind of backdrop for the pathetic element, which in turn stands for the human unconditionality ("Unbedingtes") that eludes manipulation.

The analysis identifies a fundamental and distinctive paradox of the plays, but leaves many questions unanswered. The cabal against Ferdinand von Walter seems the best example of an attempted manipulation that goes awry, but does Böckmann's analysis force us to the view that Ferdinand's murder of Luise is motivated by an inner force that, being an "Unbedingtes," we should assess positively? To a more skeptical view, Ferdinand is merely overlaying jealousy with religious delusions. And would Schiller have regarded Karl Moor's revolt against society as essentially incalculable? One might argue that the action of act I/2 leading up to the receipt of the letter is calculated to show the inner logic of that revolt, with the Plutarchian fantasies of heroism suddenly presenting themselves to Karl's mind as providential destiny. Again, is Böckmann led by the fashionable philosophy of existentialism to downplay the specifically Christian elements of Schiller's plots? It is a pity that Böckmann never fleshed out these remarkable reflections on Schiller's dramas with demonstrations of how they might apply to each work in detail.

We now enter the 1950s, a bumper decade for Schiller research, including the anniversary years of 1955 and 1959 and the appearance of several landmark monographs. The first of these was the revised version of Reinhard Buchwald's biography, which, although conservative in tone, is still the standard one today.[1] Buchwald's discussions of the plays are always helpful, although naturally more concerned with points of biographical interest than with formal or aesthetic aspects. Buchwald offers a perceptive defense of Schiller from the devotees of Goethe, who (as we have repeatedly seen) stigmatize Schiller's works for failing to live up to Goethe's standards. Buchwald distinguishes between the two authors' modes of appropriating the Shakespearian influence, seeing *Götz von Berlichingen* as an epic work dealing with real people in a real environment whereas *Die Räuber* (despite Schiller's disclaimer in the preface) is essentially a work conceived for the theater. Buchwald takes over and develops Böckmann's analysis of the work's stylistic duality, and suggests that both the pathetic-lyrical and the naturalistic strands can be subsumed under the heading of an intensified Shakespearianism.

Buchwald is also interesting on *Kabale und Liebe*, disputing the common view that Schiller was here consciously seeking to conform to the standards of the Mannheim theater. On the contrary, writes Buchwald, Schiller was trying to prove that his trademark style of intensified Shakespearianism enabled him to beat Iffland and the other writers of domestic drama on their own ground. He substantiates this by a careful comparison of the play with Schiller's chief model, Otto von Gemmingen's *Der deutsche Hausvater* [The German Pater Familias, 1780], and contends that Schiller consciously decided to give tragic dignity to the bourgeois figures (according to traditional theory only suitable for comedy) by accentuating the political theme of their oppression by the aristocrats. Buchwald's interpretation is more weighted toward the political sphere than some others, and he also emphasizes the historical accuracy of the charges levelled by Schiller against the German courts. Less attention is thus given to the personal and religious aspects of the play. Although placing Luise and not Ferdinand at the heart of the tragedy, Buchwald has surprisingly little to say about her.

Buchwald's discussions of the other two plays are less substantial, and he sees *Don Carlos* more as a document in the development of Schiller's *Geist* than as a text that is inherently worthy of our interest. Here Buchwald approaches the teleological method we observed in Melitta Gerhard, whereby the texts are scoured for signs of Schiller's future "Vollendung" [completion/perfection]. The figure of the

Queen is thus argued to anticipate Schiller's critique of Kantian ethics in *Über Anmut und Würde* [On Grace and Dignity, 1793].

The year 1955 brought celebrations in East and West, and among the numerous tributes that they prompted pride of place must go to Thomas Mann's valedictory *Versuch über Schiller*. Although in no sense a scholarly text, the essay remains a noble and courageous statement that invokes Schiller's humanism against the ideological divisions of the Cold War. Of relevance here are Mann's appreciation of *Don Carlos*, recalling the one he had offered fifty years before in *Tonio Kröger*, and also the following anecdote illustrating Schiller's unrivalled power to move audiences in the theater, even in the most inauspicious circumstances:

> Ich habe *Kabale und Liebe* nach dem ersten Weltkrieg in München — die Räterepublik war gerade gefallen — vor einem äußerst bürgerlichen, äußerst rückschlägig-konservativ gestimmten Publikum in mittelmäßiger Aufführung gesehen und es erlebt, daß dieses Publikum durch den Atem des Werkes in eine Art von revolutionärer Rage versetzt wurde. Es wurde zum Schiller-Publikum, wie noch ein jedes es geworden ist vor seinen Stücken. (31–32)

> [I saw *Kabale und Liebe* in Munich after the First World War — the Republic of Councils had just fallen — in a mediocre performance for an audience in an extremely bourgeois, reactionary-conservative mood, and I witnessed how this audience was transported by the breath of the work into a kind of revolutionary fury. It became a Schiller audience, such as every audience has become before his plays.]

Less personal views were expressed in two nonetheless highly intelligent contributions of the same year. In an article that shows the continued influence of Kierkegaardian existentialism during this period, Adolf Beck offers a strikingly negative view of Karl Moor and Ferdinand von Walter, discerning an essential bad faith in their actions at the turning points of the plays. Karl's response to the letter (I/2) indicates that his own letter to his father was insincere; his request for forgiveness was contingent on the assumption that it would be granted, and was hence "bedingt" [conditional] and not "unbedingt." Karl's wild reaction and his faulty rationalization of that reaction points to an underlying lack of trust and a half-conscious awareness that he is merely venting his wounded pride. As for Ferdinand, his courageous stand in acts I and II turns, again through a lack of trust, into an egoism and power mania that lead him to deny Luise's autonomous existence. Paradoxically enough, Ferdinand's behavior reproduces the aristocratic arrogance against which he claims to be protesting. In each play, Beck sees the "conditional" behavior of the male protagonist as being shown up by the "unconditional" behavior of the female (a view that fits *Kabale und Liebe* better than *Die Räuber*). Beck's interpretation, which is based on a careful consideration of the texts, strikes at the heart of the once customary assumption that Schiller's "young idealists" are figures whom we ourselves are supposed to idealize. His article was to prove influential, and it should be mentioned here that, following a remark of Schiller's in his "Selbstrezension" [self-review] to *Die Räuber* (622), these characters have increasingly been seen by postwar critics as "sublime criminals." The description is clearly preferable to "idealist" in that it reflects the protagonists' active (as opposed to speculative) dispositions as well as their moral ambiguity. It also accords with the way in which these characters were seen by Hegel (see chapter 2 above).

Preoccupations similar to Beck's are manifested in a fine article of the same year by Paul Böckmann, who explores the paradox that Schiller's dramas generally have a political subject matter without ever becoming "Thesenstücke" [plays propounding a thesis]. In an analysis reminiscent of von Wiese's 1938 monograph (and drawing also on the insights of Kommerell's 1934 article on Schiller as portrayer of action), Böckmann portrays the political sphere not as one in which ideals are realized but as an ambiguous sphere in which general conceptions are confronted by unique and opaque human situations. In this world of tragic irony, individuals are forced to act on the basis of imperfect knowledge and are punished by unforeseen consequences. Like Beck, Böckmann pays close attention to *Die Räuber* I/2, although he attaches less weight to character traits and moral qualities, more to decisions and actions, and this seems appropriate to the dramatic genre. The article is also noteworthy for its defense of the integrity of *Don Carlos* as a work dealing with the alienation to which the individual is subject when he engages in political action. While Böckmann's writing is always forceful, the reader cannot help observing that, with its sharp antithesis of the human and the political, he is expressing the quietism that was to be so vehemently rejected by the next generation. An author like von Wiese would, we feel, have attempted some mediation between the two spheres. (For a gentle critique of Böckmann from a later perspective, see Klaus Bohnen's 1980 article on *Don Carlos*, discussed in chapter 8.)

We must turn now to the two large monographs of 1959 by Storz and von Wiese, books that, although often criticized, have yet to be superseded despite the passage of over forty years. Although the authors adopt different methods, one cannot speak of any radical difference of opinion between them. Of the two books, von Wiese's aspires more obviously to become the standard work on the author, in that it deals with Schiller's biography and also discusses the historical and philosophical works, whereas Storz confines himself to the dramas and poems. Storz's is the more personal and wayward of the two, and its discussions sometimes even make a slightly disjointed impression. Although Storz justifies his narrower approach by linking other methods to the false "Aktualisierung" [topicalization] of Schiller, and in particular to the attempt to draw political lessons from his works, he himself could be said to be open to the same charge, and for two reasons. First, Storz's focus on the technical dimension of the works (bypassing the moral and pedagogical energies that they express) reflects the formalism of the American New Criticism and its German imitators, and this was a movement with its own political agenda; second, in identifying himself with Schiller's alleged elevation of the human over the political, Storz seems himself to be recommending such quietism to the reader.

Despite these reservations, Storz's book deserves its continued prominence. It is certainly more successful than his 1938 study in providing insights into the structure of the works, and it is less relentless in its theological emphasis. Where most scholars write about the characters, Storz stands out by his ability to describe the construction of the plots, especially such features as the management of momentum and tension. A consequence of this, in my view a weakness in the book, is a disregard of psychology. Storz discounts Schiller's intention (preface to *Die Räuber*, 484) "die Seele gleichsam bei ihren geheimsten Operationen zu ertappen" [to catch the soul so to speak by its most secret operations], and, where the figures act in an unexpected way, his usual explanation is that Schiller has sacrificed consistency of characterization to the needs of the plot. But it is more likely that Schiller, with his education in anthropology from Abel, was attentive to his characters' motivations; when, for example, Ferdinand refuses to hear Kalb's admission of the falsity of the charge against Luise, this refusal surely arises directly from Schiller's conception of the character. It should be possible to give due weight to the element of plot without going as far as Storz does here. On the other hand, there is much to be said for his view that Posa's intrigue and death in act IV of *Don Carlos* arise primarily from the needs of the plot and not from Schiller's conception of the character.

For Storz the chief formal aspect of *Die Räuber* is "Finalität," by which he means the purposive momentum directed toward the conclusion. There is none of the panoramic portrait of the age that we see in *Götz von Berlichingen*. Within this context Storz highlights the techniques of "Gliederung" [arrangement] and "Steigerung" [intensification] in the construction of the scenes and points to the contribution of the lyrical and narrative elements to the living fullness of the whole. The only episodic element in the work, Storz contends, is the figure of Spiegelberg. Storz argues that a purely formal analysis justifies the theological interpretation of the work as against a political one, but, as before, this seems to me to overextend the scope of formal analysis.

Although less dismissive of *Fiesco* than before, Storz accentuates the greater quantity of episodic content here than in *Die Räuber*, as well as Schiller's tendency to engineer dramatic situations (the Berta episode, for example) for effect rather than because of their contribution toward the whole. Regarding the play's political content, Storz emphasizes the hostility toward politics implicit in Schiller's preface, and he argues that at this stage of his career, under the influence of early modern Stoicism, Schiller regards political issues as no different from simple moral ones. Arguing here against critics who view *Fiesco* as a trial draft of *Wallenstein*, Storz stresses the abstractness of the alternatives (tyranny or republic?) presented by the play. Without explaining precisely what he means, he misses a proper *Tragik* in the work, which he regards as overpreoccupied with the mechanics of the plot.

Kabale und Liebe is in Storz's view the more worthy successor to *Die Räuber*, with the eschatological concern returning in full force. For the eighteenth century, he reminds us, the term "bürgerlich" implied "unpolitical," and hence it is wrong to overrate the work's political content. He praises the virtuosity of the exposition, with its atmosphere of breathless haste and its contrast with the massive slowness of act V. His judgment of the problem scene in act IV between Luise and Lady Milford is unsparing, but he offers some convincing suggestions as to why Schiller wrote it. He also points out Schiller's new ability to differentiate the figures by their mode of speech, as well as to make character arise naturally from milieu (in a way that it did not in *Die Räuber*). Interestingly, however, Storz argues that Ferdinand and the Lady are both exceptions to this rule, in that it is hard to imagine how they have come to be as they are. They are oddly abstract characters, and it is not coincidental that they resemble each other in their rejection of the ethos of the Residenz and their willingness to renounce their privileges.

Don Carlos, finally, benefits from the greater concreteness of character and milieu that, Storz argues, Schiller had learnt in composing the domestic tragedy. Besides, he now has a greater feel for the contingencies of history, and this makes him less prone to think in rhetorical antitheses. Storz places King Philip firmly at the centre of this play, stressing that he has no predecessor in the earlier plays. Philip's tragedy is human and not political; in Posa Philip sees a human being, not a bearer of ideas, and it is as a human being that Philip is betrayed. Storz thus discovers a dissociation between the tragic and historical contents (143), a valuable insight into this peculiar work that exemplifies the best of what Storz's structural method can achieve.

Von Wiese's *Friedrich Schiller* has stood the test of time even better than Storz's book. It is still the first work that every serious student of Schiller should read, and its appeal is enhanced by the accessible style in which it is written. As in his 1948 monograph, von Wiese places the author in the context of a series of suprapersonal *Ordnungen*. While his book could be allocated to the school of *Geistesgeschichte* (as opposed to *Werkimmanenz*), therefore, it does not belong to the type that dwells on the organic development of a personal *Geist*. (Paulsen rightly regards Buchwald as falling into this category [387].) Rather, von Wiese sees the writer as in constant interaction with a complex and evolving environment, and his book is notable for its exhaustive presentation of the religious and political culture of Württemberg. These early chapters bring a more specific content to the notion of the *Ordnungen* than was possible in the author's work on tragedy, and the discussions of the first three plays, which are fuller than those of the classical dramas, benefit particularly from this historical research. (I shall pass over the account of *Don Carlos*, which strikes me as less challenging than those of the prose plays.)

Broadly speaking, von Wiese presents dialectical interpretations (he may be overfond of the term "dialectic") of the works similar to those in his earlier books, with the emphasis more on the dramatic plot as mirror of social processes than on the characters as timeless types. Where Storz tends to argue *for* a religious and *against* a political interpretation, von Wiese strives to reintegrate the two. These interpretations are now enriched, first, by the account of the growth of Schiller's dramas in the soil of Württemberg, and second, by the more expansive discussions of the texts themselves, including perceptive comments on incidental effects or flaws, so that the plays are no longer in danger of being overshadowed by the critic's abstractions.

In *Die Räuber*, von Wiese focuses on the intersection of social and religious layers in the institution of the patriarchal family, seen here as the divinely sanctioned kernel of all society. The two brothers are discussed not as psychological types but as rebels against this "Vaterordnung" [patriarchal order]. The implausibility of Franz's intrigue is conceded but makes no difference to its value as symbol of the evil "Schein" [semblance] by which the family is threatened. Karl is rightly distinguished from Franz in that he never fundamentally renounces his loyalty to the "Vaterordnung." Where Franz is always a solitary figure, Karl's outburst in I/2 is followed at once by the forging of a new social entity, the firm bonds of which are supposed to show up the debility of lawful society. Von Wiese gives a particularly perceptive reading to the last two acts; for example, he attributes key importance to Karl's song about Brutus and Caesar for highlighting the elevation of the family theme to political significance. He also stresses the necessity of the theological conclusion, in which the ancient motif of nemesis returns in the Christian form of the Last Judgment. He dismisses the view that, in making Karl surrender to the authorities, Schiller shows that he lacks the courage of his Storm and Stress convictions. The theme of judgment is implicit in the story from the outset, as a sign that no human life is possible outside a moral *Ordnung*, and the earthly authorities are merely the symbol of the divine one. At the same time, however, in a further twist of the dialectic, von Wiese shows that the action evinces an internalizing of the traditional motifs of Heaven and Hell, which become as much forces within the tragic individual as transcendent realities. While it is right to speak of the Baroque heritage in these motifs, therefore, it is important to remember that it is the Baroque in a secularized version.

In a perhaps unconscious wordplay, von Wiese compares *Fiesco* to a fresco, that is, to a colorful but lightweight work after the great tragedy of *Die Räuber*. In general, he is content to look for echoes of the earlier play and anticipations of the next two. The chapter, however, contains some helpful comments on Schiller's use of the nemesis motif ("sowohl eine naturhafte, in der Geschichte wirkende, wie auch wieder eine moralische Macht," 180 [both a natural power that works in history and again a moral power]) and also a thoughtful passage on the implications of the scene with the painter Romano (II/17) for Schiller's notion of the relation of stage and history. With *Kabale und Liebe*, he faults the Marxist and the existentialist critics for their unhistorical readings. Starting once again from the *Ordnung* of the family, he warns the reader against trusting his/her spontaneous impressions of the characters. Von Wiese defends not only Luise's language ("halting" [stockend], not "artificial" [künstlich]) but also Ferdinand's supposed selfishness in love, on the grounds that these criticisms will not occur to a reader aware of the centrality of the *Ordnung*. Von Wiese does not mention that similar criticisms had been made by Schiller's contemporaries (see chapter 1 above), and, in general, is too confident that a "historical" view of the play can make its problems disappear. Luise is the play's central figure since she recognizes the validity of both obligations, of love and of family, whereas Ferdinand (the "Karl Moor of love") recognizes only love. Von Wiese rejects Korff's view that Luise is limited by her narrow class horizons, or that Ferdinand is intended to display aristocratic features in spite of himself. As with the conclusion of *Die Räuber*, von Wiese integrates the apocalyptic, political and psychological moments in a dense interpretation of the play's climax.

Some articles of these years offer specific insights not found in the longer studies though without contradicting their essential arguments. A posthumously published lecture by Wolfgang Kayser (1960) deals concisely with the motif of greatness ("Größe") in Schiller's work and draws attention to Schiller's perennial irresolution as to whether greatness is intrinsically linked to morality or not. This topic, which is inescapable especially with respect to the early works, was first broached by Dilthey, and it was to become popular among scholars such as Staiger (1967) and Guthke (1994) who wish to defend Schiller from the charge of moral didacticism. Oskar Seidlin's analysis of the letter motif in the early plays (1960) complements von Wiese remarks on "Schein" as symbol of evil, but connects this topic with Schiller's views on language, for which the mediation of sign and signified stands for the necessary mediation between the phenomenal and the absolute. Characters who commit the hubris of demanding immediate access to the absolute are those who are most vulnerable to deception by forged letters. The merit of Seidlin's article is to alert us to a serious theological meaning in an aspect of these plays that we might be tempted to dismiss as melodramatic. On a related topic, Schunicht's analysis of the intrigues (1963) remains close to the texts, but argues for a growing tendency for Schiller to embed his dramatic intrigues in historical realities; hence *Don Carlos* marks an advance over *Fiesco*, while the maximum is not reached until *Wallenstein*. (The point seems related to Storz's discovery of a new concreteness in *Don Carlos*.) Schunicht's article is helpful also on the clash between the metaphysic of sympathy and materialistic psychology in *Die Räuber*.

Von Wiese's argument on the theological roots of Schiller's dramas is developed by Rohrmoser (1959) in a taxing article on theodicy and tragedy. Schiller is situated here in a philosophical progression running from Friedrich Christoph Oetinger, a speculative Württemberg theologian mentioned only cursorily by von Wiese, and the early Hegel. Rohrmoser exemplifies a continued tendency in some modern scholarship to dwell excessively on the philosophical determinants of literary works. Nothing is said here about the plays as works for the theater; instead, they are viewed as a complicated attempt to reconcile a residual faith in divine providence with an equal faith in the autonomy of reason. The processes of crime and judgment are said to emerge from this dialectical process rather than from any literary tradition. Although far more persuasive, Rohrmoser's Hegelian decoding of Schiller is nonetheless somewhat reminiscent of Hinrichs's work of the 1830s.

A less extravagant example of the theological approach is offered by Scheibe (1966) in his exploration of the themes of "Schöpfertum" and "Geschöpflichkeit" [the qualities of creator and creature] in the four plays. He detects a pattern by which the villains — Franz, the President, Philip — arrogate to themselves a blasphemous status equivalent to that of the Creator. But they provoke the heroes into an equally blasphemous response, until all are finally forced to acknowledge their "Kreatürlichkeit." The article leaves some questions unaddressed: Is this process merely the mechanism of hubris and nemesis disguised in Christian costume? What is the relation between the theme of Creation and that of the Last Judgment, which is no less prominent? Although not a major contribution, and despite arbitrary interpretations of some passages, Scheibe's article is supported by plenty of textual material and contains some worthwhile insights.

To complete our survey of theologically oriented discussions of these plays, we should mention here a much later contribution by Arthur McCardle (1986), who attempts to provide the systematic investigation of the links between Schiller and the Swabian Pietists for which von Wiese had called. Despite his thoroughness, however, McCardle hardly achieves impressive results in his discussions of *Die Räuber* and *Kabale und Liebe*. There are several difficulties inherent in such an approach to these dramas: one is the uncertainty as to what Schiller had actually read or been taught, and another is how to disentangle the strands of the Christian education that Schiller received, for, besides Pietism, one must give due weight to the Leibnizian so-called "Neology" as well as to orthodox Lutheranism. Lastly, how are we to know to what extent the theological motifs are sincerely used, to what extent they are exploited for literary effect? McCardle does not get to grips with these problems, and as a result his discussion is diffuse and never goes beyond making piecemeal comparisons.

Returning now to the bicentenary year of 1959, we should also mention two French contributions. Anstett offers a concise and eloquent discussion of the four early plays from the perspective of generational conflict. Of greater importance (and a welcome change from the prevailing concern with theology) is Masson's attempt to approach *Die Räuber* from the angle of Schiller's medical writings. The presentation of Karl and Franz as psychological cases, whose behavior can be understood in terms of Schiller's theory of the interaction of body and mind, is highly original and is, as the author notes, equally applicable to the other prose plays. This materialistic side to Schiller, always obscured by the image of the idealist, was in danger of being overlooked altogether by the scholarship of the 1950s.

Marxist Scholarship

It is time to look at some contributions of the German Democratic Republic to the understanding of these works. We should start by noting that, in two sections of his *Minima Moralia* (1951), Theodor Adorno had suggested that Schiller's idealism was the distorted reflection of the most deplorable tendencies in German history: "Im innersten Gehäuse des Humanismus, als dessen eigene Seele, tobt gefangen der Wüterich, der als Faschist die Welt zum Gefängnis macht" (111). [In humanism's innermost core, as its own soul, rages the imprisoned tyrant who, as a fascist, turns the world into a prison.] Somewhat implausibly, Adorno alleges that the line "Amalia für die Bande" (*Die Räuber* V/2; 615), by which the robbers call upon Karl to renounce Amalia in order to free himself from his oath of loyalty, is indicative of a failure on Schiller's part to delineate individuals, and that this failure is part and parcel of his idealism. True, Adorno never taught in the GDR and his ideas were never adopted there. However, they show that one possible response of Marxist criticism to Schiller's works is to reject them outright as belonging to a repressive tradition.

That was not the path taken by East German scholarship. On the contrary, in line with the governmental policy of appropriating the nation's cultural heritage, Schiller was portrayed as a champion of the revolutionary and humane values that were ultimately to be realized by the communist regime. The latter's intentions are revealed in a remarkable volume of 1959 edited by Günther Dahlke. (The title, *Der Menschheit Würde* [The Dignity of Humanity], alludes to Schiller's poem "Die Künstler" [The Artists, 1789].) Besides a collection of statements on Schiller by Marx and Engels and a reprint of Mehring's *Lebensbild* of 1905 (discussed in chapter 3), the volume contains some more recent statements including a "Declaration of the Schiller Committee of the German Democratic Republic" (319–26) which presents Schiller as a champion of humanism and (surprisingly) national unity, as well as a fearless opponent of "feudal absolutism," of which the great capitalistic concerns are of course the modern heirs. (For a discussion of the failure of East and West to engage in dialogue during the two anniversaries, see Nutz 1990.)

While most East German scholars are thus at pains to accentuate the positive, we are still often left with a sense of disappointment in Schil-

ler's life and work, a disappointment that can be traced back to the belief that the failure of the German bourgeoisie in 1848 was linked to its
idolization of Schiller. The presuppositions underlying the mainline
Marxist discussion of Schiller can be extracted from some remarks by
Georg Lukács in his volume of essays on German literature (1964). On
the one hand, the literature of the eighteenth and early nineteenth
centuries must be seen (Lukács cites Franz Mehring as his authority
here) as the ideological preparation for the bourgeois-democratic
revolution in Germany (46). On the other, since the revolutionary opportunity was in fact missed, some signs of this failure, or of the weaknesses that led to it, must be detectable in the literary texts that
reflected the political movement. Once more following Mehring, Lukács cites Marquis Posa (along with some other Schillerian figures) as
symptomatic of the flawed relationship between literature and life in
Germany. The dramatic work is the outcome of such an extreme process of abstraction from the historical reality experienced by poet and
audience that, despite all the enthusiasm aroused by the stage hero, the
work leads to no consequences:

> Dieses Pathos erschuf dann eine Popularität der Mißverständnisse: die
> menschheitliche Allgemeinheit wurde in Zitate zerschlagen und zum
> Wechselgeld eines flachen Gedankenaustausches im Reich der Spieß-
> bürger umgeprägt. (12–13)

> [This *Pathos* then created a popularity consisting of misunderstand-
> ings: the humanistic universality was broken up into quotations and
> recast as the small change of superficial chit-chat in the petit bourgeois
> realm.]

While credit is thus due to Schiller for the progressive tendencies in his
works, blame must also be apportioned for the later political failure,
and this must be shared between the author, the audience and the general circumstances. Lukács explicitly rejects the views of some unnamed
progressive writers (perhaps Adorno is one of them) who, by means of
selective quotation and distortion, try to make Goethe and Schiller into
precursors of German reaction (45). It is clear that these assumptions
can be reconciled with positive as well as negative assessments of Schiller's works, depending on whether the stress falls on the opportunity or
the failure, and it is a matter for individual discretion which course a
scholar chooses to take. But evidently, the experience of 1848 still casts
a long shadow over these discussions.

    An early and influential expression of the Marxist view is Alexander
Abusch's volume on Schiller's life and works (1955). Abusch signals his
intention by taking as epigraph some words from Goethe's poetic

obituary of Schiller, "Denn er war unser" [For he was ours], thus proclaiming Schiller to be a forefather of the socialist state. The book has the unmistakable feel of an official work written for public edification, and the interpretation never wavers from serving the needs of the class struggle, with literary arguments taking second place to political ones. Abusch is heavily influenced by Mehring; he echoes, for example, the latter's interpretation of Karl and Franz Moor as embodying revolutionary enthusiasm and materialism respectively. His view of this play is inevitably one-sided, and is not free of distortions: it is a work of "flammende Empörung" and "soziale Anklage" (34) [burning indignation and social accusation], to which the (interpolated) motto "In tyrannos" is entirely commensurate. Karl's use of the term "Republik" in I/2 is taken as a call for a German republic based on Rousseau's theory of popular sovereignty, and the law against which Karl inveighs in the same scene is asserted to be "das herrschende Gesetz tyrannischer Willkür der Fürsten" (41) [the prevailing law of the princes' arbitrary tyranny]. But Abusch departs from Mehring's view, and shifts from the negative to the positive tack, when he argues that the play's conclusion, far from being a meek surrender to authority, in fact reflects Schiller's mature recognition that "Räubertum" ["robberdom"] is an inadequate form of revolution. This is to confuse ex post facto interpretation with the reconstruction of the author's intention. In accordance with East German cultural policy, realism is the watchword in Abusch's discussion of *Die Räuber*, as it is also of *Kabale und Liebe*, from which he quotes the whole of the famous second scene of act II between Lady Milford and the servant. With *Don Carlos*, his attention falls on the *Thalia* version with its greater revolutionary potential; Schiller's removal of the more anticlerical passages is said to be a result of his political alignment with the reformist rather than the revolutionary branch of the German bourgeoisie. But Abusch applauds the greater humanity in Schiller's portrayal of King Philip in the final version, arguing (with dubious consistency) that this accords with the program of realism. Abusch goes on to deplore Schiller's development in the 1790s, which he sees as a surrender to political pressure and to the lure of metaphysical speculation. Summarizing the paradox of Schiller's career, he writes: "Der Schöpfer großer revolutionärer Werke schauderte von den revolutionären Stürmen zurück, die sie mitentfesselt hatten" (165). [The creator of great revolutionary works shrank back from the revolutionary storms that they had helped to unleash.] Sadly, like so many Marxist critics in both East and West, Abusch thus emerges as an apologist for political violence.

Two papers of a more academic kind were written by Joachim Müller (1972), the doyen of East German scholars of the *Goethezeit*, although here his political affiliation is barely perceptible. In his formal
analysis of "Der Held und sein Gegenspieler" [The Hero and his An-
tagonist], Müller starts with an impressive Hegel-inspired account of
the role of collision and decision in dramatic structure in general. Next,
after prefatory sections on the prose dramas, he offers a long account of
the audience scene of *Don Carlos*, which he classifies as one of three
classic Schillerian collisions. (The other two are between Wallenstein
and Max and between Elisabeth and Maria Stuart.) Although this
seems a promising approach, Müller's article is disappointing in that it
devotes too much space to renarrating the action of the collision
scenes, too little to analyzing their function in the works as a whole or
to asking what decisions result from them. Of *Fiesco*, he notes correctly
that the conflict between the protagonist and Verrina is only one of
several in the play, and that there is even one within the protagonist
himself. (The same could be said of the other plays.) Instead of examining the shifting of the main conflict during the course of the play,
however, Müller only deals with the one conflict, thus achieving less
than he might have done. For an East German scholar, Müller also
shows surprising attention to religious motifs, and this is true also of his
later article listing the allusions to Heaven and Hell in the prose plays.
Here as before, he is conscientious with regard to textual detail but
modest in drawing conclusions.

Ursula Wertheim's monograph on *Fiesco* and *Don Carlos* (1958)
can be passed over quickly, in that, beyond repeating much familiar
material on the genesis of the plays and their various versions, she limits
herself to the political value of their subject matter to the exclusion of
aesthetic aspects. Her conclusion, hardly a surprising one, is that *Don
Carlos* is genuinely historic whereas *Fiesco* merely deals with the past
(216). Content also predominates in an article of 1959 by the same
author, which asks to what extent Schiller's plays are "Zeitstücke"
[plays reflecting their time]. Predictably, she praises *Kabale und Liebe*,
but she fails to pose the question that, for Marxists, is most acute, that
is, why Schiller turned his back on the German present in his later
works. A more substantial argument is contained in an article of the
same year by Hans-Günther Thalheim, who traces the relationship
between the dramatic hero, with his mission of self-help, and the people, without whose aid the hero can accomplish nothing. Thalheim
finds that this relation becomes stronger as the plays succeed each
other: Karl Moor is entirely isolated from the lower classes and can only
surrender at the end of act V, while *Kabale und Liebe* contains a refer-

ence to the American War of Independence and hence holds out the hope that the lovers' death will be part of a meaningful process of general liberation. This historical contextualization of the private events on the stage is then magnified in *Don Carlos* by the much stronger integration of the plot with the Dutch revolt against the Spanish throne. Turning against the example of Abusch, Thalheim continues by seeking the positive potential in the later dramas also, hence claiming the later as well as the younger Schiller for the side of the angels. We should mention finally that, in a striking insight on a perennial problem, Thalheim proposes that Verrina in *Fiesco* should be seen as a satirical figure, in that he embodies the true spirit of republicanism and thus shows up the inadequacy of both the Genoese people and the would-be hero, for whereas the former are unprepared for the revolutionary challenge, the latter is nothing but a demagogue.

The best monograph about Schiller to emerge from East Germany, and a more scholarly book than Abusch's, is by Eike Middell (1980), who reconciles the ideological requirements of a socialist scholar with a high standard of argument and fidelity to the texts. Middell is one of a number of East German scholars to question the blanket condemnation of Weimar Classicism by an earlier generation of Marxists, and he warns against adhering too closely to the traditional "deutsche Misere" interpretation (13–14). (Abusch is one of his targets here. Amusingly, Middell points to some Western scholars influenced by the New Left as guilty of this exaggeration also. See 300 and 452, n 60.) Naturally, it is the later and not the earlier Schiller who is affected most by this reevaluation, and so one cannot speak of a major revision in Middell's view of our four plays. But his cautious and differentiated discussions are impressive in their own right. He is of course attentive to the political implications of the works; much space is devoted, for example, to Schiller's antithesis of Brutus and Catiline in reference to Karl Moor, and Franz Moor is said to represent the "Schreckbild" [bogy] of feudal oppression (69). But Middell is careful not to reduce the works to a political statement, and he thus gives weight to the arguments of Peter Michelsen and others that, in formal terms, *Die Räuber* contains a strong Baroque component. He also does not ignore the religious side of the texts. Like many Western scholars, Middell explores the gap between the concrete historical situations portrayed in the texts and the abstractness of the perspectives (embodied especially in Verrina and Posa) that the texts then seem to offer. He pursues (73) the interesting argument (originally suggested in an article of 1960 by Thalheim) that the Brutus/Catiline duality has paradigmatic value in these texts: the figure of Brutus stands for Schiller's recognition that the situations demand real political solutions, while Catiline represents his tendency to allow himself to be distracted by the question of the moral qualification of the rebel. While we might not agree that the moral question is an idle one, this still seems a useful way of encapsulating a genuine problem in these plays. Middell follows Beck and other scholars in seeing the male protagonists as problematic, and he argues consistently that they (including the Carlos of the *Thalia* fragment) represent a critique of the Storm and Stress ideal of the *Kraftgenie* [genius of strength]. Despite a certain tendency to linguistic obscurity, Middell's book is one of the most solid monographs on Schiller to be written since 1945, and it deserves to be read alongside the more famous ones produced in the West.

Before leaving the subject of East German criticism, we should briefly note two volumes that appeared in the 1980s, the last decade of the German Democratic Republic. The first is a collection edited by Hans-Dietrich Dahnke and Bernd Leistner (1982) containing individual interpretations of each play, some of which will be discussed in chapters 5 to 8 below. The collection is unusual in that it contains no notes and no discussion of the views of other scholars, even socialist ones (although here and there the authors appear to be drawing tacitly on western scholarship). This reticence limits the book's usefulness. In one sense the themes of these essays arise naturally — and predictably — from the concerns of East German literary scholarship, the conflict, for example, between ideal and reality and the hampering effect of morality on social revolution, but in another sense the essays remain close to the text and are quite conservative in terminology and method, discussing such hoary old themes as moral purification and the *sittliche Weltordnung*. While the ideological imperative is evidently less strong than it was in the days of Abusch, this collection hardly gives the impression of being the product of a flourishing intellectual culture.

The second volume, which was edited by Helmut Brandt (1987), is the outcome of a conference held in Jena in 1984 and attended by scholars from both East and West. What concerns us here is a discussion of *Die Räuber* and *Kabale und Liebe* by Hans-Günther Thalheim, a contribution that displays East German scholarship at its most doctrinaire. The article reproduces with precision the views that Thalheim had expressed over twenty years earlier in his unpublished Berlin Habilitationsschrift (1961), which contained an interpretation of *Die Räuber* preceded by an account of Schiller's early biography and intellectual environment. In both places, Thalheim insists that the protagonists represent progressive bourgeois ideals and that the works both pillory the oppressive conditions of Germany under "feudal absolutism" and also point the way to a future based on humane values, a future that we of course infer to be identical with Thalheim's present. Needless to say, the problem is not that the plays contain no social criticism, for they contain a good deal. It is rather the stale rhetoric with which Thalheim regales us, and our awareness that he lacks the freedom to express any nuances, or indeed to consider any point of view substantially different from the 1959 "Declaration of the Schiller Committee" discussed above. When we read that "die Wirklichkeit des 18. Jahrhunderts in Deutschland erscheint als eine erstarrte, versteinerte Welt" (144) [the reality of the eighteenth century in Germany appears as a rigid, ossified world], we cannot withhold the mental riposte, "Just like the German Democratic Republic." Schiller scholars have no reason to regret the passing of this land of spies and barbed wire.

The Sociopolitical Trend

The 1960s were a fairly uneventful period in our story, since they were dominated by the work of the previous decade, while the politically radical *Germanistik* inspired by the student movement did not affect the character of scholarly publications until the 1970s. The decade saw one major event in Schiller studies, however, with the publication of Emil Staiger's *Friedrich Schiller* in 1967. The book's iconoclastic thesis (adumbrated long before in an article of 1950 on the fragmentary *Agrippina*) was that Schiller's tragedy was motivated by one purpose only: the author's desire to dominate an audience by means of powerful emotional effects.[2] The real speaker of the line "Ich bin mein Himmel und meine Hölle" (IV/5; 591) is not Karl Moor but Schiller himself. The numerous scholars who have sought to discern a consistent metaphysical view of tragedy underlying the works are therefore doomed to failure, as were those (von Wiese and his successors) who took the theodicy as their point of orientation. For Staiger, the references to divine providence in these plays are superfluous to the plots and were added by Schiller solely to make the plays acceptable to a conventionally minded audience. The psychological and the political approaches are treated no better. The characters are much too inconsistent for the former to be plausible, and there is no evidence in Schiller's letters that he had any political intentions.

Staiger is clever at making the most of the evidence that supports his case, and he points up numerous inconsistencies in the plays. Clearly, if he is right, a large number of scholars have been wasting their time. Not only that, but further investigation of these plays would be largely superfluous too; if they are what Staiger says they are, viz., loosely connected sequences of scenes, each one calculated to rouse the maximum of emotion without respect to overall continuity or consistency, they cannot contain much material requiring serious analysis or interpretation. It is hardly surprising, therefore, that subsequent interpreters have tended to reject Staiger's views. Each reader will have to decide for him/herself whether the portrait of Schiller as egocentric and power-hungry is persuasive, and whether such an author could have written these dramas. For what it is worth, my own view is that Staiger's Schiller could not have produced works that are so rich in intellectual content, even if their overall purport is hard to define; one could imagine him writing Klinger's *Die Zwillinge* but not *Die Räuber*.

In the interpretation of the young Schiller, the emergence of a radical *Germanistik* is perhaps best epitomized by the anonymous *Räuberbuch*, which appeared in 1974 and will be discussed in chapter 5 below. Surprisingly, there are no works of a comparably controversial nature that could be included in the present chapter. Herbert Kraft's 1978 study, *Um Schiller betrogen*, is the only work that might fall in this category, and, as we shall see, that is a curiously unsatisfactory book. The failure of the '68 generation, despite all their rhetoric, to challenge the von Wiese/Storz view of Schiller in a substantial new monograph is a tribute to the lasting authority of these older works.

An outstanding shorter contribution of this decade is a brief essay by Hans Mayer (1966) that is comparable to Böckmann's 1955 essay on "Politik und Dichtung." Mayer, who moved from East Germany to the West in 1965, boldly confronts the issue of the quality of Schiller's drama in the light of his unpopularity with writers and scholars. He concludes that, whereas *Die Jungfrau von Orleans* and *Die Braut von Messina* are rightly disdained by modern audiences, the four plays under discussion here have a lasting appeal on the grounds that, in contrast to the distortions of *Die Jungfrau*, "Aktualität und Historizität . . . stehen hier noch überall in einem guten Verhältnis zueinander" (490) [topicality and historicity . . . still stand here in a thoroughly good relationship with each other]. What is helpful about Mayer's remarks is that, although a Marxist, he does not stretch the evidence to produce a spurious political "realism," as had Abusch. Instead, he draws a distinction between political drama and the Schillerian drama of politics, the latter dealing with human problems engendered by engagement in political life, but not with specific political problems or solutions. Behind all the sound and fury, Mayer sees *Die Räuber* as a meditation on impulse and calculation as applied to ends and means, and he describes *Fiesco* as the tragedy of the adventurer and renegade, comparing the hero to the aristocrats who later joined the French

Revolution. In *Don Carlos* Mayer sees Philip as the central figure, again stressing the human tragedy caused by the conflicting pressures of high office. In each case the political constellation merely provides the occasion for the exploration of more personal conflicts, and yet Schiller's presentation of these conflicts is respected as having perennial significance for political existence. One wishes that some subsequent political critics of Schiller's plays had learned from Mayer how to strike such a fine balance.

Herbert Kraft's 1978 book mentioned above sets out to rescue a rebellious Schiller, knowledge of whom has been concealed from readers (hence the tendentious title of the book, which means "Cheated of Schiller") by a reactionary academic tradition that has propagated a dubious classical image of the author that poses no threat to the social order. At least that is the appearance. In fact, Kraft's distrust extends beyond the scholarly tradition to the works themselves; in his judgment, a completed work automatically falls under suspicion of being the outcome of a compromise with the status quo, while a fragmentary work is viewed as automatically embodying a challenge to that same status quo. (Why else was it not finished?) But if unfinished dramas have more integrity than finished ones, then must not the works of the most integrity of all be the ones that were never written down, even in part? This extraordinary defeatism sets Kraft's book apart from the work of the GDR scholars we have mentioned, as does the style, which emulates the oracular manner of Ernst Bloch and Theodor Adorno, often making the critic's meaning hard to fathom.

Kraft is displeased by Karl Moor's surrender at the end of *Die Räuber*, but he attempts to play off this apparent capitulation to the status quo against the fragmentary *Die Braut in Trauer* (1800), which Schiller intended as a continuation. But the remnants of *Die Braut in Trauer* lend no support at all to the theory that Schiller intended in this work to mitigate Karl's alleged meekness. With *Fiesco*, Kraft seems to view the multiple endings as conferring a kind of fragmentary status on the play, and here he is on stronger ground, since there is a genuine ambivalence in the text as to the legitimacy of Andreas Doria's rule. Kraft sees the real political contest as being between Andreas and Verrina, the feudal lord against the committed republican, with the Fiesco plot as an irrelevant distraction, and he points to moments in the play where the "real" contest seems to break through the veneer. While this kind of reading is undeniably enjoyable, it must be stressed that it rests on dogmatic foundations, in that the critic assumes that he knows what the text is really about before he starts to read it. Here we feel that, if we have been cheated of a more radical Schiller, it must have been by

Schiller himself, and that Kraft is criticizing him for not writing the plays that he, Kraft, thinks he ought to have written.

In the other two plays, Kraft is severe when he detects hints of compromise between bourgeoisie and nobility, which, for unclear reasons, he regards as the inherent ideology of the domestic tragedy. Such a compromise, he believes, was shown by the French Revolution to be historically untrue, and hence literary works expressing hope for a class rapprochement are guilty of falsehood. Kraft seems to believe both that violent class warfare has been the norm in modern European history (mercifully, it has not), and also that it is inherently more desirable than compromise. Why a senior humanities professor at a West German university should espouse such views is a mystery.

The social emphasis has, however, led to some more judicious treatments in the literary histories that appeared in great numbers during this period (including two that include the term "Sozialgeschichte" in their titles). Schiller's early plays will always present a frustrating problem for this type of criticism, and not every critic can balance the political with the nonpolitical with the expertise of Mayer. Klaus Berghahn expressed the problem as follows in 1980:

> So findet in den Jugenddramen eine intensive Auseinandersetzung mit den politisch-gesellschaftlichen Zuständen der Zeit statt, die allerdings dramatisch so vermittelt wird, daß die politische Thematik in einen sinnlich-sittlichen Konflikt verwandelt wird, in dem sich der Held moralisch bewähren wird. (164)

> [And so an intensive engagement with the sociopolitical conditions of the age occurs in the early dramas, but this is mediated dramatically in such a way that the political theme is transformed into a conflict of ethics and sensibility in which the hero will prove himself in moral terms.]

From the perspective of the political critics, it must appear that Schiller raises the vital issues only in order to evade them. The question that they themselves evade is whether tragic dramatists have ever dealt with political issues in a purely political way, and whether that is not rather the task for a different kind of writer.

Jochen Schulte-Sasse (1980) is a critic who has come to terms with this dilemma, and he offers a sympathetic treatment of the works, which he views as belonging ideologically to the Enlightenment, stylistically to the Storm and Stress. The central role of Schiller's philosophy of harmony is accepted here, and Schulte-Sasse comments (with none of the censure to which some critics are prone) that, in principle, Schiller regards all forms of government, even autocracy, as capable of being infused with a humane spirit if only the ruler embraces that philosophy. Schulte-Sasse argues that, since the catastrophes depicted in these plays are particular and not necessary, the philosophy itself is not impugned. (President von Walter, for example, accepts it at the end of *Kabale und Liebe* when he states that his son forgave him before his death.) Schulte-Sasse can thus argue that, all in all, these are optimistic plays, a surprising view, perhaps, but a well-reasoned one.

Horst Albert Glaser's account of the prose plays (1980a) is less successful. He cannot accept Schiller's commitment to a nonpolitical theory of politics, and he shakes his head over the way that private issues are "zur Menschheitsangelegenheit hochgeputscht" ("Sturm und Drang", 313) [inflated to matters of humanity]. Rather than illuminating the texts and their historical roots, this critic seems more concerned to show that Schiller's political acumen is inferior to his own. His interpretation of *Don Carlos* (1980b) as a hybrid combination of family drama and tragedy of state is more successful. Hans Gerhard Winter (1978) takes a similar approach, focusing on the political lessons that the modern radical can draw from these old texts: "Karls Aktion ist . . . nicht von der Einsicht breiter Volksschichten in ihre Interessen getragen, sondern von der moralischen Empörung einzelner." (248) [Karl's action rests . . . not on the insight of broad segments of the people into their interests but on the moral outrage of individuals.]

Gerhard Kaiser's discussion in his *Aufklärung, Empfindsamkeit, Sturm und Drang* of 1976 (an outstanding book) is likely to prove more durable than these last two, which reflect the turbulent climate of the German academy in the 1970s. Even within the short compass that such a work demands, Kaiser succeeds in producing startling new insights into the plays, integrating the religious and the social dimensions. In *Die Räuber*, he offers a strong answer to the charge that Karl's surrender represents a capitulation to the status quo. True, there is the problematic connection between earthly authorities and divine authority: "Die korrupte irdische Gerechtigkeit wird ihm durchsichtig auf das göttliche Gericht" (282). [Corrupt earthly justice allows him a glimpse of the divine court.] But this is not equivalent to a retraction of the charges; earthly justice remains corrupt. Kaiser stresses that Karl activates his own judgment, instead of having it imposed from without. What has changed is that the old patriarchal order has died with the old father and a new order is called for, based not on obedience but on the free decisions of autonomous individuals.

In *Fiesco*, Kaiser makes Bourgognino a central figure (286), which is an unusual step, but he justifies it on the grounds that this character's opposition to the tyrant is based on the latter's rape of Berta, which violates the relationship of the betrothed couple and hence the natural order. Within the terms of Schiller's philosophy of harmony, Verrina's commitment to the principle of republicanism is secondary, in that it lacks this personal dimension. Here as in the other plays, Kaiser discerns an underlying opposition between the concepts of intrigue and ideal, each of which gives rise to a kind of utopia, one of absolute calculability and the other of realized harmony. And yet, in some mysterious way, each term of the polarity is in league with the other. Hence Karl and Franz Moor each require the other, as do Ferdinand and Wurm. The pattern is more complex in *Fiesco* and *Don Carlos*, where the ideal and the intrigue seem to inhabit the same person, but it still provides a means of unlocking the plots of these two plays. All in all, this seems to me to be a highly stimulating hypothesis as to the structural groundplan of these works, the inner form as it used to be called, and is at least as convincing as Böckmann's antithesis of *Pathos* and naturalism.

Kaiser does full justice to the social criticism that *Kabale und Liebe* contains, but he rejects the left-wing view that Luise's bourgeois submissiveness is the cause of the tragedy. She is the real heart of the tragedy, and she is destroyed because unlike Ferdinand she knows that, no matter how strong their love, they need a reality within which to live. Finally, he sees *Don Carlos* as the greatest political play of German theater, emphasizing the way that the action and characterization are conceived now in specifically political and not abstractly moral terms. Unlike Schulte-Sasse, Kaiser believes that the play shows the inherent incompatibility of absolutism and humane values. Where Schulte-Sasse sees the remnants of human feelings in Philip, Kaiser points to the fact that we are shown their inevitable extinction. Kaiser might, however, agree with Schulte-Sasse that the plays are fundamentally optimistic, although where the latter sees a validation of Schiller's philosophy of harmony, Kaiser sees an irresistible progress toward autonomy and "Mündigkeit" [maturity].

Further politically oriented studies of this period should be mentioned. Anthony Williams (1974) offers a rather doctrinaire Marxist reading of *Kabale und Liebe* and *Die Räuber* (in that order, since he sees the later play as explaining the political choices of the earlier one). He repeats the thesis of Abusch that, after his republican beginnings, Schiller adopted the position of compromise with the aristocracy because he recognized that conditions were not ripe for revolution. Karl Moor's closing words thus represent not craven capitulation but rather mature insight into the objective circumstances. Williams gets himself into trouble arguing that Franz is the embodiment of feudal despotism while Karl represents the upsurging energies of the bourgeoisie. Why then, we ask, does Franz adhere to the revolutionary doctrine of materialism, while Karl wants nothing more than to marry Fräulein von Edelreich and manage his estates as his father had done before him? Similar problems can be found in a lot of the sociological interpretations of this period; scholars are prone to identify characters on inadequate grounds as representative of either the bourgeoisie or the nobility. Williams's major hypothesis is that the play's dual structure can be attributed to Schiller's insight into the social constellation: if he had brought Karl and Franz together, this would have negated the actual divorce between conservative and progressive energies in society and would have turned the plot into a purely private family quarrel, eliminating its bearing on the wider social conflict. Unlike some socialist critics of *Kabale und Liebe*, Williams sees Ferdinand as a spokesman for bourgeois ideas and as a type of aristocratic rebel actually existing at the time. He is perceptive when he brings out the combination of assertiveness and submissiveness in Luise and her father. But in claiming that the motif of the Last Judgment "anticipates the bourgeois revolution in the only form possible to the economically weak and socially oppressed bourgeoisie, that is in religious terms" (43), he reveals the basically dogmatic structure of his argument.

Walter Hinderer's account of the material (1978) is more rewarding, in that he pays more attention to Schiller's theoretical writings of this period and after, searching for the political meaning of Schiller's apparently unpolitical arguments. The concept of autonomy and the new science of anthropology come to the fore in this article, two ideas that have rightly become prominent in the discussion of the young Schiller.[3] However, this critic seems so determined to demonstrate that the four plays reflect a prerevolutionary climate that the line of thought often becomes dubious. Is the concept of "Selbstbestimmung" [self-determination] really of importance for Schiller before he encountered it in the works of Kant? I suspect that it is pushed to the foreground here, at the expense of "Vollkommenheit" [perfection], since the latter is less capable of being given a political subtext. The unspoken premise seems to be that, unless the plays can be shown to be in some sense revolutionary, there is no reason for students to read them. Klaus Berghahn's discussion of the plays (1980) seems more successful in this regard, searching for their political relevance without forcing the evidence and paying full attention to stylistic features. (Berghahn is heavily influenced by Böckmann's analysis of *Pathos*.)

Despite the rising political tide, more traditional lines of inquiry did not come to an abrupt halt in the 1970s. Rolf Linn's short monograph on Schiller's young idealists (1973) is a perceptive piece of work that rightly connects the heroes of our four plays with Max Piccolomini, Mortimer and Don Cesar of the later ones. Linn's goals are quite modest, in that he confines himself to a psychological examination of these characters while ignoring the manifold *Ordnungen* that von Wiese regards as so crucial to these works. His study is really a continuation of Beck's article of 1955, using psychological rather than metaphysical terminology, and coming to even harsher conclusions about the heroes; Karl Moor is seen as a case of immaturity, while Ferdinand is said to seek compensation in his domination of Luise for the humiliations he suffers at the hands of others. Von Wiese would no doubt object that it is anachronistic to abstract the characters from the whole work, and also that Linn analyzes them as if they were real people and not literary creations. Politically committed scholars, on the other hand, would condemn the way that the censure of the young heroes implicitly condones the social abuses against which they protest. On their own terms, however, Linn's arguments are quite persuasive, and show that, despite Schiller's evident concern with religious issues in the plays, he is also capable of character delineation that satisfies, or seems to satisfy, modern criteria of psychological coherence. While he sometimes sounds schoolmasterly in his treatment of the first three heroes (Ferdinand, for example, is compared to the nursery rhyme figure "Bruder Ärgerlich"), Linn's analysis of *Don Carlos*, the longest one, is exceptionally challenging. Here he has two cases to deal with and so his argument extends beyond psychology into a structural interpretation of the whole play. He contrasts Carlos and Posa as idealists devoted respectively to persons and to ideas, and shows that, by the end of the play, each is transformed, with Posa dying for his friend and Carlos sacrificing himself for an idea.

Another exception to the political trend is Kenneth Dewhurst and Nigel Reeves's edition and translation of Schiller's medical writings (1978). In a useful chapter on "Psychology in the Early Dramas" (in which they acknowledge the influence of Masson's article of 1959), they explore the ways in which Schiller's understanding of volition (drawn mainly from Leibniz and Ferguson and transmitted through Abel's teaching) influenced his dramatic creations. They are skeptical as to political interpretations, and they argue that the theological motifs are either a matter of convention or else are there for the purpose of characterization. Although forcefully argued, the chapter does not always keep clear of the rather fruitless terminology of idealism and realism. Like Linn's contribution (1973), it also creates the impression that, were it not for the shortcomings of the protagonists, all would be right with Schiller's world. The discussion of *Don Carlos* seems especially problematic in this regard, for the authors claim that Posa's intrigue in act IV "could have been avoided had Posa not scorned Philip's genuine offer of friendship and been content with gradual, not radical, change" (337). What evidence is there that Philip is amenable to any change at all? In general, it seems to me that the naturalistic interpretation of the young Schiller is the mirror-image of the theological. Both interpretations reflect influential components of his mental world, the one operating through his religious upbringing, the other through his medical and philosophical education, and there is no question but that the two are uncomfortable bedfellows. It is a mistake, however, to try to absolutize either component or to reduce one to the other.

In the 1980s we see a continuation of the social interest in these plays, but often combined with a less ideological approach, and in studies which discuss these plays in connection with recent historical research or in the course of investigations of wider literary questions. An example of the latter type is Helmuth Kiesel's valuable 1979 study of literary "Hofkritik" [criticism of courts], which traces this topos back to Renaissance humanism. While not offering new analytical insights into the texts themselves, Kiesel's chapter on Schiller has the merit of situating this important aspect of his work within a broader historical context.

The Danish scholar Bengt Algot Sørensen, an example of the former category, has more detailed discussions of *Die Räuber* and *Kabale und Liebe* in the course of his pioneering book (1984) on the value system of patriarchalism, as this is reflected in the dramas of Lessing and the Storm and Stress. The book alludes to studies of the history of the family, and includes primary materials from France and England as well as Germany. Sørensen's chief finding is that the patriarchal ideology was modified in the eighteenth century by a strong dose of emotionalism, leading to an ascendancy of "Zärtlichkeit" [tenderness] over "Herrschaft" [dominance], but that in itself paternal authority was not called into question. His perspective allows him to point out the centrality of the father-child relationship in both dramas, a feature that is common to the whole genre of the domestic tragedy. He also questions a view expressed sometimes by scholars that the Storm and Stress generation, including Schiller, were expressing a revolt against the patriarchal order, arguing that in this respect there is less of a gap between this generation and the previous one than is often assumed.

Perhaps a little schematically, Sørensen sees both plays as staging a conflict between the sentimental ideology of the family and the new ideal of greatness, two forces that are in alliance against courtly despotism but which exist uncomfortably together. His greatest contribution is to have situated the plays within Enlightenment debates about the family, both in itself and as a model for political authority, for this establishes the context for various terms and motifs that we might not otherwise understand.

Although apparently written without any knowledge of Sørensen's work, an article by Denis Jonnes (1987) shares Sørensen's concern with the history of the family and with the emergence of a sentimental version of patriarchy in the eighteenth century. Jonnes aims to question the view of von Wiese and his followers (a view that was in danger of becoming a dogma) that in these works the patriarchal family is assumed to be an "Urzelle" [primal cell] of human society. In an adventurous analysis that includes *Don Carlos* as well as the two plays discussed by Sørensen, Jonnes suggests that the texts actually show Schiller departing from the "sentimental paradigm" exemplified by Lessing and centred on the father-daughter relationship. Lessing's "libertine" figures who threaten that relationship are the predecessors of Schiller's "young idealists," and Schiller alters the paradigm, first, by making these young men the spokesmen for revolutionary ideas (and hence upgrading them), but second, by defining them as sons of the patriarchal figure and hence as incapable of achieving the autonomy to which they aspire. One can criticize Jonnes for presenting hypotheses that are too bold for their textual base. Also, his admission that Schiller's version of the family is in the nature of a myth or a construct leaves us wondering about the relevance of the empirical historical material that he has presented. Nonetheless, this is an impressive attempt to reexamine a critical orthodoxy and to read the texts with fresh eyes.

Harald Steinhagen (1982) and Jürgen Bolten (1985) offer a more philosophical approach to the social implications of the works, each of them participating in the debate about "Aufklärung" [enlightenment] that consumed so much energy during this decade. (This debate had both a historical and an ideological aspect. Both have been fruitful for Schiller scholarship, the one serving to integrate Schiller in his historical epoch, the other to explore the contemporary relevance of his work.) Where Sørensen warned against taking Franz's materialist views too seriously, Steinhagen sees them as central: by denying that reason is anything more than the faculty by which we devise the means to satisfy our desires, Franz poses a challenge to the social and religious order, and Schiller's whole career is portrayed as a series of attempts to refute him.

Some would no doubt criticize Steinhagen for treating the plays as philosophical texts, but he gives an absorbing discussion of the role of providence in the prose plays as the author's proposed answer to Franz. Moreover, his interest in the theological meaning of dramatic causality is a welcome change from the usual focus on the characterization. While Steinhagen may be too hasty when he concludes that in each case the outcome of the play negates the intended theodicy, he deserves credit for asking important questions in direct language.

Bolten's book is less accessible, and must indeed rank as one of the most difficult contributions to this subject ever written. The argument is fundamentally Hegelian, and like that of Hinrichs in the last century portrays Schiller's dramas as the expression of steps in a dialectical process taking place in society at large. Bolten's concern is with the social psychology of the German bourgeoisie in its (in the author's view) unimpressive attempts to free itself from feudal domination; the authority of Hegel is thus combined with that of more recent authors, notably Sigmund Freud, Reinhart Koselleck and Jürgen Habermas. The process that Bolten traces consists of a number of steps in which the sentimental bourgeois subject seeks protected areas ("Freiräume") for the exercise of virtue, first in the sphere of the family and secondly within private subjectivity. The search is vain, however, for the wider social pressures infiltrate these "Freiräume", causing division and conflict. Bolten sees the Storm and Stress dramas of fraternal strife as encapsulating such familial and subjective conflict.

What sets Schiller apart, in his view, is that his prose plays show this process rising in an ascending line to the level of consciousness. The Moor brothers, he argues, represent a single individual divided between head and heart, and Karl is himself divided, in typical fashion for this generation, between passion and melancholy; he is Prometheus and Ganymed (of Goethe's celebrated poems) at once. However, this conflict is partly reconciled by the end, while the conclusion of the *Trauerspiel* version has the two brothers momentarily embracing in token of their being two sides of a single character. (Puzzlingly, Bolten also claims that they could be played by the same actor.) Fiesco combines the two characters in one, but fails throughout to realize this unity in consciousness, and hence never manages to be more than a fool. Luise Millerin, finally, is said to achieve a higher level of subjective awareness that prepares the way for the next phase of Schiller's work, which is devoted to reflective and not practical reason. Unfortunately, Bolten's analysis of Luise's "path of knowledge" into four distinct stages is so complex that it can barely be understood. Besides, there seems to be an inherent implausibility in the use of multiple references to Herder and

Spinoza to interpret the thoughts of an uneducated sixteen-year-old girl.

Bolten has less to say about *Don Carlos*, which he sees mainly as documenting a shift toward historical reflection. The relative neglect of the more political play is symptomatic of this author's greater interest in psychology, although this is always psychology with a view to a future social emancipation rather than a concern with psychological harmony as an end in itself, which we find in some critics. In general, we can admire the boldness of Bolten's interpretation while also wondering whether his underlying premise, namely that literary works are precise indicators of dialectical movements in social psychology, is really tenable. Riding roughshod over aesthetic autonomy, for example, Bolten claims that, instead of saying that *Fiesco* is a weak play, we should recognize it as a true reflection of the weakness of the bourgeois Enlightenment (82–83). Does this mean that every bad work of art points to a defective social reality, and never to a lack of skill or a miscalculation on the part of the artist? There are dangers in this kind of analysis of which the author seems barely aware. Besides, the desire to make the works fit into a preconceived dialectical pattern leads inevitably to some inaccuracy and sleight of hand when it comes to textual detail.

Konrad Maier's dissertation of 1992 is another contribution falling into the category of the modified sociological approach, although this author turns to the psychology of religion rather than to philosophy in search of more differentiated results. In a well documented and forthrightly written account, Maier links the words and actions of the protagonists of *Die Räuber* and *Kabale und Liebe* to an analysis of Lutheran theology as seen through the lens of Freudian psychology, the latter understood in the libertarian version of Erich Fromm and Alexander Mitscherlich. The attention to Lutheranism as a concrete and specifically German cultural factor is particularly welcome here, and stands in contrast to the stress of sociological critics on the rather abstract concepts of the bourgeoisie and "feudal absolutism." Maier diverges also from other analyses of the religious dimension of the works, which usually focus either on the idea of theodicy or on the role of Swabian Pietism. His impressive analysis of the influence of Lutheranism on bourgeois character formation means that his work improves on that of Beck and Linn, who also dwelt on the problematic personalities of the protagonists, in being based on a clearly defined model of psychological integration.

Although Maier avoids the utopian perspective of much recent politically oriented scholarship, his work nonetheless has its origins unmistakably in the post-1960s preoccupation with generational conflict in the Federal Republic and with the broader phenomenon of the German "Misere." Maier's thesis thus forms part of his generation's work of settling accounts with German sociopolitical traditions, and it is not surprising that his results are not very charitable to Schiller. Karl Moor's rebellion is thus seen as infantile, while his fixation with a paternal God and his assumption of a paternal role among the robbers are said to show that he has adopted a "defensive identification" with the order that he claims to reject. Ferdinand von Walter is said to be guilty of narcissism, while Luise is prevented by paternal tyranny from achieving any kind of practical emancipation for herself. In all cases, Lutheranism has led to a hypertrophied super-ego that prevents the characters from acting in their own interests.

A fascinating aspect of Maier's thesis is that he agrees with von Wiese in making the "Vaterordnung" central to these works, but, where von Wiese regards this as relatively benign, Maier views it as inherently repressive. His demonstration of how this order leads in *Kabale und Liebe* to the victimization of the most powerless member of society is particularly striking. For Maier, a successful rebellion against the father, including against paternalistic religion, is a prerequisite to any kind of autonomy and happiness in life, and, from his point of view, these dramas tell the story of individuals broken by an ascetic socioreligious order whose attempts at self-assertion are doomed from the outset.

One might regret Maier's lack of sympathy with Schiller, but he cannot be accused of inconsistency or inaccuracy. There is also much to be said for his strategy of stating that, on the evidence of the texts, Schiller adopts a conservative standpoint, and then criticizing him for it. It is more usual, and less satisfactory, for politically radical scholars to argue that, contrary to the obfuscations of conservative scholars, the texts in fact contain a radical message. But is Maier perhaps guilty of dogmatism in his adherence to the Fromm/Mitscherlich model of psychic integration, and is he antihistorical in applying that model to the eighteenth century? True, he shows considerable attention to the historical dimension in analyzing the effects of Lutheranism. But his ideal of the secular, autonomous and happy individual owing no duties to anyone except him/herself is nonetheless open to criticism as the product of our postwar consumer society. Besides, although Maier dismisses political utopianism, might he himself be guilty of a psychological utopianism in assuming that a life led according to the approved precepts will in fact lead to happiness? Such questions, however, do not detract from the importance of this book.

Feminist Approaches

The most important subcategory of the sociological approach to these works is the investigation of Schiller's female characters and his portrayal of gender in the widest sense. This preoccupation reflects the burgeoning of feminism in the academy in recent years, which has provoked so much intellectual passion and brilliance. In scholarship on Schiller, where feminism has not been as prominent as in Lessing studies, it has led to discussions of differing character. A groundbreaking study for our period was Silvia Bovenschen's *Die imaginierte Weiblichkeit* (1979), which was critical of Schiller for lending his authority to the notion of the complementarity of gender-roles (the so-called "separate spheres" theory), which, under the guise of idealizing women, subordinates them to men and confines them to private life. (For Bovenschen's discussions of Schiller, see 71–75, 220–24, 239–56.) Helmut Fuhrmann responded in 1981 with a thoughtful article in which he conceded that Schiller's prose and lyric poetry present just such a patriarchal image, but argued that, with few exceptions, the female figures in his dramas transcend this passive role. With their moral courage and their capacity to act with boldness and decision, they anticipate the gender-neutral view of humanity for which we are still striving today. With regard to Schiller's early plays, Fuhrmann pays special attention to *Fiesco*, where Leonore's passionate republicanism (as well as her assumption of male clothing) conflict with the traditional female role, and where Julia protests against the inequality of men and women in love. He also notes Amalia's active resistance to Franz Moor, Luise's "unbestechlich[er] Blick für die Wirklichkeit der Menschen und Verhältnisse" (345) [incorruptible eye for the reality of people and situations] in contrast to Ferdinand's utopian illusions, and Elisabeth's dignified responses to King Philip's domineering behavior. Referring to Schiller's traumatized youth in the Karlsschule, Fuhrmann offers a biographical explanation for this contradiction between feminine "Bild" and "Gestalt" [image and figure]: the former, he says, is determined by Schiller's need for the domesticity and security of which he had been deprived, the latter by his no less great need for freedom. But Fuhrmann considers and rejects, perhaps too rapidly, an alternative explanation, namely that this contrast has as much to do with the requirements of tragic drama, which cannot afford passive characters, as it has with Schiller's subjective needs. (Surprisingly, he does not mention the figure of Angelika in the fragmentary *Der versöhnte Menschenfeind* [The Reconciled Misanthrope, 1790], a text which raises acutely the question of how a Schillerian "beautiful soul" could fit into a genre the essence of which is action.)

A dissertation by Rachid Jai Mansouri (1988) offers a rather limited account of Schiller's representation of women in each completed drama, rarely going beyond close description of the texts and not coming to grips with Fuhrmann's point. At the opposite extreme is an essay by Stephanie Barbé Hammer (1994) that does not address Fuhrmann's article, but praises *Die Räuber* and *Fiesco* as instructive portrayals of how male lust for power has generated a history consisting of endless cycles of violence. Hammer is unusual in that she cites parallels from recent science fiction in literature and film to show that Schiller's view of modernity is of high relevance today. A weighty feminist response to Fuhrmann came finally in 1993 with a dissertation by Karen Beyer that deals with all four plays under discussion here. Her central arguments are, first, that the female characters are consistently functionalized, that is, they live and die as a consequence of their role in the lives of the male figures who determine their fate, and second, that whereas the males live and are judged by the Enlightenment ideals of freedom and autonomy, the women remain subject to a pre-existing order that allows them at best a passive heroism in the form of virtue, endurance and renunciation. By and large, Beyer proves her first point; these females clearly live in a world devised by and for men, their choices are narrowly circumscribed, and they are subject to a double standard (although Fuhrmann's observation that Schiller's female characters are all quite different from the notorious housewife of lines 116–32 of "Das Lied von der Glocke" [The Song of the Bell, 1800] remains valid).

Her second argument is questionable, however, since it implies both that the male characters exemplify general Enlightenment standards of (male) conduct, and that these actions enjoy the endorsement of the author. Neither statement is true; both Karl Moor and Ferdinand end by abjuring their rebellions (which have after all led them to commit murder) and returning to the "sittliche Weltordnung." It is surely this return to the fold and not the preceding "sublime criminality" that will have appealed to the conformist attitudes of the bourgeois audience. If we follow Beck and his successors with their critical view of the male protagonists, then the situation of the females does not look so bad after all. Beyer also often seems not to distinguish between the action of a play and the attitude of the author. Must we assume the playwright to approve of everything he shows? A startling example is when Beyer writes (150–51) that Leonore's death in *Fiesco* is a punishment (willed by the author) for transgressing her assigned role. One could by the same logic argue that Shakespeare "punishes" Cordelia or Desdemona for imaginary misdeeds. The simple reality, perversely overlooked by Beyer, is that all three characters, Amalia, Leonore, and Luise, are blameless and fall victim to the wickedness or delusions of others. Similarly, Beyer writes (226) that Frau Millerin is punished for resisting her husband's authority by being banished from the stage after act II. True, Frau Millerin is a satirical character and the purpose of satire is to ridicule. But her disappearance from the stage surely has more to do with Schiller's clumsiness in plot construction than with a desire to discipline aberrant women. (Inge Stephan takes a more sensible as well as a more historical approach to Frau Millerin in an excellent article [1986], the influence of which Beyer acknowledges, and which discusses *Kabale und Liebe* in connection with Lessing's two domestic tragedies. For Stephan, the centrality of the father-daughter relationship in this genre is the result of bourgeois anxiety about paternal control in the family at a time when the bourgeoisie was challenging the aristocracy for ideological dominance.)

If Fuhrmann clearly writes as counsel for the defense, Beyer's desire to convict Schiller is no less obvious, and each reader will have to decide on the verdict for him/herself. Fuhrmann seems to me to have the upper hand in respect of historical awareness, in that he situates Schiller's attitude within the spectrum of opinion available in his own lifetime. Beyer's interpretation follows the principle of *Werkimmanenz* and takes account of no eighteenth-century sources apart from the texts themselves, although she cites much twentieth-century feminist theory. Like Konrad Maier, she does not avoid the risk of anachronism when she applies the modern ideal of individual self-realization to eighteenth-century characters, and, like Maier again, she displays an extreme hostility to the institution of the family, seeing it as little more than an instrument for the subjugation of women. In *Kabale und Liebe*, the play that she discusses in the greatest detail, she is exceptional in the vehemence of the criticism that she directs at Miller, accusing him not only of denying Luise her autonomy but also implicating him (as well as Schiller) in her death: "Eine Frau, die den Vater nicht glücklich macht, gehört geradezu umgebracht" (255) [A woman who does not make her father happy literally deserves to be killed]. In both Beyer's and Maier's studies, the reader often senses that Schiller is only the stalking-horse, and that the real target of the authors' anger is the society in which they have grown up.

English-Language Scholarship

I shall continue by surveying a series of general monographs on Schiller in English. They are dealt with separately because they are written for a different readership, namely the modern languages student in English-speaking countries, and hence represent a self-contained subgenre within the field.

F. W. Kaufmann's study of 1942 provides a clear and concise argument that must have been found helpful by many of the students for whom the book was designed. Kaufmann's title, *Schiller: Poet of Philosophical Idealism*, indicates his approach. His discussion is guided by the aim of making the plays accessible as philosophical statements, with the various characters each representing a principle of some kind, usually a combination of realism, idealism and sentimentalism. The common thread in Kaufmann's treatment of the four early plays is that they portray a dissociation of idealism from the reality that it wishes to change, and that they hence represent a problem that Schiller only solves in his later works, on the basis of the harmonious philosophy of his essays of the 1790s. Despite the greater simplicity of his language, Kaufmann's interpretation is a little reminiscent of that of Hinrichs (1837–39) in its desire to reduce the plays to a philosophical argument.

William Witte's lively depiction of Schiller (1949), by contrast, is descriptive rather than interpretative. The author's intention seems to be to counteract the hostile influence of Robertson with a general appreciation of Schiller's work, and hence to rehabilitate him with the English reader. Erich Heller's 1950 review of Witte's book, in which Schiller is denounced as a moralist and "a poetical disaster," shows that such hostility was still widespread in the English-speaking world at that time, as it is no doubt still. (Heller directs his scorn, however, chiefly at the classical Schiller, suggesting that, as with Mayer's essay [1966], Schiller's best chance of reaching a modern public may rest with his early works.) In general, English scholarship seems more preoccupied than German scholarship with refuting the negative image, and this often gives it an apologetic tone. In Witte's case, one notices a rather Leavisite defense of Schiller against the charge of being a philosophical poet, not surprisingly in a work from England. On the contrary, says Witte, the attitudes of the Moor brothers are presented not academically "but as elements of real experience, deeply felt" (112).

E. L. Stahl's book (1954), preceding not only the monographs of Storz and von Wiese but also Beck's article on the heroes, is more analytical but looks rather narrow nowadays. Stahl places the psychology of the flawed idealist at the heart of our four plays, arguing that each male protagonist, although initially led by selfless motives, comes increasingly to resemble his adversary, and his enterprise ultimately fails owing to "his own inability to sustain idealism at the summit of integrity" (12). But "idealism" is an imprecise notion for dealing with such different and complex characters, and the ambiguity as to its philosophical and psychological applications is vexing. Is "idealism," we wonder, perhaps nothing more than a red herring? Besides, Stahl's argument marginalizes the social and religious motifs, and dwells on the role of psychic harmony (thereby anticipating much subsequent writing on Schiller in English). This leads to some dubious statements, as when Stahl implies that Karl Moor's allusion to "die Harmonie der Welt" (V/2; 617) [harmony of the world] refers to an inner state. Stahl has an oddly lyrical view of tragedy as dealing essentially with inner and not external conflict. We need merely to recall von Wiese's stress on the objective *Ordnungen*, both in these works and in the Weltanschauung of the Enlightenment, to realize how limited Stahl's view is here.

R. D. Miller (1963) places the Kantian idea of freedom at the centre of the prose plays, and the idea of harmony, which Schiller adopted in contrast to the spirit of Kantian ethics, at the centre of *Don Carlos*. This is a strange perspective, in that Schiller's reading of Kant and his criticism of him only occurred in the next decade, so that the entire process seems to be magically prefigured in these early dramas. Miller manages to make this plausible to some extent, particularly with reference to Schiller's attempt in *Über das Pathetische* to give an implicit moral content to the immorality of the great criminal. But often the plays are made to sound like dialectical fencing matches between the concepts of freedom, nature and idealism. The value of Miller's book is also limited by its failure to take into account other scholarly work on Schiller.

H. B. Garland (1969) offers something rather unusual, a distinctively English, rigorously empirical, study of poetic style, which catalogues Schiller's developing technique and convincingly demonstrates his conscious artistry in the language of these works. Although Garland ignores the usual foci of interpretation and confines himself to the analysis of rhetoric, diction and imagery, some general insights emerge nonetheless. In his only engagement in scholarly controversy, he dismisses Auerbach's allegation (see chapter 7 below) that *Kabale und Liebe* is an aesthetic failure owing to Schiller's inability to sustain the realism of the opening scene. Garland argues that the realistic episodes, here and in the other prose plays, are only marginal, not an end in themselves. Schiller's real aim was "an intense and violently cathartic tragedy, and the means available to him were winged rhetoric and strong emphasis" (95). Moreover, even the realistic passages are satirically heightened, and are tied to the more elevated passages by the use of certain stylistic devices. As a result, the play is "a masterpiece of stylistic counterpoint," not a failed exercise in realism. In a insight that is unheard of in German scholarship, Garland suggests here that the unity of the play lies not in an idea but in a style.

Realism is a theme in Garland's treatment of the other plays also. He regards the language of *Die Räuber* as a hybrid between prose and poetry that poses an obstacle to the appreciation of a basically visionary play. The verse of *Don Carlos* is shown to accommodate a good deal of realistic language besides the more exalted passages. Garland regards Schiller's creation of what he calls a "medial" style in the final version of this play as a great achievement and again as the work's unifying feature. He finds here a tendency toward harmony rather than violent antithesis, as in the earlier plays. He concludes his discussion with the familiar view that *Don Carlos* marked a step on Schiller's path to Goethe, although, since he has supported this view through his analysis of the play's language, it sounds more persuasive here than it sometimes does.

Psychology is at the heart of a brilliant and erratic book by Ilse Graham (1974), who is inspired in part by existentialism, in part by the idea of psychic wholeness, of which she finds the later Schiller, the theorist of the "ästhetischer Zustand" [aesthetic condition], to be a champion. (There is a longer version of the interpretation of *Fiesco* in Graham's dissertation, published 1975.) Citing the biblical Jacob's theft of his father's blessing as the precedent for Karl Moor's attempt to do the same (V/1), she constructs an elaborate interpretation of *Die Räuber* on the idea of theft as symbol for existential bad faith. But the argument is built on sand, for the blessing that Karl receives is nowhere said to be exclusive, that is, gained at the expense of his brother. Of more importance, however, is that Jacob is a *younger* son, while Karl is the elder son, and so would be the rightful recipient of an exclusive blessing if any such were intended. To compare Karl, an elder son cheated by a younger, to Jacob and not Esau, is perverse.

Graham pursues her argument with a dogmatic indifference to historical plausibility that is once again reminiscent of the account by Hinrichs a century before. Where he read the plays as an allegory of the Hegelian "Weltgeist" in its interactions with nature, Graham sees them as prefiguring theories propounded by twentieth-century psychologists. A problem here is the tendency to put a mental state, psychic wholeness, at the centre of an interpretation of drama, a genre that has to do with action. Related to this is the tendency to reduce secondary characters to allegories of aspects of the protagonist's mind (for example, the Moor as expression of Fiesco's sensuality). Another problem is Graham's overinterpretation of incidental motifs and connections, as when she claims that significance of the "Kammerdiener" scene in *Kabale und Liebe* resides less in its inherent political force than in the oblique light it throws on Miller's attitude to his daughter: "the father's relation to her is as deeply anonymous as the ruler's relation to his subjects, in that neither is aware that he is related to adult beings with rights and needs of their own" (119). The parallel is spurious even on its own terms, for Graham has accused Miller of possessiveness, whereas the Duke's fault, in sending his subjects to their death in a foreign land, is indifference. In her overall view of the play as portraying "the gradual strangulation of an adult relationship [!] caught in the coils of a filial entanglement" (111), Graham is blind to the actual pressures, economic, social and religious, on Luise, treating the play rather like a case history from a modern work of popular psychology.

T. J. Reed's essay of 1991 is a work of advocacy, defending Schiller from a new generation of doubters, and his strategy is to present a liberal Schiller, a moralist but not a moralizer, locked in a struggle against despotism. As Reed realizes, however, the texts do not always cooperate in this strategy, and what makes his discussion especially fascinating is his refusal to overstate his case, his scrupulousness in making necessary qualifications, and his admission of dramatic weaknesses. He regards *Kabale und Liebe*, with its combination of elevated language and bourgeois subject matter, as "a mismatch of temperament and mode" (30), and he does not believe that the unity of *Don Carlos* can be rescued ("Time had undone art," 49). Reed's formulations of the plays' political meanings are circumspect: *Die Räuber* poses the vital question "How can a flawed humanity put ideals into practice?" (20), and *Fiesco* asks, "Is today's liberator not almost bound to be tomorrow's new tyrant?" (28). Reed does not pretend that the plays provide answers. Despite its brevity, this is a fine analysis that, like those of Böckmann and Mayer, makes a strong case for the dramas by recognizing the way in which they intermesh political questions with the psychological and ethical quandaries encountered in political life.

The most recent monograph in this series from England is by Lesley Sharpe (1991), who, more than any of her predecessors, seeks to give a well-rounded account of her subject, situating Schiller in his own age and integrating the views on the plays put forward by recent scholarship. If as a result her book is a little less incisive, a little more cautious than some of its predecessors, it is perhaps all the more useful for the student. Like Reed, Sharpe feels obliged to defend Schiller against the stigma of being a moralist. In *Die Räuber*, for example, she concedes that the characters are perpetually "judged and judging," but argues that, instead of dictating a verdict, Schiller makes us "experience the enormous difficulty of reaching final judgment, indeed of even finding the criteria by which to judge" (13). Is that perhaps too much of a concession to modern skepticism? One could argue that Karl's references in the last scene to the "Bau der sittlichen Welt" and the "Harmonie der Welt" bespeak a greater degree of moral certainty than Sharpe will admit.

Sharpe resembles Reed also in addressing the political aspect of these works, even including the term "politics" in her title. But, like him, she is careful not to overstate the ideological content of the works. A common theme running through her discussions is an "unresolved element" (23), a "tension between hope for a better order and yet disquiet about the agents of change" (44) and "a deep disquiet about the implications of the exercise of human freedom" (53), all good formulations of the dilemma we have repeatedly encountered. But other aspects are not ignored. The discussion of *Die Räuber* includes a careful analysis of the points of departure from the Prodigal Son theme; this section proceeds from but also goes beyond von Wiese's account of the family as keystone of a socioreligious *Ordnung*. To balance the religious dimension of the play, however, Sharpe also pays attention to the influence of Schiller's medical studies on his approach to motivation. This recognition of both the theological and the anthropological levels in this play is perhaps the most important aspect of her interpretation.

Kabale und Liebe is presented here chiefly in psychological terms, as the tragedy of a lost generation; Ferdinand and Luise are seen as caught between the received outlook of their class, from which they have only partially freed themselves, and the new ideas — and emotions — of the Enlightenment. In the first half of the play, the opposition to the lovers is external, and the play's theme seems to be social division. In the second half, however, the internal obstacles come to the fore as the lovers' underlying loyalty to their background asserts itself. The result is violence, in Luise's case against herself, in Ferdinand's against Luise. On the central crux, Sharpe denies that Schiller intended us to approve of Luise's renunciation of Ferdinand, arguing instead that this decision betrays the timidity of her class. Sharpe also makes a good case for the inner necessity of the Lady Milford episode, suggesting that the character's decision to abandon her false role and to regain her dignity through private moral regeneration shows what might have been a positive way out of the lovers' plight.

Sharpe's treatment of *Don Carlos* is the most contentious. First, she strives to vindicate the work's artistic unity, which she says resides in the nature imagery and in the paralleling of scenes. More importantly, she firmly rejects the view that, following Schiller's *Briefe*, condemns Posa as a moral despot. She works hard to absolve Posa of the various charges against him, and, in doing so, portrays the play as the successful resolution of the dilemma underlying the earlier ones. In this respect, Schiller has won through in her view to a historical optimism. If political action entails some loss of personal integrity, this loss is not boundless and is justified by the outcome. However, as Sharpe argues, the experience of the French Revolution was soon to put an end to this phase in Schiller's thought, leaving *Don Carlos* as a unique and isolated document of political hope.

There has been little American writing on Schiller since Kaufmann (1942), but I shall conclude with a recent monograph by the United States scholar Steven Martinson (1996), an ambitious attempt to subsume Schiller's works in all genres under the heading of "harmonious tensions." Martinson's book is an effort to press home the suggestion of Dewhurst and Reeves (1978) that Schiller's early medical writings are the key to his life's work. Martinson argues for the primacy of the anthropological dimension, and he attributes paramount importance to the symbol of the stringed musical instrument, whether as metaphor or as actual object on the stage, as denoting the ideal harmony of mind and body. But Martinson allows his pursuit of this and related metaphors to get in the way of his investigation of the plays as demonstrations of the author's anthropological tenets. This leads to eccentric and disjointed interpretations in which the verbal imagery receives more attention than the events. Scenes involving music are assumed *ex hypothesi* to be of high importance, while the theological implications of the metaphor of harmony are overlooked. Two further eccentricities are the unexplained omission of *Fiesco*, and the use of the second edition of *Die Räuber* as basis for the discussion, apparently on the sole ground that it supports the author's thesis better than the first edition. All in all, the book does not present a strong case for the anthropological and naturalistic view of Schiller.

Three Heavyweights

I shall conclude by looking at recent contributions by three prominent German scholars who stand aside from the trend, noted above, toward examining these plays as part of a wider socioliterary investigation. Instead, they attempt to take stock of Schiller and his works in the light of the current state of scholarship. A common feature of the first two discussions is a desire to locate Schiller in his age, and to this end both draw on the recent development of a detailed and empirical research into the German Enlightenment, as opposed to the more abstract and ideological research that came about in the 1970s. Hence we hear less about Enlightenment as a criticism of authority and a quest for autonomy, more about the intellectual climate generated by the interest in empirical psychology and "anthropology." The first of the three scholars is Gerhard Kluge, who, as editor to two volumes of the new Frankfurt edition (1988, 1989), has provided highly intelligent introductions to the works under discussion. A particular strength of his analyses is his frequent allusions to contemporary texts that illuminate the intellectual background and may have served as Schiller's sources, for instance, Abel's writings on psychology, and Adam Ferguson's *Essay on the History of Civil Society*. Kluge's observation that, as a term for the heroes of all four plays, the concept of the "Schwärmer" [enthusiast] may be more useful than that of the idealist, strikes me as helpful, not least since Kluge avoids committing himself to a narrowly psychological interpretation of the plays; hence he argues that the concept of the "Schwärmer" entails social and moral consequences, social, in that the "Schwärmer" isolates himself from society, and moral, in that his immoderate actions trigger the avenging machinery of nemesis. At the same time, Kluge is careful not to define "Schwärmertum" itself too narrowly, a step that would run the risk of obscuring the differences between the three works. He thus allows for some variety of types of "Schwärmer," and notes that the term includes extremes of enthusiasm and melancholy. Kluge stresses several further common features, all of which are indeed indispensable to a comprehensive characterization of the plays. These are: Schiller's preoccupation with personal greatness as a quality that appears to challenge the validity of normal morality; his concern with precise motivation; the quality of the plays as a "Theater der Grausamkeit" [theater of cruelty] involving extremes and implausibilities; and the plays' experimental character, underlined in the Frankfurt edition by the decision to publish all variant versions in full. It might be objected that not all of these features are mutually compatible, especially psychological precision and "Theater der Grausamkeit." Against this one could assert that a broad perspective like Kluge's is needed to do justice to works of this complexity. Kluge also considers the view, expressed by both conservative and radical critics, that the conclusions to the plays imply a tacit legitimation of the status quo, and rejects it on the ground that the latter has been so radically challenged by the protagonists' deeds that no return is possible.

In his essays on the individual works, we notice that Kluge makes an effort, first, to include all the characters of the play and all aspects of the plot, second, to address most of the issues at the forefront of recent discussion, mediating between alternative points of view, and third, as befits an editor, to defend the play against criticisms. He comments rightly that *Die Räuber*, in spite of being a protest against Schiller's education, is a mirror of the educational level of the age, and that it is raised above the other plays of the Storm and Stress movement by its rich intellectual content. Thus both the anthropological and the religious strands receive due emphasis without either being subordinated to the other. Kluge's discussion of the religious aspects is especially helpful, separate treatment being given to the three topics of Swabian Pietism, the plot paradigm of the Prodigal Son, and the theme of despair, while the latter is related back to the psychological concept of "Seelenstärke" [strength of soul]. Kluge downplays the element of social criticism in the play and stresses rather the pathological side of Karl's rebellion, a decision that gives his interpretation a conservative slant. This is reinforced by his judgment that the "disturbed order in a family" (981) overrides the theme of fraternal strife, a view that demonstrates the continued influence of von Wiese's analysis.

In *Fiesco*, Kluge concurs with the modern tendency to view the protagonist negatively, and he warns us against confusing Fiesco with Karl Moor, whose heroic features he lacks. Kluge's most interesting remarks here aim at vindicating Verrina's much criticized final words ("Ich gehe zu Andreas"); they are not absurd or resignatory, but may rather represent the play's tragic climax. Since Fiesco's lamentable end has shown him to be unworthy to carry the tragic weight of the play, this now shifts to Verrina, who abandons the republic as idea and accepts the necessarily imperfect form that the idea must assume. In an interesting comparison, Kluge argues that Verrina's last action resembles Karl Moor's; instead of claiming to be above the law by virtue of his dedication to a higher ideal, Verrina agrees to take his chance with earthly justice. Kluge's discussion of *Kabale und Liebe* is a delicate attempt to mediate between conservative and progressive interpretations of the work. He rejects the radical view that Luise is merely the product of a repressive upbringing, arguing that she has far more freedom than her parents and that her renunciation of Ferdinand is based on realism, not cowardice. On the other hand, Kluge accepts the criticisms of Miller's conduct that have come to be heard recently. Similarly, he makes the religious motifs central to the play without allowing these to detract from the social criticism. In *Don Carlos*, finally, Kluge emphasizes the differences between the various versions of the play, and he welcomes the recent attention that the *Briefe* have received. He argues that much of the critical literature on this work is flawed by the use of the 1805 version, which is discussed as though it were a text of the 1780s, and he makes a strong case for using the 1787 version as the standard. Contrary to the charges of artistic incoherence, Kluge views the play as being unified around the figure of the prince, who is portrayed as vacillating between enthusiasm and melancholy. Kluge sees Posa as a "Schwärmer" and as a gambler rather than an intriguer or a despot, although this does not invalidate his ideals.

Karl Guthke, the second of the two scholars referred to, has produced a formidable monograph (1994) of an unfashionable kind, in which each of Schiller's completed dramas forms the subject of a substantial and closely argued chapter. A particular virtuosity of Guthke as a writer is his ability to comment on a huge range of previous scholarship, both old and recent, without losing the thread of his own argument. His writing has a more polemical edge than Kluge's, and aims to refute the image of Schiller as idealist, to which Guthke (in my view rightly) attributes Schiller's unpopularity with generations of readers. In place of this he sets out to emphasize the skeptical intelligence that Schiller brings to bear on his characters, especially those normally thought of as idealists. Guthke links this critical quality to Schiller's anthropological studies and, in general, to the widespread interest in "Erfahrungsseelenkunde" [empirical psychology] in the late Enlightenment before the rise of idealism. (The books by Dewhurst and Reeves [1978] and Riedel [1985] both receive prominent mention in his preface.) He also pays homage to English scholars, especially to T. J. Reed (1991), as less theory-bound and, thanks to their Shakespearian schooling, as more sensitive to Schiller's psychological insight than German scholars have been.

Despite his good intentions and the high quality of his writing, it is unclear to me either that the attitude which Guthke challenges is still very widespread or that, on his own terms, he manages to overcome it. On the first point, as we have seen, there is an impressive line of postwar German commentaries on these works (starting with Beck, 1955) that explore the dark side of the so-called idealist characters, so that Guthke seems to me less of an iconoclast than he fancies. On the second point, Guthke makes the crucial decision to retain the term "idealist." Instead of dispensing with it altogether like Kluge, Guthke finds a pattern in the plays of idealistic and realistic characters occurring in mutual opposition. His strategy is to argue that, instead of "idealizing" them, Schiller treats the idealists skeptically, while the realists are treated with sympathy. What disturbs me here is that Guthke seems to have turned the quality of "Menschenkenntnis" [psychological understanding] from something flexible and empirical into something like a dogma; hence, where a truly empirical writer like Shakespeare is able to portray a wide range of well-differentiated human types, Guthke sees the most important characters of Schiller's plays as falling into one of two antithetical categories. This pattern does not really support the picture of Schiller as "Menschenkenner." Further, once Guthke has identified a character as an idealist, he feels obliged to criticize him, and the converse is true of the realists. The consequence is a certain rigidity in his analyses, as if throughout his life Schiller had understood it as his mission to warn his audiences of the dangers of idealism. Why he should have believed this is unclear. It is also ironic that Guthke makes the concept of idealism, which he claims to abhor, so indispensable to his own interpretation. He seems to have allowed the terms of his analysis to be dictated by the scholarly tradition that he opposes most vehemently, and that for that very reason he never manages to escape its influence.

The chapter dealing with *Kabale und Liebe* (published first in Hinderer, ed. 1979) is the most valuable of the four that concern us, and also one of the best existing discussions of this play. Although Guthke touches on the subject of Ferdinand's idealism, this is in the context of the broader theme of secularization. Alluding to an essay by Walther Rehm, he argues that both Ferdinand and Luise commit the error of *experimentum medietatis*, that is, that, in an age of weakening religious faith, they endow secular emotions with religious authority. Ferdinand views his love in this way, and Luise her respect for the established social order. Guthke departs here from a virtual consensus among scholars dwelling on the religious theme, who usually assume that Luise's conservatism has the author's support. Instead, Guthke regards this as a mirror-image of Ferdinand's delusion, irreconcilable with it, to be sure, but no less blind and rigid. In the case of this play, then, Guthke's focus on secularization allows him to give equal treatment to Luise, who cannot be regarded as an idealist, and also to view the themes of the play in a sociohistorical context.

The discussion of *Don Carlos* does not meet the same standards, however. In an argument of a kind that we often find among German scholars, the play is said to be a tragedy of character as opposed to a family drama or a political drama. The chapter then turns into a narrow attack on Marquis Posa as idealist and would-be artist, and it is implied that the discrediting of this character is the play's *raison d'être*. This seems to me an unbalanced view. It is compounded, moreover, by a strange paradox. Guthke rejects the traditional picture of Schiller as a moral pedagogue; in his introductory chapter (citing Kayser's essay of 1960) he brings out Schiller's lifelong fascination with amoral greatness, and in his chapter on *Die Räuber* he goes to great lengths to rehabilitate Franz as an exemplar of this quality. However, there is what I can only call an extreme moral fastidiousness about his own attack on Posa for repeatedly infringing the autonomy of other characters. Is Guthke not applying a double standard, or at least displaying a lack of proportion here? He is highly censorious about Posa's lies to Philip in the audience scene, but these seem mild indeed compared with Philip's accomplishments as a persecutor of heretics. Should we really insist that a dramatic character always tell the truth, even when he is certain to lose his life as a result?

Guthke's book receives high praise from Helmut Koopmann in the "Forschungsbericht" that concludes his *Schiller-Handbuch* (1988, 892–94), which also contains updated versions of Guthke's chapters on three of Schiller's later plays. Koopmann himself, with whom I shall conclude this chapter, contributes discussions of *Fiesco* and *Kabale und Liebe* as well as an introductory essay on Schiller and the dramatic tradition. The theme linking these essays, very different from Guthke's concern with "Menschenkenntnis," is a concept of Schiller as a virtuoso of intertextuality, constantly playing with different literary motifs and styles. This is certainly a valid way of looking at these plays, although I suspect that Koopmann overdoes it. But what is most interesting is the contrast to Koopmann's own short monograph of 1988, in which he wrote as a disciple of Jürgen Habermas rather than of Roland Barthes, and in which the reference to contemporary reality (both Schiller's and ours) was paramount. The argument running through the earlier book was Schiller's identity as *Aufklärer*, who worked to expand the rational awareness and moral autonomy of reader and audience, and who either anticipated or reflected the momentous events in France. Koopmann has been an active Schiller scholar for over thirty years, and his erudition is unsurpassed. His failure, or perhaps his refusal, to adopt a stable and consistent point of view says less about himself than it does about the subject, by which I mean both the inherent difficulty of Schiller himself and the changeable intellectual climate in which we live. These two "ineluctable modalities" of modern research on Schiller will ensure that new viewpoints and methodologies will continue to be generated for as long as young scholars choose to devote their time to studying him.

Notes

[1] Ernst Müller's biography of the young Schiller, although overshadowed by Buchwald's first volume, deserves a brief mention for its intelligent discussion of *Die Räuber*. (The treatment of *Fiesco*, the only other play discussed, is less good.) Although dependent on Stubenrauch for the story of the play's composition and on Cysarz for its Lutheran aspects, Müller offers a useful analysis of Karl's "Hamlet" speech in IV/5 and some suggestive comments as to Schiller's critical attitude to the Enlightenment's ethic of happiness. Good popular biographies of Schiller have been written subsequently by von Heiseler (1959) and Lahnstein (1981), but they will not be discussed here.

[2] A similar view of Schiller to Staiger's is expressed by Nietzsche in section 8 of *Der Fall Wagner* (1888), where he writes that Wagner desired nothing but effect ("Wirkung"). He continues: "[Wagner] hat darin die Unbedenklichkeit, die Schiller hatte, die jeder Theatermensch hat, er hat auch dessen Verachtung der Welt, die er sich zu Füßen legt!" (*Werke*, 2: 920). [In this respect [Wagner] shares the unscrupulousness of Schiller and every person of the theater; he also shares his contempt for the world that lies at his feet!]

[3] For anthropology, see the important book by Wolfgang Riedel (1985). Although it does no more than touch on the plays, it definitively sets out their intellectual background.

Works Cited

Abusch, Alexander. 1955. *Schiller: Größe und Tragik eines deutschen Genius.* 4th ed. Berlin (East): Aufbau, 1965.

Adorno, Theodor W. 1951. *Minima Moralia: Reflexionen aus dem beschädigten Leben.* Frankfurt a. M.: Suhrkamp, 1980. ("Schwabenstreiche," 110–11, and *"Die Räuber,"* 111–12).

Anstett, J.-J. 1959. "Schiller: Drames de jeunesse, drames de la jeunesse." *EG* 14: 307–12.

Beck, Adolf. 1955. "Die Krisis des Menschen im Drama des jungen Schiller." *Euphorion* 49: 163–202.

Berghahn, Klaus. 1980. "Zum Drama Schillers." In *Handbuch des deutschen Dramas,* ed. Walter Hinck. Düsseldorf: Bagel, 157–73.

Beyer, Karen. 1993. *"Schön wie ein Gott und männlich wie ein Held": Zur Rolle des weiblichen Geschlechtscharakters für die Konstituierung des männlichen Aufklärungshelden in den frühen Dramen Schillers.* Stuttgart: M & P.

Böckmann, Paul. 1949. "Die pathetische Ausdrucksform in Schillers Jugenddramen." In *Formgeschichte der deutschen Dichtung.* Vol. 1. Hamburg: Hoffmann; 2nd ed. 1965, 668–91.

——. 1955. "Politik und Dichtung im Werk Friedrich Schillers." In *Schiller: Reden im Gedenkjahr 1955,* ed. Bernhard Zeller. Stuttgart: Klett, 192–213.

Bolten, Jürgen. 1985. *Friedrich Schiller: Poesie, Reflexion und gesellschaftliche Selbstdeutung.* Munich: Fink.

Bovenschen, Silvia. 1979. *Die imaginierte Weiblichkeit: Exemplarische Untersuchungen zu kulturgeschichtlichen und literarischen Präsentationsformen des Weiblichen.* Frankfurt a. M.: Suhrkamp.

Brandt, Helmut, ed. 1987. *Friedrich Schiller — Angebot und Diskurs: Zugänge — Dichtung — Zeitgenossenschaft.* Weimar Berlin (East): Aufbau.

Buchwald, Reinhard. 1953–54. *Schiller.* 2nd ed. Wiesbaden: Insel. Vol. 1: *Der junge Schiller.* Vol. 2: *Der Weg zur Vollendung.* (First edition 1937.)

Dahlke, Günther, ed. 1959. *Der Menschheit Würde: Dokumente zum Schiller-Bild der deutschen Arbeiterklasse.* Weimar: Arion.

Dahnke, Hans-Dietrich and Bernd Leistner. 1982. *Schiller: Das dramatische Werk in Einzelinterpretationen.* Leipzig: Reclam.

Dewhurst, Kenneth and Nigel Reeves. 1978. *Friedrich Schiller: Medicine, Psychology and Literature.* Oxford: Sandford.

Fuhrmann, Helmut. 1981. "Revision des Parisurteils. 'Bild' und 'Gestalt' der Frau im Werk Friedrich Schillers." *JDSG* 25: 316–66.

Garland, H. B. 1969. *Schiller the Dramatic Writer: A Study of Style in the Plays*. Oxford: Clarendon.

Gerhard, Melitta. 1950. *Schiller*. Bern: Francke.

Glaser, Horst Albert. 1980a. "Drama des Sturm und Drang." In *Zwischen Absolutismus und Aufklärung: Rationalismus, Empfindsamkeit, Sturm und Drang 1740–1786*, ed. Ralph-Rainer Wuthenow. Vol. 4 of *Deutsche Literatur: Eine Sozialgeschichte*. Reinbek: Rowohlt, 299–322.

———. 1980b. "Klassisches und romantisches Drama." In *Zwischen Revolution und Restauration: Klassik, Romantik 1786–1815*, ed. H.A. Glaser. Vol. 5 of *Deutsche Literatur: Eine Sozialgeschichte*. Reinbek: Rowohlt. 276–312.

Graham, Ilse. 1974. *Schiller's Drama: Talent and Integrity*. London: Methuen.

———. 1975. *Schiller: A Master of the Tragic Form*. Pittsburgh: Duquesne UP.

Guthke, Karl. 1994. *Schillers Dramen: Idealismus und Skepsis*. Tübingen: Francke.

Hammer, Stephanie Barbé. 1994. "Schiller, Time and Again." *German Quarterly* 67: 153–72.

Heiseler, Bernt von. 1959. *Schiller: Dichter, Idealist, Philosoph*. Munich: Heyne, 1983.

Heller, Erich. 1950. "Friedrich Schiller: The Moralist as Poet." *Times Literary Supplement*, Nr. 2506 (10 February 1950): 81–83.

Hinderer, Walter. 1978. "Freiheit und Gesellschaft beim jungen Schiller." In *Sturm und Drang: Ein literaturwissenschaftliches Studienbuch*, ed. Walter Hinck. Kronberg: Athenäum, 230–56.

———, ed. 1979. *Schillers Dramen: Neue Interpretationen*. Stuttgart: Reclam.

Jonnes, Denis. 1987. "Pattern of Power: Family and State in Schiller's Early Drama." *CG* 20: 138–62.

Kaiser, Gerhard. 1976. *Aufklärung, Empfindsamkeit, Sturm und Drang*. 3rd ed. Munich: Franke, 1979.

Kaufmann, F. W. 1942. *Schiller: Poet of Philosophical Idealism*. Oberlin: Academy Press.

Kayser, Wolfgang. 1960. *Schiller als Dichter und Deuter der Größe*. Göttingen: Vandenhoeck & Ruprecht.

Kiesel, Helmuth. 1979. *'Bei Hof, bei Höll': Untersuchungen zur literarischen Hofkritik von Sebastian Brant bis Friedrich Schiller*. Tübingen: Niemeyer.

Kindermann, Heinz. 1948. *Theatergeschichte der Goethezeit*. Vienna: Bauer.

Kluge, Gerhard. 1988. "Kommentar." In Friedrich Schiller, *Dramen I*. Vol. 2 of *Werke und Briefe*. Frankfurt a. M.: Deutscher Klassiker Verlag. 871–80, 978–99, 1215–34, 1408–24.

———. 1989. "Kommentar." In Friedrich Schiller, *Dramen II.* Vol. 3 of *Werke und Briefe.* Frankfurt a. M.: Deutscher Klassiker Verlag. 991–96, 1149–62.

Koopmann, Helmut. 1988. *Schiller: Eine Einführung.* Munich: Artemis.

———, ed. 1998. *Schiller-Handbuch.* Stuttgart: Kröner.
Includes:

Helmut Koopmann. 1998. "Schiller und die dramatische Tradition," 137–54.

Helmut Koopmann. 1998. "*Die Verschwörung des Fiesko zu Genua,*" 354–64.

Helmut Koopmann. 1998. "*Kabale und Liebe,*" 365–78.

Kraft, Herbert. 1978. *Um Schiller betrogen.* Pfüllingen: Neske.

Lahnstein, Peter. 1981. *Schillers Leben.* Frankfurt a. M.: Fischer, 1984.

Linn, Rolf N. 1973. *Schillers junge Idealisten.* Berkeley: U of California P.

Lukács, Georg. 1964. *Deutsche Literatur in zwei Jahrhunderten.* Neuwied: Luchterhand.

Maier, Konrad. 1992. *Zerstörungsformen einer verabsolutierten Moral im Frühwerk Friedrich Schillers.* St. Ingbert: Röhrig.

Mann, Thomas. 1955. *Versuch über Schiller.* Berlin: Fischer.

Mansouri, Rachid Jai. 1988. *Die Darstellung der Frau in Schillers Dramen.* Frankfurt a. M.: Lang.

Martinson, Steven D. 1996. *Harmonious Tensions: The Writings of Friedrich Schiller.* Newark: U of Delaware P.

Masson, Raoul. 1959. "La psycho-physiologie du jeune Schiller." *EG* 14: 363–73.

May, Kurt. 1948. *Friedrich Schiller: Idee und Wirklichkeit im Drama.* Göttingen: Vandenhoeck & Ruprecht.

Mayer, Hans. 1966. "Schillers Dramen — für die Gebildeten unter ihren Verächtern." In vol. 2 of Schiller, *Werke.* 2 vols. Frankfurt a. M.: Insel, 481–95.

McCardle, Arthur W. 1986. *Friedrich Schiller and Swabian Pietism.* New York: Lang.

Middell, Eike. 1980. *Friedrich Schiller: Leben und Werk.* Leipzig: Reclam.

Miller, R. D. 1963. *The Drama of Schiller.* Harrogate: Duchy.

Müller, Ernst. 1955. *Der Herzog und das Genie: Friedrich Schillers Jugendjahre.* Stuttgart: Kohlhammer. (Earlier version appeared as *Der junge Schiller,* 1947.)

Müller, Joachim. 1972. *Von Schiller bis Heine.* Halle: VEB Niemeyer.

Includes:

"Der Held und sein Gegenspieler in Schillers Dramen," 38–82. (Earlier version in *Wissenschaftliche Zeitschrift der Friedrich-Schiller-Universität Jena: Gesellschafts- und Sprachwissenschaft* 8 [1958/59]: 451–69.)
"Himmel und Hölle," 104–15.

Nietzsche, Friedrich. 1888. *Der Fall Wagner.* In vol. 2 of *Werke*, ed. Karl Schlechta. 6th ed. 3 vols. Munich: Hanser, 1969, 901–38.

Nutz, Maximilian. 1990. "Der verhinderte Dialog: Zu den Schiller-Feiern von 1955 und 1959 im geteilten Deutschland." *Literatur für Leser* 1: 14–28.

Oellers, Norbert. 1991. "Zur Geschichte der Schiller-Nationalausgabe." In his *Friedrich Schiller: Zur Modernität eines Klassikers.* Frankfurt a. M.: Insel, 349–67.

Paulsen, Wolfgang. 1962. "Friedrich Schiller 1955–1959: Ein Literaturbericht." *JDSG* 6: 369–464.

Reed, T. J. 1991. *Schiller.* Oxford: Oxford UP.

Riedel, Wolfgang. 1985. *Die Anthropologie des jungen Schiller.* Würzburg: Königshausen & Neumann.

Rohrmoser, Günter. 1959. "Theodizee und Tragödie im Werk Schillers." *Wirkendes Wort* 9: 329–38. Repr. in Klaus Berghahn and Reinhold Grimm, ed., *Schiller: Zur Theorie und Praxis seiner Dramen.* Wege der Forschung, 323. Darmstadt: Wissenschaftliche Buchgesellschaft, 1972, 233–48.

Scheibe, Friedrich Carl. 1966. "Schöpfer und Geschöpf in Schillers Frühwerk." *GRM*, N.F. 16: 119–38.

Schulte-Sasse, Jochen. 1980. "Drama." In *Deutsche Aufklärung bis zur Französischen Revolution*, ed. Rolf Grimminger. Vol. 3 of *Hansers Sozialgeschichte der deutschen Literatur vom 16. Jahrhundert bis zur Gegenwart.* Munich: Hanser, 423–99.

Schunicht, Manfred. 1963. "Intrigen und Intriganten in Schillers Dramen." *ZfdPh* 82: 271–92.

Seidlin, Oskar. 1960. "Schillers 'trügerische Zeichen': Die Funktion der Briefe in seinen frühen Dramen." *JDSG* 4: 247–69. Repr. in Klaus Berghahn and Reinhold Grimm, ed., *Schiller: Zur Theorie und Praxis seiner Dramen.* Wege der Forschung, 323. Darmstadt: Wissenschaftliche Buchgesellschaft, 1972, 178–205.

Sharpe, Lesley. 1991. *Friedrich Schiller: Drama, Thought and Politics.* Cambridge: Cambridge UP.

Sørensen, Bengt Algot. 1984. *Herrschaft und Zärtlichkeit: Der Patriarchalismus und das Drama im 18. Jahrhundert.* Munich: Beck.

Stahl, E. L. 1954. *Friedrich Schiller's Drama: Theory and Practice.* Oxford: Clarendon.

Staiger, Emil. 1950. "Schiller: *Agrippina*." In his *Die Kunst der Interpretation*. Zurich: Atlantis, 1961, 132–60.

———. 1967. *Friedrich Schiller*. Zurich: Atlantis.

Steinhagen, Harald. 1982. "Der junge Schiller zwischen Marquis de Sade und Kant: Aufklärung und Idealismus." *DVjs* 56: 135–57.

Stephan, Inge. 1986. "'So ist die Tugend ein Gespenst': Frauenbild und Tugendbegriff bei Lessing und Schiller." In *Lessing und die Toleranz*, ed. Peter Freimark, Franklin Kopitzsch and Helga Slessarev. Munich: Text und Kritik, 357–72.

Storz, Gerhard. 1959. *Der Dichter Friedrich Schiller*. Stuttgart: Klett.

Thalheim, Hans-Günther. 1961. "Der junge Schiller." Habilitationsschrift, Humboldt-Universität, Berlin (East).

———. 1969. *Zur Literatur der Goethezeit*. Berlin (East): Rütten & Loening. Includes:

"Volk und Held in den Dramen Schillers," 85–117. (First published 1959.)

"Schillers Stellung zur Französischen Revolution und zum Revolutionsproblem," 118–45. (First published 1960.)

———. 1987. "Zeitalterkritik und Zukunftserwartung: Zur Grundkonzeption in Schillers früher Dramatik." In Brandt, ed., 1987, 141–59.

Wentzlaff-Eggebert, Friedrich-Wilhelm. 1949. *Schillers Weg zu Goethe*. 2nd ed. Berlin: de Gruyter, 1963.

Wertheim, Ursula. 1958. *Schillers "Fiesko" und "Don Carlos": Zu Problemen des historischen Stoffes*. 2nd ed. Berlin (East): Aufbau, 1967.

———. 1959. "'Zeitstück' und 'historisches Drama' in Schillers Werken — Ein aktuelles Problem für den Dichter unserer Zeit." In Braemer, Edith and Ursula Wertheim, *Studien zur deutschen Klassik*. Berlin (East): Rütten & Loening, 1960, 163–88.

Wiese, Benno von. 1948. *Die deutsche Tragödie von Lessing bis Hebbel*. 3rd ed. 1967. Hamburg: Hoffmann & Campe.

———. 1959. *Friedrich Schiller*. Stuttgart: Metzler.

Williams, Anthony. 1974. "The Ambivalences in the Plays of the Young Schiller about Contemporary Germany." In *Deutsches Bürgertum und literarische Intelligenz 1750–1800*. Literaturwissenschaft und Sozialwissenschaften 1. Stuttgart: Metzler, 1–112.

Winter, Hans Gerhard. 1978. "Antiklassizismus: Sturm und Drang." In *Geschichte der deutschen Literatur vom 18. Jahrhundert bis zur Gegenwart*, ed. Viktor Žmegač. Vol. I/1. Königstein: Athenäum, 194–256.

Witte, William. 1949. *Schiller*. Oxford: Blackwell.

5: *Die Räuber:*
A Political Play?

THE GREATEST TEMPTATION to the reader and spectator of Schiller's first drama has always been to take Karl Moor's rhetoric in the first two acts at face value. The private emotion vented in his first words, the famous "Mir ekelt vor diesem tintenklecksenden Säkulum" [This ink-blotting age disgusts me], is broadened to an ideological statement when he praises freedom as the source of "Kolosse und Extremitäten" [colossi and extremes]. Karl's titanic outburst culminates in the boast that, placed in command of an army of men equal to himself, he would turn Germany into a republic that would make Rome and Sparta look like nunneries (I/2; 503–4). Despite the well crafted dramatic context — Karl's desire to outdo the ancient republics is clearly stimulated by reading Plutarch with a glass of wine in his hand — the volcanic force of these words has persuaded many readers that they must be an expression of the author's own feelings, while the occurrence of the terms "freedom" and "republic" have prompted some critics to read a political program into the speech as well.

Even more irresistible have been Karl's actions as robber chief, which correspond neither with the anarchism implicit in his opening speech nor with the violent misanthropy that is brought on by the arrival of Franz's letter later in the same scene. In the second act we see Karl in the role of avenger, proudly punishing oppressive politicians, denouncing the hypocrisy of the Catholic church, and using his booty for charitable purposes. These actions, together with the allusions to political abuses in Kosinsky's narrative (III/2) and in Franz's deeds as ruler, raise the question whether the play is essentially an attack on the political condition of Germany in Schiller's time, or whether Karl's career is in some way an affirmation *avant la lettre* of the revolutionary movements that were shortly to engulf much of Europe (although not Germany).

This view cannot easily be dismissed, especially since the corrupt minister and financial official whom Karl boasts of killing (II/3; 552) are certainly intended as references to actual figures at the Württemberg court. The abuses were real, and were intended to be recognized. They were also the kind of thing that later seemed to many to justify the violence of the French Revolution. When the National Assembly voted to honor Schiller by making him a citizen in the new republic in 1792, even though its members had certainly never read *Die Räuber*, one cannot say that they were wholly wrong to identify its author as one of their spiritual precursors. What makes the matter so difficult is the play's conclusion. Kosinsky's narrative leads Karl not to resume the struggle for justice but to rush home to see his beloved Amalia again. In the closing acts he renounces his rebellion, first as an error due to his rash temper, then as a sin against the divine order. Hans Mayer (1968) has expressed incomparably the perplexing effect of the ending, in which Karl gives himself up to the authorities for trial and punishment. What has become, we wonder, of the injustices that Karl was fighting not so long before? The play seems to back away from the issues that it has raised so forcefully. Even if Karl is acting neurotically and in bad faith, even if he commits crimes for which he must be punished, we are still perplexed at the way in which those injustices are suddenly forgotten. Moreover, we cannot say for certain whether this problem is primarily an artistic or a political one. Does it reflect Schiller's inexperience as a dramatist, or perhaps a desire to forestall the censor? Can we solve the problem by thinking about the text alone, or must it be analyzed in terms of the sociopolitical environment in which Schiller was working?

It would be foolish to try to portray all of the numerous post-1945 publications on this work as comments on this central issue, for there is always a babel of heterogeneous claims and methods struggling for attention. The question of political evaluation of the play is probably the most interesting one, however, and the one posed most consistently and urgently in the mass of printed material. The emerging pattern that is most conspicuous to me is the appearance in West Germany in the 1970s of a left-wing challenge to a predominantly existentialist consensus for which the political motifs were secondary. That challenge, which took up arguments heard earlier in East Germany, petered out in the 1980s, partly as the result of some overstatements, partly as a reflection of the general loss of orientation of the West German intellectual left, and it was answered by authoritative new studies from Peter Michelsen and Hans-Jürgen Schings. The present situation can best be described as a somewhat fragmented search for new perspectives, marked however by a welcome resurgence of empirical scholarship. In the following, I shall trace this story by commenting on some of the best contributions to the debate.

Herbert Stubenrauch, the editor of *Die Räuber* for the Nationalausgabe (1953), made one of the earliest contributions after the Second World War and also one of the best. Besides giving an account of the genesis of the play that is still regarded as conclusive, he outlines the structure of the play in a way that is unsurpassed. Although relying largely on Böckmann (1934) for his portrayal of the conflict between a mechanistic psychology and an "unconditional" conscience, he breaks new ground with his formal analysis of the play as "Doppeltragödie" [double tragedy]. He points out, for example, Schiller's missed opportunity of uniting the stories of the two brothers when he makes Franz die (V/1) without realizing that the marauders (whom he takes for devils) in fact come from Karl. Beyond this negative point, Stubenrauch characterizes the stylistic difference between the two plots with much insight. Franz's scenes are short and dramatic, in that each one contains decision and deliberate action, while Karl's scenes are slow and discursive, containing lengthy narrative passages. Karl himself is generally passive, and when he acts it is normally as an impulsive response to someone else's action. Despite its undramatic character, Stubenrauch regards Karl's story as more tragic than Franz's, which he sees more as a didactic fable or *Moritat* [ballad] illustrating a villain's just punishment.

Hans Schwerte (1960) agrees with Stubenrauch's unpolitical approach, noting that Schiller's forewords to the play are silent on sociopolitical abuses. The play is a predominantly inward one, he writes, in which words have more weight than deeds. The external events take place in an oddly abstract world (compare it, for example, with the topographical precision of *Götz von Berlichingen*) and the real events are before the inner tribunal of the conscience. (The term "innerer Tribunal" is taken from the play [V/1; 604].) However, far from presenting it as a conventional moral parable, Schwerte underlines the play's modernity; it presents a world from which, with the failure of the father, the traditional structure of authority and meaning has suddenly vanished, with the result that individuals must struggle to find their own meanings. We can see the influence of existentialism here in Schwerte's recourse to the concept of the absurd. Schwerte also attempts to answer Stubenrauch's criticism of the play's lack of unity by arguing that, true to his name, Spiegelberg functions as a distorting mirror to the two brothers, while the two are simultaneously present in Amalia's consciousness.

Schwerte's article has the same conservative bent and the same stress on the theodicy motif as the treatments of the play by Storz (1959) and von Wiese (1948, 1959) examined above. The most substantial East German response to this approach is Günther Kraft's recourse to social history (1959). He relates the play to an actual band of robbers, led by one Krummfinger-Balthasar, that was operating in Franconia during the 1750s. Schiller's interest in the literary treatment of criminal cases is attested by his later story "Der Verbrecher aus verlorener Ehre" [The Criminal out of Lost Honor, 1786], and so it is reasonable to suggest that he knew something of the Krummfinger band. (Kraft proposes that Spiegelberg is alluding to the leader's name [Krummfinger = crooked finger] when he says that anyone who can starve "with straight fingers" ["mit *geraden* Fingern"; I/2; 507] deserves to be hanged.) Finally, Kraft presents evidence as to a series of real events that may have formed the basis for Schubart's story "Aus der Geschichte des menschlichen Herzens," and speculates that Schiller may have known more of the true story than was published. In general, the historical part of Kraft's book is well researched and is of great interest, not only in relation to Schiller's play but as a contribution to a side of German social history of which most of us know little. His inference that the play is inspired less than is normally believed by literary models and more by social reality deserves to be taken seriously. But what is assumed rather than proved by Kraft, who is in this respect typical of Marxist critics, is that the existence of this band of robbers in some way entails that Schiller's play is revolutionary in content. Even if it can be shown that an oppositional ideology of some kind was prevalent in this and other criminal bands, that would still say nothing about the political implications of Schiller's play. For that, the text itself must be our primary evidence.

In 1968 Hans Mayer was provoked by a Hamburg production of *Die Räuber* to protest against sensationalism and "Aktualisierung" [bringing up to date] as a theatrical strategy. *Die Räuber* is a work that reflects its own time, not ours, and it should be approached with the mind and not the emotions. Mayer outlines the actual historical facts that are presented satisfactorily by the play, for example, family struggles in ruling houses and the adoption of materialism by aristocratic libertines. He ends by expressing with brilliant trenchancy the objections that not only Marxists but anyone committed to enlightened politics must feel in the face of the play's twin conclusions, that is, that of the "Trauerspiel" (which ends with Karl instructing his men to seek an enlightened king to serve), as well as that of the "Schauspiel" version, which Mayer aptly calls a "Passion." Since the play presents such clear grounds for a general revolt, why does Schiller insist on the merely private occasion for Karl's decision to become a robber leader? Since the lower classes are the victims of oppression, why do the robbers acclaim a nobleman as leader? Best of all, if Karl's sin consists in having put himself in the place of God's providence, what shall we say of this providence that allows the social injustice to continue? Wisely,

Mayer does not try to answer these questions beyond stating that they are symptomatic of German backwardness and the propensity of the Germans to welcome "revolution from above." He recommends his readers to reflect upon such facts historically instead of regarding them as immutable.

In a fine discussion of 1972, Fritz Martini seeks to mediate between the concerns of the East German critics and the unpolitical and "inward" approach of scholars like Beck (1955), which he rightly regards as a departure from the more robust commentary offered by the works of nineteenth-century positivism. In a comparison of *Die Räuber* with two earlier Storm and Stress plays on the theme of fraternal strife, Martini shows first that the theme itself inherently expresses and is symptomatic of social tension, and secondly that Schiller's treatment of the theme is remarkable for his inclusion of more specific social comment and sharper criticism than the two earlier works. Schiller expanded the range of the plot to the point of destroying its formal unity, but this was the price he paid for giving some substance to Karl's story. (Guelfo, the equivalent figure in Klinger's *Die Zwillinge* [The Twins, 1775], rants and raves but, thanks to the classical unity of place, is confined to his father's castle. He thus never attains any real content or context for his complaints, as Karl does.) In one way, Martini is here merely restating the kind of synthesis that we can find in von Wiese (1959): the various moral and religious *Ordnungen* presented here include a political one. On the other hand, he goes further than von Wiese when (citing an argument of E. L. Stahl, 1954) he claims that Karl's story falls into two parts, with the political dimension prevailing in acts I to III and being suppressed in favor of the inner moral dimension in IV and V; von Wiese had argued, in my view persuasively, for the story's conceptual integrity. Martini is persuasive, however, when he warns against reading too concrete and specific a political message or program into the play. Once the characters depart from the given *Ordnungen*, the only destinations available are despotism, anarchism and utopian dreams. Beyond a general hope for peace and justice, Schiller and his contemporaries lacked a vision of the new forms of government that the next century would bring.

Despite Martini's caution, however, the views of Kraft and Thalheim (1969) were taken up in the West in the *Räuberbuch* of 1974 and in an essay of 1976 by Johannes Merkel and Rüdiger Steinlein. Both publications (the first is one of a series called "Lernen: subversiv") evoke the militant climate prevailing in West German schools and universities during that decade; Steinlein and Merkel, in a postscript that is a classic of its kind, urge teachers to overcome the usual tedium of literature classes by relating this play to the conflicts that their students experience every day, both with their families and with society at large. This advice brings home to us just how much legitimate skepticism must have been aroused by *Die Räuber*, a work absorbed as few others are with paternal authority, during a period in which the young were justifiably venting their disgust with their parents' generation.

As one would expect, the authors of both publications — those of *Das Räuberbuch* shroud themselves in anonymity — are preaching to the converted. Perhaps the most general obstacle to their interpretation of this play is that Marx's analysis applies to the early industrial society that he himself witnessed in England during his lifetime. Since such a society only came about in Germany after 1870, the application of Marxist concepts — especially the postulate of a revolutionary bourgeoisie — to a German text of the 1780s, involves, both here and in similar publications, a high degree of anachronism. There was no German industrial bourgeoisie in Schiller's time, only a rather docile and dispersed class of lawyers, administrators and scholars, and so all the talk of Karl as representative of a bourgeois revolt against "feudal absolutism" is largely a fantasy. Most of the *Räuberbuch* is actually devoted not to the play itself but to unmasking the political presuppositions of the German academic tradition, although it is odd that the focus here falls on the nineteenth rather than the early twentieth century. *Geistesgeschichte* presents a much better target for ideological critique, one would think.

Merkel and Steinlein are more scholarly and they do their best to meet the salient objections to their case. Their strongest argument pertains to the status of the father in the Moor household: what we see of that household, especially the manner in which paternal authority has been internalized by both sons, is more typical of bourgeois than of the aristocratic culture of which they are nominally a part, and hence it is legitimate to see them as really bourgeois rather than noble. Nonetheless, this interpretation remains dogmatic both in its contempt for the text's religious concerns and in its assumption that Karl is engaged in a comprehensive revolt against "feudal absolutism." As with the East German scholars discussed in chapter 4, the main justification for this view seems to be Karl's use of the term "Republik" in I/2.

The most interesting of the left-wing interpretations came in 1979 from Klaus Scherpe, who conceded the naivety of the last two contributions and aimed to better them. His reading of the play is both closer to the text and also more realistic about the actual prospects for revolution in Schiller's day. Plausibly enough, he argues that the play's reputation as a revolutionary one is due more to its stage history than to the actual text. Like his predecessors, however, Scherpe takes it as certain that Schiller's basic intention was to launch an attack on the sociopolitical system, and this intention is at the heart of Scherpe's clever essay; his critical strategy is to tease out a notional "Klartext" [clear text] that Schiller really wanted to write from behind the evasions, compromises, and moral "Überkonstruktionen" [superstructures] that allegedly make up the text that we have. This leads to some interesting observations on the different types of plot-pattern that can be discerned in the various parts of *Die Räuber*, but the existence of this underlying "Klartext" remains a matter of faith rather than of proof. Scherpe's method is actually more psychoanalytical than political, with various aspects of the play being identified as fantasies and symptoms of repression. The political argument becomes rather general as a result, hinging on a clash between a bad reality and a dream of a good society. It is arguments like this that caused German political criticism in the 1980s to become enmired in theories of utopia.

At this point we should note three interesting studies on the figure of Spiegelberg which indirectly support the revolutionary interpretation of the play in that they help to elucidate its sociohistorical background. Philip Veit (1973) establishes beyond a reasonable doubt that Schiller characterized Spiegelberg as recognizably Jewish; the best evidence here is the unusual word order of his line "warum bin ich nicht geblieben in Jerusalem" (II/3; 549) [Why didn't I remain in Jerusalem]. Veit also presents material about Messianism that goes far to explain Spiegelberg's strange proposals in the withdrawn first version of act I/2. Building on Veit's article, Hans Mayer (1973) offers a thoughtful and informative study on the literary treatment of Jews in the eighteenth century against the background of their actual social condition. Where the protagonist of Lessing's *Nathan der Weise* [Nathan the Wise, 1781] epitomizes the call for the Jews to seek integration into European societies, Spiegelberg represents the alternative option, that is, the messianic hope of a return of the Jewish nation to Palestine. Otto Best's article of 1978, by contrast, goes well beyond the evidence to suggest that, behind the figure of Spiegelberg the libertine, we can detect a first version of the play — an *Urtext* comparable to Scherpe's *Klartext* — that is far more radical than the allegedly conformist work that we have. Although Best shows himself to be very knowledgeable about the libertine tradition, his article (which seems to consist mainly of questions) is marred by the wishful thinking to which left-wing critics seem so prone.

The challenge posed by these politically oriented interpretations was soon answered by Peter Michelsen (1979) and Hans-Jürgen Schings

(1980/81, 1982), both of whom, not content to restate positions of the older scholarship, took the opportunity to push the discussion in new directions. In the first of his two studies (originally published in 1964) Michelsen presents an analysis of the dramatic style which takes up the suggestion made before, notably by Walther Rehm (1941), that Schiller's early plays have a strongly Baroque quality to them. Michelsen offers a wealth of material in support of his thesis that Schiller's visits to the opera and ballet at the court of Ludwigsburg during his Karlsschule years exposed him to a rhetorical, pathetic, and antirealistic theatrical style that, contrary to the Enlightenment standards of nature and probability, was to become his dramatic norm. This explains such wildly implausible moments as Franz's successful use of the bloody sword (II/3) to convince Amalia and the Old Moor of Karl's death.

Michelsen's second study, which itself falls into two parts, seeks to define the object or theme on which Schiller lavishes such rhetorical treatment. In the first part Michelsen states a view of the play that is not all that far from von Wiese's, although he takes pains to show how many motifs can be related to preoccupations of the whole early modern period rather than exclusively to the late Enlightenment. Hence Franz's monologue (I/1) is based on Edmund's from *King Lear* (I/2), and his philosophy owes more to Hobbes and Bacon than to the French materialists. His discussion of Karl is even more harmful to the left-wing view. Throughout, Michelsen argues, Karl remains bound to the values of the old patriarchal order. The motive for his revolt is not a rejection of these values but rather society's failure to implement them; even in his apparently revolutionary phase in the second act, Karl is merely practicing justice and benevolence, which are traditional obligations of the nobility. There is no evidence, even in Karl's preemption of divine justice, that he envisages a social order of a different kind from the old one.

As persuasive as all this is, Michelsen has so far only been heading off the Marxist challenge to the traditional interpretation, as well as Staiger's subversive suggestion (1967) that, since Schiller was concerned solely with effect, his plays lack all intellectual substance. But Michelsen too finds the traditional interpretation to be inadequate, in that it presents the play as moralistic and didactic. (Although Michelsen avoids the term *Tragik*, I understand him here to be seeking a justification for thinking of the play as a tragedy.) In the last part of his study, which seems to me akin to Hegel's view of the play (see chapter 2 above), he answers his original question by stating that the object of Schiller's rhetoric is the struggle between the patriarchal order and the great and autonomous individual, portrayed consistently by Schiller as a

Satanic being whose pursuit of self-realization is necessarily destructive and dictatorial (and here Michelsen rightly includes Karl's aspiration to found a republic in I/2). Where in the first part Michelsen differentiated Karl and Franz, here he finds them both to be Satanic rebels, and their energies are released not through a revolt against paternal severity but by the Old Moor's failure to use a firm hand in raising them. The tragic dilemma, Michelsen seems to be telling us, is the impossibility of bridging the gulf between individual autonomy and social order.

Schings, who is as keen as Michelsen to refute Staiger and the Marxists, adopts the strategy of investigating Schiller's intellectual interests at the time he wrote the play, and he tells us a great deal about some of the obscurer philosophical byways of the German Enlightenment. Schings distinguishes between the respectable philosophy of the age, which besides that of Leibniz and Wolff included Schiller's favorite Adam Ferguson, and the hermetic tradition that still clung on in such places as rural Württemberg. By some fine detective work, Schings makes it plausible that the young Schiller's philosophy of love, expressed most completely in the early "Theosophie des Julius" (Theosophy of Julius, published 1786 as part of the *Philosophische Briefe* [Philosophical Letters]), was influenced by Jakob Hermann Obereit, a hermetic medical writer. Schings expounds this philosophy and argues that it provides us with the key to *Die Räuber*, which should be seen as an experiment devised to show the consequences of suspending the laws of love that hold the cosmos and the social order together.

Although Schings has made a substantial contribution to intellectual history here, and although his stress on metaphysics counteracts the distortions of the Marxist approach, his argument has the effect of reducing *Die Räuber* to an illustration of Schiller's theories, and this seems to me to do justice neither to the difference in genre between the two works nor to the play's extraordinary power. Lesley Sharpe (1990) has expressed some doubts about seeing too close a relationship between the two works. As she says, the idea of harmony underlies the cosmic vision of the "Theosophie des Julius," but *Die Räuber* presents a desolate universe, more a negative counterpart than an illustration. As an alternative model she suggests the Neoplatonic dialectic of exile and return. (This was placed at the heart of Romanticism by M. H. Abrams in his *Natural Supernaturalism* [1971], a book that has never been adequately recognized in Germany.)

One can think of further reservations about Schings's thesis. Can we really speak of the play as an *experiment*, when the action so clearly unfolds under the signs of fate, nemesis and judgment (concepts of which the "Theosophie des Julius" makes no mention)? To say that

Karl's surrender in act V is connected to the statements about sacrifice in the "Theosophie" may be true, but it will hardly allay the objections of left-wing critics to this act of surrender. Most important, there is a clear incommensurability of stature between Schiller's self-indulgent early speculations and the mighty drama that has gripped readers and audiences ever since its first appearance. It runs counter to our intuition to suggest that a great tragedy could be the outgrowth of such a light-weight philosophical text. Michelsen is surely on firmer ground when, resisting a didactic interpretation, he takes the tragic effect for granted and seeks to explain it.

Although a good deal has been published about *Die Räuber* since the studies of Michelsen and Schings, little new ground has been broken. The authors usually seem to be playing variations on themes that have already been stated more forcefully by others. Dieter Borchmeyer (1987), for example, remains within the line of scholars concerned with the role of the patriarchal order (*Vaterordnung*, *Vaterwelt*) as core of society, but makes the theme more topical by relating it the topics of Enlightenment and *Mündigkeit* [legal maturity], which were often the focus of discussion in left-liberal circles during this decade of political defeat. Perhaps reflecting the disillusioned spirit of the time, Borchmeyer sees Schiller as the "Aufklärer mit einem gebrochenen Flügel" (174) [enlightener with a broken wing], hopeful of progress toward a society that is not reliant on patriarchal authority but cripplingly conscious of the dialectic of enlightenment that turns all such hopes to dust.

All discussions of the *Vaterordnung* show themselves aware that Schiller had originally intended to call the play "Der verlorene Sohn" [The Prodigal Son], and the significance of the biblical parable, to which the characters more than once allude explicitly, has been often reflected upon. (The standard early study is by Elisabeth Blochmann, 1951.) Klaus Weimar (1988) offers an engaging postmodern variation on this theme when he comments on the profusion of textual allusions in *Die Räuber* and suggests that Karl Moor's fate can be seen as a series of attempts to escape from the pre-text of the parable and to seek self-determination by detextualizing his life altogether. His view has been criticized by Richard Matthias Müller (1989), who argues that Karl does not willingly give up the role of prodigal in act I, but is in fact determined to play it until he receives the forged letter. The point is well taken, but it is unclear whether Weimar would regard the objection as conclusive. (Müller's own interpretation of the play is rather weak, however, consisting seemingly in an attempt to read Schiller's play as if it had been written by Hölderlin.) Weimar can be criticized also for missing several of the other texts to which the play contains allusions. He notes the biblical stories of Esau and Jacob and of Jacob and Joseph (see Koopmann 1976), but he passes over the allusions to the Passion of Christ in acts IV and V, as well as to Shakespeare's *Timon of Athens* in I/2 (see Cersowsky 1990). The tremendous intertextual density of Schiller's play, the extent to which it is a collage of previous literary texts, is a aspect about which more can and no doubt will be said.

Wolfgang Riedel's article on Franz Moor (1993) shows that detective work can still be fruitfully pursued into the less familiar corners of the intellectual history of the period. Starting with a characterization of Franz's philosophy as an assault on the "Theosophie des Julius" (a view that does not go substantially beyond Schings), Riedel continues by questioning the often heard criticism that Franz's psychological collapse in acts IV and V is inadequately motivated. By recourse to the writings of Johann Georg Sulzer, which he shows were known at the Karlsschule, Riedel claims that Schiller is operating here with a theory of mind as divided between conscious and unconscious elements, with the latter exercising more power than reason; Franz's knowledge of the vacuity of Christian theology and morality is thus overcome by the remembered prejudices of childhood. As Riedel says, such a theory of mind signifies a repudiation of the monistic concept propagated by Wolffian rationalism, the official school philosophy for most of the century. His most striking discovery concerns Franz's statement (IV/2) that the source of religion is the fairy tales told to children by their nurses; this has a precise parallel in a medical dissertation by Schiller's friend Wilhelm von Hoven.

Riedel concludes that Schiller is working here with a well developed theory of the unconscious, and hence that Franz's collapse is not at all poorly motivated. But Riedel seems not to realize that his argument has further and more subversive implications, namely, that it vindicates Franz's whole philosophy. Franz is overcome in this view, not by conscience or fear of coming judgment, but rather by the childhood prejudices, *the sources and operations of which have been correctly identified by Franz himself* and which were merely too strong for him to resist. If that is right, then the entire theological plot of the play is reduced to absurdity, for, if Franz's suicide is based on illusions, then so must the whole of Karl's career also. It is an appealing thought that the action of the play might be accessible not only to theological interpretation (that is, from Karl's point of view) but also to interpretation in terms of the nihilistic psychology espoused by Franz. The divided plot, of which Stubenrauch wrote, would then be paralleled by a duality of underlying philosophies, and the play's turbulence could be attributed to a profound conflict of beliefs in Schiller himself, with each brother standing simultaneously as spokesman and as guinea pig for a philosophy. No wonder Schiller did not want to bring the brothers on to the stage at the same time!

Richard Brittnacher's fine essay for the new *Schiller-Handbuch* (1998) is emphatic in its rejection of the political interpretation (although he takes up Scherpe's idea of a flawed moralistic superstructure in act V). Karl's opening tirades are too much the frustrated outpourings of a spoilt young nobleman, the robbers are too strongly motivated by hatred and destructiveness, for them to carry any conviction as rebels against social injustice or as agents of improvement. Brittnacher relies on Michelsen and Schings, but goes beyond them at two points. First, in addition to the play's borrowings from Shakespeare, Baroque and Storm and Stress, he draws attention to the appearance of motifs drawn from Greek tragedy, notably that of sacrifice, as well as the fusion of the robbers into a chorus in the last act and the occurrence of ritual gestures such as the tearing of garments. Our understanding of Schillerian drama could be enriched, I feel, if research into Schiller's intellectual environment (practiced with such distinction by Schings and Riedel) could be complemented by a deeper grasp of the tragic genre in its various historical manifestations, especially ancient tragedy. Brittnacher points the way here. (I shall mention here my own essay of 1994, in which I point out that, in aiming to punish parricide only to commit it himself, Karl Moor is following in the path of Oedipus.)

Brittnacher's second contribution is his attention to the frequency of the Satanic and Luciferian motifs in the play, and he explores the different types of devil available in the tradition and their applicability to different characters. His treatment of Spiegelberg as a crude medieval devil and as mirror to Karl and Franz is very helpful. (This mirroring function, as well as the verbal echoes between Karl and Franz, to which Brittnacher draws attention, goes some way to overcome the problem of the play's duality.) But Brittnacher leaves readers to draw their own conclusions as to the sheer strangeness of a play that can simultaneously evoke the cultic aspects of ancient tragedy while also enlisting Christian theology.

Although the political interpretations of the 1970s seem to have been refuted, this does not mean that from now on all will be bland consensus. The end of the German Democratic Republic means that the old Marxist argument is unlikely to return, but the kind of analysis developed by the Foucault-inspired cultural studies movement in the English-speaking world has been recently applied to *Die Räuber* by

Richard T. Gray (1995). Gray proceeds from Foucault's argument in *Les mots et les choses* as to a succession of semiotic paradigms in Western culture, and also from Seidlin's 1960 article on the "treacherous signs" in these plays. By means of a somewhat questionable recourse to Schiller's later theory of the naive and the sentimental, Gray posits that Franz stands for a new capitalistic semiotic of abstraction and mediation whereas his older brother stands for the naive directness of an earlier age. Karl's surrender is a surrender to the capitalistic norms that are henceforth to prevail, but his surrender is in fact ironic. Within, he aims to preserve his naive semiotic, even as he outwardly conforms to the new, thus helping to bring about the "divided subject" alluded to in the title of Gray's book. (The fact that Karl is shortly to die apparently makes no difference.) Gray's argument seems to me to involve a good deal of distortion and overinterpretation, but its central flaw is surely the almost comical implausibility of the claim that the play's wildly flamboyant plot serves to mask something as dull as a conflict between two semiotic systems. As with Hinrichs in the last century and Ilse Graham in our own, this is to subordinate Schiller's work to the critic's own abstruse intellectual hobbyhorse. Gray's book has not yet drawn a response from scholars in Germany, but a sustained challenge from this direction would lead to a beneficial debate between two scholarly cultures that appear to be growing apart. Whatever happens, we can be sure that *Die Räuber*, by virtue of its intellectual depth and its aesthetic power, will never cease to provoke the most gifted scholars of each generation to engage in debate over its meaning.

Works Cited

Abrams, M. H. 1971. *Natural Supernaturalism: Tradition and Revolution in Romantic Literature*. New York: Norton.

Anon. 1974. *Das Räuberbuch: Die Rolle der Literaturwissenschaft in der Ideologie des deutschen Bürgertums am Beispiel von Schillers "Die Räuber."* Frankfurt a. M.: Roter Stern.

Best, Otto F. 1978. "Gerechtigkeit für Spiegelberg." *JDSG* 22: 277–302.

Blochmann, Elisabeth. 1951. "Das Motiv vom verlorenen Sohn in Schillers Räuberdrama." *DVjs* 25: 474–84.

Borchmeyer, Dieter. 1987. "Die Tragödie vom verlorenen Vater: Der Dramatiker Schiller und die Aufklärung — Das Beispiel der *Räuber*." In *Friedrich Schiller: Angebot und Diskurs*, ed. Helmut Brandt. Weimar/Berlin (East): Aufbau, 160–84.

Brittnacher, Hans Richard. 1998. "*Die Räuber*." In *Schiller-Handbuch*, ed. H. Koopmann. Stuttgart: Kröner, 326–53.

Cersowsky, Peter. 1990. "Schillers *Räuber* und Shakespeares *Timon von Athen*." *Arcadia* 25: 127–36.

Gray, Richard T. 1995. "Righting Writing: Semiotic Conflict, Hermeneutical Disjunction, and the Subl(im)ation of Revolt in Schiller's *Die Räuber*." In his *Stations of the Divided Subject: Contestation and Ideological Legitimation in German Bourgeois Literature, 1770–1914*. Stanford: Stanford UP, 102-45.

Koopmann, Helmut. 1976. "Joseph und sein Vater. Zu den biblischen Anspielungen in Schillers *Räubern*." In *Herkommen und Erneuerung: Essays für Oskar Seidlin*, ed. Gerald Gillespie and Edgar Lohner. Tübingen: Niemeyer, 150–67.

Kraft, Günther. 1959. *Historische Studien zu Schillers Schauspiel "Die Räuber": Über eine mitteldeutsch-fränkische Räuberbande des 18. Jahrhunderts*. Weimar: Arion.

Martini, Fritz. 1972. "Die feindlichen Brüder: Zum Problem des gesellschaftskritischen Dramas von J. A. Leisewitz, F. M. Klinger und F. Schiller." *JDSG* 16: 208–65.

Mayer, Hans. 1968. "Schillers *Räuber* 1968." *Theater heute* 9, H. 10: 1–6.

———. 1973. "Der weise Nathan und der Räuber Spiegelberg: Antinomien der jüdischen Emanzipation in Deutschland." *JDSG* 17: 253–72.

Merkel, Johannes and Rüdiger Steinlein. 1976. "Schillers *Die Räuber*: Modell-versuch bürgerlich-revolutionärer Umgestaltung des feudal-absolu-tistischen Deutschland." In *Der alte Kanon neu: Zur Revision des literari-schen Kanons in Wissenschaft und Unterricht*, ed. Walter Raitz and Erhard Schütz. Wiesbaden: Westdeutscher Verlag.

Michelsen, Peter. 1964. "Studien zu Schillers *Räubern*: Teil 1." *JDSG* 8: 57–111.

———. 1979. *Der Bruch mit der Vaterwelt: Studien zu Schillers "Räubern."* (*Beihefte zum Euphorion* 16.) Heidelberg: Winter.

Müller, Richard Matthias. 1989. "Nachstrahl der Gottheit: Karl Moor." *DVjs* 63: 628–44.

Pugh, David. 1994. "Tragedy and Providence: *Die Räuber* and the End of the Enlightenment." In *Hinter dem schwarzen Vorhang: Die Katastrophe und die epische Tradition. Festschrift für Anthony W. Riley*, ed. Friedrich Gaede, Patrick O'Neill and Ulrich Scheck. Tübingen: Francke, 63–74.

Riedel, Wolfgang. 1993. "Die Aufklärung und das Unbewußte: Die Inversio-nen des Franz Moor." *JDSG* 37: 198–220.

Scherpe, Klaus. 1979. "*Die Räuber.*" *Schillers Dramen: Neue Interpreta-tionen*, ed. Walter Hinderer. 2nd ed. Stuttgart: Reclam, 1983. 9–36.

Schings, Hans-Jürgen. 1980/81. "Philosophie der Liebe und Tragödie des Universalhasses: *Die Räuber* im Kontext von Schillers Jugendphiloso-phie I." *Jahrbuch des Wiener Goethe-Vereins* 84/85: 71–95.

———. 1982. "Schillers *Räuber*: Ein Experiment des Universalhasses." In *Fried-rich Schiller: Kunst, Humanität und Politik in der späten Aufklärung*, ed. Wolfgang Wittkowski. Tübingen: Niemeyer, 1–21.

Schwerte, Hans. 1960. "Schillers *Räuber.*" *DU* 12, H.2: 18–41. Repr. in *Deut-sche Dramen von Gryphius bis Brecht: Interpretationen*, ed. Jost Schillemeit. Frankfurt: a. M. Fischer, 1965, 147–71.

Sharpe, Lesley. 1990. "Die Reisen des Verlorenen Sohnes: Eine These zu Schillers *Räubern.*" *ZfdPh* 109, Sonderheft: 3–15.

Stubenrauch, Herbert. 1953. "Einführung." In *Die Räuber*. Vol. 3 of *Schillers Werke*. Nationalausgabe. Weimar: Böhlau, vii–xxxi.

Veit, Philip F. 1973. "Moritz Spiegelberg: Eine Charakterstudie zu Schillers *Räubern.*" *JDSG* 17: 273–90.

Weimar, Klaus. 1988. "Vom Leben in Texten: Zu Schillers *Räubern.*" *Merkur* 42: 461–71.

6: *Fiesco*:
The "Republican Tragedy"

*F*IESCO HAS ALWAYS BEEN REGARDED AS INFERIOR to the works that precede and follow it, and in view of the strange story of its changing endings, this is probably inevitable. (The book edition ends with Fiesco's assassination as he attempts to claim the title of Duke, the Mannheim stage version ends with him renouncing his ambition.) Debate has revolved most often around Schiller's description of the work on the title page of the printed edition (1783) as "Ein republikanisches Trauerspiel" [A Republican Tragedy], a genre that he appears to have inaugurated himself (although the name harks back to some earlier works, notably Johann Christoph Gottsched's *Sterbender Cato* [The Death of Cato, 1732]. In one sense the description is obvious, for the play concerns a failed restoration of republican government in a Renaissance city-state under ducal rule. But in another sense it is problematic, for not only is the protagonist's allegiance to the republican idea (at least in the printed version) merely opportunistic, the portrayal of Verrina, who is the champion of the republican idea, is so peculiar that Schiller's attitude to him must be said to be uncertain. In addition, the regime that the plotters are hoping to overthrow is a divided one. True, there is an archetypal tyrant in the person of Gianettino, but his uncle, the Doge Andreas Doria, appears (if we leave aside his indulgence to his nephew) to be a just and a wise ruler. When the play ends, after the deaths of both Gianettino and Fiesco, with Verrina's notorious line "Ich geh zum Andreas" (V/17; I: 751) [I am going to Andreas], we do not know whether to take this as tragic, pusillanimous, absurd, or merely sensible.

Although it has not attracted as many discussions as the other two prose plays, *Fiesco* clearly offers great scope to the interpreter, and there are a number of astute and learned contributions that should be considered. The play is discussed in an influential article on the nemesis motif by Clemens Heselhaus (1952). Nemesis is certainly an important topic, although it is not named explicitly as it is in *Die Räuber* (IV/5: 588); Verrina uses instead the Christian term "Weltgericht" (V/16: 750) [day of judgment]. But Heselhaus proposes the somewhat dubious argument that, in *Fiesco*, nemesis occurs as a supernatural and malign ("tückisch") force, similar to the one that appears in ancient tragedy, and he then contrasts it with a later "naturalized" concept of nemesis, which Schiller allegedly learned from Herder and went on to apply in his later plays. Heselhaus is thus using *Fiesco* as a foil in order to show up Schiller's greater achievement later on, a strategy that is hardly calculated to do justice to the earlier play, and he is besides committed to the argument that Schiller's development is toward an ever strengthening belief in a harmonious law of nature. This seems to me a distortion of Schiller's intellectual biography.

The first major article of the postwar period devoted to this play alone is by Kurt Wölfel (1957), who shows the strong influence of Paul Böckmann's 1934 study of "inner form." Wölfel discovers a disunity in the play caused by the inner division in the author which I have called the moral-immoral dilemma: on the one hand Schiller, in line with his "Titanism" or passion for "greatness," identifies himself with his amoral hero, and, on the other, he retains his commitment to a moral world-order. From this psychological premise, Wölfel tries to find formal elements in the play that correspond to these contrary attitudes, with the moral purpose tied to the onward movement of the plot and the identification tied to the static, even statuesque, moments of self-glorification by the hero. This neat antithesis is complicated somewhat when Wölfel concedes that the conspiracy has its own amorality and that Verrina has a fanatical side to him, and his argument never quite regains its balance. One could add that Fiesco's superiority is expressed not only in static moments but also in his effortless control of the logistics of the conspiracy. Wölfel's essay is nonetheless a notable attempt to identify the underlying forces shaping this strange work.

Publications on this play became more frequent in the 1970s. As we have seen, the application of existentialist ideas to Schiller is nothing new, but Walter Hinderer (1970), inspired perhaps by Käte Hamburger's much discussed comparison of Schiller to Sartre (1959), attempts it once again, although relying more on Heidegger than on Sartre or Kierkegaard; his starting point is Fiesco's line "Ein Augenblick Fürst hat das Mark des ganzen Daseins verschlungen" (III/2; 698) [A moment as prince has consumed the marrow of all existence], which lends itself to analysis in terms of Heidegger's concept of authenticity (*Eigentlichkeit*) and the theory of time to which it gives rise. Hinderer's essay is notable for its detailed discussion of previous contributions, and he engages in close debate with Böckmann's theory of *Pathos*. As I noted above, Böckmann appears to stretch this concept well beyond its proper sphere, that is, the rhetorical expression of emotion, and so the introduction of a distinct body of theory concerning existential states seems an interesting alternative. The emphasis thus falls on not on the success or justifiability of the protagonist's political ambitions but rather on his *Existenzproblematik,* specifically in his tendency to be swallowed up by the various roles that he plays, and attention is paid to the metaphors of masks, play, comedy, etc. (One is reminded here of Sartre's play of 1954 about the famous English actor Edmund Kean.) In his conclusion, however, Hinderer concedes that the existential *Problematik* is subordinate to the religious one, an admission that seems to leave his study as little more than a *jeu d'esprit,* full of interesting comments on various parts of the text, but not compelling in the last resort. Perhaps its most significant aspect is Hinderer's manifest skepticism, despite the political agitation of the age, as to the feasibility of a coherent political interpretation of the play.

Without any reference to Heidegger or existentialism, Frank Fowler (1970) interprets the play in quite a similar manner to Hinderer. Starting with the aim of defending the political coherence of the 1783 version of the play, Fowler introduces the Aristotelian concept of the tragic flaw (*hamartia*) to argue that this version fits the established theory of tragedy. But rather than some conventional vice like stubbornness or ambition, Fiesco's flaw is a theatrical temperament that leads him to seek the most glorious role for himself and to assume wrongly that other people will fall into the roles that he has devised for them. (This view seems to be compatible with Hinderer's focus on the concept of authenticity.) Fowler's interpretation ends in a rather different register from where it begins, for, instead of legitimating the drama in conventional terms, he shifts to the problem of Schiller's possible self-identification with his protagonist, so that, whereas Fiesco is a political man whose flaw is that he views his actions under the aspect of theater, his creator is a man of the theater who takes his creation as a political deed. With such a confusion of author and hero, it is hard to see how a play can subsist as a free-standing Aristotelian structure.

Two articles by Reginald Phelps (1974) and Paul Michael Lützeler (1978) try to restore the discussion to the sphere of political theory. Phelps's argument is mainly negative: as political terms like "republic" are used in the play without any conceptual precision, it thus makes more sense, despite Schiller's subtitle, to see the play's subject as freedom in general. Lützeler does not give up so easily, and argues that the play is indeed a political *Lehrstück* [pedagogical play]. He provides a learned commentary on the cult of Plutarch in Schiller's time and on the various types of political agent (Brutus, Caesar, Catiline) that arise from Plutarch's writings. He points out that for Rousseau (whom Schiller read in 1781–82) a republic is any state governed by laws, and so there is nothing absurd or inconsistent about Verrina putting himself at the elder Doria's service once the nephew is dead. Lützeler's comparison of Schiller's painter Romano to Jacques Louis David is also pleasing (although, since David's *Oath of the Horatii* was not painted until 1784, a direct influence is hardly possible). The problem with his interpretation is that it cannot explain why Schiller chose to make Fiesco and not Verrina the hero. Lützeler thus seems to be expounding a text that he wishes Schiller had written, not the one that he in fact wrote.

Rolf-Peter Janz (1979) attempts a more differentiated discussion of the political implications, turning for support to the historian Reinhart Koselleck, whose *Kritik und Krise* [Critique and Crisis, 1959] contains a powerful analysis of the political consciousness of the German middle class. For Janz, the key to the play is the antithesis between the morality of private life and the amorality of public life; as Koselleck argues, absolutist rulers insisted that this gulf was unbridgeable, a belief to which the bourgeoisie responded with the demand that the sphere of power be subordinated to the moral standards underlying private life. Janz portrays Schiller's play as an experimental attempt at such a subordination in the medium of drama (and we might thus compare his interpretation to Schings's "experimental" reading of *Die Räuber* [1982]), but in my view he does not quite justify this approach, in that his discussion is unfocused and leads to no clear result. For Janz, the character who best represents the subordination of politics to morality seems to be Verrina, whom he judges negatively, both for his treatment of his daughter and because his final response to the political crisis is inadequate: true to his bourgeois respect for legality, instead of pressing ahead with the installation of a republic, Verrina permits the restoration of the feudal ruler. Does this mean that Fiesco's amorality and contempt for law are to be endorsed? Janz does not quite say this openly, although, as in Scherpe's discussion of *Die Räuber* (which appeared in the same collection), he hints (46) at a political subtext that would enable Fiesco to appear as the true champion of the bourgeoisie. It is here that Janz, and the literature on *Fiesco* in general, come closest to expressing the Marxist-Leninist view that the revolutionary should dispense with all moral scruples. Even the East German scholar Wolfgang Hecht brands as reactionary (1982; 57) the theory that political morality is different from that of everyday life. (One wonders whether Lenin would have agreed with him.) Although Janz ultimately backs away from explicitly endorsing immoral means in the service of a political goal, his article ends with a general condemnation of the play on the grounds that its mixture of public and private themes is doomed to fail. This again seems to reflect the troubling view that those who engage in political activity should leave their moral principles at home. One can only feel grateful that Germany is not being governed (again) by people who agree with Janz on this matter.

The most successful analyses of *Fiesco* in recent years are those by Albert Meier (1987) and Peter Michelsen (1990). Meier wishes to preserve the notion that the play was intended to convey a positive political message to its audience, and he concedes that the plot, when subjected to rational analysis, lends no support to such a view. (In particular he rejects Lützeler's positive view of Verrina.) Meier's strategy is to shift from rational to emotional analysis, for which he finds legitimation in Schiller's aesthetic writings of the time, notably in the "Erinnerung an das Publikum" (Message to the Audience, 1784) written for a performance of this play (in its stage version) in Mannheim. For Meier, the text has the character of an appeal, and it is structured as an "Aggregat von kalkulierten Impulsen" (132) [aggregation of calculated impulses], calculated, that is, to arouse the audience to a condition that is conducive to moral and political behavior in the pursuance of republicanism. Vital steps in the argument are, first, that Schiller adhered to the moral sense theory, with the implication that the arousal of emotion automatically meant the arousal of *moral* emotion; and second, that Schiller believed republicanism to be merely the putting into practice of the moral precepts associated with the *Empfindsamkeit* [sentimentality] movement. Meier makes his case with a good deal of learning and subtlety, and he has interesting things to say about Schiller's position relative to the Baroque drama of admiration and the Enlightenment drama of sympathy. His basic premise, however, that rational coherence and emotional effectiveness are alternative rather than complementary means for a drama to succeed, seems to me rather debatable. Can a play really generate high emotion in the audience if its story does not make sense, or if its characters are not psychologically consistent?

Peter Michelsen's discussion — an exceptionally subtle one that, like his interpretation of *Die Räuber*, seems influenced by Hegel — highlights the play's modernity. Michelsen thus rejects the approach based on the ancient concept of nemesis (which has led to an energetic debate on *Wallenstein*). Like *Die Räuber*, *Fiesco* deals with the conflict between a modern autonomy-seeking consciousness and the traditional *Ordnungen* that have ceased to have meaning for it. As before, Michelsen is waging war on two fronts. Against the left-wing critics, he denies that Fiesco has any political aims that deserve serious consideration; he reminds us that, in Fiesco's animal fable (II/8), the democratic constitution is treated with contempt, and he argues plausibly that Fiesco's renunciation of the purple at the end of the Mannheim stage version is merely another expression of his will to personal greatness. Against Staiger (who, as we recall, argues that Schiller writes for effect alone), Michelsen argues that this desire for greatness should be seen not merely as expressing the author's own lust for power over the audience, but as representing the breakthrough of a modern awareness whose problematic nature is encapsulated in the term "sublime criminal." We thus might summarize his approach as an attempt to make Staiger's reading of the early Schiller less destructive by reinterpreting it in a Hegelian light.

Of the modern awareness that Fiesco represents Michelsen has three things to say: first, it has a *schwärmerisch* [enthusiastic] quality, unthinkable in a true Machiavellian, in that he insists on enjoying things in advance of their achievement; second, Fiesco sees and speaks of himself as an artist (hence the identification of author and hero); last, his desire to determine every element of the plot himself leaves him vulnerable to the operation of chance ("Zufall"). Here we might ask whether Michelsen is right to reject the concept of nemesis so firmly. After all, chance does not operate at random in the play, but punishes Fiesco with the death of his wife. Perhaps Fiesco's desire for control, which is the misapplication of the artist's forming impulse to real life, is a (or even *the*) modern form of hubris, which is punished by events in a manner consistent with the concept of nemesis. As sometimes happens, I feel here that the ancient/modern antithesis is based on an inaccurate conception of the ancient.

As in chapter 5, I shall conclude with a glance at a recent North American contribution. True to the Foucauldian spirit of cultural studies, Dorothea von Mücke (1987) focuses not on the substantive issues of politics but on the politics of representation and role play. With Fiesco's artistic self-understanding and his theatrical language, the play certainly contains plenty of fuel for such an interpretation, and the reconciliation of the political and private plots, to which von Mücke's method seems to promise a path, is a long-standing desideratum. Does she succeed? Although it would be nice to welcome the insights arising from an innovative methodology, I must admit that, as with Gray's interpretation of *Die Räuber*, I find this approach unilluminating, both in its placing of medium over message and in its generally obscure style of argumentation. As with so many earlier discussions, this is essentially an attempt to read the play as if it were the demonstration of a thesis devised by a later theorist, or as the answer to somebody else's question. Such a methodology leads inevitably to distortion. On the evidence of von Mücke's article, it seems unlikely that the new style of Anglo-

American scholarship will be able significantly to reorient the debate over this play.

Works Cited

Fowler, Frank M. 1970. "Schiller's *Fiesko* Re-examined." *PEGS*, N.S. 40: 1–29.

Hamburger, Käte. 1959. "Schiller und Sartre: Ein Versuch zum Idealismus-Problem Schillers." *JDSG* 3: 34–70.

Hecht, Wolfgang. 1982. "Aufstieg und Fall des Grafen von Lavagna: *Die Verschwörung des Fiesko zu Genua*." In *Schiller: Das dramatische Werk in Einzelinterpretationen*, ed. Hans-Dietrich Dahnke and Bernd Leistner. Leipzig: Reclam, 42–63.

Heselhaus, Clemens. 1952. "Die Nemesis-Tragödie: *Fiesco — Wallenstein — Demetrius*." *DU* 4, H. 5: 40–59.

Hinderer, Walter. 1970. "'Ein Augenblick Fürst hat das Mark des ganzen Daseins verschlungen': Zum Problem der Person und Existenz in Schillers *Fiesco*." *JDSG* 14: 230–74.

Janz, Rolf-Peter. 1979. "*Die Verschwörung des Fiesco zu Genua*." In *Schillers Dramen: Neue Interpretationen*, ed. Walter Hinderer. 2nd ed. Stuttgart: Reclam, 1983, 37–57.

Koselleck, Reinhart. 1959. *Kritik und Krise: Ein Beitrag zur Pathogenese der bürgerlichen Welt*. Freiburg: Alber.

Lützeler, Paul Michael. 1978. "'Die große Linie zu einem Brutuskopf': Republikanismus und Cäsarismus in Schillers *Fiesko*." *Monatshefte* 70: 15–28.

Meier, Albert. 1987. "Des Zuschauers Seele am Zügel: Die ästhetische Vermittlung des Republikanismus in Schillers *Die Verschwörung des Fiesko zu Genua*." *JDSG* 31: 117–36.

Michelsen, Peter. 1990. "Schillers Fiesko: Freiheitsheld und Tyrann." In *Schiller und die höfische Welt*, ed. Achim Aurnhammer et al. Tübingen: Niemeyer, 341–58.

Mücke, Dorothea von. 1987. "Play, Power and Politics in Schiller's *Die Verschwörung des Fiesko zu Genua*." *Michigan German Studies* 13: 1–18.

Phelps, Reginald H. 1974. "Schiller's *Fiesco*: A Republican Tragedy?" *PMLA* 89: 442–53.

Wölfel, Kurt. 1957. "Pathos und Problem: Ein Beitrag zur Stilanalyse von Schillers *Fiesko*." *GRM*, N.F. 7: 224–44.

7: *Kabale und Liebe*:
The Domestic Tragedy

IN SOME WAYS THE POST-1945 RECEPTION of *Kabale und Liebe* parallels that of *Die Räuber* as outlined in chapter 5 above, going from a period of rather introverted existentialism, through one of political challenge, to a subsequent and still current period of reorientation and search for new perspectives. But von Wiese's statement (1959, 193) that this is the most controversial of all Schiller's plays, a view endorsed by Koopmann (1982, 75), is probably justified. The interplay of social and private themes is exceptionally hard to unravel, and the visionary religious language in which both lovers experience and express their love adds to the difficulties of assessment. Is the reader/spectator supposed to take the truth of Christian doctrine for granted, and if so, in which version? Conversely, if this is basically a play about people in a finite world (and there is after all no *deus ex machina*), how far can we go in trying to discern "real" motivations behind the religious ones? Some critics (Janz 1976, Huyssen 1980) have taken to psychoanalyzing Luise, and have discerned repressed sexual desires behind her religious utterances. As for the political motifs, the situation is similar to that concerning *Die Räuber*; on the one hand the play alludes to actual scandals such as the German princes' sale of soldiers in order to finance their lavish lifestyles, on the other the plot seems to get sidetracked into private areas of experience, and the play ends with a reconciliation, despite all his crimes, between President von Walter and his rebellious son Ferdinand.

At the most basic level, it has been a matter of controversy whether Luise or Ferdinand is the real protagonist, and the assessment of each of them is deeply problematic. With Ferdinand, it is impossible to say for certain whether Schiller regarded him as hero, victim or villain: on the one hand, he shows admirable courage in standing up to his father, who is unquestionably a tyrant and a scoundrel; on the other, the way in which Ferdinand falls for a transparent intrigue raises strong questions about the nature of his love for Luise; finally, he succumbs to the most alarming religious delusions when he resolves to punish her. Similar issues bedevil the interpretation of Luise: are we supposed to commend her for her courage and realism in renouncing Ferdinand or, with Korff (1923, 211), deplore her lack of religious and social freedom? Even the figure of Luise's father is not free from controversy. After his plucky demeanor toward the President in act II, which disposes us in his favor, he is easily manipulated by Ferdinand's gold in act V, hence opening the path to murder. His pressuring of his daughter earlier in the same act has seemed problematic to many, although one can mitigate his moral blackmail of Luise (for that is what it is) in that he is seeking, first, to dissuade her from committing suicide, and later, to end a relationship that he believes can only end in disaster for her.

Genre is a frequently discussed aspect of the play, which Schiller's subtitle identifies as a domestic tragedy. The work thus grows out of a well established eighteenth-century tradition, which remains the subject of vigorous research and debate among German scholars. Research on Lessing, who as author of *Miss Sara Sampson* (1755) and *Emilia Galotti* (1772) is the real founder of the genre in Germany, has been particularly lively. This is not the place to summarize that debate, however, and I merely refer the reader here to the latest edition of Karl Guthke's authoritative survey of it in the Sammlung Metzler series (1994). Another aspect is the ongoing debate over the Storm and Stress movement, which used to be regarded as an irrationalistic (and laudable) reaction to the Enlightenment, but is now more commonly regarded as a continuation of the latter by a younger generation, with its slightly different priorities. A symptom of uncertainty about the allocation of the play to a literary period is the fact that it is discussed in each of the two volumes of the Winkler series "Kommentar zu einer Epoche" dealing with the drama of the Enlightenment and the Storm and Stress (Koopmann 1979, Huyssen 1980).

A further particularity of the reception of *Kabale und Liebe* concerns its aesthetic standard. In 1980, Andreas Huyssen wrote that the play was generally accepted as the highpoint of Schiller's early work (206). Gerhard Fricke (1930, 15), however, had regarded the play as the weakest of Schiller's early works from the point of view of *Tragik*, and soon after the Second World War the play's quality was once again impugned in *Mimesis* (1946), Erich Auerbach's classic survey of the portrayal of reality in western literature. Schiller's domestic tragedy had earned its inclusion in Auerbach's work by the realism of its representation of the Miller family in its opening scenes, which Auerbach rightly praises for their precision and vigor. However, he judges that the play fails to live up to its promising start; not only is it packed with melodramatic exaggerations and manipulations, the contingent idiosyncrasies of the characters and the extremism of its depiction of the social circumstances also prevent us from accepting it as a typical representation of its time.

How fair are these strictures? Auerbach seems to me to err when he accuses Schiller of having an unclear conception of Luise, allowing her to present the appearance of a self-sacrificing heroine when the facts of the story show her to be guilty of "narrowness and pusillanimity" (443). Although many scholars have sided with Auerbach on the score of pusillanimity, it is not at all clear that Schiller would have agreed with them. Auerbach prejudges this intractable question when he comes down so firmly against Luise. In a wider sense, however, his criticism seems fair and apposite. Although Germanists may not like to hear one of their canon of great works being referred to as "a fairly bad play" (441), Auerbach actually supports his judgment rather well, arguing that Schiller has not succeeded in achieving a convincing synthesis between sentimental love, on which he wished to confer the highest tragic dignity, and the realistic portrayal of milieu in the recent manner of the Storm and Stress.

This remains a powerful analysis, but all too often Germanists have casually brushed it aside. I cannot help suspecting that a kind of guild mentality, which prevents scholars from taking seriously views expressed by members of other disciplines (Auerbach was a scholar of comparative literature), must bear some of the blame for this. But Auerbach also referred prominently to H. A. Korff, whose sociopolitical view of the play (see chapter 3 above) was in disfavor among western critics at this time. (Not among East German scholars of course; see Joachim Müller, 1955.) A more influential early discussion was E. M. Wilkinson and L. A. Willoughby's introduction to an British edition of the play (1945), which caught the spirit of the time in its subordination of the political and religious dimensions. For these critics the play depicts "the fate of absolute love in this world of compromise" (xiii). The political is no more than a veneer; in spite of condemning the courtly ethos for preventing the free pursuit of love, Schiller actually suggests that the latter would not be possible even in a reformed society. As Luise fails the existential test posed by her love because she cannot free herself from her bourgeois conscience, Ferdinand, although braver than Luise, fails by concocting an ideal of love that loses sight of its object.

Despite their more affirmative attitude, Wilkinson and Willoughby agree with some of Auerbach's criticisms. For example, they write of a disunity of conception in the character of Luise: Schiller the moralist condemns her for her cowardice even as the tragedian seeks to portray her as tragic heroine. For these critics Ferdinand is thus a more suitable tragic hero, a view that has provoked many rejoinders. They argue also that it is the juxtaposition of rhetorical *Pathos* and a naturalistic milieu which creates the impression of bombast. While many early critics had accused Schiller of bombast (*Schwulst*), none identified its sources with such care. Wilkinson and Willoughby's Introduction contains numerous valuable observations as to the play's structure and language, and, despite a certain stylistic floridity, it still commands a good deal of respect.

We should next look at three canonical discussions of the 1950s. Fritz Martini (1952) offers a sensitive reading that focuses on the inner experience of the lovers and carefully enumerates the plot's multiple tragic ironies. Although he aims to integrate the sociological, religious and psychological perspectives, it is the psychological that comes out on top. He is thus critical of von Wiese's overhasty assumption that the metaphysical *Ordnungen* are intended to be taken as objective realities. For Martini, it is the refraction of the religious convictions through the contingent subjectivities of the lovers that is paramount; their respective visions thus mirror Ferdinand's impetuousness and Luise's dreaminess. Martini's view of the rights and wrongs of the story are diametrically opposed to that of Wilkinson and Willoughby. In an insight that was to be often repeated in the 1970s, Martini brings out the extent to which, even in his revolt, Ferdinand thinks and acts like an aristocrat. He cleverly points out that the President's statement "daß ich, wenn ich einmal glaube, hartnäckig glaube, rase, wenn ich zürne" (I/5; 768) [that, when I believe, I believe stubbornly, that I rage when I am angry] applies with equal force to his son. Martini thus regards Luise as basically justified in renouncing him. A valuable lesson that emerges here is that, whereas interpretations from the religious and sociological angles tend to condemn Luise, respectively for deficient faith and social conformism, the psychological interpretation tends to vindicate her on the grounds of her insight into Ferdinand's instability. Critics who take this view are of course able to point out that Schiller's first choice was to name the play after the heroine, not the hero.

Luise is also at the heart of Walter Müller-Seidel's interpretation (1955), which focuses on the artistic use of language and speechlessness in order to bring out the work's tragic quality. This critic's argument is directed equally against Korff's sociopolitical interpretation and Fricke's diagnosis of a clash between tragedy and moralism. Müller-Seidel takes over the Kierkegaardian term "unconditionality" from Fricke and Böckmann, and he follows Wilkinson and Willoughby in identifying an existential dilemma at the core of the play. But the fact that this is now a different dilemma, namely "die Antinomien menschlichen Handelns" (143) [the antinomies of human action] and not the English critics' "fate of absolute love in this world of compromise," makes us pause to wonder whether there is not a certain arbitrariness behind all this profundity. Skepticism has also been provoked by Müller-Seidel's exaggeration of Luise's alleged speechlessness, when in fact for much of the play she is rather articulate, and astoundingly so in her scene with Lady Milford (IV/7) (see Michelsen 1984, n 9). However, the thesis derives some validity from the verbal hesitancy that Luise normally displays in her scenes with Ferdinand.

The last of these three accounts is that by Wolfgang Binder (1958), who offers yet another existentialist definition of the play as "die Tragödie des endlichen Menschen" (267) [the tragedy of the finite human being] in his striving for the absolute from his situation of having being "cast" ("geworfen," a Heideggerian echo) into an imperfect existence. In Binder's discussion, this kind of metaphysical language preempts a more empirical psychology. Like the other critics, he is still worried by Fricke, and thus insists on the superiority of Schiller's achieved *Tragik* to any moral aspects of the work. He is alone, however, in taking Lady Milford seriously, and also in striving to make Schiller's later aesthetic concepts, such as the naive and the sentimental, relevant to the play. In this sense, he can be said to be part of the existentialist reinterpretation of Schiller's aesthetics that has been attempted sporadically since the Second World War. Binder's essay contains further an elaborate and subtle system of distinctions pertaining to the play's language, the discussion of which is divided into various "dimensions" (social, intellectual, moral); further triadic categorizations pertain to the kinds of conflict experienced by the characters, to the kinds of relationship they can have to "the absolute," and to the possible "Seinsweisen" [modes of being] entertained by the play. As ingenious as all this no doubt is, the reader feels that the life of the drama is constrained rather than illuminated by such a fine mesh of theoretical classifications.

The most prominent interpretation of the next decade was a lengthy and sophisticated discussion by Wilfried Malsch (1965).[1] Malsch follows Binder in accentuating the moment in which Ferdinand and Luise fell in love, and which both lovers describe (Luise in I/3, Ferdinand in V/7) as an essentially religious and paradisaical experience. Although this moment occurs three months before the start of the play, and hence falls outside the stage action, its importance has to be grasped if one is to understand the power of the obligation that Ferdinand feels toward Luise, as well as his rage when he feels that she has betrayed him. Malsch thus dwells more than other critics on the meaning of Ferdinand's oath, arguing that this is the precondition for his deluded self-identification with an avenging deity (the *deus iratus* of Malsch's title) in the last two acts.

The greater part of Malsch's argument (which is not always easy to follow) is concerned with precisely recreating the changing dramatic situations, bringing out to this end no fewer than eight dramatic conflicts and their interrelationships; in this, he is no doubt reacting against some of the abstractness of the scholarship of the previous decade. But Malsch's conclusion strikes me as a slightly perilous balancing act. On the one hand, he rejects Korff's view of the play as "a dagger-thrust into the heart of absolutism." Malsch finds the attack on the state of contemporary society to be only peripheral (208), and argues like his predecessors of the 1950s for the centrality of the metaphysical dimension; his own formula for this is that the play enacts a "die Probe der Wirklichkeit, der konkreten Gegenwart, aufs Paradies" (204) [the test of reality, of the concrete present, against paradise]. On the other hand, he pleads for the interdependence of the religious and social themes, and speaks of the way in which the social themes and the story of thwarted love are integrated with each other (205). The subject thus entails a powerful religious critique of misgovernment without holding out any utopian expectations of how a reformed society might look. Although Malsch's article is clearly one of the essential discussions of the past few decades, one must question whether he has successfully reconciled the political and nonpolitical strands of his argument here.

A less weighty article from the same decade is that by Robert Heitner (1966). (In an article of 1958 Heitner had made a good case for regarding *Der Landesvater* by Johann Georg Brandes [1782] as Schiller's most important model.) Heitner is still concerned to defend Luise from the earlier critics who had denigrated her; his argument is that her renunciation of Ferdinand is taken partly on religious grounds that should command respect, partly out of a realistic sense of what is possible in her society. Beyond this he aims to show that, despite the extremes of passivity and adventurousness that Luise displays, Schiller has a coherent conception of her character. At this point Heitner draws a comparison between Luise, Karl Moor and Don Carlos, arguing that all three are fundamentally divided characters, and that they all change from one mode of behavior to another after experiencing a great shock. Thus Karl Moor changes from passive obedience to active rebellion on receiving his brother's letter, and Carlos changes in the opposite direction on being rebuffed by his father (II/2). Luise's shock, which causes her to change from passive to active conduct, is her confrontation with Ferdinand's father in II/6. The chief purpose of this argument seems to be to help us come to terms with Luise's eloquence in her scene with Lady Milford (IV/7), but the simple antithesis of active and passive seems too mechanical to deal satisfactorily with the very different and complex characters to which Heitner applies it.

Rolf-Peter Janz's article of 1976 sets the tone for the more socio-politically oriented scholarship of the next generation of critics. He begins by arguing that the genre of domestic tragedy was inherently concerned with the conflict of nobility and bourgeoisie, and continues that, even where the discourse of the play is moral and religious rather than political, the political tensions of the age provide the general framework, and should thus be placed more in the foreground than they were by Malsch and others. In so far as a play consists of actions, whereas the religious dimension concerns only words and beliefs, this stress on the real and not the imaginary determinants of the action seems appropriate. Janz makes a telling charge when he says that, despite their claims to mediate between religious and social dimensions, Malsch and the others had in fact left religion at the heart of their interpretations.

Janz's first main point is Ferdinand's aristocratic nature, even though he is in revolt, and the typicality of his claim to exercise power over Luise. (But do his plans for flight in III/4 really resemble the young nobleman's grand tour?) Of more interest is his discussion of Miller, a figure who has come increasingly into the forefront of critical attention, in line with the trend toward criticism of the bourgeois family. As is often the case in Marxist interpretations, Janz's treatment of the bourgeoisie is ambivalent; it receives sympathy for its struggle against the court, but censure in so far as it shows it is itself capable of becoming a repressive class. Janz accuses Miller of sharing in the guilt for Luise's death. His wish to determine whom she will marry is dictated as much by material as by religious interests, for he needs a son-in-law who will look after him in his old age. There is some truth in this; after all, there were no pensions in Schiller's time, and this was how parents expected to support themselves in their old age.

But Janz's argument (which others have repeated) seems to me unduly harsh when he accuses Miller of suppressing his daughter's erotic desires. In fact, in the first act, Miller sends Wurm packing when the latter asks him to influence Luise in his favor, and he speaks with some emotion of his daughter's right to choose her own future husband (I/2). Schiller seems to portray Miller in this way precisely in order to show that his opposition to the relationship with Ferdinand does *not* stem from a general wish to dominate her life. The point, which Janz does not sufficiently allow for, is Miller's perfectly reasonable fear that Luise's fate will be that of a discarded mistress, namely unmarriageable, forced to earn her living as a prostitute, and with the certain prospect of a miserable and early death. His concern is as much for her as for himself. Like other scholars, Janz seems to me to compare Luise's choices with those open to a young woman in the twentieth century, not in Schiller's, and his unforgiving attitude toward the bourgeoisie again seems to reflect the concerns of our own time.

The concept of the domestic tragedy is also the focus of Helmut Koopmann's 1979 discussion of the play, although, where Janz stresses conflict between classes, Koopmann brings out the internal contradictions of the bourgeois family. Like Martini, Koopmann is taking aim here at von Wiese's view of these plays in terms of a sacrosanct metaphysical *Ordnung* vested in the existing social order; instead he argues that, in contrast to earlier authors, who had portrayed the family as a sacred refuge from the outer world, Schiller regards the family both as prone to self-destruction and also as a threat to individual self-determination. (The theme of self-determination is also at the heart of Koopmann's discussion of the play in 1986, in which he opposes Guthke's accentuation of the religious argument.) While it may be true that Schiller problematizes the father-daughter relationship in act V, it is doubtful whether Luise ever claims a right of individual self-determination, which seems altogether too secular a notion to suit this character. This part of Koopmann's argument alludes to the wider debate about enlightenment and autonomy in Germany in the 1970s and 80s. A comparison with his discussion of the same play in the *Schiller-Handbuch* of 1998, with its very different emphasis (see chapter 4 above), shows the extent to which Koopmann's 1979 treatment reflects the time in which it was written.

Huyssen (1980) raises many of the same themes as Janz and Koopmann, although he favors the former's stress on conflict between classes as opposed to within the family. While drawing attention to the French author Sebastien Mercier's *Du Théâtre, ou nouvel essai sur l'art dramatique* (1773) as intellectual source for the more politically radical approach to the domestic tragedy in the 1770s and 80s, Huyssen argues that Schiller went beyond merely showing how social pressures destroy the lovers' relationship; instead, the social conflict is transformed into an internal conflict in each of them, hence demonstrating that the religious agonies that each of them experiences are in fact caused by the confrontation of irreconcilable class ideologies. This is an ingenious argument, although, as Huyssen himself admits, he is going well beyond any possible authorial intentions is pushing his analysis so far.

The year 1979 saw the first appearance of Guthke's outstanding interpretation of the play in the context of secularization (discussed in chapter 4 above). Both Guthke and Huyssen are grappling with the problem of how to take account of both religious and social dimensions, and Guthke's answer, that is, that the extremity of the lovers' religious language is in fact symptomatic of declining faith at all levels of society, has perhaps superior plausibility to Huyssen's stress on class struggle. Two further discussions appeared in 1984 that support Guthke in this regard. Peter Michelsen's article (an exceptionally strong piece that was in fact written in 1963) starts by pointing out that in act I Miller is planning to alert the President to Ferdinand's attentions to Luise. If Schiller had allowed him to carry out his plan, Michelsen writes, there would be no intrigue and no drama, for the two fathers have a common interest in stifling the relationship, and in act I Luise is already prepared to end it. So where, he asks, is the class conflict? (The point is perhaps a little overstated. The President fears a mésalliance but would condone a seduction of Luise by Ferdinand; Miller, who fears a seduction, would presumably accept a marriage but is too realistic to think it possible, even for a moment.)

Michelsen differentiates between, on the one hand, the surface — and conventional — conflict of human feeling and court intrigue (to which the play's title alludes) and the deeper conflict between those who uphold the established order and the two characters who set it aside in their pursuit of selfish goals. The characters he means are Ferdinand and his father; despite their mutual contempt, Michelsen argues, father and son are mirror-images in their neglect of the responsibilities imposed upon the nobility by the social order. (This alludes to a point made repeatedly by Michelsen and it deserves wider attention. The traditional feudal ideal of the *societas civilis*, the despotic corruption to which that order is prone, and the absolutistic concentration of power in the hands of the ruler are all different phenomena, and they get blurred when scholars write blandly of "Feudalabsolutismus.") Like Guthke, Michelsen regards the lovers' exaltation as a sign of faltering belief, not of firm conviction; he goes so far as to write of a corruption of religious faith. To focus a religious emotion on the possession of the beloved, as Ferdinand does, is an abuse of religion and an act of hubristic *Eigensinn* [self-will].

Michelsen asks next why the surface structure obscures the deeper one, and his answer is that, since Schiller's artistic roots were in the Baroque drama and opera (see his 1964 interpretation of *Die Räuber* discussed in chapter 5 above), he has reinvented the genre of domestic tragedy in the Baroque idiom, including both the exalted rhetoric that so offended the play's early critics and the omnipresence of a transcendent dimension in the play's imagery. The character Wurm, for example, he sees as derived from the figure of the *Intrigant* from the

Baroque stage, and the theological overtones of his name (Wurm = serpent) confirm this. The result is that the conflict of court and bourgeois society is presented as a conflict of virtue and vice, the latter being enhanced by hair-raising abuses and by exaggerated characterizations. All of these elements (which Auerbach had described as melodramatic) distract attention from the redundancy of the intrigue. The inconsistency of Ferdinand's role — within the surface structure, he figures as champion of virtue against courtly vice, in the deeper structure as epitome of hubristic *Eigensinn* — indicates the young Schiller's insoluble clash of values, on the one hand viewing the *societas civilis* as fundamentally legitimate, on the other fascinated by and sympathizing with the "sublime criminals" whom he portrayed in all his early plays.

In a fine discussion, appearing also in 1984, Gerhard Kaiser concurs with Michelsen in downplaying the importance of class conflict. Kaiser is interested in the crisis of the family in the late eighteenth century, a topic that remains in the forefront of research but that has rarely been discussed with the perceptiveness on display here. In the course of the century, Kaiser argues, the family began to be thought of as an autonomous unit, a refuge of love and virtue within a harsh world, but simultaneously to be challenged by a new ideology of individual autonomy. In contrast to Lessing in *Emilia Galotti*, therefore, Schiller shows the challenge to the family coming not from a typical noble seducer but from a nobleman fresh from the university, where he has absorbed the individualism associated with the bourgeois Storm and Stress movement. Kaiser thus implicitly rejects Janz's view of Ferdinand and his "absolutism of love." In line with his interest in the bourgeois family, Kaiser examines the role of Miller, one of a line of weak fathers in German drama at this time, and he differentiates finely between Miller's conservative side, which is rooted in the old *Ständestaat* [state ordered by degree or estate] and his new *empfindsam* [sentimental] propensities, a contrast that results in a loss of orientation and a failure to meet the challenge posed to fathers in the emerging new society. There is an insightful discussion of the "eroticization" of the father-daughter relationship here and in *Emilia Galotti* as well. Kaiser finally has worthwhile things to say about the lovers themselves; Luise's superiority to Ferdinand, whose passion he describes as abstract and obsessive, is a symptom of the emerging feminine role in modern literature, that is, as closer to nature than men, and, although less articulate, gifted with a more robust intuition.

In a third prominent contribution of the year 1984, Hans Peter Herrmann covers much of the same ground as Kaiser, although attempting to define the play's sociohistorical location more closely, which proves to be rather a mixed blessing. Herrmann portrays Miller as representative of the old "third estate" confronted with a new bourgeois ideology that it cannot comprehend, but like Kaiser Herrmann shows that Miller also bears traits of that new ideology, most notably in his desire to allow Luise to choose her future husband. In general, however, Herrmann views the play as a demonstration of the inadequacy of Miller's hidebound Weltanschauung compared to that of the rising liberal bourgeoisie with its ideology of individual self-realization, of which Herrmann sees Ferdinand as the spokesman. In this he differs from Janz and Huyssen's view of Ferdinand as essentially aristocratic. But even if Ferdinand's ideas cannot be linked to the aristocracy, it is surely more plausible to see him with Kaiser as an isolated "aesthetic" individual than as a representative for a confident rising middle class, or as a stand-in for the Prussian reformers Hardenberg and Stein. Herrmann seems overeager here to fit the play into a somewhat rigid conception of German social history. Again, his desire to see the play's religious theme through the lens of social class leads him to interpret the "third place" mentioned in Luise's letter (V/1) as the place of the progressive bourgeoisie (227). Unfortunately the text tells us quite clearly that this third place is the grave, while the progressive bourgeoisie itself, on which Herrmann's interpretation hinges, remains wholly invisible. We feel here that the critic is forcing Schiller's play to do duty as a political manifesto.

Bernd Fischer's short monograph (1987), in some ways reminiscent of Brittnacher's interpretation of *Die Räuber* (1998), represents an advance on the contributions of Guthke, Michelsen and Kaiser, and takes the debate to the highest level so far attained. Refusing to be overawed by his subject, Fischer goes back to the negative contemporary response to the play, admitting elements of incoherence, inconsistency or even absurdity in it. Earlier critics had seen the play as an attempted synthesis of incompatibles, hence Böckmann's analysis (1949) of the clash of naturalism and *Pathos* and Michelsen's (1984) of the crossing of bourgeois drama with Baroque opera. Fischer goes further in this direction, identifying a variety of dramatic modalities, including comedy, martyr tragedy and Diderotian *tableau*, all of which are alluded to or integrated in the drama. This approach, which regards the work as a synthesis of various components, leads to a welcome sobriety in this discussion and a resistance to emotional arguments pro or contra different characters or actions.

But Fischer too is working with a master-antithesis, that of skepticism and melodrama. (One must comment on the strange infrequency with which the topic of melodrama has arisen in the reception of the play in this century.) If Schiller displays skepticism in his noncommittal play with the available genres, he ultimately falls into a melodramatic mode as a result of his wish to impose a high tragic, as opposed to a sentimental or a socially critical, conclusion on the work. Although Fischer is oddly unwilling to offer a definition of melodrama, he seems to be referring chiefly to Schiller's use of "pathetic" language to distract attention from implausibilities of plot, as well as to a premature appeal to the audience to identify emotionally with the characters. He criticizes Schiller's conclusion, in that it not only implies resignation to the immutability of a particular social order, but also depends too much on the beliefs and actions of Luise with which we can only partially identify. Although Fischer's conclusion is thus in some respects a "deconstruction" of the play into its components, he acknowledges the work's achievement as having pushed the form of bourgeois drama to its limits, implying that there is after all a *Tragik* of some sort at work here. He has interesting things to say about two characters who both in different ways represent loose ends in the play's texture: Wurm, who as a "genialer Beamte" (112) [official of genius] exposes the workings of the state with exemplary precision, and Lady Milford, whose departure represents a utopian way out (141) of the tragic problem in the form of a nobility of soul that transcends the intractable social situation. In Lady Milford, he concludes, we can see the future development of Schillerian tragedy, a most stimulating suggestion.

Three feminist interpretations should be mentioned in order to convey the tenor of some current scholarship. The first is a perceptive discussion by Gabriele Wickert of the changing relationship between the innocent bourgeois girl and the corrupt and aristocratic courtesan-figure. *Kabale und Liebe* appears here as the end of a development, in which Luise and Lady Milford vary a theme that was introduced into German drama by Lessing. Wickert, following a groundbreaking study by Andreas Huyssen (1977) on women victims in German bourgeois drama, is concerned with the passivity that seems to be the bourgeoisie's feminine ideal, and she shows that, in different degrees, the noble mistresses represent a more assertive alternative. Unfortunately she has nothing to say about Luise herself. The second (alluded to in chapter 4 above) is by Inge Stephan (1986), who argues rather convincingly that *Kabale und Liebe*, together with Lessing's two domestic tragedies, are symptomatic of a decline in the status of women in the later eighteenth century. (For this thesis see Bovenschen 1979.) Whereas the early Enlightenment favored a more pragmatic and social concept of virtue, these dramas epitomize a narrower and more repressive view, such that a woman's virtue is identical to her sexual "purity" and must be controlled by the family. Stephan comments acutely on the voyeuristic interest that the texts display in the question of virginity, on the subliminal eroticism of the father-daughter relationship, as well as on the way in which the heroines preserve or regain their "purity" in death, whereupon the survivors acclaim them as angels. Although, as said above with reference to Janz (1976), I think it is a mistake to overdraw the picture of Miller as a tyrannical father, there are clearly some good observations here pertaining to the unsavory aspects of the bourgeois image of femininity. The last feminist contribution is by Thomas Barry (1989), who outdoes Stephan in the vehemence of his denunciation of Schiller without contributing any new insights. In the contrast between Stephan and Barry we can see academic feminism ceasing to be a source of new insights and hardening instead into a rigid set of attitudes that obscure rather than illuminate the text.

I shall conclude this chapter with a chapter of a book by Günter Sasse (1996) that bears a certain resemblance to the work by Sørensen (1984) discussed in chapter 4 above. Both books attempt to situate the bourgeois dramas of Enlightenment and Storm and Stress in the context of social shifts as explored in recent work by social psychologists and historians. Where the Danish scholar addressed the change in the family role of the father from domination to tenderness, Sasse is looking at the rising ideal of marriage based on love (as opposed to social and economic advantage), but the similarity of approach is perhaps more striking than the difference. Sasse takes issue with Sørensen in one matter, reaching a far more negative judgment on Ferdinand; where the latter was seen by Sørensen as the spokesman for the philosophy of love advanced by Schiller in his *Philosophische Briefe* (1786), Sasse accentuates instead the blind and monomaniacal aspects of this character. (He has also devoted a separate article [1997] to distinguishing between the role of this philosophy of love in the two texts.) This is a useful book, and Sasse's discussion of the play is remarkable for the dispassionateness with which he views all the protagonists and their respective situations and mentalities. Rather than exonerate one figure at the expense of the others, or idealize any particular ideas or qualities, he takes a sober look at all of the characters and finds plenty to criticize everywhere. His conclusion is that the play deconstructs its own title, in that it discredits the idea of love as a possible realm of private experience immune to the wider social forces epitomized by the court and its cabals; the reason is that the manner in which all characters experience and act on their love is saturated with social content. Sasse's discussion may lack Fischer's awareness of the structuring power of the different types of drama available to Schiller, but this is still an

excellent contribution. If, together with Fischer's study, it heralds a period of "new objectivity" in Schiller studies, then this is surely to be
welcomed.

Notes

[1] Malsch is alone in making the Mannheim stage version the basis of his discussion. This version, the so-called "Mannheimer Soufflierbuch," was published by Herbert Kraft in 1963, and is included also in the 1988 Frankfurt
edition edited by Gerhard Kluge.

Works Cited

Auerbach, Erich. 1946. "Miller the Musician." In *Mimesis: The Representation of Reality in Western Literature*. Trans. Willard R. Trask. Princeton,
N. J.: Princeton UP, 1953, 434–53.

Barry, Thomas F. 1989. "Love and the Politics of Paternalism: Images of the
Father in Schiller's *Kabale und Liebe*." *CG* 22: 21–37.

Binder, Wolfgang. 1958. "Schiller: *Kabale und Liebe*." In *Das deutsche Drama I*, ed. Benno von Wiese. Düsseldorf: Bagel, 248–68.

Fischer, Bernd. 1987. *"Kabale und Liebe": Skepsis und Melodrama in Schillers
bürgerlichem Trauerspiel*. Frankfurt a. M.: Lang.

Fricke, Gerhard. 1930. "Die Problematik des Tragischen im Drama Schillers."
JFDH: 3–69.

Guthke, Karl S. 1994. *Das deutsche bürgerliche Trauerspiel*. 5th revised ed.
Sammlung Metzler. Stuttgart: Metzler.

Heitner, Robert R. 1958. "A Neglected Model for *Kabale und Liebe*." *JEGP*
57: 72–85.

——. 1966. "Luise Millerin and the Shock Motif in Schiller's Early Plays."
GR 41: 27–44.

Herrmann, Hans Peter. 1984. "Musikmeister Miller, die Emanzipation der
Töchter und der dritte Ort der Liebenden: Schillers bürgerliches Trauerspiel im 18. Jahrhundert." *JDSG* 28: 223–47.

Huyssen, Andreas. 1977. "Das leidende Weib in der dramatischen Literatur
von Empfindsamkeit und Sturm und Drang: Eine Studie zur bürgerlichen
Emanzipation in Deutschland." *Monatshefte* 69: 159–73.

——. 1980. "Friedrich Schiller: *Kabale und Liebe*." In his *Drama des Sturm
und Drang: Kommentar zu einer Epoche*. Munich: Winkler, 202–24.

Janz, Rolf-Peter. 1976. "Schillers *Kabale und Liebe* als bürgerliches Trauerspiel." *JDSG* 20: 208–28.

Kaiser, Gerhard. 1984. "Krise der Familie: Eine Perspektive auf Lessings *Emilia Galotti* und Schillers *Kabale und Liebe*." *Recherches germaniques* 14: 7–22.

Koopmann, Helmut. 1979. "Friedrich Schiller: *Kabale und Liebe*." In his *Drama der Aufklärung: Kommentar zu einer Epoche*. Munich: Winkler, 143–55.

——. 1982. *Schiller-Forschung 1970–1980: Ein Bericht*. Marbach am Neckar: Deutsche Schillergesellschaft.

——. 1986. "*Kabale und Liebe* als Drama der Aufklärung." In *Verlorene Klassik?*, ed. Wolfgang Wittkowski. Tübingen: Niemeyer, 286–303.

——. 1998. "*Kabale und Liebe*." In *Schiller-Handbuch*, ed. Koopmann. Stuttgart: Kröner, 365–78.

Korff, Hermann August. 1923. *Geist der Goethezeit, I. Teil. Sturm und Drang*. Leipzig: Weber.

Malsch, Wilfried. 1965. "Der betrogene Deus iratus in Schillers Drama *Louise Millerin*." In *Collegium Philosophicum: Studien Joachim Ritter zum 60. Geburtstag*. Basel/Stuttgart: Schwabe, 157–208.

Martini, Fritz. 1952. "Schillers *Kabale und Liebe*: Bemerkungen zur Interpretation des 'Bürgerlichen Trauerspiels.'" *DU* 4, H. 5: 18–39.

Michelsen, Peter. 1984. "Ordnung und Eigensinn: Über Schillers *Kabale und Liebe*." *JFDH*: 198–221.

Müller, Joachim. 1955. "Schillers *Kabale und Liebe* als Höhepunkt seines Jugendwerkes." In his *Wirklichkeit und Klassik: Beiträge zur deutschen Literaturgeschichte von Lessing bis Heine*. Berlin East): Verlag der Nationen, 116–48.

Müller-Seidel, Walter. 1955. "Das stumme Drama der Luise Millerin." *Goethe Jahrbuch* 17: 91–103. Repr. in Klaus Berghahn and Reinhold Grimm, ed., *Schiller: Zur Theorie und Praxis seiner Dramen*. Wege der Forschung, 323. Darmstadt: Wissenschaftliche Buchgesellschaft, 1972, 131–47.

Sasse, Günter. 1996. *Die Ordnung der Gefühle: Das Drama der Liebesheirat im 18. Jahrhundert*. Darmstadt: Wissenschaftliche Buchgesellschaft.

——. 1997. "'Der Herr Major ist in der Eifersucht schrecklich, wie in der Liebe': Schillers Liebeskonzeption in den *Philosophischen Briefen* und in *Kabale und Liebe*." In *Konflikt Grenze Dialog: Kulturkonstrastive und interdisziplinäre Textzugänge. Festschrift für Horst Turk zum 60. Geburtstag*, ed. Jürgen Lehmann, Tilman Lang and Thorsten Unger. Frankfurt a. M.: Lang, 173–84.

Stephan, Inge. 1986. "'So ist die Tugend ein Gespenst': Frauenbild und Tugendbegriff bei Lessing und Schiller." In *Lessing und die Toleranz*, ed. Peter Freimark, Franklin Kopitzsch and Helga Slessarev. Munich: Text und Kritik. 357–72.

Wickert, Gabriele. 1984. "Late Eighteenth-Century 'Women's Liberation': Aristocratic Courtesan versus Bourgeois Innocent in German Melodrama." *Monatshefte* 76: 45–57.

Wiese, Benno von. 1959. *Friedrich Schiller*. Stuttgart: Metzler.

Wilkinson, E. M. and L. A. Willoughby. 1945. Introduction to Friedrich Schiller, *Kabale und Liebe*. Oxford: Blackwell, ix–lvi.

8: *Don Carlos*: The Drama of Freedom

WITH DON CARLOS WE HAVE REACHED the end of Schiller's prose trilogy and are now dealing with a transitional work that, in its form and subject matter, looks forward to the verse dramas on historical subjects that he wrote during his classical decade. As we saw in chapter 1, an early reviewer set it beside Lessing's *Nathan der Weise* and Goethe's *Iphigenie auf Tauris*, an apt comparison in that, besides the shared blank verse form, each of the plays contains a confrontation between the powerful and the powerless, with the latter pleading their cause in the name of the Enlightenment values of humanity and tolerance. (Indeed, the famous audience scene at the center of *Don Carlos* [III/10] is almost certainly meant to echo Lessing's equally famous scene in which Nathan tells Saladin the parable of the three rings.) Hence we already have four possible categorizations for *Don Carlos* that can be made the focus of critical study: the classical or preclassical drama, the historical drama, the drama of humanity, and the drama of the Enlightenment.

Next we must recall the work's status as favorite text of the German nineteenth-century liberals, although we suspect that the only part of the play that really counted for them was Posa's plea to the King "Geben Sie Gedankenfreiheit" (3213–14; 126) [Grant freedom of thought]. In this connection it is possible either to examine the idea of freedom of thought historically (its meaning, Schiller's sources, and so forth), or to consider the scene and Posa's speeches from a formal point of view. We might thus ask to what extent the speeches have the character of an appeal from the stage to the audience, that is, whether we should think of them more as a political pamphlet framed in a drama but essentially independent of it, or whether on the other hand we must understand the speeches as the words of one dramatic figure addressed to another in particular circumstances, and assume that whatever validity we attribute to the speeches should be contingent on how we assess all the characters and events of the play. Schiller's own words can be cited in favor of both procedures, for in the tenth of the *Briefe über Don Carlos* (1788) he appears to affirm Posa's ideas, while in the eleventh he attacks his personality and methods.

There are further issues that will continue to be discussed for as long as *Don Carlos* is the subject of scholarly attention. The first is the work's protracted genesis, starting with the first epistolary references to the material in 1782, going through the Bauerbach plan for a drama in five acts (spring 1783) and the *Thalia* phase (Schiller published three huge fragments in his journal, which was originally called the *Rheinische Thalia*, between 1785 and early 1787, amounting to over 4000 lines in all and still reaching only the brink of the audience scene), and ending with the book edition of June 1787 with its 6282 lines. Schiller prepared stage versions for use in Hamburg and Riga in 1787, and he shortened the play for book editions in 1801, 1802 and 1805, so that the standard text is now a mere 5370 lines long.[1] Among other things this situation has given rise to severe editorial problems. It has until recently been customary to treat the 1805 version as definitive, but as we saw in chapter 4 this has been questioned by Gerhard Kluge, who edited *Don Carlos* for the Deutscher Klassiker Verlag (1989). In an article of 1984, Kluge argued forcefully that this editorial practise is dictated by the interpretative paradigm of Schiller's progressive "purification" in the direction of classicism. This in turn leads to an interpretation of the play that sees Carlos similarly "purified" in the final scene. (Kluge's own reading of the last act is rather different.) Although he himself favors the 1787 version, Kluge austerely refuses to say that there is any one authoritative text of this play, merely the variant versions, each of which brings out a different aspect of the rather amorphous material, and he insists that scholars familiarize themselves with all of them. In a separate study (1982) he argues that we are bound to misunderstand the function of Princess Eboli in the play unless we study the *Thalia* version.

Even before bequeathing these problems to his editors, Schiller himself seems to have been uncertain about the project; in his foreword to the first *Thalia* installment (1785) he admits that he does not know how to complete the play, and three years later he acknowledges in the first *Brief* that the protracted period of composition had put a strain on the work's unity of conception. According to the now standard view, the play started as a tragedy of love, went through a phase as one of friendship, and ended as a tragedy of a political idea. (One should note here the critics' tendency to try to classify the play as a tragedy *of* something or other. It is not clear why this sort of pigeonholing is called for. What is *King Lear* a tragedy *of*?) Two consequences of this extended process are the complexity of the plot, especially in act IV, and the large number of main characters. Such issues have been discussed at length, as has the question of how much importance to attach to the *Briefe* in principle. Was Schiller here honestly explaining what he had intended to say, or was he merely concocting an opportunistic retrospective defense of the work against unwelcome criticism? (For a succinct statement of the skeptics' case against the *Briefe*, see Koopmann 1977, 56–57.) This is no mere question of philology, for the *Briefe* have the effect of discrediting Posa, at least in part, and are as such unwelcome to the many readers who feel unreserved admiration for this character and his political objectives.

The story of the critical reception of *Don Carlos* is slightly different from that of the prose plays, and by and large the debate has been less heated. A strand of the story that we can usefully isolate here, before proceeding to the central issues, has been the succession of studies dealing with the more extraneous aspects of the work, including the sources and contexts of Schiller's political ideas, the meanings of terms, etc. Regarding philosophical sources, there is now little controversy that the main one is Montesquieu, to whom Schiller refers prominently in the tenth *Brief.* This thesis was set out by Roger Ayrault (1948), who argued powerfully that the play reflected the analysis in *L'Esprit des Lois* (1748) of the relation between forms of government and individual psychology; Posa's *Tugend* [virtue] thus has to be seen in relation to republicanism. The theory is qualified somewhat by Dushan Bresky (1961), who questions whether Schiller had read Montesquieu before 1788 but underlines the intermediary role of Adam Ferguson; Bresky helpfully stresses the latter's *Essay on the History of Civil Society* (1767, German translation 1768), besides the more frequently cited *Institutes of Moral Philosophy* (1769, German translation 1772). Paul Böckmann tried in his 1974 edition of the purported "original version" of *Don Carlos* (490–507) (to which we shall return below) to reduce the role of Montesquieu in favor of Rousseau, but this attempt has been rejected by Schings (1996, 110) in the most recent major study of the play. Schings, who does not deal with Bresky's allusion to Ferguson, points (110–12) to the intermediary role of Thomas Abbt's essay *Vom Verdienste* [On Merit, 3rd edition 1772]. In addition, Böckmann (1974, 508–28) gives a sweeping account of the intellectual and religious debates in England and France that were the context for Posa's plea for freedom of thought. Henry Fullenwider (1976) fills in the picture by pointing out two earlier occurrences of the German term "Gedankenfreiheit" (previously thought to have been coined by Schiller himself), while leaving open whether Schiller was actually aware of them. Bärbel Becker-Cantarino (1975) contextualizes Schiller's depiction of sixteenth-century Spain by giving a helpful outline of the so-called "black legend," that is, the widespread stereotyping of Philip's regime by Enlightenment authors as the archetype of cynical ecclesiastical tyranny. Finally, in one of the few studies of Schiller by a scholar from the postmodern camp, Friedrich Kittler (1984) suggests some fascinating parallels between the action of the play and some of the odder goings-on at the Karlsschule, which he views through the prism of Michel Foucault and Jacques Lacan. After our brief survey of these more contextual studies, we can now turn to the debate about the more intrinsic issues raised by the text.

In some ways the most important post-1945 article has been André von Gronicka's early character study of Posa (1951), expressing the rather extreme view that the Marquis is a fanatic and "despot of the idea" (211) who manipulates and instrumentalizes others in his quest to realize his political goals. On the one hand, the article merely repeats more forcefully Schiller's own views as expressed in the *Briefe*. On the other, it is clearly a product of its own age, for Gronicka alludes in his conclusion to the tensions of the early Cold War era when he warns his readers against the seductions of ideology. The strength of his argument is that it enables us to view the play as an integrated and well constructed tragedy (which was of course Schiller's intention in the *Briefe* also). Posa emerges as the main protagonist, and his tragic flaw is his excessive devotion to the cause of freedom. The weaknesses of Gronicka's view are, first, that Carlos, and even more Philip, have at least equal claims to be thought of as the play's protagonist. Instead of identifying the problem of the play with the problem of Posa, should we not try to grasp his function within the broader dramatic structure? Second, and more important, it strains our credulity to suggest that Schiller could have composed Posa's incomparable denunciations of tyranny, the finest ideals of the age hurled with such courage into the tyrant's face, while all the while thinking of their speaker in basically negative terms. If Schiller had planned this character as "despot of the idea," would he not have signalled his intentions earlier on, ensuring that the audience could see his darker side even when the other characters could not? Even the fourth act monologue ("Gott sei gelobt! . . . "), composed subsequently by Schiller for a stage production in 1796, is concerned with illuminating Posa's intentions in the complex intrigue and not with portraying him as despotic.

Frances Ebstein's answer to Gronicka (1961) is in one way a naive piece of work, in that she writes as though Posa were a real person and not a literary creation. But she still points up some aspects in which the Gronicka view is too harsh. Carlos, she correctly states, was never in the dark about Posa's political ideals, and he still wanted to be his friend, and so the talk of "instrumentalizing" others is overdone. More generally, she suggests that by subsuming the play under the heading of tragedy, we force ourselves needlessly to fit Posa into the mould of tragic hero. In fact, as she points out, in the 1805 edition the play is defined by its subtitle not as a tragedy but as "Ein dramatisches Gedicht" [A Dramatic Poem]; and besides, Posa's motives and actions are simply too enigmatic and impulsive to conform to the traditional type of tragic figure.

The early contributions by German critics were rather different from these North American views, and concentrated on matters of form and genre. In 1952, Friedrich Sengle devoted a couple of pages of his study of German historical drama to *Don Carlos*, and these were to prove influential. Sengle places great emphasis on the shift from the private conception of the Bauerbach plan to the public concerns of the finished work. However, he distinguishes between the concepts of a political play, (that is, one of intrigue like *Fiesco*), a historical play (for which Goethe's *Egmont* is his exemplar), and a play of ideas. In Sengle's view, *Don Carlos* falls short of *Egmont* because of the abstract nature of Posa's devotion to freedom of thought in comparison with Goethe's attention to the Dutch milieu. He regards the portrait of King Philip as the most "historical" part of the play in his understanding of the word, in that Schiller has here shown how the figure has come to be what he is through the influence of an accurately described historical ethos.

An East German voice (and a fairly predictable one) is heard in 1955 with Joachim Müller's essay on the idea of humanity in history. Taking aim at Sengle, Müller defends Posa from the charge of espousing an abstract ideal, and he also cautions his readers against exaggerating the amount of pure humanity to be found in the King. The priority here is clearly with assessing the political rights and wrongs and not with an accurate reading of the text. Besides criticizing von Wiese (1948) for discovering a religious dimension in the work, Müller surpasses all rivals in counting the kinds of tragedy that the play is supposed to exemplify. It is, he solemnly tells us (108–9), a tragedy of friendship, of trust, of humanity in human history, of state despotism and of ecclesiastical omnipotence. The list, one feels, could be extended *ad infinitum* without throwing much light on the play.

A comparable approach to Sengle's is taken by Gerhard Storz (1960), who restates the arguments of his 1959 monograph (see chapter 4 above) at greater length in a fine account of the play's genesis and structure. In Storz's version, structural and dramaturgical considerations have precedence over ideological ones. He finds that King Philip is both more central to the play and a more subtle artistic creation than Posa, and he is able to quote some statements from Schiller's prologue to the first installment of the play in support of this appraisal of the King. For Storz, Posa's antics in act IV and his death in act V are necessary not because Schiller wished to create a certain type of character but because he had to kill Posa off in order to avoid doing violence to the broader historical truth. (As we saw in chapter 3, Kühnemann took a similar view in 1905.) A drama in which Philip II is converted to eighteenth-century liberalism would have been as absurd as one in which Carlos escapes to lead the Dutch revolt, and it would have been banal to restrict Posa, the servant of the idea, to the domestic task assigned him by Philip, that is, to bringing about a private reconciliation within the royal house. Although it was legitimate to take some liberties with the historical record, there clearly were limits, and so it was necessary for Schiller to devise a worthy death for the revolutionary Marquis. Although he does not directly take issue with Gronicka, Storz would presumably accuse him of putting the cart before the horse.

A short book by Graham Orton (1967) restates the Gronicka thesis with some variations. While agreeing that the play hinges on this character, Orton argues that Posa's besetting sin is not so much idealistic despotism as vanity. In a careful reading of the audience scene, Orton shows that what prompts Posa to open his mind to Philip, thus putting all his own plans at risk, is the fear of being thought a fool. As perceptive as this is, we still wonder if it makes Schiller sound too much like the Ibsen of *The Wild Duck*. Orton places more emphasis than many critics on the late revelation (V/8) of Posa's intrigue with the Turks, and he considers its problematic implications for all his previous deeds during the play, with which it hardly seems consistent. He does not consider the possibility, in my view quite likely, that Schiller simply added this material in order to provide a late *coup de théâtre*, without fully realizing the difficulties it would raise for how we understand what came before. Orton is also a particularly harsh judge of Posa's treatment of the Queen. What emerges most forcefully from this book, however, is the demands that *Don Carlos* places upon the reader (for the spectator has not the opportunity to ponder the work's ambiguities during the course of a performance). Orton is obliged to discuss a number of scenes in some detail, quoting and weighing the possible meanings of numerous lines spoken by Posa in the serpentine course of his intrigue. For readers wishing to enter this debate there is no short cut around this arduous task, and it is unlikely that the questions can ever be fully resolved. Orton's book concludes with helpful discussions in the Anglo-Saxon mode of Schiller's method of characterization and on the play's structure, technique and language. While German critics might find his approach a little unserious, Orton's articulation of Schiller's struggle with the dramatic form as an architectural problem ("the vast Eboli wing was of unmanageable proportions," 40) seems to me illuminating as well as amusing.

As we have seen, the 1970s saw the consensus pertaining to the prose plays challenged by Marxist interpretations from West German scholars, but there is no real equivalent for this with *Don Carlos*. The play features prominently, however, in Dieter Borchmeyer's sociological study of Schillerian tragedy and the public sphere (1973), one of the most stimulating books on our subject to appear during this decade. Using a theoretical framework drawn primarily from Habermas's *Strukturwandel der Öffentlichkeit* (1962), Borchmeyer locates Schiller's work within a model of social and aesthetic change, postulating a shift from the traditional *societas civilis*, which was mirrored in the old aesthetic norms of rhetoric and decorum, toward the modern administered state, in which a new autonomous and private aesthetic of beauty compensates for the loss of the former public realm. He views the domestic tragedy as an unsuccessful attempt to design a tragedy reflecting the new private ethos, and goes on to argue that Schiller's post-1795 dramas aim to reinvent a public drama in the changed conditions and on a new theoretical foundation. *Don Carlos* features in this argument (78–90) as a first draft of this new public tragedy, but as an unsatisfactory one because of its inadequate grasp of courtly existence and its faulty integration of public and private themes, of *Familiengemälde* and *Staatsaktion*. Although some of Borchmeyer's strictures seem to reflect a fundamental lack of sympathy with drama on private themes, his diagnosis of the play's problems is still plausible, and he has some perceptive remarks on the latent political meaning that the work confers on private emotions.

The longest contribution to scholarship on *Don Carlos* during this decade is also one of the oddest. In 1974, forty years after his article on inner form in Schiller's early dramas, Paul Böckmann, who had already edited the *Don Carlos* volumes of the Nationalausgabe, published a volume containing what purported to be the "original version" of the play. This turned out to be the *Thalia* text up to III/9, the point at which it breaks off, with the rest of the play appearing as in the first published edition of 1787. The problem here is not so much the length (7044 lines) but rather the absence of any authority for Böckmann's version. Schiller published the 1787 version as a integral whole, in which the first two acts and the first part of the third had undergone extensive revision since their first appearance in the *Thalia*. Böckmann has unilaterally rejected Schiller's revisions, making the unwarrantable assumption that the second half of the 1787 version fits harmoniously with the unrevised first half. (For detailed criticism of Böckmann's edition, see Kluge 1984. Kluge points out that there were some precedents in the nineteenth century for Böckmann's attempt to reconstruct an original text.)

Böckmann's editorial decision seems to be determined by his view of the play as revealed in his lengthy essay that appears in the same volume. He argues here that the form of the work reflects Schiller's wish to compose a *tableau*, in the sense in which Diderot had used this term. This is not so much the vague meaning of *Gemälde* [painting], as it was used in German theatrical circles at the time, as a quite precise concept involving, first, "situations" as opposed to strong individual portraits, and secondly, relatively independent scenes as opposed to sudden shocks, or *coups de théâtre*. With its long scenes, the *Thalia* text seems to correspond to this plan better than do any of the completed versions. Besides, the second half of the play contains a number of striking *coups de théâtre*, for instance, Posa's revelation of his antimonarchical views to the King (III/10), his arrest of Carlos (IV/17), and the incomparable "Der König hat geweint" (IV/23) [The King wept], the line that made such an impression on the young Tonio Kröger. Whatever validity Böckmann's *tableau* conception has thus seems to be confined to the *Thalia* text. But even beyond this objection, as Koopmann points out at some length (1982, 81–86), the Diderot thesis is speculative and implausible. There is a shortage of evidence for any real preoccupation with Diderot on Schiller's part, and the idea that, at this desperate time of his career, he would have been concerned with vindicating Diderot's theory of the *tableau* lacks all biographical plausibility. (In a publication of 1982, Böckmann restates the main themes of his 1974 essay, but argues in addition that the theme of Carlos's technically incestuous desire for the Queen exerts a powerful influence over the action. This is a somewhat bizarre view, and Böckmann does not make his case very convincingly.)

Although taking issue with Böckmann, Helmut Koopmann (1979) seems to fall into the same trap of trying to interpret this complex work by means of a genre term. Koopmann starts by expressing his impatience with the usual story of a shift in conception from tragedy of love to one of politics or of ideas, and he sets out to vindicate the play by showing that, in keeping with the traditional requirement of aesthetic unity, it is based not on a number of conceptions but on a single one, that of the *Familiengemälde*. Koopmann seems unclear as to what his real target is here, for he attacks both the *Methodenpluralismus* [pluralism of method] then fashionable in German universities and the idea of

Vielschichtigkeit [many-layeredness] in the literary work itself. But these are not the same thing; even if critics who espouse the former are more prone to discover the latter, a work may still be many-layered irrespective of any reader's favored methodology, and there are surely good reasons for taking *Don Carlos* as such. Moreover, most people would take "many-layered" to be a term of aesthetic appreciation, not of blame. Critics such as Oskar Seidlin (1983) have often praised *Don Carlos* precisely for showing the human dimension in political events, and they are surely right to do so. Koopmann's animus against an academic fad leads him into an oddly one-eyed discussion, in which he is at pains to play up the family theme and to play down its political aspects, in the belief that a good drama cannot contain both.

Koopmann's article has not persuaded many readers. It is criticized by Klaus Bohnen (1980) for separating unnecessarily the public and the private spheres, as well as for its imprecise concept of the political. Bohnen's thoughtful article is written out of homage to Paul Böckmann's contributions to Schiller scholarship, but it directs some criticism toward Böckmann himself by suggesting that his "crisis of the spirit" (proposed in Böckmann's 1955 article on "Politik und Dichtung" discussed in chapter 4 above) should be extended from its existential focus to take into account the findings of recent work in social history. Calling mainly on the work of Rudolf Vierhaus, Bohnen redefines Böckmann's contrast between *Politik* and *Moral* as one between the absolutist court and the civil society that was emerging in Schiller's time. Bohnen's discussion adds a welcome concreteness to Böckmann's work which, for all its erudition and sensitivity, is often troublingly abstract. Klaus-Detlef Müller (1987) is another critic who targets Koopmann's handling of the public-private dichotomy, arguing persuasively for a Hegelian resolution according to which, by means of the dialectical gambit of *Aufhebung* ["sublation"], Schiller turns domestic drama into a vehicle of political critique. Where Lessing had written of the power of such drama to portray princes as human beings, Schiller's play shows precisely how the court ethos must destroy whatever human impulses a prince may feel. The argument elegantly bridges the gulf between the political and private sides of the plot.

Regine Otto's essay (1982), which for an East German publication is refreshingly free of propaganda, can be usefully set alongside the foregoing discussions of genre and personality. Citing *Briefe über Don Carlos* 8–10, she points out that Schiller himself situated the play's unity in its "Hauptidee" [main idea], namely, the ideal of a society achieving the highest possible degree of communal happiness and individual freedom, and that in advocating this ideal Posa is acting as the author's mouthpiece. This of course provides a different perspective on the work, but one that surely does not misrepresent Schiller's intentions. A strength of Otto's discussion is that it addresses a formal peculiarity of the work, namely the way in which the play's center of gravity seems to lie outside itself. This is true both spatially and temporally: spatially, in that the action, although taking place in Spain, is largely determined by events in the Netherlands, and temporally, in that Posa's friendship with Carlos is based on their student days when Carlos was a very different person (169–79; 14–15). Moreover, both Posa (3076–78; 121) and the King (5080–85; 207) speak suggestively of a future in which Posa's vision will be realized, a future that Schiller's audience, and perhaps we ourselves, are to understand as a task still to be accomplished. The corollary of this decentering is of course a certain disunity in the play, in that Posa's failure in act IV arises more by chance than necessity, and Otto's solution, like Ebstein's (1961), is to deny that the play is a typical tragedy. But this may be a concession that is worth making if the alternative, as with Gronicka (1951) and Orton (1967), is to turn Posa into the villain.

To include here all the valuable recent discussions of *Don Carlos* would cause this chapter to swell to an unreasonable length, and I shall therefore conclude by looking in some detail at three that seem likely to achieve a kind of canonical status for the brilliance and directness with which they debate the issues raised by the play. These are Karl Konrad Polheim's attack on Posa (1985), Wilfried Malsch's defense (1988), and Hans-Jürgen Schings's attempt (1996) to outflank the textual dilemmas by means of a detour into biographical research. (See also Malsch's interesting *Rezeptionsgeschichte* of the *Briefe über Don Carlos* [1990].) Polheim's article is in one sense a restatement of the old argument (unfortunately he refers neither to Gronicka nor to Orton) that Posa is a warning example of the dangers of an excessive adherence to an ideology. He even calls him a "Fanatiker" (94). Polheim is not driven by a distaste for ideology, however, as Gronicka seemed to be, but rather by a desire to vindicate the unity of the text in its 1805 version, centered around Posa as protagonist. (King Philip gets short shrift in his reading.) Polheim thus defends the coherence of the intrigue in act IV, and treats the *Briefe* as reliable on all points. In the course of this effort, supported throughout by close reading, he makes a number of new contentions, most notably that, in the much ridiculed scene (IV/16) in which Posa comes close to killing Princess Eboli, the former's motivation is fear, not that Carlos has revealed that he loves Elisabeth (which Eboli of course knows already from act II), but that he might have revealed details of Posa's political plans. Although Polheim argues the case heroically, the objection remains that Carlos is largely in the dark about these plans, and so Posa's action appears as not much more rational than it had done under the old hypothesis. Polheim also devotes attention to the late revelation of Posa's plans in the last act, arguing that this is not an afterthought but a careful calculation by the author. By withholding vital information until the end, he argues, Schiller is approximating the technique of the criminal novel; a second hallmark of this genre is the long final conversation between Carlos and Posa in act V, in which the events of act IV, which had been so mysterious to both Carlos and the audience when they occurred, receive a retrospective explanation.

A number of more general points should be made about Polheim's article. First, while he claims to be using the findings of depth psychology to interpret Posa's words and actions — his Posa is thus inhibited by a halfconscious sense of guilt from revealing his plans to Carlos in IV/5 — his interpretation makes me wonder if the dramatic form can tolerate too great a degree of psychological subtlety. When characters are driven by intentions or fears that they cannot justify or even articulate, the result on the stage is confusion, and a reconstruction of the character's intentions in a learned journal, no matter how plausible, does not help the audience in the theater. Polheim's interpretation has the odd effect of pushing the great audience scene to the sidelines in psychological terms; here, he says, both Posa and King Philip speak and act out of character under the unique pressures to which they are subject, and both of them forget about the conversation as soon as it is over (Posa at least partially so). Again, this may be imaginable in the real world, but such inconsistency seems barely tolerable within drama, which, as the neoclassical critics saw, requires a certain coherence and predictability in its characters and sequence of events in order to be comprehensible to the audience.

The second comment is a formal one. Polheim admits that it is an odd perspective that turns Posa, the spokesman of the Enlightenment, into a dramatic villain, and his article ends by judging that the play glorifies the ideas of freedom and humanity while also highlighting the danger of turning them into ideology. His final sentence then aims to convert this contrast into an artistic triumph: "Diese Doppelschichtigkeit . . . macht das Drama so spannungsreich, festigt aber auch, da die Schichten unlösbar miteinander verschränkt sind, die künstlerische Einheit" (100). [This double-layeredness . . . makes the drama so exciting, but also, since the layers are indissolubly intertwined with each other, strengthens the artistic unity.] However, this problem is more serious than the coexistence of political and family levels in the plot, which caused Koopmann such difficulty, and suggests rather a structural discrepancy between the play's ideal and psychological meanings. While some readers may find Polheim's conclusion illuminating, to me it sounds rather like describing a problem and stating that it is the solution. Besides, has Polheim not already undermined his endorsement of the work's artistic quality by his comparison of it to a criminal novel?

Writing in Posa's defense, Malsch (1988) starts by presenting a good deal of evidence, both internal and external, for Schiller's fundamental adherence during this decade to the kind of political and moral perspectives that Posa embodies, and he also underlines the horrors for which King Philip, as a result of his own free decisions, is responsible. Here Malsch has undoubtedly found an Achilles heel of the Gronicka-Polheim view; even if Posa is guilty of some lying and manipulation, what does this amount to when set against King Philip's mass murders? Malsch argues that in some respects Posa is a surrogate figure for William of Orange (whom the author could not transport to Madrid to appear in his own right), and that the political solution that Posa advocates is not as utopian as many believe, not at least before the escalation represented by Philip's dispatch of Alba to the Netherlands. (One must contradict Malsch, however, when he says [209] that religious toleration was on offer in the England of Queen Elizabeth I.) The new state, the "Traumbild"[dream-image] of which Posa speaks to the Queen (4278; 173), is a regulative idea and has the force of a general moral appeal, not of a rigidly conceived constitution of which Posa should be seen as the blinkered ideologue.

While doing his best to put Posa's individual actions in a favorable light, Malsch is also prepared to admit some fault in him. In a subtle argument, he presents Posa, Carlos and the Queen as members of a pact dedicated at once to private friendship and to the realization of humane values in the public realm; hence Posa's reference to the new state as "Der Freundschaft göttliche Geburt" (4279; 173) [the divine offspring of friendship]. For Malsch (as for Regine Otto) this project represents the real heart of the play. Carlos and Posa each fall short of the ideal but in different ways, with Carlos becoming so obsessed with his private emotion that he loses sight of the public goal, and Posa becoming so devoted to the public goal that he is prepared to override the claims of friendship. The Queen alone maintains the proper poise throughout. This strikes me as a persuasive attempt to bring the play's diffuse action under a single theme. It takes account, among other things, of the strange quirk of the plot by which Posa arranges, and not once but twice, for Carlos to receive his marching orders from the Queen. Although Malsch does not adequately address the prominent role allotted to King Philip (a fault of which Polheim is also guilty), his reading is still superior to Polheim's rather rough-and-ready argument that the first half of the play deals with private and the second half with public themes. Regarding the question of morality and politics, Malsch acknowledges that Posa acts foolishly, and even falls momentarily into something like fanaticism, but he refuses to locate the moral or message of the play in this aberration, as do Gronicka and Polheim. For him, the enthusiastic vision of a new state and the appeal to make that vision a reality remain in force at the end of the play.

We turn finally to Schings's 1996 book on Schiller's contacts with the secret society of the Illuminati. This is a brilliantly researched and wonderfully readable book that has sent shockwaves through the ranks of Schiller scholars. The affair of the Illuminati, a radical subgroup of the Freemasons that was banned in 1786, is clearly of first importance for the literature of this decade, and the pattern of indolence and incuriosity about the subject that Schings discovers among earlier scholars is indeed hard to deny or excuse, especially since Schiller himself refers to the Illuminati in the tenth *Brief*. Despite the allusion to Marquis Posa in his title, however, Schings's findings are primarily in the biographical field. Only the first half of the book deals with the period of *Don Carlos*, and only one chapter deals with the play itself (101–29). Schings's claims pertaining to the play can be summarized as follows: Schiller's contacts with members of the Illuminati induced him to expand Posa's role from the modest one allotted him in the Bauerbach plan to the one that we see in the *Thalia* fragments and the 1787 version; the play alludes to various topics that were in the air in connection with the Illuminati; Posa's political philosophy, with its emphasis on human rights, closely resembles the radical Enlightenment stance of the Illuminati; the portrayal of Posa shows the psychological process by which a proponent of the Enlightenment can become a despot, a development that Schiller had been able to observe at first hand in Illuminati circles; and lastly, Schiller's account of his intentions in the *Briefe* is truthful and accurate. Beyond these points are numerous suggestive details, such as Posa's secret warrant to arrest Carlos, a possible allusion to the notorious *lettres de cachet* that were a stock grievance of the Illuminati against the status quo.

Regarding our play, then, what Schings has given us is in essence a new statement of the Gronicka thesis, expanded to be sure with a mass of fascinating new information, but not leading to a fundamentally different reading of the play. The tacit assumption behind his account is that Posa is the central figure, and that once Posa has been explained the play has been explained also. I am not at all certain that this is the case. Must not an interpretation address the whole text? Besides the striking parallels between Posa and the Illuminati, there are also differences. As Schings himself states, Posa is a "Sonderling" (125) [maverick], not a member of a secret society, and there are no cases on record in which an Illuminatus confronted a ruling monarch as Posa does. Conversely, we are not required to resort to the Illuminati to explain Posa's philosophy, for the group's doctrine was a distillation of Enlightenment theories that were in general circulation; as Schings himself shows, most of Posa's statements can be satisfactorily derived from the writings of Montesquieu and Thomas Abbt. But even if Posa reflects, and was supposed to be seen to reflect, an extraliterary reality, he had still to be accommodated to the inner workings of the literary work, and this obeys different rules from reality. While Schings has indisputably made a great contribution to literary history and biography, he has almost certainly been overhasty in declaring the *Don Carlos* case closed. Once his book has been digested, the critical debate, enriched of course by his findings, will no doubt continue as vigorously as before. My own wish is that scholars would return to Gerhard Storz, causing the focus of the discussion to shift away from Posa and toward King Philip, who would finally receive the attention he deserves as the figure at the heart of this tragedy.

Notes

[1] For a facsimile of the Bauerbach plan, together with a commentary on the circumstances of its composition, see Storz (1964), who places the plan (which lacks a political dimension) in close proximity to Schiller's French source, a novelistic treatment of the subject by the Abbé de Saint Réal. Storz's study illuminates Schiller's dilemma of the years 1783–84, when Dalberg, the intendant of the Mannheim theater, was pressing him to revive political tragedy in the seventeenth-century French style, while he himself still inclined more toward "bourgeois" drama. Schiller's statement in a letter to Dalberg (7 June 1784), and repeated with slight variation two years later in a footnote in the *Thalia*, that the play would be a "Familiengemälde in einem fürstlichen Haus" [family tableau in a royal house] is interpreted by Storz as an attempt at a compromise. Paul Böckmann (1974) takes issue with some aspects of Storz's interpretation. Schiller's precise intentions with the Bauerbach plan will probably always remain a matter for conjecture.

Works Cited

Ayrault, Roger. 1948. "Schiller et Montesquieu: Sur la Genese du *Don Carlos*." *EG* 3: 233–40.

Becker-Cantarino, Bärbel. 1975. "Die 'Schwarze Legende': Ideal und Ideologie in Schillers *Don Carlos*." *JFDH*: 153–73.

Böckmann, Paul. 1974. "Untersuchungen zur Entstehungsgeschichte des *Don Carlos*." In *Schillers Don Carlos: Edition der ursprünglichen Fassung und entstehungsgeschichtlicher Kommentar*, ed. P. Böckmann. Stuttgart: Klett, 377–623.

——. 1982. "Strukturprobleme in Schillers *Don Karlos*." *Sitzungsberichte der Heidelberger Akademie der Wissenschaften*, Philosophisch-historische Klasse, Bericht 3.

Bohnen, Klaus. 1980. "Politik im Drama: Anmerkungen zu Schillers *Don Carlos*." *JDSG* 24: 15–31.

Borchmeyer, Dieter. 1973. *Tragödie und Öffentlichkeit: Schillers Dramaturgie im Zusammenhang seiner ästhetisch-politischen Theorie und die rhetorische Tradition*. Munich: Fink.

Bresky, Dushan. 1961. "Schiller's Debt to Montesquieu and Adam Ferguson." *Comparative Literature* 13: 239–53.

Ebstein, Frances. 1961. "In Defense of Marquis Posa." *GR* 36: 205–20.

Fullenwider, Henry F. 1976. "Schiller and the German Tradition of Freedom of Thought." *Lessing Yearbook* 8: 117–24.

Gronicka, André von. 1951. "Friedrich Schiller's Marquis Posa: A Character Study." *GR* 26: 196–214.

Kittler, Friedrich A. 1984. "Carlos als Carlsschüler: Ein Familiengemälde in einem fürstlichen Haus." In *Unser Commercium: Goethes und Schillers Literaturpolitik*, ed. W. Barner et al. Stuttgart: Cotta, 241–73.

Kluge, Gerhard. 1982. "Um Eboli betrogen: Vom Auf- und Abbau einer dramatischen Figur in Schillers *Don Karlos*." In *Genio huius loci: Dank an Leiva Petersen*, ed. Dorothea Kuhn and Bernhard Zeller. Vienna: Böhlau, 79–109.

——. 1984. "Fehlgeleitetes Verstehen: Kritische Anmerkungen zu Edition und Interpretation von Schillers *Don Karlos*." *Neophilologus* 68: 81–97.

——. 1989. "Kommentar." In Friedrich Schiller, *Dramen II*. Vol. 3 of *Werke und Briefe*. Frankfurt a. M.: Deutscher Klassiker Verlag. 991–96, 1149–62.

Koopmann, Helmut. 1977. *Friedrich Schiller I: 1759–1794*. Sammlung Metzler. 2nd revised ed. Stuttgart: Metzler.

———. 1979. *"Don Carlos."* In *Schillers Dramen: Neue Interpretationen*, ed. Walter Hinderer. 2nd ed. Stuttgart: Reclam, 1983, 87–108.

———. 1982. *Schiller-Forschung 1970–1980: Ein Bericht*. Marbach am Neckar: Deutsche Schillergesellschaft.

Malsch, Wilfried. 1988. "Moral und Politik in Schillers *Don Karlos.*" In *Verantwortung und Utopie: Zur Literatur der Goethezeit*, ed. Wolfgang Wittkowski. Tübingen: Niemeyer, 207–35.

———. 1990. "Robespierre ad Portas? Zur Deutungsgeschichte der *Briefe über Don Karlos* von Schiller." In *The Age of Goethe Today: Critical Reexamination and Literary Reflection*, ed. Gertrud Bauer and Sabine Cramer. Munich: Fink, 69–103.

Müller, Joachim. 1955. "Die Humanitätsidee in der Geschichte: Eine Betrachtung zu Schillers *Don Carlos.*" In his *Das Edle in der Freiheit: Schillerstudien*. Leipzig: Koehler & Amerlang, 1959, 108–23.

Müller, Klaus-Detlef. 1987. "Die Aufhebung des bürgerlichen Trauerspiels in Schillers *Don Karlos.*" In *Friedrich Schiller — Angebot und Diskurs: Zugänge — Dichtung — Zeitgenossenschaft*, ed. Helmut Brandt. Weimar Berlin (East): Aufbau, 218–34.

Orton, Graham. 1967. *Schiller: Don Carlos*. London: Arnold.

Otto, Regine. 1982. "Familiengemälde und Weltbürgerdrama: *Don Carlos.*" In *Schiller: Das dramatische Werk in Einzelinterpretationen*, ed. Hans-Dietrich Dahnke and Bernd Leistner. Leipzig: Reclam, 89–121.

Polheim, Karl Konrad. 1985. "Von der Einheit des *Don Karlos.*" *JFDH*: 64–100.

Schings, Hans-Jürgen. 1996. *Die Brüder des Marquis Posa: Schiller und der Geheimbund der Illuminaten*. Tübingen: Niemeyer.

Seidlin, Oskar. 1983. "Schillers *Don Carlos* — nach 200 Jahren." *JDSG* 27: 477–92.

Sengle, Friedrich. 1952. *Das deutsche Geschichtsdrama: Geschichte eines literarischen Mythos*. Stuttgart: Metzler.

Storz, Gerhard. 1960. "Die Struktur des *Don Carlos.*" *JDSG* 4: 110–39.

———. 1964. "Der Bauerbacher Plan zum *Don Carlos.*" *JDSG* 8: 112–29.

9: Conclusion

As Friedrich Schlegel noted in 1812, Schiller was the true founder of the German theatrical tradition. As such, he is an inescapable figure for anyone concerned with German culture, and the four plays we have considered will continue to be discussed for as long as German literature finds readers. And yet, with their unwieldy plots and their overstrained rhetoric, they are all flawed works, written by a young man hungry for fame but possessing strange ideas as to what constituted theatrical effect. (We cherish the anecdote of Schiller's appalling "Brüllen, Schnauben und Stampfen" [roaring, snorting and stamping] when he took on the title role in a performance of Goethe's *Clavigo* at the Karlsschule in 1780. See Buchwald 1953–54, 1: 242) And as if the works themselves were not sufficiently overwrought, the story of their reception by the German academy adds a good measure of hysteria of its own, with nationalism, existential theology, and Marxism causing new emotional spasms that have stimulated and also distorted each generation's effort to come to grips with these landmark texts. This is not to decry the efforts of German scholars, often men (and more recently women) of great brilliance, merely to point out that the confrontation of such overwrought texts with a scholarly tradition that shared the neuroses and traumas of post-Bismarckian German has led to a strange and distorted critical history.

It would be silly and presumptuous if, at this late stage of this book, I were to produce a theory of my own as to the proper interpretation of our four dramas and announce that all problems are therewith solved. These plays do not admit of such solutions. Where I have offered criticism of the views of others, I have tried to respond to inherent weaknesses of argument rather than to guide the reader surreptitiously toward an unstated view of my own as to the correct meanings of the texts. The critical reception of great literary works is, in any case, not a process that can reach a natural end. Each intelligent individual who studies and reflects on such works develops a personal perspective on them in the light of his/her own character and experience, and the change of generations brings into play new viewpoints, terminologies, criteria of plausibility and styles of argument. Not even the most erudite and persuasive interpretation, therefore, can have the power to shut off debate, and even the discovery of new historical facts, such as

Schiller's relations with the Illuminati, merely adds fuel to the endless conversation. None of the numerous methods of valid literary investigation (for example, close textual study, the relation of the text to others of its genre, the socio-political context and implications, the psychology of the author) has in my view exhausted its power to throw fresh light on these works. Regarding future research, therefore, I shall confine myself to expressing the modest hope that the scholarship of the next generation will continue to be informed by the spirit of sobriety, clear argument, and the avoidance of extreme conclusions that I have noted in the best work of the 1980s and 1990s, for example, in Brittnacher's study of *Die Räuber* (1998) or Fischer's of *Kabale und Liebe* (1987). As a united Germany strives for acceptance as a normal member of the family of nations, it is to be hoped that its scholars will play their part by continuing to promote the values of patient research, dispassionate analysis, and liberal dialogue in order to help the young to reach a balanced view of their country's literary past.

Works Cited

Primary Sources

Schiller, Friedrich. 1867–76. *Sämmtliche Schriften* in 15 vols., ed. Karl Goedeke. Stuttgart: Cotta.

Includes:

Vol. 2: *Die Räuber* (Schauspiel and Trauerspiel), ed. Wilhelm Vollmer, 1867.

Vol. 3: *Fiesco* (book and Mannheim versions), *Kabale und Liebe*, ed. Wilhelm Vollmer, 1868.

Vol. 5/1: *Don Carlos* (*Thalia* version), ed. Hermann Sauppe, 1869.

Vol. 5/2: *Don Carlos* (composite prose version and 1805 version), ed. Hermann Sauppe, 1869.

——. 1904–5. *Sämtliche Werke* in 16 vols. (Säkular-Ausgabe), ed. Eduard van der Hellen. Stuttgart: Cotta.

Includes:

Vol. 3: *Die Räuber, Fiesco, Kabale und Liebe*, ed. Erich Schmidt, 1905.

Vol. 4: *Don Carlos*, ed. Richard Weissenfels, 1905.

——. 1943– . *Werke* (Nationalausgabe), founded by Julius Petersen, currently ed. Norbert Oellers. Weimar: Böhlau.

Includes:

Vol. 3: *Die Räuber* (Schauspiel and Trauerspiel), ed. Herbert Stubenrauch, 1953.

Vol. 4: *Fiesco* (book and Mannheim versions), ed. Edith Nahler and Horst Nahler, 1983.

Vol. 5: *Kabale und Liebe*, ed. Heinz Otto Burger and Walter Höllerer, 1957.

Vol. 6: *Don Carlos* (*Thalia* version and 1787 edition), ed. Paul Böckmann and Gerhard Kluge, 1973.

Vol. 7/1: *Don Carlos* (Hamburg and Riga stage versions, 1805 edition), ed. Paul Böckmann and Gerhard Kluge, 1974.

Vol. 7/2: Commentary to *Don Carlos*, ed. Paul Böckmann and Gerhard Kluge, 1986.

——. 1963. *Kabale und Liebe: Das Mannheimer Soufflierbuch*, ed. Herbert Kraft. Mannheim: Bibliographisches Institut.

——. 1969. *Sämtliche Werke* in 5 vols., ed. Gerhard Fricke and Herbert G. Göpfert. Munich: Hanser.

Includes:

Vol. 1: *Die Räuber, Fiesco, Kabale und Liebe.*

Vol. 2 *Don Carlos* (1805 version, *Briefe über Don Carlos, Thalia* version).

———. 1974. *Don Carlos: Edition der ursprünglichen Fassung und entstehungs-geschichtlicher Kommentar*, ed. Paul Böckmann. Stuttgart: Klett.

———. 1988– . *Werke und Briefe* in 12 vols., ed. Klaus Harro Hilzinger et al. (Frankfurter Ausgabe). Frankfurt a. M.: Deutscher Klassiker Verlag.

Includes:

Vol. 2 (Dramen I): *Die Räuber* (Schauspiel and Trauerspiel); *Fiesco* (book and Mannheim stage versions); *Kabale und Liebe* (published version and Mannheim stage version), ed. Gerhard Kluge, 1988.

Vol. 3 (Dramen II): *Don Carlos* (*Thalia* version, 1787 version, *Briefe über Don Carlos*, Hamburg and Riga stage versions, 1805 version), ed. Gerhard Kluge, 1989.

Secondary Sources

Saint-Réal, César Vichard, Abbé de. 1672. *Dom Carlos: Nouvelle Historique.* Repr.: Geneva: Slatkine Reprints, 1979.

Schubart, Christian Friedrich Daniel. 1775. "Zur Geschichte des menschlichen Herzens." In *Werke in einem Band*, ed. Ursula Wertheim and Hans Böhm. Weimar: Volksverlag, 1962, 241–46.

Timme, Hermann. 1781. [Review of *Die Räuber.*] *Erfurtische Gelehrte Zeitung*, 24.7.1781. Cited in Schiller, Frankfurter Ausgabe, 2: 950–57.

Knigge, Adolf, Freiherr von. 1782. [Review of *Die Räuber.*] *Allgemeine deutsche Bibliothek* 49, 1: 127. Cited in Schiller, Frankfurter Ausgabe, 2: 958–59.

Anon. 1783. [Review of *Fiesco.*] *Nürnbergische gelehrte Zeitung* 47: 377–79. Cited in Schiller, Frankfurter Ausgabe, 2: 1196–98.

Eschenburg, J. J. (?). 1783. [Review of *Die Räuber.*] *Jahrbücher des Geschmacks und der Aufklärung.* Cited in Kurrelmeyer 1919.

Klein, P. 1783–84. [Review of *Die Räuber.*] *Pfälzisches Museum* 1: 225–90. Cited in Braun 1882, 1: 32–64.

Knigge, Adolf, Freiherr von. 1783. [Review of *Fiesco.*] *Allgemeine Deutsche Bibliothek* 56, 1: 959. Cited in Schiller, Frankfurter Ausgabe, 2: 1198–99.

Anon. 1784. [Review of *Kabale und Liebe.*] *Gothaische gelehrte Zeitung*, 29.5.1784. Cited in Schiller, Frankfurter Ausgabe, 2: 1371–72.

Eschenburg, J. J. 1784. [Review of *Kabale und Liebe.*] *Allgemeine deutsche Bibliothek* 58, 2: 477–80. Cited in Schiller, Frankfurter Ausgabe, 2: 1381–85.

Moritz, Karl Philipp. 1784. [Review of *Kabale und Liebe.*] *Königlich privile-gierte Berlinische Staats- und gelehrte Zeitung*, 4.9.1794. Cited in Schiller, Frankfurter Ausgabe, 2: 1373–79.

Anon. 1786. [Review of excerpts of *Don Carlos* in *Rheinische Thalia.*] *Neue Bibliothek der schönen Wissenschaften und der freyen Künste* 32, 1: 289–323. Cited in Braun 1882, 1: 147–69.

Anon. 1787. [Review of *Don Carlos.*] *Ephemeriden*, 10 and 17.11.1787. Cited in Braun 1882, 1: 185–88.

Anon. 1787. [Review of *Don Carlos.*] *Jenaische Zeitungen von gelehrten Sa-chen*, 1787, 708. Cited in Koch 1962, 179–80.

Jünger, Johann Friedrich (?). 1788. [Review of *Don Carlos.*] *Allgemeine Lite-ratur-Zeitung* 139–140a: 529–42. Cited in Schiller, Frankfurter Ausgabe, 3: 1116–21.

Kindervater, Christian Viktor. 1788. [Review of *Don Carlos.*] *Kritische Ueber-sicht der neusten schönen Litteratur der Deutschen* 1, 2: 9–62. Cited in Schiller, Frankfurter Ausgabe, 3: 1122–31.

Schreiber, Aloys Wilhelm. 1788. "Ueber *Kabale und Liebe.*" *Tagebuch der Mainzer Schaubühne* 3: 44f., 5: 68–74. Cited in Schiller, Frankfurter Aus-gabe, 2: 1395–1400.

Hagemeister, Gottfried Lucas. 1792. [Review of *Fiesco.*] *Dramaturgisches Wochenblatt für Berlin und Deutschland*. Cited in Grawe 1982, 13–30.

Canning, George, et al. 1798. Preface to *The Rovers.* Cited in Ewen 1932, 17.

Schink, Johann Friedrich. 1803. [Review of *Don Carlos.*] *Neue allgemeine deutsche Bibliothek* 83, 1: 86–102. Cited in Oellers, ed. 1970, 98–109.

Horn, Franz. 1804. "Andeutungen für Freunde der Poesie." Cited in Oellers, ed. 1970, 109–13.

Anon. 1805. "Über Friedrich von Schiller." *Allgemeine Literatur-Zeitung, Intelligenzblatt* 98 (19 June), 785–806. Cited in Oellers, ed. 1970, 181–99.

Brandes, Ernst. 1806. [Review of *Theater von Schiller*, 2 vols., 1805.] Cited in Guthke 1965, 139–47.

Schwaldopler, Johann. 1806. *Uiber Friedrich von Schiller und seine poetischen Werke.* Leipzig: Liebeskind.

Schlegel, August Wilhelm. 1811. *Über dramatische Kunst und Literatur.* Cited in Oellers, ed. 1970, 129–32.

de Staël, Germaine. 1813. *De l'Allemagne.* 2 vols. Paris: Garnier, 1932.

Brentano, Clemens. 1814. [Review of *Kabale und Liebe.*] Cited in Oellers, ed. 1970, 153–56.

Goethe, Johann Wolfgang von. 1815. "Über das deutsche Theater." Cited in Oellers, ed. 1970, 321–23.

Schlegel, Friedrich. 1815. *Geschichte der alten und neuen Literatur.* Vol. 6 of *Kritische Friedrich-Schlegel-Ausgabe,* ed. Hans Eichner. Paderborn: Schöningh, 1961.

Solger, Karl Wilhelm Ferdinand. 1819. "Ueber dramatische Kunst und Literatur: Vorlesungen von August Wilhelm Schlegel." In *Erwin: Vier Gespräche über das Schöne und die Kunst,* ed. W. Henckmann. Munich: Fink, 1970, 396–471. Cited in Oellers, ed. 1970, 156–58.

Taylor, William. 1821–22. "Schiller." *Monthly Magazine* 52: 223–26, 393–96; 53: 402–3, 300–3.

Carlyle, Thomas. 1825. *The Life of Friedrich Schiller Comprehending an Examination of his Works.* 2nd ed. Philadelphia: Hazard, 1859.

Tieck, Ludwig. 1827. *Dramaturgische Blätter.* Cited in Oellers, ed. 1970, 172–77.

Menzel, Wolfgang. 1828. *Die deutsche Literatur.* Cited in Oellers, ed. 1970, 240–45.

Humboldt, Wilhelm von. 1830. "Über Schiller und den Gang seiner Geistesentwicklung." In Oellers, ed. 1970, 287–309.

Wolzogen, Caroline von. 1830. *Schillers Leben verfaßt aus Erinnerungen der Familie, seinen eignen Briefen und den Nachrichten seines Freundes Körner.* 2 vols. Stuttgart: Cotta.

Carlyle, Thomas. 1831. "Schiller." In *Critical and Miscellaneous Essays.* 4 vols. in 2. London: Chapman, n.d., 2: 182–219.

Heine, Heinrich. 1833. *Die Romantische Schule.* In vol. 5 of *Sämtliche Schriften,* ed. Klaus Briegleb. 12 vols. Frankfurt a. M.: Ullstein, 1981, 357–504.

Gervinus, Georg Gottfried. 1835–40. *Geschichte der deutschen Dichtung.* 5th ed. revised by K. Bartsch. 5 vols. Leipzig: Engelmann, 1874.

Hegel, Georg Wilhelm Friedrich. 1835. *Vorlesungen über die Ästhetik.* Vols. 12–14 of *Sämtliche Werke,* ed. Hermann Glockner. 20 vols. Stuttgart: Fromann, 1928.

Eckermann, Johann Peter. 1836–48. *Gespräche mit Goethe in den letzten Jahren seines Lebens.* Munich: Beck, 1982.

Streicher, Andreas. 1836. *Schiller-Biographie,* ed. Herbert Kraft. Mannheim: Bibliographisches Institut, 1974. (First published as *Schiller's Flucht von Stuttgart und Aufenthalt in Mannheim von 1782 bis 1785.*)

Hinrichs, H. F. W. 1837–39. *Schillers Dichtungen nach ihren historischen Beziehungen und nach ihrem inneren Zusammenhang.* 3 vols. Leipzig: Verlag der Hinrichsschen Buchhandlung.

Hoffmeister, Karl. 1838. *Schillers Jugendgeschichte und Periode der jugendlichen Naturpoesie bis zum Don Karlos 1786.* Vol. I of *Schiller's Leben, Geistesentwickelung und Werke im Zusammenhang.* 5 vols. Leipzig: P. Balz'sche Buchhandlung, 1838–42.

Hoven, Friedrich Wilhelm von. 1840. *Autobiographie.* Cited in Hecker, ed. 1904, 140–46.

Schwab, Gustav. 1840. *Schiller's Leben.* Stuttgart: Lieschung.

Grün, Karl. 1844. *Friedrich Schiller als Mensch, Geschichtsschreiber, Denker und Dichter.* Leipzig: Brockhaus.

Engels, Friedrich. 1847. [Review of Karl Grün, *Über Goethe vom menschlichen Standpunkte,* 1846.] Cited in Marx/Engels 1968, 1: 457–83.

Hettner, Hermann. 1850. *Die romantische Schule in ihrem inneren Zusammenhange mit Goethe und Schiller.* Repr. in his *Schriften zur Literatur,* ed. Jürgen Jahn. Berlin (East): Aufbau, 1959, 51–165.

Fontane, Theodor. 1853. "Unsere lyrische und epische Poesie seit 1848." In vol. 21/1 of *Sämtliche Werke.* Munich: Nymphenburger Verlagshandlung, 1963, 7–33.

Hettner, Hermann. 1856–70. *Geschichte der deutschen Literatur im achtzehnten Jahrhundert.* 3rd revised ed. Vol. 3/1. Braunschweig: Vieweg, 1879.

Palleske, Emil. 1858. *Schillers Leben und Werke.* Revised ed. Berlin: Weichert, 1912.

Marx, Karl. 1859. Letter to Ferdinand Lassalle. Cited in Marx/Engels 1968, 1: 179–82.

Freytag, Gustav. 1863. *Die Technik des Dramas.* In vol. 14 of *Gesammelte Werke.* 22 vols. Leipzig: Hirzel, 1887.

Schmidt, Julian. 1863. *Schiller und seine Zeitgenossen.* Leipzig: Grunow.

Vilmar, August Friedrich Christian. 1871. *Geschichte der deutschen National-Literatur.* 14th ed. Marburg: Elwert.

Ludwig, Otto. 1874. "Schiller." In vol. 5 of *Gesammelte Schriften.* 6 vols. Leipzig: Grunow, 1891, 285–323.

Bulthaupt, Heinrich. 1880. *Lessing, Goethe, Schiller, Kleist.* Vol. 1 of his *Dramaturgie des Schauspiels.* 11th ed. Oldenburg: Schulzesche Hofbuchhandlung, 1906.

Braun, Julius W. 1882. *Schiller und Goethe im Urtheile ihrer Zeitgenossen. Abteilung 1: Schiller.* 3 vols. Leipzig: Schicke.

Scherer, Wilhelm. 1883. *Geschichte der deutschen Literatur.* 8th ed. Berlin: Weidmann, 1899.

Engels, Friedrich. 1885. Letter to Minna Kautsky. Cited in Marx/Engels 1968, 1: 484.

Schmidt, Julian. 1886. *Geschichte der deutschen Literatur von Leibniz bis auf unsere Zeit*. Vol. 3: 1781–1797. Berlin: Hertz.

Bellermann, Ludwig. 1888–91. *Schillers Dramen: Beiträge zu ihrem Verständnis*. 3rd ed. 3 vols. Berlin: Weidmann, 1905.

Brahm, Otto. 1888–92. *Schiller*. 2 vols. Berlin: Hertz.

Nietzsche, Friedrich. 1888. *Der Fall Wagner*. In vol. 2 of *Werke*, ed. Karl Schlechta. 6th ed. 3 vols. Munich: Hanser, 1969, 900–38.

——.1889. *Götzendämmerung*. In vol. 2 of *Werke*, ed. Karl Schlechta. 6th ed. 3 vols. Munich: Hanser, 1969, 941–1033.

Minor, Jakob. 1890. *Schiller: Sein Leben und seine Werke*. 2 vols. Berlin: Weidmannsche Buchhandlung.

Wychgram, Jakob. 1895. *Schiller: Dem deutschen Volke dargestellt*. Bielefeld: Velhagen.

Burggraf, Julius. 1897. *Schillers Frauengestalten*. 2nd ed. Stuttgart: Krabbe, 1900.

Weitbrecht, Carl. 1897. *Schiller in seinen Dramen*. Stuttgart: Fromann.

Eloesser, Arthur. 1898. *Das bürgerliche Drama. Seine Geschichte im 18. und 19. Jahrhundert*. Berlin: Hertz.

Harnack, Otto. 1898. *Schiller*. Berlin: Hofmann.

Weltrich, Richard. 1899. *Friedrich Schiller: Geschichte seines Lebens und Charakteristik seiner Werke*. Vol. 1. Stuttgart: Cotta.

Thomas, Calvin. 1901. *The Life and Works of Friedrich Schiller*. 2nd ed. New York: Holt, 1906.

Weitbrecht, Carl. 1901. *Schiller und die deutsche Gegenwart*. Stuttgart: Bonz.
Includes:
"Schiller in der Gegenwart," 51–92.
"Der junge Schiller und das moderne Drama," 147–75.

Mann, Thomas. 1903. *Tonio Kröger*. In his *Sämtliche Erzählungen*, Frankfurt a. M.: Fischer, 1963, 213–66.

Hecker, Max, ed. 1904. *Schillers Persönlichkeit. Urtheile der Zeitgenossen und Dokumente*. Vol. I. Weimar: Gesellschaft der Bibliophilen.

Petersen, Julius. 1904. *Schiller und die Bühne*. Berlin: Mayer und Müller. Repr. 1967.

Berger, Karl. 1905/1909. *Schiller. Sein Leben und seine Werke*. 2 vols. Munich: Beck.

Kühnemann, Eugen. 1905. *Schiller*. 5th ed. Munich: Beck, 1914.

Mann, Heinrich. 1905. *Professor Unrat*. Hamburg: Rowohlt, 1951.

Mann, Thomas. 1905. "Schwere Stunde." In his *Sämtliche Erzählungen*, Frankfurt a. M.: Fischer, 1963, 294–300.

Mehring, Franz. 1905. *Schiller: Ein Lebensbild für deutsche Arbeiter*. Leipzig: Leipziger Buchdrückerei.

Petsch, Robert. 1905. *Freiheit und Notwendigkeit in Schillers Dramen*. Munich: Beck.

Robertson, John G. 1905. *Schiller after a Century*. Edinburgh: Blackwood.

Schmidt, Erich. 1905. "Einleitung." Vol. 3 of Schiller, *Sämtliche Werke*. Säkular-Ausgabe. Stuttgart: Cotta, v–xlviii.

Weissenfels, Richard. 1905. "Einleitung." Vol. 4 of Schiller, *Sämtliche Werke*. Säkular-Ausgabe. Stuttgart: Cotta, v–xliv.

Rea, Thomas. 1906. *Schiller's Dramas and Poems in England*. London: Fisher.

Ludwig, Albert. 1909. *Schiller und die deutsche Nachwelt*. Berlin: Weidmann.

Böhtlingk, Arthur. 1910. *Schiller und Shakespeare*. Vol. 3 of his *Shakespeare und unsere Klassiker*. Leipzig: Eckardt.

Gundolf, Friedrich. 1911. *Shakespeare und der deutsche Geist*. 8th ed. Berlin: Bondi, 1927.

Strich, Fritz. 1912. *Schiller: Sein Leben und sein Werk*. Vol. 13 of *Sämtliche Werke*. Tempel-Klassiker. Leipzig: Tempel, n.d.

Gundolf, Friedrich. 1916. *Goethe*. Berlin: Bondi.

Kurrelmeyer, W. 1919. "A Contemporary Critique of Schiller's *Räuber*." *JEGP* 18: 72–79.

Strich, Fritz. 1922. *Deutsche Klassik und Romantik: oder Vollendung und Unendlichkeit, ein Vergleich*. Munich: Meyer & Jessen.

Korff, Hermann August. 1923. *Geist der Goethezeit. I. Teil. Sturm und Drang*. Leipzig: Weber.

Brüggemann, Fritz. 1925. "Der Kampf um die bürgerliche Welt- und Lebensanschauung in der deutschen Literatur des 18. Jahrhunderts." *DVjs* 3: 94–127.

Liepe, Wolfgang. 1926. "Der junge Schiller und Rousseau. Eine Nachprüfung der Rousseaulegende um den *Räuber*-Dichter." *ZfdPh* 51: 299–328. Repr. in Liepe, *Beiträge zur Literatur- und Geistesgeschichte*. Neumünster: Wachholtz, 1963, 29–64.

Fricke, Gerhard. 1927. *Der religiöse Sinn der Klassik Schillers: Zum Verhältnis von Idealismus und Christentum*. Munich: Kaiser.

Kommerell, Max. 1928. *Der Dichter als Führer in der deutschen Klassik*. 2nd ed. Frankfurt a. M.: Klostermann, n.d.

Borcherdt, Hans Heinrich. 1929. *Schiller: Seine geistige und künstlerische Entwicklung.* Leipzig: Quelle und Meyer.

Fricke, Gerhard. 1930. "Die Problematik des Tragischen im Drama Schillers." *JFDH*: 3–69.

Korff, Hermann August. 1930. *Geist der Goethezeit. II. Teil. Klassik.* Leipzig: Weber.

Ewen, Frederic. 1932. *The Prestige of Schiller in England: 1788–1859.* New York: Columbia UP.

Fabricius, Hans. 1932. *Schiller als Kampfgenosse Hitlers: Nationalsozialismus in Schillers Dramen.* Bayreuth: N. S. Kulturverlag.

Spengler, Wilhelm. 1932. *Das Drama Schillers: Seine Genesis.* Leipzig: Weber.

Dilthey, Wilhelm. 1933. *Schiller*, ed. Hermann Nohl. Göttingen: Vandenhoeck & Ruprecht, n.d.

Bertram, Ernst. 1934. "Schiller." *Jahrbuch der Goethe-Gesellschaft* 20: 213–49.

Böckmann, Paul. 1934. "Die innere Form in Schillers Jugenddramen." *Euphorion* [*Dichtung und Volkstum*] 35: 439–80. Repr. in Berghahn/Grimm, ed. 1972, 1–54.

Cysarz, Herbert. 1934. *Schiller.* Tübingen: Niemeyer.

Deubler, Werner. 1934. "Umrisse eines neuen Schillerbildes." *Jahrbuch der Goethe-Gesellschaft* 20: 1–64.

Kommerell, Max. 1934. *Geist und Buchstabe der Dichtung.* 5th ed. Frankfurt a. M.: Klostermann, 1962.
    Includes:
    "Schiller als Gestalter des handelnden Menschen," 132–74.
    "Schiller als Psychologe," 175–242.

Pongs, Hermann. 1935. *Schillers Urbilder.* Stuttgart: Metzler.

Schmid, Karl G. 1935. *Schillers Gestaltungsweise: Eigenart und Klassik.* Frauenfeld: Huber.

Smith, Herbert. 1935. "Present-Day Tendencies in the German Interpretation of Schiller." *PEGS*: 20–36.

Unger, Rudolf. 1937. "Richtungen und Probleme neuerer Schiller-Deutung." *Nachrichten von der Gesellschaft der Wissenschaften zu Göttingen: Philologisch-historische Klasse: Neue Folge: Fachgruppe IV: Neuere Philologie und Literaturwissenschaft*, I, 9: 203–42.

Buchwald, Reinhard. 1938. *Wandlungen unseres Schillerbildes.* Leipzig: Liebisch.

Storz, Gerhard. 1938. *Das Drama Friedrich Schillers.* Frankfurt a. M.: Societäts-Verlag.

Nadler, Josef. 1938. *Literaturgeschichte des deutschen Volkes: Dichtung und Schrifttum der deutschen Stämme und Landschaften.* 4th ed. Vol. II: Geist. Berlin: Propyläen. (First ed. 1912–28.)

Wiese, Benno von. 1938. *Die Dramen Schillers: Politik und Tragödie.* Leipzig: Bibliographisches Institut.

Keferstein, Georg. 1939. "Zur Wiedergeburt Schillers in unserer Zeit." *GRM* 27: 165–91.

Rehm, Walther. 1941. "Schiller und das Barockdrama." *DVjs* 19: 55–107. Repr. in Berghahn/Grimm, ed. 1972, 55–107.

Kaufmann, F. W. 1942. *Schiller: Poet of Philosophical Idealism.* Oberlin: Academy Press.

Taylor, A. J. P. 1945. *The Course of German History.* 2nd ed. London: Methuen, 1961.

Wilkinson, E. M. and L. A. Willoughby. 1945. Introduction to Friedrich Schiller, *Kabale und Liebe.* Oxford: Blackwell, ix–lvi.

Auerbach, Erich. 1946. "Miller the Musician." In *Mimesis: The Representation of Reality in Western Literature,* trans. Willard R. Trask. Princeton, NJ: Princeton UP, 1953, 434–53.

Ayrault, Roger. 1948. "Schiller et Montesquieu: Sur la Genese du *Don Carlos.*" *EG* 3: 233–40.

Kindermann, Heinz. 1948. *Theatergeschichte der Goethezeit.* Vienna: Bauer.

May, Kurt. 1948. *Friedrich Schiller: Idee und Wirklichkeit im Drama.* Göttingen: Vandenhoeck & Ruprecht.

Wiese, Benno von. 1948. *Die deutsche Tragödie von Lessing bis Hebbel.* 3rd ed. 1967. Hamburg: Hoffmann & Campe.

Böckmann, Paul. 1949. "Die pathetische Ausdrucksform in Schillers Jugenddramen." In *Formgeschichte der deutschen Dichtung.* Vol. 1. Hamburg: Hoffmann; 2nd ed. 1965, 668–91.

Wentzlaff-Eggebert, Friedrich-Wilhelm. 1949. *Schillers Weg zu Goethe.* 2nd ed. Berlin: de Gruyter, 1963.

Witte, William. 1949. *Schiller.* Oxford: Blackwell.

Gerhard, Melitta. 1950. *Schiller.* Bern: Francke.

Heller, Erich. 1950. "Friedrich Schiller: The Moralist as Poet." *Times Literary Supplement,* Nr. 2506 (10 February 1950): 81–83.

Prawer, S. S. 1950. "The Schiller-Cult in 'Biedermeier' Times." *Modern Language Review* 45: 189–94.

Staiger, Emil. 1950. "Schiller: *Agrippina.*" In *Die Kunst der Interpretation.* Zurich: Atlantis, 1961, 132–60.

Adorno, Theodor W. 1951. *Minima Moralia: Reflexionen aus dem beschädigten Leben*. Frankfurt a. M.: Suhrkamp, 1980. ("Schwabenstreiche," 110–11, and "*Die Räuber*," 111–12).

Blochmann, Elisabeth. 1951. "Das Motiv vom verlorenen Sohn in Schillers Räuberdrama." *DVjs* 25: 474–84.

Gronicka, André von. 1951. "Friedrich Schiller's Marquis Posa: A Character Study." *GR* 26: 196–214.

Heselhaus, Clemens. 1952. "Die Nemesis-Tragödie: *Fiesco — Wallenstein — Demetrius.*" *DU* 4, H. 5: 40–59.

Mann, Klaus. 1952. *Der Wendepunkt: Ein Lebensbericht*. Munich: Nymphenburger Verlagshandlung, 1969.

Martini, Fritz. 1952. "Schillers *Kabale und Liebe*: Bemerkungen zur Interpretation des 'Bürgerlichen Trauerspiels.'" *DU* 4, H. 5: 18–39.

Müller-Seidel, Walter. 1952. "Zum gegenwärtigen Stand der Schiller-Forschung." *DU* 4, H.5: 97–115.

Sengle, Friedrich. 1952. *Das deutsche Geschichtsdrama: Geschichte eines literarischen Mythos*. Stuttgart: Metzler.

Buchwald, Reinhard. 1953–54. *Schiller*. 2nd ed. Wiesbaden: Insel. Vol. 1: *Der junge Schiller*. Vol. 2: *Der Weg zur Vollendung*. (First edition 1937.)

Stubenrauch, Herbert. 1953. "Einführung." In *Die Räuber*. Vol. 3 of *Schillers Werke*. Nationalausgabe. Weimar: Böhlau, vii–xxxi.

Wiese, Benno von. 1953. "Schiller-Forschung und Schiller-Deutung von 1937 bis 1953." *DVjs* 27: 452–83.

Stahl, E. L. 1954. *Friedrich Schiller's Drama: Theory and Practice*. Oxford: Clarendon.

Abusch, Alexander. 1955. *Schiller: Größe und Tragik eines deutschen Genius*. 4th ed. Berlin (East): Aufbau, 1965.

Beck, Adolf. 1955. "Die Krisis des Menschen im Drama des jungen Schiller." *Euphorion* 49: 163–202.

Böckmann, Paul. 1955. "Politik und Dichtung im Werk Friedrich Schillers." In *Schiller: Reden im Gedenkjahr 1955*, ed. Bernhard Zeller. Stuttgart: Klett, 192–213.

Mann, Thomas. 1955. *Versuch über Schiller*. Berlin: Fischer.

Mayer, Hans. 1955. "Schillers Vorreden zu den *Räubern*." In his *Von Lessing bis Thomas Mann: Wandlungen der bürgerlichen Literatur in Deutschland*. Pfüllingen: Neske, 1959, 134–53.

Müller, Ernst. 1955. *Der Herzog und das Genie: Friedrich Schillers Jugendjahre*. Stuttgart: Kohlhammer. (Earlier version appeared as *Der junge Schiller*, 1947.)

Müller, Joachim. 1955. "Die Humanitätsidee in der Geschichte: Eine Betrachtung zu Schillers *Don Carlos*." In his *Das Edle in der Freiheit: Schillerstudien*. Leipzig: Koehler & Amerlang, 1959, 108–23.

——. 1955. "Schillers *Kabale und Liebe* als Höhepunkt seines Jugendwerkes." In his *Wirklichkeit und Klassik: Beiträge zur deutschen Literaturgeschichte von Lessing bis Heine*. Berlin (East): Verlag der Nationen, 116–48.

Müller-Seidel, Walter. 1955. "Das stumme Drama der Luise Millerin." *Goethe Jahrbuch* 17: 91–103. Repr. in Berghahn/Grimm, ed. 1972, 131–47.

Wellek, René. 1955. *The Romantic Age*. Vol. 2 of *A History of Modern Criticism, 1750–1950*. 2nd ed. Cambridge: Cambridge UP, 1981.

Wölfel, Kurt. 1957. "Pathos und Problem: Ein Beitrag zur Stilanalyse von Schillers *Fiesko*." *GRM*, N.F. 7: 224–44.

Binder, Wolfgang. 1958. "Schiller: *Kabale und Liebe*." In *Das deutsche Drama I*, ed. Benno von Wiese. Düsseldorf: Bagel, 248–68.

Heitner, Robert R. 1958. "A Neglected Model for *Kabale und Liebe*." *JEGP* 57: 72–85.

Wertheim, Ursula. 1958. *Schillers "Fiesko" und "Don Carlos": Zu Problemen des historischen Stoffes*. 2nd ed. Berlin (East): Aufbau, 1967.

Anstett, J.-J. 1959. "Schiller: Drames de jeunesse, drames de la jeunesse." *EG* 14: 307–12.

Dahlke, Günther, ed. 1959. *Der Menschheit Würde: Dokumente zum Schiller-Bild der deutschen Arbeiterklasse*. Weimar: Arion.

Demetz, Peter. 1959. *Marx, Engels und die Dichter*. Stuttgart: Deutsche Verlags-Anstalt.

Frey, John R. 1959. "American Schiller Literature: A Bibliography." In *Schiller 1759/1959. Commemorative American Studies*, ed. J. R. Frey. Urbana: U of Illinois P, 203–13.

Hamburger, Käte. 1959. "Schiller und Sartre: Ein Versuch zum Idealismus-Problem Schillers." *JDSG* 3: 34–70.

Heiseler, Bernt von. 1959. *Schiller: Dichter, Idealist, Philosoph*. Munich: Heyne, 1983.

Koselleck, Reinhard. 1959. *Kritik und Krise: Eine Studie zur Pathogenese der bürgerlichen Welt*. Frankfurt a. M.: Suhrkamp, 1973.

Kraft, Günther. 1959. *Historische Studien zu Schillers Schauspiel "Die Räuber": Über eine mitteldeutsch-fränkische Räuberbande des 18. Jahrhunderts*. Weimar: Arion.

Masson, Raoul. 1959. "La psycho-physiologie du jeune Schiller." *EG* 14: 363–73.

Mayer, Hans. 1959. "Schillers Nachruhm." *EG* 14: 374–85.

Rohrmoser, Günter. 1959. "Theodizee und Tragödie im Werk Schillers." *Wirkendes Wort* 9: 329–38. Repr. in Berghahn/Grimm, ed. 1972, 233–48.

Storz, Gerhard. 1959. *Der Dichter Friedrich Schiller*. Stuttgart: Klett.

Thalheim, Hans-Günther. 1959. "Volk und Held in den Dramen Schillers." In Thalheim 1969, 85–117.

Vulpius, Wolfgang. 1959. *Schiller-Bibliographie 1893–1958*. Weimar: Arion.

Wertheim, Ursula. 1959. "'Zeitstück' und 'historisches Drama' in Schillers Werken — Ein aktuelles Problem für den Dichter unserer Zeit." In Braemer, Edith and Ursula Wertheim, *Studien zur deutschen Klassik*. Berlin (East): Rütten & Loening, 1960, 163–88.

Wiese, Benno von. 1959. *Friedrich Schiller*. Stuttgart: Metzler.

Kayser, Wolfgang. 1960. *Schiller als Dichter und Deuter der Größe*. Göttingen: Vandenhoeck & Ruprecht.

Seidlin, Oskar. 1960. "Schillers 'trügerische Zeichen': Die Funktion der Briefe in seinen frühen Dramen." *JDSG* 4: 247–69. Repr. in Berghahn/Grimm, ed. 1972, 178–205.

Schwerte, Hans. 1960. "Schillers *Räuber*." *DU* 12, H.2: 18–41. Repr. in *Deutsche Dramen von Gryphius bis Brecht: Interpretationen*, ed. Jost Schillemeit. Frankfurt a. M.: Fischer, 1965, 147–71.

Storz, Gerhard. 1960. "Die Struktur des *Don Carlos*." *JDSG* 4: 110–39.

Thalheim, Hans-Günther. 1960. "Schillers Stellung zur Französischen Revolution und zum Revolutionsproblem." In Thalheim 1969, 118–45.

Bresky, Dushan. 1961. "Schiller's Debt to Montesquieu and Adam Ferguson." *Comparative Literature* 13: 239–53.

Ebstein, Frances. 1961. "In Defense of Marquis Posa." *GR* 36: 205–20.

Pick, R. 1961. "Schiller in England 1787–1960: A Bibliography." *PEGS*, N.S. 30.

Thalheim, Hans-Günther. 1961. Der junge Schiller. Habilitationsschrift, Humboldt-Universität, Berlin (East).

Vansca, Kurt. 1961. "Das Ernte der Schiller-Jahre 1955–59." *ZfdPh* 79: 422–41.

Witte, William. 1961. "Das neue Schillerbild der britischen Germanistik." *JDSG* 5: 402–13.

Koch, Herbert. 1962. "Zwei unbekannte Schiller-Rezensionen." *JDSG* 6: 178–83.

Paulsen, Wolfgang. 1962. "Friedrich Schiller 1955–1959: Ein Literaturbericht." *JDSG* 6: 369–464.

Raabe, Paul and Ingrid Bode. 1962. "Schiller-Bibliographie 1959–1961." *JDSG* 9: 465–53.

Miller, R. D. 1963. *The Drama of Schiller*. Harrogate: Duchy.

Schunicht, Manfred. 1963. "Intrigen und Intriganten in Schillers Dramen." *ZfdPh* 82: 271–92.

Lukács, Georg. 1964. *Deutsche Literatur in zwei Jahrhunderten*. Neuwied: Luchterhand.

Michelsen, Peter. 1964. "Studien zu Schillers *Räubern*: Teil 1." *JDSG* 8: 57–111.

Storz, Gerhard. 1964. "Der Bauerbacher Plan zum *Don Carlos*." *JDSG* 8: 112–29.

Guthke, Karl. 1965. "Lessing-, Goethe- und Schiller-Rezensionen in den *Göttingischen Gelehrten Anzeigen* 1769–1836." *JFDH*: 88–167.

Malsch, Wilfried. 1965. "Der betrogene Deus iratus in Schillers Drama *Louise Millerin*." In *Collegium Philosophicum: Studien Joachim Ritter zum 60. Geburtstag*. Basel/Stuttgart: Schwabe, 157–208.

Wellek, René. 1965a. *The Age of Transition*. Vol. 3 of *A History of Modern Criticism, 1750–1950*. 2nd ed. Cambridge: Cambridge UP, 1983.

———. 1965b. *The Later Nineteenth Century*. Vol. 4 of *A History of Modern Criticism, 1750–1950*. 2nd ed. Cambridge: Cambridge UP, 1983.

Bode, Ingrid. 1966. "Schiller-Bibliographie 1962–65." *JDSG* 10: 465–505.

Heitner, Robert. 1966. "Luise Millerin and the Shock Motif in Schiller's Early Plays." *GR* 41: 27–44.

Mayer, Hans. 1966. "Schillers Dramen — für die Gebildeten unter ihren Verächtern." In vol. 2 of Schiller, *Werke*. 2 vols. Frankfurt a. M.: Insel, 481–95.

Scheibe, Friedrich Carl. 1966. "Schöpfer und Geschöpf in Schillers Frühwerk." *GRM*, N.F. 16: 119–38.

Wittkowski, Wolfgang. 1966. "Friedrich Schiller 1962–65: Ein Literaturbericht." *JDSG* 10: 414–64.

Lämmert, Eberhard. 1967. "Germanistik — ein deutsche Wissenschaft." In *Germanistik — eine deutsche Wissenschaft*, ed. E. Lämmert. Frankfurt a. M.: Suhrkamp, 7–41.

Oellers, Norbert. 1967. *Schiller: Geschichte seiner Wirkung bis zu Goethes Tod*. Bonn: Bouvier.

Orton, Graham. 1967. *Schiller: Don Carlos*. London: Arnold.

Staiger, Emil. 1967. *Friedrich Schiller*. Zurich: Atlantis.

Vulpius, Wolfgang. 1967. *Schiller-Bibliographie 1959–1963*. Berlin (East): Aufbau.

Marx, Karl and Friedrich Engels. 1968. *Über Kunst und Literatur*, ed. Manfred Kliem. 2 vols. Berlin (East): Dietz. (Lizenzausgabe Frankfurt a. M.: Europa Verlag.)

Mayer, Hans. 1968. "Schillers *Räuber* 1968." *Theater heute* 9, H. 10: 1–6.

Garland, H. B. 1969. *Schiller the Dramatic Writer: A Study of Style in the Plays.* Oxford: Clarendon.

Thalheim, Hans-Günther. 1969. *Zur Literatur der Goethezeit.* Berlin (East): Rütten & Loening.

Bode, Ingrid. 1970. "Schiller-Bibliographie 1966–69." *JDSG* 14: 584–636.

Fowler, Frank M. 1970. "Schiller's *Fiesko* Re-examined." *PEGS*, N.S. 40: 1–29.

Hinderer, Walter. 1970. "'Ein Augenblick Fürst hat das Mark des ganzen Daseins verschlungen': Zum Problem der Person und Existenz in Schillers *Fiesco*." *JDSG* 14: 230–74.

Oellers, Norbert, ed. 1970. *Schiller — Zeitgenosse aller Epochen: Dokumente zur Wirkungsgeschichte in Deutschland. Teil I: 1782–1859.* Frankfurt a. M.: Athenäum.

Abrams, M. H. 1971. *Natural Supernaturalism: Tradition and Revolution in Romantic Literature.* New York: Norton.

Berghahn, Klaus and Reinhold Grimm, ed. 1972. *Schiller: Zur Theorie und Praxis seiner Dramen.* Wege der Forschung, 323. Darmstadt: Wissenschaftliche Buchgesellschaft.

Martini, Fritz. 1972. "Die feindlichen Brüder: Zum Problem des gesellschaftskritischen Dramas von J.A. Leisewitz, F.M. Klinger und F. Schiller." *JDSG* 16: 208–65.

Müller, Joachim. 1972. *Von Schiller bis Heine.* Halle: VEB Niemeyer.

Includes:

"Der Held und sein Gegenspieler in Schillers Dramen," 38–82. (Earlier version in *Wissenschaftliche Zeitschrift der Friedrich-Schiller-Universität Jena: Gesellschafts- und Sprachwissenschaft* 8 [1958/59]: 451–69.)

"Himmel und Hölle," 104–15.

Borchmeyer, Dieter. 1973. *Tragödie und Öffentlichkeit: Schillers Dramaturgie im Zusammenhang seiner ästhetisch-politischen Theorie und die rhetorische Tradition.* Munich: Fink.

Linn, Rolf N. 1973. *Schillers junge Idealisten.* Berkeley: U of California P.

Mayer, Hans. 1973. "Der weise Nathan und der Räuber Spiegelberg: Antinomien der jüdischen Emanzipation in Deutschland." *JDSG* 17: 253–72.

Veit, Philip F. 1973. "Moritz Spiegelberg: Eine Charakterstudie zu Schillers *Räubern*." *JDSG* 17: 273–90.

Anon. 1974. *Das Räuberbuch: Die Rolle der Literaturwissenschaft in der Ideologie des deutschen Bürgertums am Beispiel von Schillers "Die Räuber."* Frankfurt a. M.: Roter Stern.

Böckmann, Paul. 1974. "Untersuchungen zur Entstehungsgeschichte des *Don Carlos.*" In *Schillers Don Carlos: Edition der ursprünglichen Fassung und entstehungsgeschichtlicher Kommentar*, ed. P. Böckmann. Stuttgart: Klett, 377–623.

Graham, Ilse. 1974. *Schiller's Drama: Talent and Integrity*. London: Methuen.

Hannich-Bode, Ingrid. 1974. "Schiller-Bibliographie 1970–73." *JDSG* 18: 642–701.

Phelps, Reginald H. 1974. "Schiller's *Fiesco*: A Republican Tragedy?" *PMLA* 89: 442–53.

Williams, Anthony. 1974. "The Ambivalences in the Plays of the Young Schiller about Contemporary Germany." In *Deutsches Bürgertum und literarische Intelligenz 1750–1800*. Literaturwissenschaft und Sozialwissenschaften, 1. Stuttgart: Metzler, 1–112.

Becker-Cantarino, Bärbel. 1975. "Die 'Schwarze Legende': Ideal und Ideologie in Schillers *Don Carlos.*" *JFDH*: 153–73.

Graham, Ilse. 1975. *Schiller: A Master of the Tragic Form*. Pittsburgh: Duquesne UP.

Prawer, S. S. 1975/76. "What *Did* Marx Think of Schiller?" *GLL*, N.S. 29: 122–37.

Fullenwider, Henry F. 1976. "Schiller and the German Tradition of Freedom of Thought." *Lessing Yearbook* 8: 117–24.

Henning, Hans, ed. 1976. *Schillers Kabale und Liebe in der zeitgenössischen Rezeption*. Leipzig: Zentralantiquariat der Deutschen Demokratischen Republik.

Janz, Rolf-Peter. 1976. "Schillers *Kabale und Liebe* als bürgerliches Trauerspiel." *JDSG* 20: 208–28.

Kaiser, Gerhard. 1976. *Aufklärung, Empfindsamkeit, Sturm und Drang*. 3rd ed. München: Franke, 1979.

Koopmann, Helmut. 1976. "Joseph und sein Vater. Zu den biblischen Anspielungen in Schillers *Räubern.*" In *Herkommen und Erneuerung: Essays für Oskar Seidlin*, ed. Gerald Gillespie and Edgar Lohner. Tübingen: Niemeyer, 150–67.

Merkel, Johannes and Rüdiger Steinlein. 1976. "Schillers *Die Räuber*: Modellversuch bürgerlich-revolutionärer Umgestaltung des feudal-absolutistischen Deutschland." In *Der alte Kanon neu: Zur Revision des literarischen Kanons in Wissenschaft und Unterricht*, ed. Walter Raitz and Erhard Schütz. Wiesbaden: Westdeutscher Verlag.

Oellers, Norbert, ed. 1976. *Schiller — Zeitgenosse aller Epochen: Dokumente zur Wirkungsgeschichte in Deutschland. Teil II: 1860–1966.* Munich: Beck.

Huyssen, Andreas. 1977. "Das leidende Weib in der dramatischen Literatur von Empfindsamkeit und Sturm und Drang: Eine Studie zur bürgerlichen Emanzipation in Deutschland." *Monatshefte* 69: 159–73.

Koopmann, Helmut. 1977. *Friedrich Schiller I: 1759–1794.* Sammlung Metzler. 2nd revised ed. Stuttgart: Metzler.

Wersig, Peter. 1977. *Schiller-Bibliographie 1964–1974.* Berlin (East): Aufbau.

Best, Otto F. 1978. "Gerechtigkeit für Spiegelberg." *JDSG* 22: 277–302.

Dewhurst, Kenneth and Nigel Reeves. 1978. *Friedrich Schiller: Medicine, Psychology and Literature.* Oxford: Sandford.

Hinderer, Walter. 1978. "Freiheit und Gesellschaft beim jungen Schiller." In *Sturm und Drang: Ein literaturwissenschaftliches Studienbuch,* ed. Walter Hinck. Kronberg: Athenäum, 230–56.

Kraft, Herbert. 1978. *Um Schiller betrogen.* Pfüllingen: Neske.

Lützeler, Paul Michael. 1978. "'Die große Linie zu einem Brutuskopf': Republikanismus und Cäsarismus in Schillers *Fiesko.*" *Monatshefte* 70: 15–28.

Winter, Hans Gerhard. 1978. "Antiklassizismus: Sturm und Drang." In *Geschichte der deutschen Literatur vom 18. Jahrhundert bis zur Gegenwart,* ed. Viktor Žmegač. Vol. I/1. Königstein: Athenäum, 194–256.

Bovenschen, Silvia. 1979. *Die imaginierte Weiblichkeit: Exemplarische Untersuchungen zu kulturgeschichtlichen und literarischen Präsentationsformen des Weiblichen.* Frankfurt a. M.: Suhrkamp.

Hannich-Bode, Ingrid. 1979. "Schiller-Bibliographie 1974–78 und Nachträge." *JDSG* 23: 549–612.

Hinderer, Walter, ed. 1979. *Schillers Dramen: Neue Interpretationen.* 2nd ed. Stuttgart: Reclam, 1983.

Includes:

Janz, Rolf-Peter. "*Die Verschwörung des Fiesco zu Genua,*" 37–57.

Koopmann, Helmut. "*Don Carlos,*" 87–108.

Scherpe, Klaus. "*Die Räuber,*" 9–36.

Kiesel, Helmuth. 1979. *'Bei Hof, bei Höll': Untersuchungen zur literarischen Hofkritik von Sebastian Brant bis Friedrich Schiller.* Tübingen: Niemeyer.

Koopmann, Helmut. 1979. "Friedrich Schiller: *Kabale und Liebe.*" In his *Drama der Aufklärung: Kommentar zu einer Epoche.* Munich: Winkler, 143–55.

Michelsen, Peter. 1979. *Der Bruch mit der Vaterwelt: Studien zu Schillers "Räubern." (Beihefte zum Euphorion* 16.) Heidelberg: Winter.

Ruppelt, Georg. 1979. *Schiller im nationalsozialistischen Deutschland: Der Versuch einer Gleichschaltung.* Stuttgart: Metzler.

Ashton, Rosemary. 1980. *The German Idea: Four English Writers and the Reception of German Thought, 1800–1860.* Cambridge: Cambridge UP.

Berghahn, Klaus. 1980. "Zum Drama Schillers." In *Handbuch des deutschen Dramas,* ed. Walter Hinck. Düsseldorf: Bagel, 157–73.

Bohnen, Klaus. 1980. "Politik im Drama: Anmerkungen zu Schillers *Don Carlos*". *JDSG* 24: 15–31.

Glaser, Horst Albert. 1980a. "Drama des Sturm und Drang." In *Zwischen Absolutismus und Aufklärung: Rationalismus, Empfindsamkeit, Sturm und Drang 1740–1786,* ed. Ralph-Rainer Wuthenow. Vol. 4 of *Deutsche Literatur: Eine Sozialgeschichte.* Reinbek: Rowohlt, 299–322.

——. 1980b. "Klassisches und romantisches Drama." In *Zwischen Revolution und Restauration: Klassik, Romantik 1786–1815,* ed. H.A. Glaser. Vol. 5 of *Deutsche Literatur: Eine Sozialgeschichte.* Reinbek: Rowohlt, 276–312.

Huyssen, Andreas. 1980. "Friedrich Schiller: *Kabale und Liebe.*" In his *Drama des Sturm und Drang: Kommentar zu einer Epoche.* Munich: Winkler, 202–24.

Middell, Eike. 1980. *Friedrich Schiller: Leben und Werk.* Leipzig: Reclam.

Schings, Hans-Jürgen. 1980/81. "Philosophie der Liebe und Tragödie des Universalhasses: *Die Räuber* im Kontext von Schillers Jugendphilosophie I." *Jahrbuch des Wiener Goethe-Vereins* 84/85: 71–95.

Schulte-Sasse, Jochen. 1980. "Drama." In *Deutsche Aufklärung bis zur Französischen Revolution,* ed. Rolf Grimminger. Vol. 3 of *Hansers Sozialgeschichte der deutschen Literatur vom 16. Jahrhundert bis zur Gegenwart.* Munich: Hanser, 423–99.

Fuhrmann, Helmut. 1981. "Revision des Parisurteils. 'Bild' und 'Gestalt' der Frau im Werk Friedrich Schillers." *JDSG* 25: 316–66.

Lahnstein, Peter. 1981. *Schillers Leben.* Frankfurt a. M.: Fischer, 1984.

Böckmann, Paul. 1982. "Strukturprobleme in Schillers *Don Karlos.*" *Sitzungsberichte der Heidelberger Akademie der Wissenschaften,* Philosophisch-historische Klasse, Bericht 3.

Dahnke, Hans-Dietrich and Bernd Leistner, ed. 1982. *Schiller: Das dramatische Werk in Einzelinterpretationen.* Leipzig: Reclam.

Includes:

Hecht, Wolfgang. "Aufstieg und Fall des Grafen von Lavagna: *Die Verschwörung des Fiesko zu Genua,*" 42–63.

Otto, Regine. "Familiengemälde und Weltbürgerdrama: *Don Carlos,*" 89–121.

Grawe, Christian. 1982. "Zu Schillers *Fiesko*: Eine übersehene frühe Rezension." *JDSG* 26: 9–30.

Kluge, Gerhard. 1982. "Um Eboli betrogen: Vom Auf- und Abbau einer dramatischen Figur in Schillers *Don Karlos.*" In *Genio huius loci: Dank an Leiva Petersen*, ed. Dorothea Kuhn and Bernhard Zeller. Vienna: Böhlau, 79–109.

Koopmann, Helmut. 1982. *Schiller-Forschung 1970–1980: Ein Bericht.* Marbach am Neckar: Deutsche Schillergesellschaft.

Schings, Hans-Jürgen. 1982. "Schillers *Räuber*: Ein Experiment des Universalhasses." In *Friedrich Schiller: Kunst, Humanität und Politik in der späten Aufklärung*, ed. Wolfgang Wittkowski. Tübingen: Niemeyer, 1–21.

Sharpe, Lesley. 1982/83. "National Socialism and Schiller." *GLL*, N.S. 36: 156–65.

Steinhagen, Harald. 1982. "Der junge Schiller zwischen Marquis de Sade und Kant: Aufklärung und Idealismus." *DVjs* 56: 135–57.

Hannich-Bode, Ingrid. 1983. "Schiller-Bibliographie 1979–82 und Nachträge." *JDSG* 27: 493–551.

Seidlin, Oskar. 1983. "Schillers *Don Carlos* — nach 200 Jahren." *JDSG* 27: 477–92.

Herrmann, Hans Peter. 1984. "Musikmeister Miller, die Emanzipation der Töchter und der dritte Ort der Liebenden: Schillers bürgerliches Trauerspiel im 18. Jahrhundert." *JDSG* 28: 223–47.

Kaiser, Gerhard. 1984. "Krise der Familie: Eine Perspektive auf Lessings *Emilia Galotti* und Schillers *Kabale und Liebe.*" *Recherches germaniques* 14: 7–22.

Kittler, Friedrich A. 1984. "Carlos als Carlsschüler: Ein Familiengemälde in einem fürstlichen Haus." In *Unser Commercium: Goethes und Schillers Literaturpolitik*, ed. W. Barner et al. Stuttgart: Cotta, 241–73.

Kluge, Gerhard. 1984. "Fehlgeleitetes Verstehen: Kritische Anmerkungen zu Edition und Interpretation von Schillers *Don Karlos.*" *Neophilologus* 68: 81–97.

Michelsen, Peter. 1984. "Ordnung und Eigensinn: Über Schillers *Kabale und Liebe.*" *JFDH*: 198–221.

Sørensen, Bengt Algot. 1984. *Herrschaft und Zärtlichkeit: Der Patriarchalismus und das Drama im 18. Jahrhundert.* Munich: Beck.

Wickert, Gabriele. 1984. "Late Eighteenth-Century 'Women's Liberation': Aristocratic Courtesan versus Bourgeois Innocent in German Melodrama." *Monatshefte* 76: 45–57.

Bolten, Jürgen. 1985. *Friedrich Schiller: Poesie, Reflexion und gesellschaftliche Selbstdeutung.* Munich: Fink.

Polheim, Karl Konrad. 1985. "Von der Einheit des *Don Karlos.*" *JFDH*: 64–100.

Riedel, Wolfgang. 1985. *Die Anthropologie des jungen Schiller*. Würzburg: Königshausen & Neumann.

Koopmann, Helmut. 1986. "*Kabale und Liebe* als Drama der Aufklärung." In *Verlorene Klassik?*, ed. Wolfgang Wittkowski. Tübingen: Niemeyer, 286–303.

McCardle, Arthur W. 1986. *Friedrich Schiller and Swabian Pietism*. New York: Lang.

Stephan, Inge. 1986. "'So ist die Tugend ein Gespenst': Frauenbild und Tugendbegriff bei Lessing und Schiller." In *Lessing und die Toleranz*, ed. Peter Freimark, Franklin Kopitzsch and Helga Slessarev. Munich: Text und Kritik. 357–72.

Brandt, Helmut, ed. 1987. *Friedrich Schiller — Angebot und Diskurs: Zugänge — Dichtung — Zeitgenossenschaft*. Weimar/Berlin (East): Aufbau.

Includes:

Borchmeyer, Dieter. "Die Tragödie vom verlorenen Vater: Der Dramatiker Schiller und die Aufklärung — Das Beispiel der *Räuber*," 160–84.

Müller, Klaus-Detlef. "Die Aufhebung des bürgerlichen Trauerspiels in Schillers *Don Karlos*," 218–34.

Thalheim, Hans-Günther. "Zeitalterkritik und Zukunftserwartung: Zur Grundkonzeption in Schillers früher Dramatik," 141–59.

Fischer, Bernd. 1987. *"Kabale und Liebe": Skepsis und Melodrama in Schillers bürgerlichem Trauerspiel*. Frankfurt a. M.: Lang.

Hannich-Bode, Ingrid. 1987. "Schiller-Bibliographie 1983–86 und Nachträge." *JDSG* 31: 432–512.

Jonnes, Denis. 1987. "Pattern of Power: Family and State in Schiller's Early Drama." *CG* 20: 138–62.

Meier, Albert. 1987. "Des Zuschauers Seele am Zügel: Die ästhetische Vermittlung des Republikanismus in Schillers *Die Verschwörung des Fiesko zu Genua*." *JDSG* 31: 117–36.

Mücke, Dorothea von. 1987. "Play, Power and Politics in Schiller's *Die Verschwörung des Fiesko zu Genua*." *Michigan German Studies* 13: 1–18.

Jonas, Gisela, ed. 1988. *Schiller-Debatte 1905*. Berlin (East): Akademie.

Includes:

Kautsky, Karl. "Die Rebellionen in Schillers Dramen," 149–78.

Kluge, Gerhard. 1988. "Kommentar." In Friedrich Schiller, *Dramen I*. Vol. 2 of *Werke und Briefe*. Frankfurt a. M.: Deutscher Klassiker Verlag, 871–80, 978–99, 1215–34, 1408–24.

Koopmann, Helmut. 1988. *Schiller: Eine Einführung*. Munich: Artemis.

Malsch, Wilfried. 1988. "Moral und Politik in Schillers *Don Karlos*." In *Verantwortung und Utopie: Zur Literatur der Goethezeit*, ed. Wolfgang Wittkowski. Tübingen: Niemeyer, 207–35.

Mansouri, Rachid Jai. 1988. *Die Darstellung der Frau in Schillers Dramen*. Frankfurt a. M.: Lang.

Pape, Walter. 1988. "'Ein merkwürdiges Beispiel produktiver Kritik': Schillers *Kabale und Liebe* und das zeitgenössische Publikum." *ZfdPh* 197: 190–211.

Ugrinsky, Alexej. 1988. Preface to *Friedrich von Schiller and the Drama of Human Existence*, ed. A. Ugrinsky. New York: Greenwood Press, vii–viii.

Weimar, Klaus. 1988. "Vom Leben in Texten: Zu Schillers *Räubern*." *Merkur* 42: 461–71.

Barry, Thomas F. 1989. "Love and the Politics of Paternalism: Images of the Father in Schiller's *Kabale und Liebe*." *CG* 22: 21–37.

Bärwinkel, Roland, Natalija I. Lopatina, and Günther Mühlpfordt. 1989. *Schiller-Bibliographie 1975–1985*. Berlin: Aufbau.

Kluge, Gerhard. 1989. "Kommentar." In Friedrich Schiller, *Dramen II*. Vol. 3 of *Werke und Briefe*. Frankfurt a. M.: Deutscher Klassiker Verlag, 991–96, 1149–62.

Müller, Richard Matthias. 1989. "Nachstrahl der Gottheit: Karl Moor." *DVjs* 63: 628–44.

Cersowsky, Peter. 1990. "Schillers *Räuber* und Shakespeares *Timon von Athen*." *Arcadia* 25: 127–36.

Malsch, Wilfried. 1990. "Robespierre ad Portas? Zur Deutungsgeschichte der *Briefe über Don Karlos* von Schiller." In *The Age of Goethe Today: Critical Re-examination and Literary Reflection*, ed. Gertrud Bauer and Sabine Cramer. Munich: Fink, 69–103.

Michelsen, Peter. 1990. "Schillers Fiesko: Freiheitsheld und Tyrann." In *Schiller und die höfische Welt*, ed. Achim Aurnhammer et al. Tübingen: Niemeyer, 341–58.

Nutz, Maximilian. 1990. "Der verhinderte Dialog: Zu den Schiller-Feiern von 1955 und 1959 im geteilten Deutschland." *Literatur für Leser* 1: 14–28.

Sharpe, Lesley. 1990. "Die Reisen des Verlorenen Sohnes: Eine These zu Schillers *Räubern*." *ZfdPh* 109, Sonderheft: 3–15.

Hannich-Bode, Ingrid. 1991. "Schiller-Bibliographie 1987–90 und Nachträge." *JDSG* 35: 387–459.

Oellers, Norbert. 1991. "Zur Geschichte der Schiller-Nationalausgabe." In his *Friedrich Schiller: Zur Modernität eines Klassikers*. Frankfurt a. M.: Insel, 349–67.

Reed, T. J. 1991. *Schiller*. Oxford: Oxford UP.

Sharpe, Lesley. 1991. *Friedrich Schiller: Drama, Thought and Politics.* Cambridge: Cambridge UP.

Maier, Konrad. 1992. *Zerstörungsformen einer verabsolutierten Moral im Frühwerk Friedrich Schillers.* St. Ingbert: Röhrig.

Beyer, Karen. 1993. *"Schön wie ein Gott und männlich wie ein Held": Zur Rolle des weiblichen Geschlechtscharakters für die Konstituierung des männlichen Aufklärungshelden in den frühen Dramen Schillers.* Stuttgart: M & P.

Riedel, Wolfgang. 1993. "Die Aufklärung und das Unbewußte: Die Inversionen des Franz Moor." *JDSG* 37: 198–220.

Albert, Claudia, ed. 1994. *Deutsche Klassiker im Nationalsozialismus: Schiller — Kleist — Hölderlin.* Stuttgart: Metzler.

Includes:

Stilla, Gabriele. "Gerhard Fricke: Literaturwissenschaft als Anweisung zur Unterordnung," 18–47.

Grawe, Christian. 1994. "Das Beispiel Schiller: Zur Konstituierung eines Klassikers in der Öffentlichkeit des 19. Jahrhunderts." In *Wissenschaftsgeschichte der Germanistik im 19. Jahrhundert,* ed. Jürgen Fohrmann and Wilhelm Vosskamp. Stuttgart: Metzler, 638–68.

Guthke, Karl S. 1994. *Das deutsche bürgerliche Trauerspiel.* 5th revised ed. Sammlung Metzler. Stuttgart: Metzler.

——. 1994. *Schillers Dramen: Idealismus und Skepsis.* Tübingen: Francke.

Hammer, Stephanie Barbé. 1994. "Schiller, Time and Again." *German Quarterly* 67: 153–72.

Pugh, David. 1994. "Tragedy and Providence: *Die Räuber* and the End of the Enlightenment." In *Hinter dem schwarzen Vorhang: Die Katastrophe und die epische Tradition. Festschrift für Anthony W. Riley,* ed. Friedrich Gaede, Patrick O'Neill and Ulrich Scheck. Tübingen: Francke, 63–74.

Gray, Richard T. 1995. "Righting Writing: Semiotic Conflict, Hermeneutical Disjunction, and the Subl(im)ation of Revolt in Schiller's *Die Räuber.*" In his *Stations of the Divided Subject: Contestation and Ideological Legitimation in German Bourgeois Literature, 1770–1914.* Stanford: Stanford UP, 102-45.

Hannich-Bode, Ingrid. 1995. "Schiller-Bibliographie 1991–94 und Nachträge." *JDSG* 39: 463–531.

Martinson, Steven D. 1996. *Harmonious Tensions: The Writings of Friedrich Schiller.* Newark: U of Delaware P.

Sasse, Günter. 1996. *Die Ordnung der Gefühle: Das Drama der Liebesheirat im 18. Jahrhundert.* Darmstadt: Wissenschaftliche Buchgesellschaft.

Schings, Hans-Jürgen. 1996. *Die Brüder des Marquis Posa: Schiller und der Geheimbund der Illuminaten.* Tübingen: Niemeyer.

Sasse, Günter. 1997. "'Der Herr Major ist in der Eifersucht schrecklich, wie in der Liebe': Schillers Liebeskonzeption in den *Philosophischen Briefen* und in *Kabale und Liebe*." In *Konflikt Grenze Dialog: Kulturkonstrastive und interdisziplinäre Textzugänge. Festschrift für Horst Turk zum 60. Geburtstag*, ed. Jürgen Lehmann, Tilman Lang and Thorsten Unger. Frankfurt a. M.: Lang, 173–84.

Koopmann, Helmut, ed. 1998. *Schiller-Handbuch*. Stuttgart: Kröner.

Includes:

Albert, Claudia. "Schiller im 20. Jahrhundert," 773–94.

Boerner, Peter. "Schiller im Ausland: Dichter-Denker und Herold der nationalen Befreiung," 795–808.

Brittnacher, Hans Richard. "*Die Räuber*," 326–53.

Gerhard, Ute. "Schiller im 19. Jahrhundert," 758–72.

Koopmann, Helmut. "Forschungsgeschichte," 809–932.

——. "Schiller und die dramatische Tradition," 137–54.

——. "*Die Verschwörung des Fiesko zu Genua*," 354–64.

——. "*Kabale und Liebe*," 365–78.

Index

Abbt, Thomas 184, 195
Abel, Jakob Friedrich 75, 99, 118, 133
Abrams, M. H. 152, 214
Abusch, Alexander 28, 106–107, 109, 110, 112, 116, 210
Adorno, Theodor 105, 106, 113, 210
Albert, Claudia xix, 86, 221, 222
Anstett, J.-J. 104, 211
anthropology 99, 117, 131, 132, 133, 134, 135, 138
Aristotle 1, 2, 47, 161
Ashton, Rosemary 51, 217
Auerbach, Erich 128, 167–168, 175, 209
Ayrault, Roger 184, 209

Baroque 2, 5, 73, 78, 84, 85, 93, 102, 109, 151, 155, 163, 174–175, 176
Barry, Thomas 178, 220
Barthes, Roland 137
Bärwinkel, Roland xix, 220
Beck, Adolf 97–98, 110, 118, 122, 125, 127, 135, 148, 210
Becker-Cantarino, Bärbel 184–185, 215
Beethoven, Ludwig van xi
Bellermann, Ludwig 47–48, 206
Berger, Karl 58–59, 86, 206
Berghahn, Klaus 114, 117, 214, 217
Bertram, Ernst 71, 208
Best, Otto 150, 216
Beyer, Karen 125–126, 221
Biedermeier 23
Binder, Wolfgang 170, 211

Bismarck, Otto von xv, xvi, xvii, 67
Bloch, Ernst 113
Blochmann, Elisabeth 153, 210
Böckmann, Paul 57, 79–81, 82, 85, 91, 94–95, 96, 98, 112, 117, 130, 146, 160, 169, 176, 184, 188–189, 190, 195, 201, 202, 208, 209, 210, 215, 217
Bode, Ingrid (Hannich-Bode) xix, 213, 214, 215, 216, 218, 219, 220, 221. See also Raabe, Paul.
Boerner, Peter xix, 222
Bohnen, Klaus 98, 190, 217
Böhtlingk, Arthur 49, 207
Bolten, Jürgen 120, 121–122, 218
Borcherdt, Hans Heinrich 57, 75–76, 80, 208
Borchmeyer, Dieter 153, 188, 214, 219
bourgeoisie xv, 27, 28, 31, 51, 50, 61–62, 72, 77, 84, 94, 96, 97, 106, 107, 110, 114, 116, 117, 121, 122, 125–126, 130, 149, 162, 168, 172–173, 175, 176, 177
Bovenschen, Silvia 124, 177, 216
Brahm, Otto 45–46, 58, 206
Brandes, Ernst 21, 203
Brandes, Johann Georg 171
Brandt, Helmut 110, 219
Braun, Julius W. 205
Brecht, Bertolt xiii
Brentano, Clemens 21–22, 203
Bresky, Dushan 184, 212
Brittnacher, Richard 155, 176, 200, 222
Brüggemann, Fritz 57, 76–77, 207

Buch, Hans Christoph xiii
Büchner, Georg xiii; *Dantons Tod*, xii
Buchwald, Reinhard xviii, 58, 69, 81, 91, 96–97, 101, 138, 199, 208, 210
Bulthaupt, Heinrich 49, 205
bürgerliches Trauerspiel (see "domestic tragedy")
Burggraf, Julius 49, 206

Canning, George 51, 203
Carlyle, Thomas 16–18, 51, 204
Cersowsky, Peter 154, 220
classicism xi, xii, xiii, xiv, xxvi, 1, 2, 26, 27, 30, 44, 49, 62, 69, 77, 92, 101, 109, 113, 127, 148, 182, 183
Coleridge, Samuel Taylor 51
cultural studies 155–156, 164
Cysarz, Herbert 57, 69, 71–73, 138, 208

Dahlke, Günther 105, 211
Dahnke, Hans-Dietrich and Bernd Leistner 110, 217
Dalberg, Karl Theodor von xxi, 195
David, Jacques Louis 162
Demetz, Peter 51, 86, 211
Deubler, Werner 57, 73, 74, 208
Dewhurst, Kenneth, and Nigel Reeves 118–119, 132, 135, 216
Diderot, Denis 176, 189
Dilthey, Wilhelm 63, 65, 69, 87, 103, 208
domestic tragedy 47, 49, 52, 73, 82, 84, 96, 100, 114, 119, 167, 173, 174, 177
ducal academy (see "Karlsschule")
Düntzer, Heinrich 47

East Germany (GDR) xvi, 87, 91, 92, 105–111, 113, 145, 146, 148, 149, 155, 186, 190
Ebstein, Frances 185–186, 191, 212
Eckermann, Johann Peter xiv, 13–14, 68, 204
Eloesser, Arthur 49, 206
Engels, Friedrich 27–28, 51, 61, 66, 86, 105, 205, 214
Enlightenment (*Aufklärung*) xvii, 3, 4, 6, 16, 20, 21, 44, 60, 67, 68, 69, 71, 75, 76, 81, 83, 92, 114, 120, 122, 125, 128, 131, 133, 135, 137, 138, 151, 152, 153, 163, 167, 177, 178, 182, 185, 192, 194–195
Erlebnis, Erleben 58, 63, 65, 66, 68, 69, 71, 73, 87, 92
Eschenburg, Johann Joachim 3, 5, 202
Euripides 3
Ewen, Frederic 51, 208
existentialism 69, 91, 95, 97, 102, 129, 145, 146, 160–161, 166, 169, 170, 190, 199

Fabricius, Hans 57, 69, 74, 208
fate 32, 37, 38, 69, 79, 84, 86, 152
feminist scholarship 124–126
Ferguson, Adam 69, 75, 118, 133, 152, 184
Fischer, Bernd 176–177, 178–179, 200, 219
Flaubert, Gustave 49
Fontane, Theodor 41–42, 205
Foucault, Michel 156, 164, 185
Fowler, Frank 161, 214
freedom xiii, xv, xxii, xxiv, xxv, 13, 24, 30, 35, 38, 48, 58–59, 60–61, 62, 64, 67, 68, 70, 74, 78, 95, 125, 128, 144, 161, 182, 192

French Revolution 20, 24, 26,
112–113, 114, 132, 137, 144
Freud, Sigmund 121
Frey, John R. xix, 211
Freytag, Gustav 42, 205
Fricke, Gerhard xxvi, xxix, 57, 68–
69, 71, 77–79, 81, 92, 93, 167,
169, 170, 201, 207, 208
Fromm, Erich 122–123
Fuhrmann, Helmut 124–126, 217
Fullenwider, Henry 184, 215

Garland, H. B. 128–129, 214
Geistesgeschichte xvi, 50, 57–87,
92, 93, 101, 149
Gemmingen, Otto von 96
George, Stefan xiv, 63, 64, 71, 92
Gerhard, Melitta 92, 96, 209
Gerhard, Ute xix, 222
German Democratic Republic (see
"East Germany")
Gervinus, Georg Gottfried 25–26,
40, 61, 204
Glaser, Horst Albert 115, 217
Goedeke, Karl 44, 201
Goethe, Johann Wolfgang von xi,
xii, xiii, xiv, xvii, 13–14, 17, 19,
21, 23, 24, 25, 26, 27, 35, 41,
42, 48, 63, 64, 67, 68, 70, 77,
78, 81, 92, 93, 106, 129
Goethe, Johann Wolfgang von,
works by:
Clavigo 199
Dichtung und Wahrheit 92
Egmont 186
Faust 35
"Ganymed" 121
Götz von Berlichingen 3, 92, 96,
99, 146
Iphigenie auf Tauris 6, 182
"Prometheus" 121
Über das deutsche Theater 12,
204

Göpfert, Herbert G. xxvi, xxix,
201
Gottsched, Johann Christoph 2,
80, 159
Graham, Ilse 129–130, 156, 215
Grawe, Christian xv-xvi, 4, 218,
221
Gray, Richard T. 156, 164, 221
greatness xii, 63, 68, 84, 94, 103,
133, 136–137, 151, 160, 164
Greek tragedy 38, 42, 46, 82, 155
Grimm, Reinhold. See Berghahn,
Klaus.
Gronicka, André von 185, 187,
191, 193, 194, 210
Grün, Karl 27, 41, 205
Gundolf, Friedrich xiv, xv, 57, 63–
65, 70, 71, 77, 92, 207
Guthke, Karl 103, 135–137, 173–
174, 176, 213, 221

Habermas, Jürgen 121, 137, 188
Hagemeister, Gottfried Lucas 4,
203
Haller, Albrecht von 6
Hamann, Johann Georg 67, 69
Hamburger, Käte 160, 211
Hammer, Stephanie Barbé 125,
221
Hannich-Bode, Ingrid. See Bode,
Ingrid.
Harnack, Otto 45, 58, 206
Hecht, Wolfgang 162, 217
Hecker, Max xii, 206
Hegel, Georg Wilhelm Friedrich
33–37, 38, 39, 40, 41, 51, 98,
103–104, 108, 121, 129, 151,
163, 190, 204
Heidegger, Martin 160, 161, 170
Heine, Heinrich xiii, 24–25, 51,
204
Heinse, Johann Jakob Wilhelm 78
Heiseler, Bernt von 138, 211

Heitner, Robert 171–172, 211, 213
Heller, Erich 127, 209
Henning, Hans 10, 215
Herder, Johann Gottfried 67, 76, 121, 160
Herrmann, Hans Peter 175–176, 218
Herwegh, Georg 51
Heselhaus, Clemens 159–160, 210
Hettner, Hermann 44, 47, 205
Hinderer, Walter 117, 160–161, 214, 216
Hinrichs, H. F. W. 33, 38–40, 41, 63, 104, 121, 127, 129, 156, 204
Hitler, Adolf xviii, 74
Hoffmeister, Karl 12, 29–33, 37–39, 40, 41, 47, 63, 205
Hölderlin, Friedrich 153
Horn, Franz 21, 203
Hoven, Wilhelm von 12, 154, 205
Humboldt, Wilhelm von xi, 12, 81, 204
Huyssen, Andreas 166, 167, 173, 176, 177, 216, 217

Ibsen, Henrik 187
idealism, idealists xvi, xvii, 17, 25, 26, 27, 30, 38–39, 42–43, 45, 57, 59, 61, 63, 66, 68, 69, 78, 85, 86, 92–93, 98, 105, 118, 120, 127, 128, 133, 135–136
Iffland, August Wilhelm 21, 94, 96
Illuminati 3, 62, 194–195, 200
inner form 78, 79–80, 84, 87, 94, 116, 160
irrationalism 67, 79–80, 83, 91, 167

Janz, Rolf-Peter 162–163, 166, 172–173, 175, 176, 178, 215, 216

Jews 74, 150
Jonas, Gisela 62, 219
Jonnes, Denis 120, 219
Jünger, Johann Friedrich 7, 203

Kaiser, Gerhard 115–116, 175, 176, 215, 218
Kalb, Charlotte von 49
Kant, Immanuel, xi, 27–28, 39–40, 49, 68, 95, 97, 117, 128
Karlsschule (ducal academy) xxvi, 16, 30, 60, 65, 82, 95, 124, 151, 154, 185, 199
Kaufmann, F. W. 127, 132, 209
Kautsky, Karl 62, 219
Kayser, Wolfgang 63, 103, 136, 212
Keferstein, Georg xviii, 209
Kierkegaard 69, 79, 97, 160, 169
Kiesel, Helmuth 119, 216
Kindermann, Heinz 94, 209
Kindervater, Christian Viktor 8–9, 203
Kittler, Friedrich 185, 218
Klages, Ludwig 73
Klein, P. 2–3, 202
Kleist, Heinrich von xiii, 77
Klinger, Friedrich Maximilian 78, 112, 148
Klopstock, Friedrich Gottlieb 19
Kluge, Gerhard 7, 11, 133–135, 179, 183, 189, 201, 202, 218, 219, 220
Knigge, Adolf 3–4, 202
Koch, Herbert 6, 212
Kommerell, Max 57, 63, 70–71, 73, 87, 98, 207, 208
Koopmann, Helmut xix, 137, 154, 166, 167, 173, 184, 189–190, 193, 215, 216, 218, 219, 222
Korff, Hermann August 57, 63, 66–68, 77, 80, 103, 166, 168, 171, 207, 208
Körner, Christian Gottfried xiv, 66

Koselleck, Reinhard 84, 121, 162, 211
Kotzebue, August 21
Kraft, Günther 146–147, 148, 211
Kraft, Herbert 112, 113–114, 179, 201, 216
Kühnemann, Eugen 59–60, 64, 86, 187, 206
Kurrelmeyer, W. 3, 207

Lacan, Jacques 185
Lahnstein, Peter 138, 217
Lämmert, Eberhart xix, 57, 86, 213
Lassalle, Ferdinand 28
Leibniz 104, 118, 152
Leistner, Bernd (see "Dahnke, Hans-Dietrich")
Lenz, Jakob Michael Reinhold 78
Lessing, Gotthold Ephraim 1, 2, 3, 5, 19, 119, 177, 190
Lessing, Gotthold Ephraim, works by:
    Emilia Galotti 8, 167, 175
    Miss Sara Sampson 167
    Nathan der Weise 6, 7, 49, 150, 182
liberalism, liberals xi, xv, xvi, xxv, 21, 23–28, 35, 43, 58, 61, 74, 130, 182, 187
Liepe, Wolfgang 44, 57, 75, 207
Linn, Rolf 118, 119, 122, 214
Lohenstein, Daniel Casper von 6, 7
Ludwig, Albert xviii, 9, 26, 39, 42, 207
Ludwig, Otto 42, 43, 205
Lukács, Georg 106, 213
Luther, Lutheranism xv, 69, 73, 104, 122–123, 138
Lützeler, Paul Michael 161–162, 163, 216

Maier, Konrad 122–123, 126, 221

Malsch, Wilfried 170–171, 179, 191, 193–194, 213, 220
Mann, Heinrich xv, 206
Mann, Klaus xiii, 210
Mann, Thomas xiii, 97, 206, 207, 210
Mansouri, Rachid Jai 125, 220
Martini, Fritz 148, 169, 173, 210, 214
Martinson, Steven 132, 221
Marx, Karl 27–28, 51, 86, 105, 149, 205, 214
Marxism (see "socialism")
Masson, Raoul 104–105, 118, 211
materialism xviii, 61, 66, 69, 76, 103, 105, 107, 117, 147
May, Kurt 92–93, 209
Mayer, Hans xiii, xviii, 86, 112–113, 127, 130, 145, 147, 150, 210, 211, 213, 214
McCardle, Arthur 104, 219
Mehring, Franz 61, 84, 86, 105, 106, 107, 207
Meier, Albert 163, 219
Mengs, Adolf 2
Menzel, Wolfgang 25, 204
Mercier, Sebastien 173
Merkel, Johannes and Rüdiger Steinlein 148–149, 215
Michelsen, Peter 85, 109, 145, 150–152, 153, 155, 163–164, 170, 174–175, 176, 213, 216, 218, 220
Middell, Eike 109–110, 217
Miller, R. D. 128, 213
Milton, John 67
Minor, Jakob 45, 46, 47, 58, 59, 206
"Misere" 27, 61, 66, 109, 123
Mitscherlich, Alexander 122–123
Montesquieu 75, 184, 195
moral-immoral dilemma 68, 71, 79, 160

"Moraltrompeter von Säkkingen"
    xiii, xxvi, 28, 65
Moritz, Karl Philipp 4–5, 203

Mücke, Dorothea von 164, 219
Müller, Ernst 138, 210
Müller, Joachim 108, 168, 186,
    211, 214
Müller, Klaus-Detlef 190, 219
Müller, Richard Matthias 153, 220
Müller-Seidel, Walter xix, 169–
    170, 210, 211

Nadler, Josef 57, 74–75, 209
Napoleon 23, 26
nationalism xv, 24, 25, 48, 57, 62,
    70, 73, 74, 86, 91, 199
naturalism 2, 37, 38, 45–46, 62,
    63, 95–96, 116, 119, 132, 168,
    176
Nazism. See Third Reich.
nemesis 66, 80, 83–85, 93, 102,
    104, 133, 152, 159–160, 163–
    164,
neoclassicism 1, 2, 7, 8, 9, 14, 21,
    22, 30, 47
Nicolai, Friedrich 3
Nietzsche, Friedrich xiii, xxvi, 28,
    63, 64–65, 138, 206
Nutz, Maximilian 91, 105, 220

Obereit, Jakob Hermann 152
Oellers, Norbert xviii, 12, 19, 20,
    21, 44, 57, 59, 91, 201, 213,
    214, 216, 220
Oetinger, Friedrich Christoph 103
Ordnung 93, 101–102, 118, 131,
    148, 163, 169, 173
Orton, Graham 187–188, 191,
    213
Otto, Regine 190–191, 193, 217

Palleske, Emil 45, 205
Pape, Walter 4, 220

Pathos 22, 46, 58, 64, 80–81, 94–
    95, 106, 116, 117, 160, 168,
    176
patriarchalism (Vaterordnung)
    101–102, 115, 119, 120, 123,
    124, 151, 153
Paulsen, Wolfgang xvi, xix, 101,
    212
Petersen, Julius 49, 86, 201, 206
Petsch, Robert 60–61, 207
Phelps, Reginald 161, 215
Pick, R. xix, 212
Pietism 104, 122, 134
Plutarch 52, 144, 161
Polheim, Karl Konrad 191–193,
    219
Pongs, Hermann 57, 73, 74, 208
positivism xvi, 41, 44, 49, 58, 59,
    61, 66, 148
postmodernism 153, 185
Prawer, Siegbert 23–24, 51, 209,
    215
Protestantism 26, 69, 71
providence (theodicy) xii, xvii,
    xviii, 37, 77, 83, 93, 95, 103,
    111, 121, 122, 146, 147
Pugh, David 155, 221

Raabe, Paul, and Ingrid Bode xix,
    213
Raphael 2
Räuberbuch 148–149, 157, 215
Rea, Thomas 51, 207
realism xiii, 1, 2, 40, 41–44, 85,
    92–93, 107, 112, 118, 127,-
    128–129, 134, 135–136
Reed, T. J. 130, 131, 135, 220
Reeves, Nigel. See Dewhurst,
    Kenneth.
Rehm, Walther 57, 85, 93, 136,
    151, 209
Rembrandt 2

republic, republicanism 107, 109, 113, 116, 124, 134, 144, 145, 149, 152, 159–165
Riedel, Wolfgang 135, 138, 154–155, 219, 221
Rietschl, Ernst xi
Robertson, John 62, 127, 207
Rohrmoser, Günter 103–104, 212
Romantics, Romanticism xiii, 18–23, 77
Rousseau, Jean Jacques 28, 44, 45, 46, 52, 63, 67, 75, 107, 161, 184
Ruppelt, Georg xviii, 69, 217

Saint-Réal, Abbé de xxiv, 195, 202
Sartre, Jean Paul 160, 161
Sasse, Günter 178, 221, 222
Scheffel, Johann Viktor xxvi
Scheibe, Friedrich Carl 104, 213
Scherer, Wilhelm 44, 205

Scherpe, Klaus 149–150, 155, 162, 216
Schiller, Friedrich, works by:
   Agrippina 111
   "An die Freude" xi
   Briefe über Don Carlos, xii-xiii, 43, 48, 132, 134, 182, 183, 184, 185, 190, 191, 194
   "Das Ideal und das Leben" 72
   "Das Lied von der Glocke" 125
   "Der Eroberer" 71
   "Der Verbrecher aus verlorener Ehre" 147
   Der versöhnte Menschenfeind 124
   Die Braut in Trauer 113
   Die Braut von Messina xxvi, 21, 112, 118
   Die Jungfrau von Orleans xxv, 17, 112
   "Die Künstler" 105

   "Die Theosophie des Julius" 152–154
   Die Malteser 70
   Maria Stuart 108, 118
   Philosophische Briefe, 152, 178
   Über Anmut und Würde 97
   Über Bürgers Gedichte 42
   Über das Pathetische 95, 128
   Über die ästhetische Erziehung des Menschen 92
   Über naive und sentimentalische Dichtung xiv, 14, 28, 81, 156, 170
   Versuch über den Zusammenhang . . . 46, 79
   Wallenstein xi, xii, xiii, xiv, 15, 19, 20, 22, 38, 42, 48, 63, 84, 85, 100, 103, 108, 118, 163
   Wilhelm Tell 38
   "Würde der Frauen" 18
Schings, Hans-Jürgen 46, 145, 150, 152–53, 154, 155, 162, 184, 191, 194–195, 217, 218, 221
Schink, Johann Friedrich 6, 203
Schlegel, August Wilhelm 18–19, 203
Schlegel, Friedrich 18, 19–20, 22, 199, 204
Schmid, Karl G. 57, 81, 208
Schmidt, Erich 58, 201, 207
Schmidt, Julian 42–43, 44, 47, 205, 206
Schreiber, Aloys Wilhelm 5–6, 203
Schubart, Christian Friedrich Daniel 12, 147, 202
Schulte-Sasse, Jochen 114–115, 116, 217
Schunicht, Manfred 103, 213
Schwab, Gustav 40, 205
Schwaldopler, Johann 28–29, 203
Schwerte, Hans 146, 212

Seidlin, Oskar 103, 156, 190, 212, 218

Seneca 3

Sengle, Friedrich 186, 197, 210

Shakespeare, William xii, xiv, xv, 2, 3, 4, 6, 17, 21, 22, 23, 28, 37, 42, 44, 45, 49, 64–65, 70, 72, 82, 83, 96, 135, 136, 155

Shakespeare, William, works by:
 Hamlet 41, 65
 King Lear 64, 151, 183
 Macbeth 64
 Othello 65
 Richard III 65
 Timon of Athens 154

Sharpe, Lesley 70, 130–132, 152, 218, 220, 221

Smith, Herbert xviii, 208

socialism, socialists (Marxism, Marxists) 27, 61, 102, 105–111, 112, 116, 147, 151, 152, 155, 162, 172, 188, 199

sociopolitical scholarship 111–124

Solger, Karl Wilhelm Ferdinand 19, 204

Sørensen, Bengt Algot 119–120, 178, 218

Spengler, Wilhelm 82, 87, 208

Spinoza 122

de Staël, Mme. 15–16, 24, 203

Stahl, E. L. 127–128, 148, 210

Staiger, Emil 27, 63, 71, 103, 111–112, 138, 151, 152, 164, 209, 213

Steinhagen, Harald 120–121, 218

Steinlein, Rüdiger. See Merkel, Johannes.

Stephan, Inge 126, 177–178, 219

Stilla, Gabriele 69, 221

Storm and Stress xvii, 2, 3, 26, 59, 65, 67, 68, 76, 80, 102, 110, 114, 119, 121, 134, 155, 167, 168, 175, 178

Storz, Gerhard 57, 76, 81–83, 85, 98–101, 112, 127, 146, 186–187, 195, 208, 212, 213

Streicher, Andreas 12, 204

Strich, Fritz 57, 65–66, 79, 207

Stubenrauch, Herbert 138, 145–146, 154, 201, 210

sublime criminals 36, 52, 65, 72, 98, 125, 164, 175

Sulzer, Johann Georg 154

Taylor, A. J. P. xv, 209

Taylor, William 51, 204

Teniers 2

Thalheim, Hans-Günther 108–109, 110–111, 148, 212, 214, 219

theodicy (see "providence")

Third Reich xv, xviii, 57, 69, 74, 81, 91

Thomas, Calvin 46–47, 206

Tieck, Ludwig 22–23, 204

Timme, Hermann 2–3, 202

tragedy, *Tragik* 5, 33–39, 42, 46, 48, 59, 60, 61, 62, 69, 72, 73, 75, 77–79, 80, 83–85, 86, 93–94, 98, 100, 103, 111, 124, 128, 151, 152, 153, 155, 161, 167, 168, 169, 170, 177, 185, 186 (See also "domestic tragedy.")

Ugrinsky, Alexej xiii, 220

unconditionality (*Unbedingtheit*) 69, 79–80, 93, 97–98, 169

Unger, Rudolf xviii, 208

Vansca, Kurt xix, 212

Vaterordnung (see "patriarchalism")

Veit, Philip 150, 213

Vierhaus, Rudolf 190

Vilmar, August Friedrich Christian 26–27, 40, 61, 205

Voltaire 3, 62–63

Vormärz 23
Vulpius, Wolfgang xix, 212, 213

Wedekind, Frank 60
Weimar xi, xiii, xiv, 15, 92
Weimar, Klaus 153–154, 220
Weissenfels, Richard 58, 201, 207
Weitbrecht, Carl xv, 45, 48–49,
   206
Wellek, René 25, 33, 87, 211, 213
Weltrich, Richard 46, 58, 206
Wentzlaff-Eggebert, Friedrich-
   Wilhelm 92, 209
Werkimmanenz xvi, 91, 101, 126
Wersig, Peter xix, 216
Wertheim, Ursula 108, 211, 212
Wickert, Gabriele 177, 218
Wieland, Christoph Martin 7, 19
Wienbarg, Ludolf 23
Wiese, Benno von xix, 57, 76, 81,
   83–85, 93–94, 98, 101–103,
   104, 112, 118, 127, 128, 131,
   134, 146, 148, 166, 186, 209,
   210, 212
Wilkinson, E. M., and L. A.
   Willoughby 168–169, 209
Williams, Anthony 116–117, 215
Willoughby, L. A. See Wilkinson,
   E. M.
Winter, Hans Gerhard 115, 216
Witte, William xix, 127, 209, 212
Wittkowski, Wolfgang xix, 213
Wölfel, Kurt 160, 211
Wolff, Christian 152, 154
Wolzogen, Caroline von 12, 204
Württemberg 75, 101, 103, 144,
   152
Wychgram, Jakob 45, 58, 206